CORRECTIONAL EDUCATION CHRONOLOGY

Thom Gehring, Ph.D. and Carolyn Eggleston, Ph.D.

Published by

**CALIFORNIA STATE UNIVERSITY
SAN BERNARDINO**

Published in San Bernardino, California,
by California State University, San Bernardino.

Special thanks for the support from the California Department of Corrections and Rehabilitation, Division of Juvenile Justice Education Unit.

How this Book is Presented

The California State University, San Bernrdino mountain logo indicates when an entry ends, so the next one can be expected. We hope this will move readers easily through the book's transitions.

Printed in the United States of America by
Wirz & Company Printing
444 Colton Avenue
Colton, CA 92324

ISBN 0-9776008-0-7

This book is printed on permanent/durable paper.

Photo credits:

Front Cover: Walnut Street Jail, 1787. Used with permission of Pennsylvania
& Illustration: Prison Society, URL www.prisonsociety.org

Back Cover: Thom Gehring and Carolyn Eggleston at local juvenile facility
by Robert Whitehead. Used with permission.
Front door of Center for the Study of Correctional Education,
California State University, San Bernardino, California by Lori
Krueger. Used with permission.

CONTENTS

Page

Foreword by Randall Wright, Ph.D. iii

Preface ix

1787 to the Present: Historical Overview x

Introduction 1

Period One: 1787-1875 4

Period Two: 1876-1900 105

Period Three: 1901-1929 145

Period Four: 1930-1940 199

Period Five: 1941-1945 231

Period Six: 1946-1963 236

Period Seven: 1964-1980 252

Period Eight: 1981-1988 286

Period Nine: 1989-The Present 296

References 299

Acknowledgements 313

Walnut Street Jail, Philadelphia, 1787.
Used with permission of Pennsylvania Prison Society
URL www.prisonsociety.org

Foreword: The Roots and Routes of Correctional Education
by Randall Wright, Ph.D.

> Nurture your professional identity as you improve your professional excellence. Keep your eye on the big picture to improve each of the smaller ones. (Gehring and Hollingsworth, 2002, p. 94).

This *Chronology* makes an important contribution to the study of correctional education because teachers in prisons generally seem to suffer from a collective amnesia when it comes to understanding the social, historical, philosophical and educational roots of their profession. The historian Gustavson (1955) wrote: ". . . so many practices and ways of thinking are born out of past experience that unless these are known, present conduct becomes a riddle" (p.80). This work will contribute to what Gustavson describes as "historical mindedness." The term refers to an empathetic appreciation and connoisseurship of the past. It is an attitude that helps us re-live events and issues from the perspective of those living in their period. Part curiosity, it is an attitude that compels readers and researchers to look beneath the surface of events so as to discover the reasons, forces, and patterns that have contributed to the way things are today. Readers may be struck by the fact that "correctional education" appears at the juncture of many fascinating social, political and educational ideas, personalities and events.

This work is particularly important for correctional educators because they struggle with issues of personal and professional validation both inside and outside prisons. Knowing our history supports and validates us as correctional educators as we come to understand that we have a history, body of literature, methods and schools of thought that have been shaped by over more than two centuries of theory and practice. (The first period of correctional education began in 1787.) Furthermore, going to teach in prison is so disorienting and dislocating that many teachers experience culture shock (Wright, 2005). Knowing our professional ancestry helps us anticipate what to expect on the inside and should help facilitate success in this troubled transition period. It should help us find our current social and psychological place in a professional context informed by the past, and thereby reduce the professional drift we experience when we cross through the prison gates.

Hopefully, readers will appreciate that many of our professional riddles are recurring despite disparate geographical locations and historical contexts. The purpose and function of prisons in society is one of these enigmatic riddles that infuse our practice. As Skyes remarked:

> The 'prison problem' would seem to be a hardy perennial, unfortunately, for it has managed to survive every new storm of public indignation and concern. Jeremy Bentham, John Howard, Sir James Mackintosh, Elizabeth Fry–these were but the first of a long series of persons who have raised their voices

in protest against the penitentiary, and today the criticisms continue with undiminished force. Yet the problem remains. (1970, p. vii).

Remembering the past is not simply a retrospective act for there often is a transformative energy that is released when we become aware of previous, significant accomplishments in correctional education. Given the exigencies of the present (tightening budgets, larger prisons, and a "meaner world" with hardened social and judicial lines between criminals and society), educators often feel incapable of expressing visionary or utopian energies—energies that propel them into the future. The danger of any profession (and for society) is to be trapped in a "present-mindedness" that sees the world naively. Ironically, without a historical perspective we cannot take a reasoned and passionate stand against the excesses of the present and prevent future catastrophes. This is the point of Orwell's classic novel of the totalitarian state *1984*. Orwell was fearfully conscious of the relationship of historical consciousness to political control. Winston, the protagonist in this novel, is confronted by his inquisitor whose task is to efface Winston's past so as to reshape his present to suit the totalitarian needs of the state. Orwell wrote: "Who controls the past controls the future; Who controls the present controls the past. . . . "

This *Chronology* does not "sum it all up" for the reader—that is not its purpose. Using the language of post-structuralism, this is not a "writer" text but a "reader" text. In other words, the authors do not attempt to impose on the reader a continuous historical narrative that "tidies up" history by making it conform to a causal chain of events. Rather, the encyclopedic style suggests there are patterns, derivations, genealogies, and coincidences of events, ideas and persons that invite readers into the work to make connections for themselves. Its style resists a thin description of history, where events are attributed (weakly) to singular causes. For example, in some history of education books we read how the ". . . period of the Reformation formally began in 1517 when Martin Luther, an Augustinian monk and professor of religion, nailed his Ninety-five Theses questioning the authority of the Catholic Church, to the door of the court church in Wittenberg, Germany" (Webb, Metha, and Jordan, 2003, p.135). Explanations such as these do not provide the reader with a thick description of the multiple events and complex social conditions that prepared the population for Luther's religious stance. (A more complete description of the Reformation would include for example, the dissatisfaction of poor people with over taxation by the Catholic Church and their collective envy with it because it was the largest landowner at the time, the self-interests of an emerging mercantile class and bourgeoisie who desired religious tolerance so as to further their commercial interests, and so on.)

As this example of Luther's role in the Reformation illustrates, there is always a danger in history to discuss unfolding events as an outcome of the heroic efforts of great personalities.Sometimes the reader is left with this impression in this work but it may be because in correctional education, there are many "great men and women" who *do* qualify as agents of change so it would be damaging or inaccurate to our view of correctional education if we did not take up this intriguing interpretation of historical events. Fortunately, the encyclopedic style of the *Chronology* also steers us toward a broader, contextual interpretation of correctional education that counterbalances a history populated solely by heroes.

Clearly this book is not to be read from beginning to end in one sitting. Encyclopedic in style, it is meant to be mined as a valuable resource to further one's thinking about the field and to answer questions that arise with regard to particular personalities and events. For correctional education historians this text will inevitably suggest fruitful lines of inquiry. Nevertheless, it is not without an underlying and cohesive premise. The text is sustained by utopian energies as it reveals the "hidden, democratic heritage" (Eggleston & Gehring, 2000, p.306) of correctional education, a heritage that can serve as an intellectual resource to support prison teachers who are weary, disillusioned, frustrated and alienated. As a rear view mirror of our practice, this work should confirm our identities as transformative agents in prisons because it helps us ponder our deeply embedded assumptions about our roles there.

Correctional education history is an unfolding tale of "roots" and "routes." As indigenous, embedded practices, correctional education reflects the local and national cultures of the period–it is "rooted" there. But correctional education also is a cross-cultural phenomenon–the outcome of migratory patterns of ideas, people, goods (and prisoners) and thus shaped by the "routes" of emerging nation states and the interrelated processes of imperialism, colonialism, and mercantilism.

Clearly, this work speaks to a global story of correctional education—in some respects it reads like a deeply informed travelogue of persons, ideas and practices. One could argue that historically, prisons have formed a node or a connection point for tourists and intellectual sojourners (sociologists, writers, social workers, political activists, politicians–and educational reformers), who used the prison to express their views about society, culture, punishment, and of course, education. Charles Dickens and the famous sociologist, Alexis De Tocqueville graced the prison landscape and gained wide audience with their insightful comments about prison life. These "intellectual tourists" often become the primary vehicles for the production and dissemination of knowledge about prisons and correctional education. (De Tocqueville for example, came to the United States to study the prison and returned to France to share his knowledge.) Other important "tourists" appear in this work too. John Howard's visit to Holland prisons impressed him so greatly that, when he became Sheriff of Bedford, he began an educative tour of other European prisons, gathering the ideas that were later to become the foundation for his prison reforms.

Given this interpretation of the prison as a temporary collecting place for people and as a node for the dissemination of ideas, we can appreciate how Maconochie for example, working at an island penal colony in the British Pacific, along with Crofton (an Irish prison reformer), influenced the work of

Zebulon Brockway. Brockway in turn, had a formative influence on Thomas Mott Osborne. Osborne trained Austin MacCormick, whose work, *The Education of Adult Prisoners,* is still a classic and widely read today. McCormick's efforts as an editor laid the foundation for *The Journal of Correctional Education,* the official publication and vibrant voice of the Correctional Education Association internationally. These are but a few examples of the "routes" and "roots" of correctional education.

Researchers may want to consider the social contexts of correctional education more thoroughly once they become familiar with some of the key figures in correctional education described here. Of particular significance is the role of "societies" in correctional education and prison reform. "Societies" are broadly distinguished from other groups by mutual interests, shared institutions, a common culture or profession. The term also refers to the rich, privileged, and fashionable social class or the socially dominant members of a community. Societies have played an important role in prison reform. For example, New York City's Society for the Prevention of Pauperism raised over $18,000 for prison reform for children, an enormous sum in 1823. The Boston Prison Discipline Society, formed in 1825, sought to reform prisons by opposing the Pennsylvania System of prison management which relied on the total isolation of the prisoner to maintain order. They argued instead for solitary confinement at night with hard labor and human contact during the day.

We should not imagine, however, that correctional educators have always been the vanguard of holistic institutional resistance and change. Rather, as Gehring and Eggleston note in their work: "The history of the correctional education movement is a record of step-by-step improvement." In the long march toward humanized prisons (if this is not an oxymoron), the restorative efforts of teachers may indeed seem small. Sometimes the worldviews of the period severely limited what the teacher might do. In the Sabbath school years (when prisoners were taught only on the Sabbath), ministers performed restorative work as they sought to reconnect the prisoner to the spiritual world, with God, and through God, with fellow human beings. Over time, correctional educators offered prisoners a broader curriculum and provided greater opportunities for prisoners to come to know themselves and the world. Today, correctional educators are mediators between the inside and the outside worlds, offering students comprehensive, state-recognized curricula comparable to those provided in traditional, local schools.

It might come as a surprise for some readers to realize that correctional education is a widespread and influential movement that intersects "traditional" philosophies and philosophers of education. Influenced by Rousseau's naturalism, Pestalozzi put his ideas of a child-centered, sensory experience into practice in his experimental farm/school for beggars and vagabonds which opened its doors in 1774. Pestalozzi's theoretic and practical work responded to the needs of disenfranchised Swiss children in a country caught up in Bonaparte's imperialist designs on Europe. (The French overran Switzerland in

1798.) He refined many of his influential philosophical principles of education working with these disenfranchised youth, as a correctional educator.

Even as we applaud the efforts of educators in prison (and their enormous contribution to prison/social reform), we must be cautious, too, because correctional education is situated in a penal history which alternately sought to either punish the body or win over the souls and, today, the minds of prisoners. Without a doubt, correctional educators humanized prisons, but they also sought to reform, convert and proselytize prisoners. We must appreciate that the history and current practice of correctional education is grounded in contradictions; it is a tale drawn from the intersection of different, competing storylines. Tracing the routes and roots of correctional education, critical researchers may want to undertake studies that unpack these "biases" in correctional history and practice so as to more fully appreciate the social and historical context of the field. Certainly there is interpretive room for readers to examine correctional education and the correspondences with modernization, strategies of social order and control, and world views that support dividing practices (the labeling and treatment of un/desirables). In this way, readers are invited to engage not simply in remembering the past, but a critical remembering of it, so as to disclose epistemological, ontological and ethical presuppositions we share now that echo past practices and theories (Grumet, 1981). The open style of the text leaves conceptual room for readers to shape their own, perhaps more critical interpretation of correctional education.

We should probably judge the efforts of correctional education reformers and our practice by the opinions and actions of student/prisoners. Throughout this *Chronology*, one of the prominent riddles that persists and requires explanation in our profession, and that requires further research, is the question of the "successes" of correctional education. Why is it that prisoners always seem to appreciate the efforts of teachers, ministers and volunteers who teach them? Certainly there are characteristics and skills that teachers in prison must have if they are to be successful (Gehring, 1992). Still, it seems that the rewards of going to school in prison are largely intrinsic. In this history of correctional education it appears that students were highly motivated, respectful of teachers, well-behaved in classrooms, and generally showed enormous improvement in their academic abilities and personal comportment. At Auburn prison students were so motivated they would often set their food aside in the evening, preferring to take advantage of the remaining evening light to read, and then eat later in the dark.

In conclusion, this work should help correctional educators shape their schools of thought because it opens up so many interpretative spaces from which to appreciate the history of correctional education and their current practice. There is so much that has been done in this work in this regard, and there is so much to be done, for others who wish to take up the challenges of exploring the rich heritage of correctional education. This work should at least provide the reader with historical capital to respond to those who argue that correctional education is not a specialized educational field with its own literature and practice, or that correctional teachers are not "real teachers." Surveying the vast historical, conceptual and practical landscape that defines and shapes schooling in prisons should enable teachers who struggle with professional identity issues as "correctional educators" to discover their professional place in the world. Readers will be struck with a sense that this *Chronology* of correctional education is well worth reading, researching and applying to their correctional education practice.

References

Eggleston, C., and Gehring, T. (September, 2000). Carolyn Eggleston and Thom Gehring presented at the EPEA conference Athens, Greece, October, 1999. *The Journal of Correctional Education*, 51(3), pp. 306-310.

Gehring, T., and Hollingsworth, T. (September, 2002). Coping and beyond: Practical suggestions for correctional educators. *The Journal of Correctional Education*, 53(3). pp. 89-95.

Gehring, T. (1992). Correctional teacher skills, characteristics, and performance indicators. In S.L. Swartz (Ed.). *Journal of teacher education*. 1(2), pp. 22-42.

Grumet, M. (1981). Restitution and reconstruction of educational experience: An autobiographical method for curriculum theory. In M. Lawn and L. Barton (Eds.). *Rethinking Curriculum studies: A radical approach*. New York: Halstead Press. pp. 115-130.

Gustavson, G. (1955). *A preface to history*. New York: McGraw-Hill.

Orwell, G. (1983). *1984*. Toronto, Canada: Plume (Penguin Group).

Sykes, G. (1970). *The society of captives: A study of a maximum security prison*. New York: Antheneum.

Webb, L.D., Metha, A., and Jordon, K.F. (2003). *Foundations of American education*. Columbus, Ohio: Merrill Prentice Hall.

Wright, R. (March, 2005). Going to teach in prisons: Culture shock. *The Journal of Correctional Education*, 56(1), pp. 19-36.

Preface

This is a chronology—a documentary history compendium—of correctional education reform. It is not exhaustive, but it is reasonably comprehensive for the years 1787 to 1987. By that we mean it is sufficient to introduce interested readers to the major trends and contributions of the field. We believe that, in a pinch, the *Chronology* can substitute for a library on correctional education.

One problem is that correctional educators lack a "grounding" in correctional education history and literature. In teacher preparation programs, public school counterparts learn about the major contributors to their field, the current paradigm that the field follows, and the support the new teacher has when joining the discipline. This is not true in correctional education, as educators come into prison work (many describe "falling into" the work) unprepared in correctional and alternative education. They have trained in diverse educational disciplines, such as special education, reading education, elementary education, or technical education. These influences foster feelings of isolation and vulnerability in an already difficult setting, so it is important for correctional educators to learn about the history and literature of their own field. Readers of this book may discover for the first time that others faced similar problems in different places and times. There is strength in having a foundation in the field; that is why public school educators learn about who came before them. We hope readers can dispel feelings of separation and isolation, and feel confirmed in their own teaching situations. Reading about the activities of one's predecessors may provide an important underpinning to the professionalization of one's field.

Readers not currently involved in correctional and alternative education may find it surprising that this history is so closely linked to the social movements of the times: public school efforts, and compulsory school attendance; concerns about immigration, segregation, and intelligence testing, etc. Although institutions seem isolated from general society, they truly reflect issues of the culture. This is one of the things that makes correctional education and prison reform important, yet no one is aware of the entire range of applicable history, documents, and heroes. Therefore, if readers are alert to materials and ideas that are not addressed in this book, we welcome information that can be added. Our addresses, phones, and emails are listed below.

Thom Gehring, Ph.D.   and   Carolyn Eggleston, Ph.D.
Directors, Center for the Study of Correctional Education
California State University, San Bernardino
5500 University Parkway
San Bernardino, CA 92407-2397
Thom's phone (909) 537-5653   Carolyn's phone (909) 537-5654
tgehring@csusb.edu   eggleso@csusb.edu

Dedication

We dedicate this book to each other; "still crazy after all these years."

It is clear that in whatever it is our duty to act, those matters also it is our duty to study (Arnold, in Quick, 1916, p. xiii).

The North American correctional education movement began in 1787, when clergyman William Rogers first offered instruction at Philadelphia's Walnut Street Jail. The warden was worried that a riot might result from this revolutionary initiative, so he required that two guards attend the meeting, armed with muskets and a loaded cannon aimed directly at the convict students. Everything was peaceful, of course. This incident was symbolic of the struggle that has characterized teaching within prison walls ever since. Nevertheless, adult and juvenile correctional education has been on the "leading edge" of publicly funded education for more than 200 years, as this volume demonstrates.

Special Education

During the 1880s and '90s, Elmira (New York State) Reformatory superintendent Zebulon Brockway implemented educational programs for disabled learners of every description. The special education staff included physicians, craftsmen, professors, attorneys, and teachers. The program had these features:

a. Systematic linkages between academic, social, and vocational learning experiences.

b. Early morning individually tutored remedial instruction. It was believed that students were more receptive to learning in the early hours.

c. Individual diets and calisthenics, prescribed by the institutional physician. Even the cut of the clothes was sometimes prescribed, for purposes of what we now call physical therapy. Multi-modal instruction was applied, with an emphasis on tactile and auditory learning.

d. Completely individualized student education files, including 56 bodily measurements that were recorded monthly.

e. Special hot and cold baths and "the new scientific Swedish massage techniques," implemented by workers hired specifically for that purpose.

f. Follow-up and aftercare programs, implemented through interagency collaboration.

Many of these special education components at Elmira paralleled modern practice. One view suggests that the major difference between 19th century correctional education prototypes and current practice was in the names that were applied to educationally disabling conditions. Even today those early Elmira school programs for learners with disabilities would be considered sophisticated.

The Systematic Development of Individualized Instruction

Aristotle taught students individually and "little red schoolhouse" teachers used individualized activities, but the individually prescribed instruction (IPI) method was systematically applied and subsequently perfected at correctional schools like the one at Elmira. Prison reformers advocated individualization because it facilitated the classification of prisoners. Classification, in turn, could result in meaningful treatment programming and the reformation of criminals. Closely linked in theory to the medical model of corrections and the diagnostic-prescriptive approach to special education, the IPI method we know today started as a correctional education innovation and was later adopted by local public schools. Consider these events:

a. The New York State law that established Elmira Reformatory, drafted by Zebulon Brockway himself, required that school records would be maintained on each individual student.

b. As early as 1929, Austin MacCormick wrote on the systematic individualization of correctional education in the draft of his book, *The Education of Adult Prisoners*. It included what we might call an "IPI handbook."

c. The history of IPI was reviewed by William Grady, New York City associate superintendent of schools, who wrote in 1939 that "...the pioneers in...classification and individualization of personality were the prisons rather than the schools. My hat's off to the prisons."

d. During the 1960s and '70s, when IPI was becoming accepted widely in the local schools, Dr. John McKee's experiments at Draper Correctional Institution (Alabama) documented its success in correctional education. The IPI method was designed to address the severe basic skill deficits and extreme heterogeneity typically identified in correctional populations. It was a by-product of the evolving correctional education movement.

Many Modern School Practices Began in Correctional Education

A group of prominent urban school reformers developed local public school district delivery patterns during the pre-World War I period. David Snedden was very influential in this group, and his information consisted largely of the principles he gleaned from correctional education practice. He researched education in juvenile institutions to identify prototypic models which could be replicated in other educational settings. Originally, Snedden and other urban school reformers were interested in reformatories and training schools because they provided laboratories in which compulsory attendance was possible. They aspired to implement and enforce compulsory education for children nationwide.

Soon, however, the reformers found additional reasons to study correctional education. Snedden correctly assumed that programs which could succeed in the most restrictive educational environment would flourish elsewhere. In his 1907 book, *Administration and Educational Work of American Juvenile Reform Schools,* he reported on pioneer correctional education models in vocational (especially trade and industrial), physical, and military education (what we would call "boot camp"). Snedden also offered summaries about what public school educators could learn from correctional education. Many of these models were replicated and became the antecedents of contemporary local school practice.

The interest of public school practitioners in correctional education models was demonstrated at the 1938 national American Association of School Administrators conference, in Atlantic City. Fully 2,000 people attended the correctional education session on "Reduction in Crime Through Improved Public Educational Programs and the Educational Rehabilitation of Prison Inmates"—despite the fact there were only seats and room for 700. An improvised loud speaker system was provided in the corridors, lobbies, and adjoining rooms, so the other interested people could hear the program. Articles about this workshop appeared in both *Harper's Magazine* and *School Executive.* At the conference in Cleveland the next year the correctional education session had over 8,000 attendees.

This sort of interest was common. Public school educators knew that their colleagues in correctional education successfully addressed the same problems that they themselves found so frustrating every day—in an institutional setting that was even more difficult than local schools. Today correctional education professionals work with (a) students who have dropped out, been pushed out, or experienced repeated failure in the regular schools, (b) embittered and apathetic or alienated learners, (c) a high incidence of educationally disabling, emotional, and/or drug-related problems, and (d) students who lack study skills, often with a history of violence and poor self-concept. In addition, the environments in our training schools, court schools, reformatories, jails, and prisons are often bleak and antithetical to the educational mission. Outside observers expect these conditions to minimize student learning. Yet most correctional education programs demonstrate outstanding success according to all traditional measures of learning gain. In 1980, these facts prompted the U.S. Education Department to implement a Correctional Education Association proposal which included this language:

...programs which can succeed in this most difficult setting can be replicable in less restrictive environments. Toward this end, correctional education should be viewed as a laboratory for testing relevant models which can be disseminated to other contexts. (Gehring, 1980, p. 6).

Major Themes of the Correctional Education Movement

Correctional educators operate on the principle that attitudes, ideas, and behavior can be corrected—that humans are capable of learning and growing. This is what makes correctional education correctional.

The field of correctional education is part of the prison reform movement. This relationship is not limited to a theoretical perspective. It is expressed in the historic links between prison reform and correctional education, and in the daily experiences of correctional education professionals who are dedicated to student learning. This point is embodied in the mutual goals and contacts of the major contributors over the decades.

The original North American prison reformers shared a strong religious orientation. They wanted to teach convicts literacy skills so they could read the Bible and be "saved" for Christ. Foremost among this group were the part-time volunteer chaplains who organized the first correctional education programs according to the "Sabbath school" model. Jared Curtis (fl. c. 1825), one of the most famous chaplains, implemented prototypic Sabbath schools in New York and Massachusetts. Early professional associations in the U.S. shared the same advocacy work and were devoted to the prison reform/correctional education link: the Philadelphia Society for the Alleviation of the Miseries of Public Prisons, the Boston Prison Discipline Society, and the Prison Association of New York.

Zebulon Brockway "inherited" the correctional education improvements that Curtis and these early prison reform societies introduced throughout the Northeast. Brockway's success was largely attributable to his combination of reforms developed by Alexander Maconochie (at an island penal colony in the British Pacific) and Sir Walter Crofton (in Ireland), and won the devotion of the North American prison "Establishment." For 50 years, Brockway had prison reform advocates and tough-minded prison managers working together to implement better correctional education programs—a feat that seems nearly impossible today. His efforts were part of what is called the reformatory movement (1870 to about 1900), an effort to change prisons for young adults into schools by emphasizing education. Brockway helped influence Thomas Mott Osborne to pursue a career in penology. Osborne subsequently became the greatest prison reformer of the early 1900s.

A millionaire industrialist and politician, Osborne dressed himself as a prisoner in 1913 to learn firsthand about conditions at Auburn, the prison in his upstate New York home town. Within a few weeks, Osborne helped organize the Mutual Welfare League, a democratic, inmate-run organization that managed every dimension of the prison with the warden's permission. Disciplinary problems were nearly eliminated and production in the prison shops expanded dramatically. By providing experiences for inmates in the daily routines of democracy and responsible social interaction, Osborne successfully transformed a loathsome maximum security prison into an uplifting educational institution. He became warden at Sing Sing, and later at the U.S. Naval Prison at Portsmouth, New Hampshire. At Sing Sing, the inmates established a flourishing school, the Mutual Welfare Institute.

Osborne also trained Austin MacCormick, who based his correctional education theories on those of Brockway and Osborne. In turn, MacCormick's book formed the conceptual foundation for a correctional education renaissance in the 1930s. He was the first assistant director of the Federal Bureau of Prisons, and went around the country establishing and expanding correctional schools and libraries. MacCormick was first editor of what later became the *Journal of Correctional Education*. For approximately 50 years he headed up The Osborne Association, Inc., one of the nation's most active prison reform organizations.

The events, processes, and contributions introduced above merely indicate part of the general direction of the prison reform/correctional education link. However, they are sufficient to demonstrate that these companion fields of human activity have been mutually supportive, generation after generation. This relationship has been expressed in a common history and parallel goals.

There are nine major periods of correctional education history, each with its own identifiable theme(s):

1. 1787-1875: Sabbath school period; Pennsylvania (solitary) and Auburn (factory) systems of prison management; correctional education is recognized as possible.

2. 1876-1900: Zebulon Brockway's tenure at Elmira Reformatory; based on the work of Maconochie (prison reform in the South Pacific), Crofton (Irish prison reform), and the Pilsburys (prison management in the U.S.); the beginnings of correctional/special education; reformatory movement efforts to transform prisons into schools.

3. 1901-1929: Libraries, reformatories for women, and democracy. Thomas Mott Osborne, Katherine Bement Davis, and Austin MacCormick.

4. 1930-1940: The golden age of correctional education; early influence of MacCormick, especially in the New York and Federal Bureau of Prisons experiments; rebirth of correctional/special education.

5. 1941-1946: World War II, which interrupted the development of correctional education.

6. 1946-1964:   Limited recovery from the interruption.

7. 1965-1980:   "Hot spots" in correctional education—the Federal influence in education; postsecondary programs; correctional school districts; special education legislation; correctional teacher preparation programs.

8. 1981-1988:   Conservative trend in Federal programs and many states; rise of the Correctional Education Association's influence; continued refinement of trends from the previous period.

9. 1989-   :   The current period; Canadian Federal paradigm; contributions by the Ross and Fabiano team, Stephen Duguid, David Werner, and others; greater international cooperation.

The history of the correctional education movement is a record of step-by-step improvement. The correctional education profession is a great frontier with a promising future, a window through which we can observe and encourage human progress. For more than 200 years people from many walks of life have recognized this fact. Hosts of clergymen, sociologists, psychologists, novelists, professionals and community volunteers, bleeding hearts and law and order advocates, have utilized the intense correctional education context to help foster an understanding of the human adventure. Indeed, the historical record suggests that correctional education professionals themselves may be the last to appreciate the importance of their own work.

Correctional educators have always been slow to identify professionally with the correctional education field. Instead, they identified with the related disciplines. Because education originally came under the chaplaincy, correctional educators identified as Sunday school teachers. Later, higher education delivery patterns dominated. While common schools were flourishing in the outside communities, their influence was also felt inside. However, adult education, social work, and correspondence courses each had their heyday before public secondary education became a fixture on the North American scene. In recent times, particular aspects of the public school model have predominated, almost like fads: adult basic education, educational counseling, career, vocational, instructional technology, and special education. Correctional educators have always been eager to accept the identity of any professional discipline except the one that fits best—correctional education. This phenomenon is called the "confused identity problem." The Correctional Education Association (CEA) has launched a vigorous program to provide information and professionwide leadership to overcome that problem, and to consolidate the field. Readers who are interested in the improvement and professionalization of correctional education should contact the outstanding professionalization organization in the field. The CEA had its origin in 1930, when Austin MacCormick founded the Standing Committee on Education of the American Prison Association (now the American Correctional Association, ACA).

The Correctional Education Association established a national headquarters with a leadership staff near Washington, D.C. Legislative action to improve correctional education services has resulted in some important successes, even during times of budgetary cutbacks. CEA has undergone intensive, participatory self-study, with products in the forms of resolutions and long-range plans. Our Association is a network of professionals, complete with its own *Journal of Correctional Education,* national newsletter, a host of local newsletters, regional and international conferences, and membership benefits. The Correctional Education Association is affiliated with the ACA. CEA members receive frequent updates about events at the national, regional, and state levels, and may participate in professional special interest group(s) in their particular branch of the correctional education field (special education, jails, libraries, postsecondary, and so forth). For more information, contact

Dr. Stephen Steurer
CEA Executive Director
8182 Lark Brown Road, Suite 202
Elkridge, MD 21075
(800) 783-1232 or (443) 459-3080
FAX (443) 459-3088
www.ceanational.org

Introduction

The first Norwegian house of correction was established in Trondheim around 1630...From the very outset, education has been an important aspect of the [Norwegian] prison system. Educational methods have always been one of the instruments used to socialise prisoners, as well as to give them knowledge. The prison authorities have always had responsibility for prison education. (Nordic Council of Ministers, 2005, p. 66).

In 1682, William Penn and the Quakers of Philadelphia took quite a step forward and began to plan houses of correction as an instrument of justice. Houses of correction similar to the one established in Philadelphia were duplicated in Boston in 1699 and Hartford in 1727...Norfolk Prison in Virginia (1784), Newgate Prison in New York (1796), Charlestown Prison in Maine (1804), and prisons in Baltimore (1804), Windsor, Vermont (1809), and Richmond (1809) became models for the nation....Gradually four distinct penal systems emerged. One for solitary confinement, one for labour [see 1816 entry], houses for correction for those charged with misdemeanors, and a system of reform schools to take children out of the jails and prisons. The early reformatories were at first nothing more than miniature prisons. (Angle, 1982, p. 4).

Philadelphia's Walnut Street Jail was established in 1773 to improve the criminal justice system. Quakers advocated this reform as a holding facility, to replace punishments such as mutilation, staggering fines, and public humiliation (Carney, 1973, pp. 79-82). The Philadelphia Society for Alleviating the Miseries of Public Prisons (PSAMPP) was organized in 1776.

An account by Caleb Lowes written in 1779 indicates that cell study progress was being made. 'The prisoners are generally desirous of attending and always conduct themselves in decency and some appear to be benefited. The afternoon of the day is mostly spent, by many of them, in reading; proper texts being furnished for that purpose.' (Angle, 1982, p. 4).

In 1790 the Jail was converted into a State penitentiary, and remodeled by legislative act (Carney, 1973, pp. 79-82).

A group of Philadelphia Quakers, brimming with revolutionary optimism, began the experiment in a renovated downtown jail. They were bent on 'such degrees and modes of punishment... as may...become the means of restoring our fellow creatures to virtue and happiness.' (Anderson, 1982, p. 38).

Also in 1790, the PSAMPP began distributing Bibles. "Prisoners at first were able to read the Bible in their cells, then visitations were allowed. By the turn of the century some prisons were ready for educational instruction." (Angle, 1982, p. 4). The Jail was operated according to the solitary plan, known as the Pennsylvania system, in which each prisoner was isolated to prevent the contaminating influence of crime. The purpose of all reformative efforts was spiritual redemption. (Freedman, 1981, p. 9).

English prison reformer **John Howard**, visiting in Holland in 1784, found that "great care is taken to give the prisoners moral and religious instruction and reform their manners, for their own and the public good" (Howard, in Grunhut, 1973/1948, p. 231). Howard was born in 1726 (Bellows, 1948, p. 7). In 1773 he was appointed Sheriff of Bedford (p. 22). Since he knew nothing about prisons, Howard began visiting institutions in other jurisdictions and countries (p. 29). "**Mr. Popham**, member [of Parliament] from Taunton, had brought a Bill into the House of Commons abolishing gaoler's [jailer's] fees, and substituting for them fixed salaries, payable out of the county rates [taxes]." Howard and Popham met, "and probably agreed on some plan of joint action" (p. 33; emphasis added). John Howard is known as the founder of the prison reform movement.

Problems of English corrections were hastened by the American Revolution. During the age of imperialism criminal justice policy, combined with colonialism, impacted peoples everywhere.

> The loss of the American colonies temporarily halted transportation [banishment of criminals], with a consequent overcrowding of the gaols in which felons were held for safe custody, but on August 18, 1786, after years of fruitless searching for a suitable base to take the place of the one lost by the American Revolt, Lord Sydney informed the Lords Commissioners of the Treasury that the Government had decided to dump its surplus felons on the territory discovered by Captain Cook [Australia and the nearby islands] sixteen years previously. (Barry, 1958, p. 35).

On the afternoon of January 26, 1788 "a fleet of eleven vessels carrying 1,030 people, including 548 male and 188 female convicts," entered what later became known as Sydney Harbor, Australia (Hughes, 1987, p. 2). More than 730 of these convicts were from the Metropolis (London), and of that number 431 were exiled or transported for minor theft (p. 72). The overwhelming majority were 35 years old or less. Typical among the crimes was that of Thomas Gearing, "who created a brief sensation in Oxford in 1786 by breaking into the chapel of Magdalen College and stealing some ecclesiastical plate. For this sacrilege, he was condemned to death, reprieved and then transported for life." (p. 73).

> Convict assignment in Australia differed, in law, from its earlier form in America. Many respectable Americans railed at

2

the influx of felons, which they thought polluted their society. 'In what can Britain show a more Sovereign contempt for us,' wrote an irate Virginian in 1751, 'than by emptying their Jails into our settlements; unless they would likewise empty their Jakes on our tables!' But the fact was that most farmers and merchants in Maryland or Virginia, when offered a chance of convict labor, grabbed it—and paid handsomely for it. The American colonist owned his indentured servants. He had paid for their transportation across the Atlantic, and he expected to be safeguarded against financial loss if they were set free by some 'unforeseen exercise of the Royal Mercy.' Convicts were capital, like slaves, and had been freely traded as such since the early seventeenth century. 'Our principall wealth consisteth in servants,' wrote the Virginia settler John Pory in 1619. Under the transportation acts of the seventeenth and early eighteenth centuries, therefore, the Crown was bound to pay a convict's owner should it remit his sentence. Such a release was unlikely but possible. In any case, Virginia and Maryland were not penal colonies, but free ones that used felon slaves. In Australia, which had been settled as a jail, no free settler ever paid for a convict's passage from England; and that, in the official view, disposed of the settler's claim to a right of property in the convict's labor. All such rights belonged to the government. Nevertheless, disputes over the 'right' of settlers to sell or reassign their convicts kept raising colonial hackles for decades. (Hughes, 1987, p. 287; emphasis in original).

In Australia, however, the

> life of a serving convict, bad as it was, was still easier than a rank-and-file soldier's....To get out of the army [Joseph] Sudds and [Patrick] Thompson robbed a Sydney shop and made no effort to escape arrest. They were tried and sentenced to 7 years in a penal establishment. (p. 448).

Like John Howard's reform work in England, the development of the Australian penal colonies had a profound influence on North American corrections and correctional education systems. Nevertheless, those systems were unique, and Philadelphia's Walnut Street Jail is known as "the cradle of the penitentiary." Hughes wrote "The idea of the penitentiary was seen as an American invention" (p. 426).

1787 — Clergyman **William Rogers** announced that he would begin instruction at Philadelphia's Walnut Street Jail. He thus became the United States' first correctional education classroom teacher. Officials brought a loaded cannon into the Jail, placed it beside Roger's pulpit, and aimed it directly at the prisoner students. Armed guards were stationed there, ready to fire the cannon if instruction prompted rebellion. (Teeters, 1955, pp. 32-34; see also Wallack, 1939, p. 9, and Gaither, 1982, p. 19). △

1792 — In Paris, France,

> the killing of at least fourteen hundred people in cold blood was the consequence of some sort of phobic condition brought on by the military crisis [after the Revolution, when the Austrians and Prussians were said to be mobilizing against France] and the apocalyptic rhetoric of prison conspiracy....the trash to be disposed of comprised all...specified sources of contamination: gilded aristocrats, venal priests, diseased whores and court lackeys... (Schama, 1989, p. 631).

> ...the Minister of Justice was turning a blind eye to the violence he clearly knew was about to take place in Paris. When the inspector of prisons, Grandré, came to the Hotel de Ville [the seat of the revolutionary government], where the Minister was in a meeting with the Commune, to voice his concerns about the prisoners' vulnerability, Danton brushed him off with a curt...'I don't give a damn about the prisoners; let them fend for themselves.' On the third of September, as reported by Brissot, Danton claimed that the 'executions were necessary to appease the people of Paris...an indispensable sacrifice...' (pp 632-633).

> The Abbaye [which was serving as a prison] was the site of the first mass killing. A party of twenty-four priests taken there under armed escort from the mairie only just escaped violent assault from the crowd at the rue de Buci. When they reached the prison, however, another crowd (possibly the same group that had attacked them earlier, swollen by reinforcements) demanded summary 'judgment.' A grotesquely perfunctory interrogation was followed by their being pushed down the steps and into the garden, where their killers waited armed with knives, axes, hatchets, sabers and, in the case of a butcher (by trade) called Godin, a

4

carpenter's saw. In an hour and a half, nineteen of the group were hacked to pieces. The five who survived to bear witness to the atrocity included the Abbé Sicard, who had been spared only through the intervention of a grocer National Guardsman named Monnot. Later on the second, the sanguinary scene was repeated at the Carmelite convent used as a holding cell for another hundred and fifty priests. Assembled there by the ex-monk turned Jacobin Joachim Ceyrat, they were subjected to a roll call, each name being followed by the briefest questioning, a 'sentence' and murder carried out with the usual assortment of weapons. The fortunate ones were shot. In a desperate attempt to escape from the convent garden, some climbed trees and threw themselves over the wall to the street below; others ran into the chapel, from which they were dragged, then bludgeoned and stabbed. In the midst of the carnage the commissaire of Luxembourg section, Jean-Denis Violette, arrived, briefly halting the proceedings. A slightly more formal manner of judicial proceeding actually produced some 'acquittals,' but by the end of the day one hundred and fifteen persons had been subject to the...axe of vengeance..., including the Archbishop of Arles, the bishops of Saints and Beauvais and the royalist Charles de Valfons. In the days that followed, return visits were made to the Abbaye, where the murderers subsequently referred to their... labor...—for which evidently they had been promised specific wage rates. According to the army officer Jourgniac de Saint-Méard, who somehow survived and whose story of what he called his 'thirty-eight hours of agony' is one of the best accounts of the slaughter, the horror was compounded by the 'profound and sombre silence' in which the executioners worked. About two thirds of the prisoners at the Abbaye were killed....At two thirty on the morning of the third of September, the General Council of the Commune was told by its secretary, Tallien (also one of the commissaires), that though safe-conducts had been issued to protect the prisoners, there were simply too many able-bodied citizens on military duty at the barriers to ensure their safety. This was a prime instance of the conspiracy of disingenuousness that enabled those few members of the Assembly still sitting to exercise a Pilatic impartiality while the massacre continued. Another commissaire, Guiraut, was even more self-exonerating when he claimed that 'by exercising vengeance the people are doing justice.' To the Legislative Assembly he claimed there was a serious mutiny of prisoners under way at another of the prisons, Bicétre, that had to be dealt with before it became a security threat to the whole city. What was really taking place at Bicétre was the systematic butchering of adolescent boys. While the inmates at the Abbaye, the Carmelites and another holding cell at the Monastery of Saint-Firmin, were nearly all priests and political prisoners rounded up over the previous two weeks, those at Bicétre, La Force and La Salpétriére, the scenes of similar slaughters, were common criminals, beggars and persons detained at the request of their own families under the conventions of the old regime. Forty-three of the one hundred and sixty-two persons killed at Bicétre were under eighteen, including thirteen age fifteen, three age fourteen, two age thirteen and one twelve-year-old. It appears that the chief warden of the house, one Boyer, participated vigorously in killing his own inmates. At Saint-Bernard another seventy or so convicts waiting to be taken to the hulks [old ships converted into prisons] were murdered; at La Salpétriére over forty prostitutes were killed after being, in all likelihood, subjected to physical humiliation at the hands of their killers. (pp. 633-635).

One of the ladies in waiting to the Queen at La Force, the Princess de Lamballe, had been

Required to swear an oath of loyalty to Liberty and Equality and one of hatred to the King, Queen and monarchy…she accepted the first but refused the latter. A door was opened off the interrogation room, where she saw men waiting with axes and pikes. Pushed into an alley she was hacked to death in minutes. Her clothes were stripped from her body to join the immense pile that would later be sold at public auction, and her head was struck off and stuck on a pike. Some accounts, including that of Mercier, insist on the obscene mutilation and display of her genitals…What is certain is that her head was carried through the streets of Paris to the Temple, where one of the crowd barged into the King's rooms to demand that the Queen show herself at the window to see her friend's head, 'so you may know how the people avenge themselves on tyrants.' Marie-Antoinette spared herself this torment by fainting on the spot, but the valet de chamber Cléry peered through his blinds to see the blond curls of the Princess de Lamballe bobbing repellently in the air. (p. 635).

1792
(cont'd.)

> Approximately one half of all the prisoners in Paris died in the September massacres. In some places like the Abbaye and the Carmelites, 80 per cent or more of the inmates perished. There were signs of remorse and even desperation among the helpless members of the Legislative and even among some of the Commune.... But the Commune never pursued the killers, and a number of its members actually praised the deeds as a useful purge of a fifth column. (p. 636).

In the countryside, similar massacres were evident.

> A batch of forty-odd prisoners was being sent from Orléans to Paris, and the Legislative Assembly decided to divert the party to Saumur for its own safety. But one of the most militant of the Paris sectionnaires, Fournier 'the American,' actually set out with a company of armed men to ensure that the prisoners kept to the original plan. At Versailles the whole party, including the...Minister of Foreign Affairs de Lessart, were massacred in what looks remarkably like a premeditated plan. For days the sites were carefully scrubbed down and doused with vinegar, though at some prisons, like La Force, some of the bloodstains were not expungeable. (p. 637).

> In the urban centers...[as late as] December [1793 there was]...exceptional brutality. Two hundred prisoners were executed at Angers in December alone, two thousand at Saint-Florent. Others were brought from the crowded prisons at Nantes and Angers to places like Pont-de-Cé and Arvillé, where three to four thousand were shot in one long, relentless slaughter. (p. 788).

> The most notorious massacres were at Nantes, where the representant-en-mission [the local representative of the revolutionary government], Jean-Baptiste Carrier, supplemented the guillotine with what he called 'vertical deportations' in the river Loire. Holes were punched in the sides of flat-bottomed barges below the waterline, over which wooden planks were nailed to keep the boats temporarily afloat. Prisoners were put in with their hands and feet tied and the boats pushed into the center of the river to catch the current. The executioner-boatmen then broke or removed the planks and made haste to jump into boats that were alongside, while their victims helplessly watched the water rise about them. Anyone attempting to survive

7

<table>
<tr><td>1792
(cont'd.)</td><td>by jumping in was sabered in the water. At first these drownings were confined to priests and took place, almost guiltily, by night. But what the sans-culotte 'Marat company' [revolutionary enthusiasts] conspicuous in the repression humorously called 'the republican baptisms' or the 'national bath' became routinized and were executed in broad daylight, where some witnesses survived to describe them. In some cases, prisoners were stripped of their clothes and belongings (always an important source of perquisites for the soldiers), giving rise to accounts of 'republican marriages': young men and women tied naked together in the boats. Estimates of those who perished in this manner vary greatly, but there were certainly no fewer than two thousand and quite possibly as many as forty-eight hundred. (p. 789). ⌒</td></tr>
</table>

1794 — The State of Pennsylvania abolished capital punishment for all crimes except premeditated murder (Osborne, 1975/1916, p. 87). "In 1795 New York followed her example" (Osborne, 1975/1916, p. 96). ⌒

1797 — New York's Newgate Prison was opened. It became the site of the first prison industries in which convicts manufactured goods for the general market. (Murton, 1976, p. 12).

> In the years 1791 and 1795, **Thomas Eddy**, a New York philanthropist and Quaker who...later...was called the 'John Howard of America,' visited...the famous Walnut Street Prison...A prison was being planned for the State...and the New York Quakers had heard of the remarkable success of the Philadelphia prison [see Introduction]. In 1796, Eddy secured...a bill 'for...the erecting of State prisons.' The...first board of governors of the prison [was] composed mainly of Quakers. New York adopted...the Philadelphia system...and Eddy himself became the prison's first warden (Chenault, 1949-1951, p. 4; bold emphasis added).

In 1815 two additional buildings were constructed. "On the second floor of one of them was the chapel, for religious services and likely some form of instruction." (Start, in Angle, 1982, p. 4). Chaplain **John Stanford** and selected convict teachers offered instruction in "the elementary branches of education" in 1821; in 1825 lessons were held on winter evenings as well as Sundays (Chenault, 1949-1951, p. 4). By 1828 Newgate was closed—replaced by Auburn Prison (Chenault, 1949-1951, p. 3—see 1816 entry). ⌒

1798 — At more than 50 years of age, **John Henry Pestalozzi** came to the realization that he needed to show his ideas in action, in addition to writing about them (Monroe, 1912, p. 310). Pestalozzi was profoundly influenced by Rousseau's *Emile*, the French Revolution, and humanitarianism. Originally prepared for the ministry, then for law, he finally became a farmer. He had "the double purpose of improving a waste tract of land through new methods of cultivation and of living a life in accord with the prevalent naturalistic ideals" (Monroe, 1912, p. 309). His farmhouse was called "Neuhof," and it was funded by extensive loans (Quick, 1916, pp. 295-296). Students were first enrolled in 1774. Pestalozzi wrote "Our position entailed much suffering on my wife...but nothing could shake us in our resolve to devote our time, strength and remaining fortune to the simplification of the instruction and domestic education of the people." (Quick, 1916, p. 297). "Very often the little beggars whom he had gathered up waited only till they had received from him new clothing, and then ran away and resumed their vagabond life" (Compayre, 1907, p. 421). Pestalozzi's work in education has been summarized as an emphasis on "the point of view of the developing mind of the child." In addition he substituted experimentation for tradition. (Monroe, 1912, pp. 308-309).

From 1775-1780 Pestalozzi conducted what was probably the first 'industrial school for the poor.' The children were engaged in raising special farm products, in spinning and weaving of cotton and in other occupations....they also spent some time in reading and in committing passages to memory and especially in arithmetical exercises....But the combined functions of manager, farmer, manufacturer, merchant, schoolmaster, were beyond the ability of the reformer, and the experiment failed. During the next eighteen years, 1780-1798, Pestalozzi, as a participant in the revolutionary movement, devoted himself chiefly to literary activity....Social and political reforms were to be brought about by education—not the current education, but a new process of development that would result in the moral and intellectual reform of the people....The most popular of all Pestalozzi's writings, the one that exerted the most influence, was his *Leonard and Gertrude*, the first volume of which was published in 1781. Written as a novel, it popularized the idea that he initiated in practical reform...later. The purpose of the book was to depict the simple village life of the people and the great changes caused therein by the insight and devotion of a single ignorant woman, Gertrude. By her industry and patience and skill in educating her children she saves her husband, Leonard, from idleness and drink. Neighbors, children

9

and neighboring families are finally brought within the influence of the new ideas; and by the simple methods of this peasant woman this new purpose in education effects the reform of the entire village....This was his mission in life: to work out in detail the methods of this education that was to effect the regeneration of society by securing for every child that moral and intellectual development which was his natural right and inheritance. (Monroe, 1912, pp. 309-310).

From 1787 to 1797 Pestalozzi published nothing. He had become famous, and was frequently in the company of men such as Goethe and Fichte; he was declared a "Citizen of the French Republic," despite the fact of his Swiss nationality, "together with Bentham, Tom Payne, Wilberforce, Clarkson, Washington, Madison, Klopstock, Kozciusk, etc." (Quick, 1916, p. 310). Fichte urged him to complete his works and philosophy of education, and in 1797 Pestalozzi's books appeared in quick succession: *Inquiry into the Course of Nature in the Development of the Human Race,* then a book on the ABCs, and another of fables. (Quick, 1916, pp. 311-312). The French overran Switzerland in 1798 and established a Directory of five persons to run the country. Pestalozzi began writing material to support the new government. Several directors favored his approach to education, and Pestalozzi's school was funded. (Quick, 1916, pp. 314-315). He launched a new career as schoolmaster, and his influence expanded steadily. (Monroe, 1912, p. 310). But many of the Catholic Swiss cantons resisted the French, and the revolutionary soldiers were fierce in their retaliatory massacres (Quick, 1916, p. 315). Pestalozzi took charge of education in a district of Switzerland that had a large number of recently orphaned children. At Stanz, on the shores of Lake Lucerne, he worked out the core of his program, combining learning activities with work to establish a milieu in which students were "immediately interested." (Monroe, 1912, pp. 310-311). To the students

he seemed no philanthropist, but only a servant of the devil, an agent of the wicked government which had sent its ferocious soldiers and slaughtered the parents...a Protestant who came to complete the work by destroying their souls. Pestalozzi, who was making heroic efforts on their behalf, seems to have wondered at the animosity shown him by the people of Stanz... And yet in spite of enormous difficulties of every kind Pestalozzi triumphed. (Quick, 1916, p. 316).

Pestalozzi's five months' experiment at Stanz proved one of the most memorable events in the history of education. He was now completely satisfied that he saw his way to giving children a right education, and 'thus raising the beggar out of the dung-hill'; and

<table>
<tr>
<td valign="top">1798
(cont'd.)</td>
<td>seeing the right course he was urged by his love of the people into taking it. (Quick, 1916, p. 333).</td>
</tr>
</table>

The institution Pestalozzi established at Stanz was an orphan asylum (Compayre, 1907, p. 423).

> Children instructed children; they themselves tried the experiment; all I did was to suggest it. Here again I obeyed necessity. Not having a single assistant, I had the idea of putting one of the most advanced pupils between two others who were less advanced. (Pestalozzi, in Compayre, 1907, p. 424—see 1805 entry).

In 1799 the very French soldiers whose behavior had brought him to Stanz "drove him away again." They needed the school buildings for a hospital. (Quick, 1916, p. 317). Pestalozzi taught at Burgdorf. He developed the principle of the object lesson for mental development. "Here Pestalozzi first announced his great aim, 'I wish to psychologize education'" (Monroe, 1912, p. 312; Quick, 1916, p. 336). "Pestalozzi was thinking not so much of the children of Burgdorf as of the children of Europe. For Burgdorf...could not contain him" (Quick, 1916, p. 336).

> Focusing on his new challenge to the existing education Establishment, he wrote *How Gertrude Teaches her Children* in 1801. Great public attention was directed to his work, which was assisted by the government, and was widely discussed through pamphlet and magazine controversy. (Monroe, 1912, p. 312).

But the program was impacted by the withdrawal of funds and disagreement among the Institute's directors, and eventually abandoned.

1801 — "Meritorious inmates" in New York were allowed to participate in elementary school during the winter months (Roberts, 1971, p. 4). This was seen as a great step forward at the time.

> Pennsylvania law required that boots made by prisoners at Walnut Street Jail must be branded with the words "State Prison" (Reagen and Stoughton, 1976, p. 58—see entries for 1888, 1921, and 1935.) The event, a result of a long process of argument between merchants and civic leaders, began a protracted dialogue regarding the sale of goods made in institutions.

1802 — Around 1802

> **Pestalozzi** made a journey to Paris, as a member of the consulta called by Bonaparte to decide the fate

<table>
<tr>
<td>1802
(cont'd.)</td>
<td>of Switzerland. He hoped to take advantage of his stay in France to disseminate his pedagogical ideas. But Bonaparte refused to see him, saying that he had something else to do besides discussing questions of a,b,c. Monge, the founder of the Polytechnic School, was more cordial, and kindly listened to the explanations of the Swiss pedagogue. But he concluded by saying, 'It is too much for us!' More disdainful still, Talleyrand had said, 'It is too much for the people!' (Compayre, 1907, pp. 434-435; bold emphasis added; exclamation emphasis in original).</td>
</tr>
</table>

In 1803 the Swiss government took over the castle of Burgdorf, which Pestalozzi had converted to a school. In exchange, the government gave him the convent of Munchen-Buchsee. 🔺

1805 — **Pestalozzi** moved his operation to Yverdun (Compayre, 1907, p. 434), in a French-speaking district of Switzerland at the foot of Lake Neufchatel where Pestalozzi thought he would make more headway. This experiment took 20 years and highlighted secondary education and teacher preparation. Monroe offered this summary of his life "what Rousseau had demanded in a theoretic way for one individual, Emile, Pestalozzi demanded for every child, no matter how poor and humble his surroundings or how limited his capacities" (Monroe, 1912, p. 313). Pestalozzi defined education as "the natural, progressive, harmonious development of all the powers and faculties of the human being" (p. 315). He sought to establish schools that were "transformed homes, approximating the same relationships, duplicating the same spirit, seeking the same ends..." (p. 317). Pestalozzi's instruction focused on immediately tangible objects, rather than on words, and the sense impression of the student. This was known as the object lesson.

'Mental' arithmetic, the syllabic and phonetic methods in language work, and the study of geography and of nature in direct contact with natural environment were some of the innovations in method. In general, the arrangement of all modern textbooks is a direct... outgrowth of Pestalozzi's efforts at analyzing the subject into its simplest elements and proceeding then, by a gradual increase in the complexity of the material, to build up a connected and symmetrical understanding of the subject. The old method of beginning with a mastery of rules and principles as in arithmetic, of the rules of abstract form in language, or of most general relations, as in geography, history and the natural sciences, has been gradually superseded. (pp. 317-318).

1805 Morf, one of Pestalozzi's most capable disciples, summarized the
(cont'd.) instructional method of "Father Pestalozzi." It was based on
(1) Observation or sense perception ("intuition"). (2) Language should
always be rooted in observation of an object. (3) Judgment or criticism
is inappropriate when students are learning. (4) Teaching "should
begin with the simplest elements and proceed gradually according to
the development of the child...in psychologically connected order."
(5) Enough time should be directed to the lesson to allow mastery.
(6) Teaching is not an exercise in dogmatism, but in development.
(7) Teachers must respect students. (8) "The chief end of elementary
teaching is not to impart knowledge and talent to the learner, but to
develop and increase the powers of his intelligence." (9) Knowledge
and power are related; skill results from learning information. (10) Love
should regulate the relation between teacher and student, "especially
as to discipline." (11) The higher aims of education should regulate
instruction. (p. 318). Pestalozzi was a correctional educator who
impacted the larger, more general field of elementary education. "The
great superiority of Pestalozzi over Rousseau is that he worked for the
people" (Compayre, 1907, p. 442).

In the British penal colonies of Australia, "Educated convicts—
known as Specials—took pride in their literacy and their distance from
the brutish laboring mass of felons" (Hughes, 1987, p. 339). They were
much in demand.

> Because such people were uncommon (less than half,
> probably no more than a third, of the prisoners arriving
> in Australia at any stage of its penal history could
> sign their names), they were of value to government,
> which by the mid-1820s needed a small army of clerks
> to keep track of convicts' records. The bureaucracy
> of New South Wales and Van Diemen's Land [penal
> colonies] was almost wholly made up of forgers, none
> averse to palm oil. Governor Darling complained
> that 'these people are guilty of all sorts of nefarious
> practices, altering and interpolating the Registers, and
> cannot be restrained by any fear of punishment or
> disgrace...[T]hey cannot resist a bribe.' But there were
> few free clerks, and so government demands meant
> that few Specials were assigned (p. 349)

to hard labor. Some wealthy free Australian families bragged about the
convict tutors

> who steered the children through mensa....The first
> grammar school in Sydney was started by a ruined
> Irish clergyman, **Laurence Halloran** (1765-1831),
> transported at the age of forty-six for forging a tenpenny

frank. Certainly he was a better pedagogue than John Mortlock, a former officer in the British Army who had seen service in India and who was made headmaster of a small Hobart grammar school in the 1850s: 'To impress myself with a sense of my dignity, and to lighten my spirits, I immediately belaboured several of the boys (particularly those whose parents had never been transported). This refreshed and consoled me.' Because they had known respectability, most Specials found it very difficult to accept their fate. (Hughes, 1987, p. 349; emphasis added).

"Giving themselves airs and graces, [they] were disliked—and some detested—by laboring convicts for their flashness and arrogance. Officialdom could make life difficult for those suspected of freethinking." (pp. 350-351). One uneducated convict wrote that the Specials'

'hands were very soft...[T]hey schemed and wasted their time. In the middle of work I often heard them commence to talk about the fine wine they had drunk at some of the big inns in London.' One Special was said to live by the motto "What is the use of a friend, but to take the use of him?" (p. 351).

Among some educated convicts

'relaxation, petty traffic and abuse' reigned. They seized every privilege they could get; they truckled to authority ('When an overseer spoke to him,' it was said of one Special, 'he had the appearance of a goose looking down a bottle') and made tyrannous overseers themselves....'The worst wretches that a man could be put to work under were those who had been sent to the country [transported] themselves. They were far worse than men who came out free.' (p. 439).

The Port Macquarie penal colony, which was the maximum security facility before Norfolk Island (see 1840 entry), had a high proportion of Specials. The governor sent them there so they would not cause trouble in Sydney by leaking information to faultfinding Australian newspapers.

Some of them were harmless creatures, like the Irishman James Bushelle, who, in cahoots with 'a broken-down French gambler,' had toured the jewelry shops of London masquerading as a Polish prince, with gum on his fingertips, substituting fake diamonds for real ones. He drew life in New South Wales, and on being reconvicted at Port Macquarie he found a niche as a tutor to some of the free settlers who had begun to trickle in after 1830, 'instructing the young ladies both married and single,' as he put it, 'in music, dancing, French and Italian...who met occasionally to enjoy the pleasure of a German Waltz or a Spanish Quadrille in this recent Emanation from the forest; where hitherto the sound of music, or the voice of merriment, had never been heard; where no sounds, but...the groans of the convicts under the excruciating Lash, or the croaking of the wild Cockatoo, ever pierc'd the Skies or disturb'd the Ambient Air.' Thus, the first uncertain pipings of the Muses were heard at Port Macquarie. (pp. 438-439). ᕊ

"In 1805 the Lancasterian method was introduced into [the local schools of] New York City. Within a few years almost every city from Boston to Charleston, in the South, and Cincinnati, in the West, had its monitorial or Lancasterian schools" (Monroe, 1912, p. 383). What was this new system of instruction? Monroe called it

The Monitorial System of Bell and Lancaster.—In 1797 Dr. Andrew Bell introduced into England the system of using the older boys for the instruction of the younger, which he had previously employed in an orphan asylum. By him, and especially by Joseph Lancaster (1778-1838), the system was developed until it became for England a somewhat inadequate substitute for a national system of schools. Through the use of a few conduct monitors and a sufficient number of teaching monitors drawn from the more advanced students, and through a detailed system of organization of method, it was possible for one teacher to direct a large number of pupils. With Lancaster the ideal, which he himself reached before he was twenty years of age, was for one teacher to control a school of one thousand boys. Thus in the absence of any willingness on the part of the people adequately to support schools, with the government opposed on principle to contributing for such purposes, and with the religious bodies wholly unable to cope with the needs of the times, the monitorial system made possible some general attention to public education. The Bell system found little or no footing in America, since it was connected wholly with the Church of England schools. The great service with the Lancasterian system rendered in our own country was in accustoming the people to schools for the masses of the people, to contributing to their support

15

as individuals, and in gradually educating the people to look upon education as a function of the state. In addition to this it introduced a better system of grading, since all Lancasterian schools were rigidly graded on the basis of arithmetic work, and also on the basis of spelling and reading. Hence promotion was possible in one subject when it was not in the other. Moreover, it brought in a better arrangement and classification of material and a better organization and discipline of the school. The great defects of this system were that the work was most formal; that most of the instruction was extremely superficial; that the discipline was rigid and mechanical; and that the information gained was the result of formal memory work. There was absolutely no conception of the psychological aspect of the work and no intimation whatever of the newer, broader and truer conception of education that was developing on the continent [Europe].... Lancaster himself came to this country and assisted in the New York, Brooklyn [which was a separate city then] and Philadelphia schools. In the third decade of the [19th] century, the system was introduced in New York and Boston into a new type of schools, the newly founded high schools. For this and the two following decades the system was widely popular in the many academies throughout the country. As in the case of the Fellenberg system [to fund schools that applied Pestalozzi's methods—see 1798 entry], with which it was often combined, the system disappeared in consequence of the arousing of public opinion on the subject of education, of the growing material prosperity of the people and of their growing willingness to contribute more liberally to the cause of education. (pp. 382-384). ☁

1808 — During the 1749-1808 period the number of capital convictions in the greater London area increased by about 60%, while the number of executions declined by more than 50%. The percentage of executions gradually diminished from approximately 70% of capital convictions, to approximately 16%. The reason was that transportation was brought into greater use as an alternative to the death sentence. (Hughes, 1987, p. 35).

George III took the exercise of the Royal Prerogative of Mercy (the King's power to override his courts and remit a sentence at will) very seriously. The Royal Mercy showed his subjects that their monarch cared about them. One besought it by letter, through the home secretary, enclosing whatever references and

<table>
<tr><td>1808
(cont'd.)</td><td>sub-petitions could be raised from clergymen and other respectable people, and it was quite often given. The laws were the stick, mercy the carrot. There was subtlety in maintaining the hanging laws but not automatically using them. If they had merely been repealed, the effect would not have been the same. For mercy to evoke gratitude, the ruler must be seen to <u>choose</u> mercy, so that each reprieve is a special case, to be paid for in gratitude and obedience, never taken as a right. (p. 36; emphasis in original).</td></tr>
</table>

1809 — The first ombudsman program was started, in Sweden (Geary, 1975, p. 290). In several nations ombudspersons liaise and facilitate dialogue between government and community interests.

1810 — The first "family substitute" juvenile institution was opened by **Phillip Emanuel** in Switzerland. He put **Johann Jakob Wehrli**, a 20-year old school teacher, in charge and the facility became known as "Wehrli." It started with 20 boys (Eriksson, 1976, p. 107). They were involved in lessons for two hours each day. Young teachers began coming to work as trainees, and

> from 1813 a school for country school-teachers was affiliated with the institution, eventually accommodating about 60 students. According to Wehrli's educational system, both he and the teachers were not to be regarded as...supervisors but as 'older brothers.' He included the boys in all decision-making and allowed them to take part in all discussions concerning disciplinary matters and the financial situation of the institution. **Pestalozzi** [see 1798 entry] is said to have been very interested in Wehrli and astonished that he had been able to realize Pestalozzi's own ideas, even though he had never been under the man's personal influence. Wehrli left his school in 1833 to become the principal of a teachers college in...Thurgau. He died in 1855. (p. 108; bold emphasis added).

Books about prisons were beginning to appear. In his *Remarks on Prisons,* Scotland's **Stevenson Maggill** wrote

> They [prisoners], of all classes of men, require the benefit of religious ordinances and instruction, whether you view them as unfortunate or criminal; as involved in calamity, or as under the power of ignorance, error or depravity. The ignorant require to be instructed; the erring and depraved to be reclaimed;

1810
(cont'd.)

the unfortunate to be comforted; the wisest and best to be aided, directed, and built up, in the time of trial and temptation. (Maggill, 1810, p. 60). ⌒

1813 —

Lieutenant Governor Thomas Davey...ran Van Diemen's Land [a British penal colony in Australia] from 1813 to 1816....Nicknamed 'Mad Tom' by the settlers, he would later make it his custom to broach a keg of rum outside Government House on royal birthdays and ladle it out to the passersby (Hughes, 1987, p. 369—see 1840 entry).

Australian convicts had their own traditional toasts. London's "Newgate [Prison] was called the 'whit' or 'wit,' and all flash lads drank to its destruction. 'The Wit be burnt,' ran a common criminal toast, 'the Flogging Cull (flogger) be damned, the Nubbing Chit (gallows) be curs'd.'" (p. 36). ⌒

1816 — Auburn Prison was established in New York State, under the same law that had established Newgate. [See 1797 entry.] A special wing for solitary cells was completed on Christmas Day, 1821, and by 1823 the new system was fully operational. (Chenault, 1949-1951, p. 5).

Auburn's inmates...worked together during the day in silence under an elaborate system of regimentation and surveillance which included the lockstep, striped uniforms, and extensive corporal punishment. Less concerned with spiritual redemption [than the Pennsylvania system at Walnut Street Jail—see Introduction], the Auburn system attempted to remold prisoners through 'prison discipline.' (Freedman, 1981, p. 9).

In 1820 Auburn **Chaplain Bowser** made sure that Bibles and other religious books were available to "occupy their attention." By 1822 he was providing instruction between 8:00 and 9:00 each morning, "while some of the officers get their meals," in addition to Sunday lessons. Bowser recommended longer school hours and vocational education. (Chenault, 1949-1951, p. 6—see 1826 entry). ⌒

1817 — **Elizabeth Fry** (see 1832 entry) "and her ladies" were active at England's Newgate Prison, in London, "employing, educating, and religionising women and children" incarcerated there.

The three Rs were taught on the monitorial system and Bible readings were required...A wealthy and well-connected Quaker, it was not all that difficult for Mrs. Fry to incline the ear of authority to her ideas

1817
(cont'd.)

and practices which spread widely anyway thanks to the formation up and down the country over the next twenty years or so of 'ladies' prison committees, to say nothing of 'The Society for the Improvement of Prison Discipline' [see 1837 entry] which by means of visits to and inspections of prisons and of its published findings, 'holding up to public odium local authorities which had effected no reforms,' exercised not a little influence in high places....Elizabeth Fry, traditionally regarded as the founding mother of prison education, merits an essay in her own right...Someone of her personality, single-mindedness, drive, persistence, and dedication could not really fail to make an impact on a prison at that time. This is amply borne out by the contemporary achievements of **Sarah Martin** [see 1832 entry] in Yarmouth gaol, a person in humbler circumstances by far than Mrs. Fry and who, with no 'friends at court' to help her, nevertheless pioneered educational and religious ideas and practices amongst the prisoners there which were not all that different from Mrs. Fry's at Newgate. For the fact was that...prison reform was part of a wider humanitarian movement which had been growing in strength throughout the eighteenth century and was international in scale, part of the flowering of European enlightenment. As the century turned into the nineteenth...the movement attracted to itself powerful popular support associated with evangelical piety... (Forster, 1981, p. 29; emphasis added—see 1855 entry). ⌒

1819 — Englishman **William Roscoe**'s book appeared, *Observations on Penal Jurisprudence and the Reformation of Criminals*. It described the affect of instruction from inmate teachers on their student peers: "Their improvement in many instances surpasses expectation..." (Roscoe, 1819, p. 49). ⌒

At a graduation ceremony, a Black graduate of New York City's African Free School (in the local, non-institution community) asked

Shall I be a mechanic? No one will employ me; white boys won't work with me. Shall I be a merchant? No one will have me in his office; white clerks won't associate with me. Drudgery and servitude, then, are my prospective portion. Can you be surprised at my discouragement? (Tyack, 1974, p. 123).

Patterns of discrimination against education for African Americans were well established throughout the country, not only in the slave

19

1819   states. During an 1835 riot in Washington, D.C., "shipyard workers
(cont'd.) raged through black classrooms, demolishing furniture, breaking
      windows, and burning schools to the ground." (p. 112). ⌒

1820 — "Sabbath schools became a customary feature in many of the northern
      prisons, especially during the winter months when the prisoners were
      confined....Up until the 1820's children were usually housed in a portion
      of the prison set aside for juveniles." (Angle, 1982, pp. 4-5). ⌒

1821 — In England, **George Holford**'s book was published, *Thoughts on the
      Criminal Prisons of This Country*. Holford's comments about the division
      of labor in many English prisons were revealing:

> In general, the Chaplain is not required by the rules of
> the prison to do more than read prayers and preach
> on a Sunday, and read prayers once or twice besides
> in the course of the week. Where religious books are
> furnished, he is not always the channel through which
> they pass; if instruction be given in reading or writing,
> the school is generally under the management of the
> keeper, (or perhaps, in the case of boys, under that of
> the keeper's wife,) the Chaplain does not interfere, he
> is not consulted in the arrangements made for that
> purpose, he has no voice in the selection of him who is
> to teach, and knows nothing of the proficiency of those
> who are taught... (Holford, 1821, p. 69).

Holford also wrote that the rules at some prisons "contain...a proviso,
'that... attendance [in the school] shall not interfere with the stated
hours of labour.'" (p. 69—see 1899 entry). ⌒

1822 — The New York State legislature passed a law allowing that "It shall
      be lawful...to furnish a Bible for each prisoner confined in a solitary
      cell..." By 1829 this privilege was extended to all inmates who could
      read. (Wallack, 1939, p. 3). ⌒

Rachel Perijo became the first matron in the U.S., at Baltimore
Penitentiary. She offered religious, educational, and industrial
instruction for women there. (Freedman, 1981, p. 58). Perijo "took
charge of about sixty female convicts. There had been, previously,
some vile abuses practiced among them, and as the directors state, this
department was wretchedly managed." Institutional records show that
Perijo improved morale and cut expenses by

> $1,581.66 annually...i.e. the number of days spent in the
> hospital by the sick, has been diminished, what is equal
> to the sickness of one person, more than seventeen
> years....They have also been taught to read....Fifteen,

who could not read, have been taught to read the scriptures, and all, except two aged persons, to read in the spelling book. (BPDS, 1972, vol. #1, pp. 34-35).

Perijo and her daughter served as Sabbath school teachers. (pp. 34-35). In 1836 the Boston Prison Discipline Society reported that the matron at Baltimore Penitentiary cared for 23 females; there was only one female "in the Penitentiary in Washington City;" no females were at the Tennessee or Ohio State Prisons; three were at the Penitentiary in Upper Canada, etc. "So that no Prison remains without a matron, among those mentioned, where there are more than three female prisoners, except the Prison at Bellevue, in the city of New York." (BPDS, 1972, vol. #3, p. 48). "By 1845, when **Dorothea Dix** toured American jails, she found matrons in several Massachusetts houses of correction, at Sing Sing, in Maryland and Pennsylvania jails, and at Eastern Penitentiary" (Freedman, 1981, p. 58; bold emphasis added—see 1850 entry). ⌂

New York's Society for the Prevention of Pauperism released a report that explained its rationale for establishing houses of refuge for juveniles.

These prisons should be schools of instruction rather than places of punishment like our state prisons. The youth confined there should be placed under a course of discipline....The end should be his reformation and future usefulness....The object of the charity is reformation by training its inmates to industry, imbuing their minds with the principles of morality and religion, by furnishing them with the means to earn a living, and above all by separating them from the corrupting influence of improper associates. (Snedden, in Dell'Apa, 1973b, pp. 12-13).

In its 1827 report

the [Boston] Prison Discipline Society estimated that in the state prisons of Maine, New Hampshire, Vermont, New York and Virginia, one-seventh of the inmates were under 21 years of age, while many were under 12. The report states that 'the loathsome skin, the distorted features, the unnatural eyes of some of these boys, indicate, with a clearness not to be misapprehended, the existence of unutterable abominations, which it were better for the world, if they had been foreseen and avoided.' (Osborne, 1975/1916, p. 111). ⌂

Gradually, the concept of reformatory institutions for delinquent and at-risk children attracted attention.

1822
(cont'd.)

...[In] 1822 the Society for the Prevention of Pauperism urge[d] the founding of a juvenile reformatory, to which children might be sent rather than to State Prison: These prisons should be schools of instruction rather than places of punishment, like our present State prisons....calculated to subdue and conciliate.... The end should be his [the inmate's]....reformation and future usefulness....The Society appointed a committee, of which James W. Gerard was chairman, to report on the feasibility...[Half Century, p. 44]. The committee...recommended on February 7, 1823, the erection of a building, entirely separate from the State Prison, for the imprisonment of young offenders both before and after trial....[and] the place of refuge for young delinquents after discharge....Between one hundred and two hundred persons, from seven to fourteen years of age, were annually brought before the police on charges involving...crime....The next step was...to prepare a plan for the 'house of refuge,'....All the groups... public and private...were enthusiastically united in this first civic campaign to save the criminal and delinquent children. (Lewis, O.F., 1967, pp. 295-297—see entry for 1823). ⌂

1823 — At a meeting of New York City's Society for the Prevention of Pauperism on December 19, at which

the...report was read, $800 was raised, and in a short time $18,000 was secured from private subscriptions—the first instance of a large fund being raised from citizens for institutional prison reform for children...[T]he Society was reorganized as the Society for the Reformation of Juvenile Delinquents [Half Century, p. 63]—and that society still [1922] conducts the House of Refuge in the city of New York. A board... was appointed until the Society should be incorporated, which occurred on March 29th, 1824. The State then conferred upon the Society...powers...extraordinarily broad (Act of Incorporation, Ch. 126, Laws of 1824). Heretofore...some State, county or municipal body... had managed the correctional institution. But now, there was given over to a private group the power of imprisonment and...treatment....Legal custody of the inmates was given to the Society, to which was left by the State their...superintendence (Beaumont and de Tocqueville, 1964/1833, p. 110).

....The managers were not required to submit to State authority beyond the filing of an annual report....Two distinct classes of inmates were to be received by the Society: (a) Those children convicted and sentenced for crime, and (b) the children who were not convicted of crime, but who were destitute or neglected, or both, and who were in imminent danger of becoming delinquent. No age limit was set for admission, but boys might not be held by the managers beyond majority, nor girls beyond the age of eighteen years. The institution was thus to be curative, educational and preventive. Commitments to the House of Refuge might be made by police courts...or by...commissioners...of the Almshouse....all those who would infallibly become guilty if left to themselves.... It is of special interest... how, in the formation of this first House of Refuge, the founders set up...the arguments for the reformative treatment of children that fifty years later were set forth as pertaining to young men...at Elmira... (Lewis, O.F., 1967, pp. 295-297—see entry for 1876). ⌒

Quakers started visiting women incarcerated at Philadelphia's Arch Street Prison. They established a library and classes in sewing. (Freedman, 1981, p. 22). ⌒

In England, "Statutory obligations for the provision of education were placed on certain prison authorities...some forty-seven years before similar obligations were placed on school authorities by the act of 1870 to provide universal elementary education for the community as a whole" (Forster, 1981, p. 123).

Both the teaching of reading and access to books were historically associated with the consolations of religion and therefore it is not surprising that the first prison librarians were chaplains, the social engineers of the day. Prisoners were allowed gifts of books from donors and friends and, later, governors [wardens] were permitted to purchase small collections from a meagre annual grant from public funds to supplement the staple provision of the Bible and other 'good books,' as they were described. (p. 55—see entries for 1878 and 1910). ⌒

English interest in Australian penal colonies was growing. At Cambridge University the second place award for the chancellor's gold medal in poetry went to D'Arcy Wentworth, for his heroic poem "Australasia" (Hughes, 1987, p. 364—see 1837 entry). ⌒

1824 — The Auburn Prison warden blocked an attempt to teach youthful inmates the Three Rs because he feared "the increased danger to Society of the educated convict" (Wallack, 1939, p. 17). Although this decision has often been interpreted as especially hostile today, its underlying sentiment is consistent with many modern "tough on crime" approaches. ⌂

The New York-based Society for the Prevention of Pauperism established the first juvenile training school in the United States, known as the New York City House of Refuge. It was "designed to accommodate both delinquent and dependent children. Here was set the very important precedent of placing children who had actually committed crimes together with other children, not differentiating the groups in their subsequent treatment." (Dell'Apa, 1973b, p. 11).

> The pity is that it should have been felt necessary to turn these institutions into minor prisons—where we find the same system of confinement, severity, strict obedience to autocratic authority, brutal punishments, lack of responsibility and total denial of all initiative; the same system that has been tried and has failed in older prisons (Osborne, 1975/1916, p. 112).

By 1830 the House of Refuge managers reported that out of 145 inmates

> committed during the past year, sixty only were children of American parents; while eighty-four were children of foreigners. Of these forty-one were of Irish, and twenty-three of English extraction....Since the opening of the institution six years ago, eight hundred juvenile delinquents have been received, and six hundred and fifty of these have been disposed of in different ways. (BPDS, 1972, vol. #2, p. 485). ⌂

August Zeller "proposed that prisons be true reformatories and described in detail what he had in mind for them" (Eriksson, 1976, p. 98). Approximately fifty years later this concept would become generally accepted among many prison leaders. ⌂

A series of watercolors were commissioned "to promote the beauties of Australia and attract free emigrant settlers" (Hughes, 1987, p. 339). One judge arrived there in 1834, and "was puzzled by the discrepancy between the looks and the contents of the place.... Here, Romantic belief in the therapeutic power of landscape...had to be suspended, a distressing anomaly..." (Hughes, 1987, p. 477). ⌂

1825 — **Louis Dwight** founded the Boston Prison Discipline Society, which advocated Sabbath school moral instruction as part of the Auburn

1825   system of prison discipline (Davis, 1978, p. 9—see 1816 entry). The
(cont'd.) Auburn system helped prisons advance from the cottage industries
         which characterized the Pennsylvania system [see Introduction] to the
         increased production and profits associated with factories.

> The Prison Discipline Society, a reform organization...
> with headquarters at Boston, persistently threw its
> influence for many years against the Philadelphia [or
> Pennsylvania] system. It was left, however, for an...
> English traveller, one **Charles Dickens** by name, to
> deal it [the Pennsylvania system] a staggering blow.
> (Osborne, 1975/1916, p. 100; emphasis added—see
> 1842 entry). ⚑

The English government had decided much earlier to transport criminals
to remote colonial territories rather than build prisons to contain them
in England.

> By 1825, the English authorities knew—and in fact, had
> come to accept—that their ways of dealing with crime
> had failed in the past, were not working now and would
> be unlikely to succeed in the foreseeable future. The
> crime rate in England had not dropped; thus one had
> to conclude that transportation [the exile of criminals]
> did not deter. The question of 'reformation' was not
> quite as important, since so few people came back from
> Australia. In 1826, for instance, only about 7 percent of
> the convicts freed at the end of their sentences chose to
> return to England, an eloquent comment on what they
> believed their chances were there. (Hughes, 1987, pp.
> 425-426).

In the Van Diemen's Land penal colony near Australia, during
"1822 and 1823, one man in ten disappeared. In 1824 the rate rose
to nearly one in seven." They ran "inland, trying to reach the settled
and farmed districts to the east, and most of them died....The usual
requiem was 'Supposed to have perished in the woods.'" (p. 219).
Those who escaped and survived were called bushrangers. In 1825 a
mounted police force of dragoons was organized to track and capture
escapees—hence the term "goons." (p. 236). Those that did not escape
were treated like slaves. The "first Australian railway [was] powered
not by steam but by convicts." (p. 406). Conditions became more
repressive after 1825. In 1830 the New South Wales penal colony
had 18,571 convicts; the total number of floggings was about 3,000;
the number of lashes was 124,333; and the average number of lashes
per flogging was 41. By 1837 there were 32,102 convicts; nearly 6,000
floggings were administered—over 268,000 lashes in all—and the
average number of lashes per flogging was 45. (p. 428). "[R]ecalcitrant

1825   convicts were sometimes chained in semi-starvation" (p. 292). With
(cont'd.)   regard to political dissent,

> Australia...turned the protester into a political
> eunuch without making a martyr of him. The wives
> of transported men, widowed and yet not widowed,
> taught their sons to avoid the ways of the dissenter;
> some of them were asked to do so quite specifically by
> their husbands. (p. 201). ⌂

The first U.S. reform school opened, the New York City
House of Refuge. Many children placed there were what we would
call neglected or delinquent today. These facilities were first called
"Houses of Refuge," then "reform schools," and later "training and
industrial schools." The regime focused on work, education, and
rigid discipline to help young minds gone astray. (Abbott, 1968, vol.
II, pp. 323-328). ⌂

1826 — Auburn chaplain **Reverend Jared Curtis** officially became the founder
of the first prison Sabbath school (BPDS, 1972, vol. #2, p. 618), although
he did not actually begin the job until 1827. Curtis was assigned as
the country's first resident or full-time chaplain (Gaither, 1982, p. 19),
as opposed to being a traditional visiting or part-time chaplain. The
establishment of the position was based on a needs assessment by the
keeper, funded by the Massachusetts Prison Discipline Society (BPDS,
1972, vol. #1, pp. 92-93), and filled the following year. "In May of 1827 a
Sunday School opened in Auburn Prison, the result of a report by **Judge
Powers** to the Legislature of New York. In his report he claimed that 1/8
of the prisoners were illiterate." (Angle, 1982, p. 4; bold emphasis added).
Curtis brought in a teacher from the Auburn Theological Seminary to
instruct illiterate inmates (Chenault, 1949-1951, p. 6). Auburn prisoners
had the choice of either attending classes on Sunday or staying in their
cells, confined and alone, without work or other programs (Reagen and
Stoughton, 1976, p. 52). Enrollment started at 50 (BPDS, 1972, vol. #2,
p. 618); it reached 100 before the year ended; in 1829 it was 150; by 1830
more than 300 had been instructed, cumulatively. Curtis focused on "the
benefit of the young and illiterate portion of the convicts," and offered a
writing class and arithmetic lessons (Chenault, 1949-1951, p. 6). In 1829
the Boston Prison Discipline Society reported that "At Auburn...a very
large proportion of all the convicts, as they are passed on the Sabbath,
at their cell doors, are found reading the scriptures..." (BPDS, 1972, vol.
#1, p. 301). In 1830 Curtis reported that 160 students were in 31 classes,
taught by 32 teachers. "I scarcely know which most to admire, the
devotedness of the teachers, or the ardor and industry of the scholars."
When he was asked "How can you immure yourself of so dreary a
place, and among such a class of men?" Curtis guessed the inquirer
had "yet to learn what is the richest luxury that a benevolent heart can
enjoy." Further, Curtis reported more than 140 "well authenticated cases

1826
(cont'd.)
of reformation...and the recommitals are less than one in twelve." The State legislature awarded him a $250 bonus for the good work. Curtis found that "no other punishment is more dreaded than exclusion from the school." **B.C. Smith**, who later succeeded Curtis, wrote that he had "known [students] frequently to set their supper aside, and study their book as long as they could see, and then eat in the dark." (BPDS, 1972, vol. #1, pp. 348-350—see 1832 entry). ⌒⌒

The Boston House of Reformation was opened, to incarcerate juvenile criminals (Abbott, 1968, vol. #2, pp. 323-328). Along with a teacher and a supervisor, education director **Reverend E.M.P. Wells** offered instruction to nearly 100 juveniles, including ten girls, at the new institution. "Wells...was firmly convinced of the educational value of games, in which he participated" (Eriksson, 1976, p. 132—see 1837 entry). **Beaumont** and **de Tocqueville** later wrote that the schedule at the House of Reformation included five and a half hours of day labor in four workshops: shoemaking, joiner's work, cloth making, and carpentry—four hours of school, one hour of religious study, and two and a quarter hours of recreation. "The children learn in the school, reading, writing, and arithmetic; they also receive some instruction in history and geography." (Beaumont and de Tocqueville, 1964/1833, pp. 142-143). ⌒⌒

Male and female prisoners in Philadelphia jails were separated. The purpose of this policy was to end "promiscuous and unrestricted intercourse" and "universal riot and debauchery" (Freedman, 1981, p. 47). ⌒⌒

The interests and influence of the new Boston Prison Discipline Society extended throughout the Northeastern part of the United States.

> In the Virginia Penitentiary, no provision is made by the State for religious instruction; the scriptures are not read to the men daily; nor has there been a religious service on the Sabbath, sometimes, for three months together. The chapel has been converted into solitary cells. (BPDS, 1972, vol. #1, p. 34). ⌒⌒

In Australia, during the 1822-1826 period, there were on average 245 prisoners at Macquarie Harbor, the "maximum security" penal colony (Hughes, 1987, p. 377). This facility

> would remain a colonial benchmark for some time— the nadir of punishment, until it was shut down and then exceeded by Norfolk Island (p. 380—see 1840 entry).

1826   At Macquarie, convicts were used as guards. (p. 377). Prisoners
(cont'd.) would go to extreme lengths

> to get away...even for a little while. For example, two men would arrange for one to gash the other with an ax or a hoe; the victim would then swear out a charge and other convicts would step forward as witnesses. Since there was no court at Macquarie Harbor, they would all have to be shipped back to Hobart for trial. In court, their testimony would become vague and contradictory, and in the fog of lies the case would have to be dismissed....Other prisoners would simply murder an overseer or a prisoner so they could be hanged in Hobart. (p. 379).

At another South Pacific penal colony, Van Diemen's Land, "A prisoner sank by bad conduct, and went up the rungs by good—after a time" (p. 385).

1827 — The Boston Prison Discipline Society publicly expressed opposition to the Pennsylvania system of prison management. (See Introduction and 1825 entry.)

> As the experiments have been conducted, thus far, the results are decidedly opposed to solitary confinement day and night, as the means of preventing evil communication. We are left, therefore, in view of all the facts known to us, with a preference for solitary confinement at night, and hard labor by day, with such regulations to prevent evil communication as the case requires... (BPDS, 1972, vol. #1, p. 91).

Connecticut's Wethersfield Prison was opened, replacing the abandoned cavern facilities of the gruesome Simsbury Mines Prison. **Moses Pilsbury**, previously New Hampshire State Prison warden, served as warden of the new institution for three years. Pilsbury had the hearty endorsement of the Boston Prison Discipline Society. He was succeeded by **Amos**, his son. **Amos Pilsbury** later managed the Albany (New York) County Penitentiary, the country's first industrial penitentiary for misdemeanants, beginning in 1845. Subsequently, he managed the entire New York prison system. Amos Pilsbury was known for his fair but stern leadership, and for the fact that the prisons he supervised always made a profit. He was a great supporter of **Zebulon Brockway**, who served later at Elmira Reformatory and implemented many important correctional education innovations. Amos' son, **Louis Pilsbury**, became a member of the first Elmira Reformatory board of managers. The Pilsburys were known as "the best prison people in the world" (Brockway, 1969/1912, pp. 23-34—see 1833 entry).

1827   Maine State Prison superintendent **Dr. Rose**, and the keeper, favored the
(cont'd.) establishment of a Sabbath school. Their purpose: "so that the [convicts] may leave the Prison better prepared to become useful citizens" (BPDS, 1972, vol. #1, p. 91—see 1833 entry). ⌒

Like most prison administrators in the U.S., the Auburn Prison keeper **Mr. Powers** stayed in touch with representatives of the Boston Prison Discipline Society. He recommended that

> A resident chaplain should, in all cases, and under all circumstances, strictly conform to the rules and regulations of the institution, especially in not furnishing convicts forbidden intelligence, or the great hypocrisy, and tend to insubordination. He should deal plainly with them, and dwell emphatically upon their deep depravity and guilt in violating the laws of God and their country; convince them of the justice of their sentence; awaken remorse in their consciences; press home upon them their solemn obligations; make them feel pungently the horrors of their situation; and by all other means make them realize the necessity and duty of repentance, of amendment, and of humble and strict obedience to all the regulations of the Prison. This course would tend powerfully to make them better convicts, and, when restored to their liberty, make them better citizens. (BPDS, 1972, vol. #1, p. 92).

Powers thought highly of the school: "A keeper mentioned that a whisper had not been detected in the school in five months. The chaplain's letters concerning this school are delightful." In his report to the legislature, Powers wrote that

> we believe the labors of the present excellent chaplain [**Jared Curtis**—see 1826 entry] have had a most happy effect on the minds of the prisoners. He at once enjoys the good will of the prisoners, as we found by their almost unanimous declarations, and at the same time strengthens the hands of the keepers. It seems to be the effect of truth, plain dealing, and a sincere desire for the good of the convicts...we found the prisoners attentive to their lessons, anxious to learn, and grateful for the care bestowed upon them. We look to it as a great means of reformation. (p. 93).

That year several legislators visited the Prison and its school. They "were so much pleased with it, as to request its enlargement; and it was accordingly enlarged to one hundred [student] members." (p. 93—see entry for 1832). ⌒

1828 — **Reverend James Brown**, the Norwich Castle [Prison] chaplain in Norfolk, England, reported on the 1825 enrollment in his school:

> four hundred prisoners came under my examination; of these 173 could neither read nor write; 28 merely knew the alphabet; 49 could read very imperfectly, so as not to be able to obtain information by it; 51 could read only; and 99 could read and write. (BPDS, 1972, vol. #1, p. 210).

Brown wrote that (a) "ignorance is productive of crime," and reported a "very remarkable correspondence between ignorance and crime." He found that (b) "the prisoners are generally willing to learn, and attentive to the instruction afforded them." At New York's Auburn Prison **B.C. Smith**, Sabbath school superintendent-turned-chaplain, made a strikingly similar report. He found (a) "the truth of the common remark, that ignorance and vice are closely allied," and (b) that the students "applied themselves with such diligence to their lessons," which he found "in general highly gratifying." (p. 210).

Attention to urban crime and delinquency was gradually increasing. The Philadelphia House of Refuge was established (Abbott, 1968, vol. #2, pp. 323-328).

1829 — The government of Kentucky passed legislation requiring the wardens of prisons to arrange for the teaching of reading, writing, and arithmetic for at least four hours every Sunday. The legislation even stipulated that expenses were not to exceed $250.00 per annum. This particular Act became the first one in the country formally providing for the instruction of convicts. By the early 1830's Auburn, Baltimore, Washington, Wethersfield, Charlestown, and Sing-Sing had all employed chaplains to conduct Sunday classes for the instruction of illiterates....In terms of educational progress, the 1830's and 40's were a relatively stable period for prisons and juvenile reformatories in the country. Sabbath schools were well established in many prisons, and juvenile reformatories were gradually being increased as the results of separate treatment became apparent. Of major importance was the fact that it was during this period that the idea of instructing incarcerates became firmly entrenched in the minds of government officials, prison officials, and the general public. (Angle, 1982, p. 5).

Reverend Gerrish Barrett, the chaplain at Philadelphia's Cherry Hill Prison, maintained an individualized Sabbath school

30

1829
(cont'd.)
student activity log. Of 142 prisoners, only ten "could read and write tolerably." (Teeters and Shearer, 1957, p. 158). The Prison inspectors stated in 1839 that the chaplain "visited the sick and instructed the ignorant." During this period "schooling [in the free community] was a private matter and was furnished only to the children whose parents could afford it." (p. 159—see entries for 1823 and 1845). ⚑

Contrary to the title, Charles Caldwell's book *New Views of Penitentiary Discipline and Moral Education* was based on old views. Caldwell referred to confined students as "dunces" (Caldwell, 1829, p. 34), and "depraved" (Caldwell, 1829, p. 33). He wrote that in "youthful offenders...the...brain resembles too much that of the Carib, who is perfectly animal, and never feels a virtuous emotion"(p. 31). However, Caldwell suggested that "moral and religious instructors of criminals should be themselves moral and religious..." (p. 35). He recognized that "To reform...convicts...judicious and active education is essential," but then he went on to explain why.

> [At] school, the dunce requires, for his improvement in letters, more labor in the teacher, and a greater length of time, than the boy of sprightliness; and...the wound, which has long festered, is more difficult to heal than that which is fresh. (p. 34—see 1941 entry).

Caldwell wrote that "Education, to be productive and useful, must be administered within the walls of a prison, precisely as it is within those of a schoolhouse" (p. 35). ⚑

The Industrial Revolution sharpened the perception of socio-economic class differences, prompting interest among the wealthy in curbing crime.

> The Metropolitan Police Act for the City of London... made it quite clear that the new police department was a civil force seeking to attain the objectives of peace, order, and crime control in cooperation with the people. No aspect of police work was quite as strongly stressed in these documents as the duty of every member of the force to protect the rights, service the needs, and earn the trust of the population he policed. (Geary, 1975, p. 372—see 1844 entry).

> The first organized police dates from Charles the Wise, who reigned in France from 1364 to 1380. Endeavoring to bring order into his kingdom, after the first phase of the Hundred Years War with England, he established a body of permanent officials, to enforce the law. It is

written that it was cordially hated by the people as an instrument of oppression... (Osborne, 1975/1916, p. 47). 🐾

1830 — Bibles were distributed to the prisoners at Auburn Prison (Roberts, 1971, p. 5). At Connecticut State Prison, each prisoner was furnished a Bible and other religious books, "to improve their morals and conduct" (Connecticut, 1830). In Illinois, however, the convicts "were supplied with two Bibles, three New Testaments, and several hymn books"—for the entire population (Illinois, 1834). 🐾

At Sing Sing, some convicts were identified as illiterate. The prison had been built according to the Auburn plan in 1825 to house inmates who were leaving Newgate. It was "under the supervision of Elam Lynds, who had been warden at Auburn and was a strict disciplinarian with no belief in the capacity of inmates to reform." (Chenault, 1949-1951, p. 3). Chaplain **Gerrish Barrett** (see 1829 entry) wrote in 1828

> When it was first proposed to teach them to read... the reply was, we have no convenient room, while the Prison is building, where they can be assembled for instruction. The answer to the objection was, teach them through the grated iron doors of their cells, so long as you are subject to the evil of having no room. The next objection was, we have no spelling books. The answer to this objection was, it is possible that you can learn them to read quicker without spelling books. It is at least worthy of an experiment... (BPDS, 1972, vol. #1, p. 211).

In another vein, Barrett wrote "After prayers I heard a black man read." (p. 211). "Every prisoner has a bible...the...only...school-book." In 1830, the keeper provided spelling books. By 1831 some of the officers were "employed in teaching" the 60-80 students. School was interrupted by a cholera epidemic in 1832. In 1835 Barrett suggested that "If the short time of ten minutes per day could be allowed...that they might learn to read...they would go forth into the world with a new incitement to do something for themselves..." But the opposite occurred: the chaplain was told that the school "was...ineffectual and attended with many inconveniences. Those who engaged in it as teachers became less interested as the novelty wore away; and classes of men were often brought out without any teacher appearing to instruct them." (Chenault, 1949-1951, pp. 3-4). The chaplain explained in 1836 that the school was "inadequate to our wants" (BPDS, 1972, vol. #3, p. 48). He requested that an officer might teach on Sunday, but had no authority to implement that change. In 1838 he described the "impracticability of a Sunday school" without a teacher, and suggested that the legislature

1830   provide a schoolmaster. (Chenault, 1949-1951, p. 4—see entries for 1840
(cont'd.)   and 1843). ⌒⌒

        In England, thanks to the advocacy of Elizabeth Fry in fostering
attention to the reforms of Quakers in Philadelphia and New York, the
period from

> 1830 to 1850 was the great age of the so-called 'separate
> system' of prison discipline [Pennsylvania system—
> see Introduction] and numerous publications of prison
> chaplains attest to their activities in alliance with
> schoolmasters. Pentonville [a showcase institution]
> provides what was, at least on paper, as good a
> curriculum as most national schools, if not a better and
> more varied one. So did the boys' prison at Parkhurst....
> From the 1830s onwards...a welling frenzy of deterrent
> punishment for prisoners began to grip the country,
> which endured until the end of the century... (Forster,
> 1981, pp. 30-31).

Prison inspectors were appointed in 1835, subject to a host of regulations
"on every detail of prison life." (pp. 30-31). ⌒⌒

        In London the secretary of state for the colonies feared for
the aboriginal population in the penal colony of Van Diemen's Land
(Tasmania).

> The whole race...may, at no distant period, become
> extinct....Any line of conduct, having for its avowed,
> or for its secret object, the extinction of the Native
> race, could not fail to leave an indelible stain upon the
> character of the British Government. (Hughes, 1987, p.
> 420—see 1876 entry). ⌒⌒

1831 — The inspectors of Pennsylvania's Western Penitentiary submitted the
following report:

> The inspectors of the prison are required to make
> provision for the moral and religious instruction of
> the convicts, by obtaining suitable persons for that
> object whose services are gratuitous....The importance
> of combining with the punishment of offenders the
> means of moral and religious instruction demands
> that a permanent provision be made. We urge an
> appropriation, however moderate, be made during
> the present session of the legislature, for that object...
> provision of a small library which could be placed
> under the direction of the person who might be

1831
(cont'd.)

entrusted with their religious instruction. (Angle, 1982, p. 5). 🔺

Alexis de Tocqueville declared "Nowhere was this [American] system of imprisonment crowned with the hoped-for success....It never effected the reformation of the prisoners." (Anderson, 1982, p. 38).

De Tocqueville, after all, first came to America to report on its penal system. His *Systeme Peniteniare aux Etats-Unis*, 1833...had great influence in Europe... trivia collectors might note that it is thought to be the first book to contain the word 'bureaucracy.' (Smith, 1982). 🔺

1832 — **Jared Curtis**, now serving as chaplain at Massachusetts State Penitentiary, prepared the first known statistical report on a group of convicts. His careful interviews of 256 prisoners documented a need to educate young offenders. (McKelvey, 1977, p. 20). In 1840 Curtis told a Boston Prison Discipline Society representative that "As in former years, so also during the last, he has experienced uniformly, from the warden and all the subordinate officers of the institution, all those attentions which he could wish in the discharge of his official duties" (BPDS, 1972, vol. #3, p. 438). 🔺

At Auburn Prison, where chaplain Jared Curtis had previously enjoyed the "cheerful cooperation" of the officers, approximately 550 students had been served since the school opened. Most were between the ages of 18-30. (Chenault, 1949-1951, p. 6). Thirty-five Theological Seminary students were now serving as teachers (Chenault, 1949-1951, p. 7); one of them was appointed superintendent [of the school], and had "since become the resident chaplain" (BPDS, 1972, vol. #2, p. 619). One teacher was selected by the others to become superintendent in 1833. **Chaplain B.C. Smith** reported that "Exclusion from the school is found to be one of the most effectual modes of punishment for disorderly conduct..." (BPDS, 1972, vol. #2, p. 620). While engaged in reading instruction, the teachers took "the opportunity of dropping useful incidental remarks, and of making such explanations and application of the great truths of the Bible, as calculated to enlighten the understanding and affect the heart..." The school was closed for remodeling in 1833, but reopened with an enrollment of 228. By 1837 all of the illiterates were in school, but then it was closed without explanation. Classes began again in 1839, with 45 teachers; in 1840 enrollment reached 300. Some of the students could not count to ten. (Chenault, 1949-1951, p. 7). Smith reported that 50 volunteer teachers (tutors) were serving the 300 students. "They [the teachers] are full of zeal and hope in the school, and have a special weekly prayer-meeting in behalf of it." (BPDS, 1972, vol. # 3, p. 440—see 1836 and 1843 entries). 🔺

1832　　　　　　　As a result of a scandal, a matron was hired for the Auburn
(cont'd.)　Prison women's quarters. In 1826 Rachel Welch died after childbirth.
She had become pregnant while serving time in a solitary cell, and her
death was caused by a guard's flogging. In 1828 the New York legislature
passed a law requiring separate facilities for male and female prisoners.
(Freedman, 1981, p. 15). By 1830 a legislative committee recommended

> that the females should be kept in separate apartments,
> in a manner similar to the present mode adopted with
> males, placed under the care of matrons, and rigidly
> excluded from each other.

However, the legislature postponed action. (BPDS, 1972, vol. #1,
p. 348). ⌒

In England, prison reformer/correctional educator **Elizabeth
Fry** visited **Sarah Martin** at Great Yarmouth Gaol (Banks, 1958, p.
15). Martin, known as "the Prisoner's friend," lived from 1791-1843.
She served at the Gaol as chaplain and teacher, from the age of about
15—but was not salaried until 1841. (p. 11). This, despite legislation on
the books since 1773 "authorizing the Justices at Quarter Sessions to
appoint chaplains to gaols, at salaries not exceeding 50 £ a year..." (p.
18). Many of Martin's records remain intact. The *Prison Journal* is one. It
records for each prisoner:

> Name, Crime, Religion, Waiting Trial or Convicted,
> Whether able to read when convicted, Whether able
> to write when convicted, Whether Taught in Prison,
> Confined in Gaol or Bridewell [a gaol with a work
> program], Conviction, General Observations—the last
> often occupying considerable space, and showing both
> psychological insight and often intimate knowledge of
> social background (p. 13).

Martin sometimes suffered

> distress at the depravity of one of the turnkeys. 'Yet,'
> she declares, 'even he could not deprive me of respect
> from the prisoners, nor destroy my influence over
> them. My only safe alternative was trust in God....My
> influence with the prisoners was simply supported by
> what I taught of truth.' (p. 16).

In 1838, when a more effective warden was assigned, Martin convinced
the warden's wife to become a matron to the female prisoners (p. 15).
However, "Sarah Martin's work seems to have died with her" (p. 17—
see 1817 entry). ⌒

1832   Despite the visit and report of **Beaumont, de Tocqueville,** and
(cont'd.) **Julius** (see 1826 entry), the Boston House of Reformation

> was in trouble...a commission appointed by the
> municipal authorities inspected the place. The religious
> instruction was found to be unexceptionable, but the
> general schooling program was judged...poor. The
> commission complained that the children were not
> compelled to work harder to contribute to...expenses....
> The entire institution was said to be characterized by
> excessive recreation and entertainment instead of by
> strict moral and physical discipline and correction. The
> children were kept in the institution too long, which
> made the whole operation too costly. Wells did not
> bother to stand up to his bigoted critics. He resigned,
> and the fate of this pioneer institution was sealed.
> (Eriksson, 1976, p. 134). ⌒

1833 — At the Connecticut State Prison (see 1827 entry),

> there is a resident chaplain, who receives a salary of
> four hundred dollars per annum from the state. He
> devotes from two to three hours per day to the duties
> of his office....One hour is spent in the Sabbath school,
> two hours in public worship, and from five to six hours
> in the cells. (BPDS, 1972, vol. # 2, p. 618).

The chaplain was required to

> see that every convict is furnished with a Bible, and
> may apply to the warden for a proper supply....He shall
> not furnish them with any information or intelligence,
> other than relates to their duty, without permission of
> the warden. (BPDS, 1972, vol. #4, p. 147).

He was also required to manage the school "with the cooperation
and concurrence of the warden... [and to] conform, in all cases, to the
general rules and regulations of the institution." (p. 147). The chaplain
was superintendent of the school, and was assisted by ten teachers who
were "gentlemen living in the neighborhood" (BPDS, 1972, vol. #2, p.
619). In 1842 a legislative committee reviewed the relevant State law:

> The statute provides for a chaplain to the Prison,
> and requires him to devote his whole time to the
> religious instruction and moral improvement of
> the prisoners; also that suitable apartments shall be
> provided for the introduction of a system of Sabbath
> school instruction, to be conducted under the

superintendence of the warden and chaplain, in such manner as may be prescribed by the by-laws. (BPDS, 1972, vol. #4, p. 146).

However, "There has been no Sabbath school for some years past. The principal reason assigned by the warden for the omission, is the difficulty of obtaining teachers. The chaplain instructs some of the prisoners from cell door to cell door..." (p. 146). The prison directors had their own understanding about facilities for correctional education facilities, and the institutional rules specified that the chaplain "shall... instruct, through the grating of the cell doors, all who are unable to read" (p. 147). On a related issue, the legislative committee wrote that "The opportunities for giving instruction on week days are not considerable, and most of the prisoners, on the Sabbath, prefer resting from labor rather than attending to moral or religious teaching." Of 805 prisoners incarcerated up that time, 171 were aged 12 to 20. The committee suggested that individualized instruction should be provided each day "which would not take much from the [State industry] earnings of each prisoner." The Committee recommended that the education program should be structured like that of a reformatory.

> In other states, Houses of Refuge or Reformation have been established for young offenders, where they not only work and receive instruction, but care is used to find them places for earning a living, after their discharge, removed from old associates, haunts, and temptations, instead of leaving them to their own unaided resources and resolutions. (BPDS, 1972, vol. #4, p. 146).

The Committee wanted to offer correctional education for "the more youthful and docile prisoners" (p. 147). By 1844, two new classes were in operation, one for females and the other for juveniles (p. 388). Many of the students "have at times been so anxious to receive instruction, that it has been necessary to break away from them, leaving them in tears both of joy and distress" (p. 389).

The New Hampshire Prison Sabbath school was closed, a result of the construction of the new prison, "but four convicts, who cannot read, are now learning to read, and six have been taught in the Prison" (BPDS, 1972, vol. #2, p. 619). In 1826 former warden **Moses Pilsbury** (see 1827 entry) began donating "twenty-five dollars annually, from his own means, to be added to what the State appropriates...to the...instruction of the convicts" (BPDS, 1972, vol. #1, p. 91). By 1844 **Reverend Mr. Atwood** was hired as chaplain. "He has acquired the respect and confidence of the prisoners. The discharged convicts...frequently call at his office for advice." Atwood's service was characterized "with benevolence and zeal for the reformation of the convicts." The State

1833   expressed its pleasure by raising his annual salary from $50 to $300.
(cont'd.)   (BPDS, 1972, vol. #4, p. 387). ◠

In addition to four teachers at Maine State Prison, "the chaplain superintends the Sabbath school, and the clerk and overseers of the Prison are his assistants." School sessions were one hour each week, and the average enrollment was 78. "The convicts generally take a deep interest in the school, and it is, by the most of them, highly esteemed." (BPDS, 1972, vol. #2, p. 619). In 1838 superintendent **John O'Brien, Esq.** reported "We are now about establishing a day school for the purpose of instructing those who are quite deficient in common learning" (BPDS, 1972, vol. #3, p. 218). In 1842 O'Brien wrote

> The library...is somewhat reduced, and should be replenished, by a new selection of books, early in the spring. They [the inmates] have, for the last season, been weekly furnished with temperance papers and many of them appear to be much interested in the cause. (BPDS, 1972, vol. #4, p. 141).

Chaplain **Job Washburn** reported

> Our Sabbath school consists of about 20, who are divided into two classes. I have charge of one class, and the clerk of the Prison, the other. The classes use the Union Questions. I have before my class a large map of Asia Minor, and the adjacent countries, and whenever a place is mentioned in the session, it is pointed out to them on the map. Most of them appear to be interested in the exercises. (p. 142).

By 1844, however, the chaplain reported that

> some few attend [school] with interest and delight; but we find it hard to engage a majority of them in the work of searching the Holy Scriptures....It would be very desirable to procure some Bibles of a large and fair type, as most of those now used, when new, were unfit for such a place....Some addition, also, to the library is needed; but considering the dampness of the cells, which soon renders books unfit for use, together with the want of light to read, there may be sufficient reason to delay the purchase, until these evils are removed. (p. 386).

The Boston Prison Discipline Society was concerned. "What does this mean?" the Society asked.

1833
(cont'd.)

It means that the men in the Maine State Prison are placed in pit-holes, about ten feet deep, entered by a trap-door from the top, without windows for light, without fires or stoves for heat, and that, consequently, the cells are so dark, damp, and cold, that the prisoners can scarcely be seen themselves, much less can they see the small, poor print of their Bibles, and give their attention to reading...and the ice of winter freezes in their dark pit-holes—pit-holes above ground—worse than good cellars; because good cellars will not freeze... human beings, of flesh and blood like us...shut up in cold, damp cells, during a long winter night of between fifteen and sixteen hours. (p. 386).

Dr. Buxton, one of the prison inspectors, invited a legislator to visit and observe conditions at the institution. The legislator brought his Committee, and they visited on a very cold day. (p. 386).

So it was; and they returned to Augusta [the State capital], and procured, with the help of Dr. Buxton, the passing of a law for building a new Prison, on a plan admitting good light, heat, and air. This was done, and the new Prison is now in a state of forwardness, and, when finished and occupied, it will be much less difficult to engage a majority of the men in searching the Scriptures. (p. 387).

The Boston Prison Discipline Society encouraged correctional education. However, the Society reported that "In Ohio, there is neither school nor chapel attached to the Prison; neither is there any room that it would be possible to teach in; therefore there are no Sabbath school teachers" (BPDS, 1972, vol. #2, p. 620—see 1844 entry).

The relation between prison discipline and education was emphasized by Boston Prison Discipline Society. To promote its interests the organization reported that

a Sabbath school...is generally considered...essential in a good system of Prison discipline. We estimate the number of schools in the Prisons in the United States to be not less than ten, the number of teachers about seven hundred, and the number of scholars about fifteen hundred. (BPDS, 1972, vol. #2, p. 619).

In Vermont, the chaplain was the only teacher. He taught 25 students (BPDS, 1972, vol. #2, p. 619); by 1836 the number had risen to 60 (BPDS, 1972, vol. #3, p. 48). **Rufus L. Harvey** was chaplain in 1840. He reported that

1833
(cont'd.)

The Bible is studied with increasing delight and attention, and large portions of it are committed to memory, and recited in our excellent Sabbath school....We now have but very little cause for solitary punishment among them; whereas, six years ago, before things were perfectly systematized, the solitaries...were perfectly crowded with offenders.... Indeed, there are but four or five, out of the 81 convicts now in confinement, who did not converse freely and candidly with me upon the interests of religion... (BPDS, 1972, vol. #3, p. 439).

By 1842, Harvey identified the need for assistance, at least on Sundays.

I doubt not that our Sabbath school would be far more interesting, if Christian persons from without should volunteer their services, and come in on the Sabbath, and act as teachers. But, for want of such help, some of the most confidential convicts are chosen to perform this duty. I think, however, that our school is prosperous, and doing much good. (BPDS, 1972, vol. #4, p. 143).

"In Massachusetts, the number of teachers in the State Prison Sabbath school varies from twenty to thirty. They are gentlemen from several religious societies in Boston, Charlestown, and from the Divinity School in Harvard College." The teachers used a rotating schedule for service to about 150 students. "The warden and a deputy warden attend alternately. The chaplain is the superintendent." (BPDS, 1972, vol. #2, p. 619). By 1836, fully one half of the institutional population was in school. The teachers "travel the distance of several miles, and not unfrequently when the weather is unpleasant and severe." (BPDS, 1972, vol. #3, p. 48—see entries for 1842 and 1845).

Keeper C.S. Morgan reported that "The system adopted in the Virginia Penitentiary is solitary confinement at night, labor in shops during the day in silence, with instruction allowed, but not provided." See entry for 1826. Morgan said that the law of 1833 provided that

solitary confinement is fixed at one twelfth part of the whole term of imprisonment, and that no person shall be kept therein more than one month at a time. He has, therefore, adopted the plan of placing each convict in solitude one week in every three months, except in the last year of his term, and reserving, to be inflicted in that year, one month of solitude immediately preceding his discharge. (BPDS, 1972, vol. #2, p. 813).

1833   The institutional population was 122. "Twenty-eight died of cholera
(cont'd.) in the months of October and November." (p. 813). The Boston Prison
         Discipline Society investigated the situation because "the whole number
         of convicts is very small for so large a state as Virginia, containing more
         than a million inhabitants." The Society found that

> There was a law...from...1824 to...1826, requiring each
> person to be confined in his dark and solitary cell for six
> months after being received; and, from...1826 to...1829,
> that three months at the commencement, and three
> months at the close, should be in the same manner; and,
> from...1829, to...1833, that only the three last months
> should be spent in this manner. The punishment under
> this system was awful; and, call it by what name it
> may be called, there can be no satisfactory evidence
> that a large number of convicts were not, directly or
> indirectly killed by the process. (p. 814).

Official reports indicated the number of deaths each year. The average
institutional population for the years 1824-1833 was 171, and the
average mortality rate for the same years was 22 (or 13%). In

> 1833, the law requiring this horrible punishment was
> repealed, and the frightful mortality immediately
> ceased....It seems highly probable, therefore, that a mode
> of execution was adopted in Virginia, unintentionally,
> which took the life of a great number of prisoners,
> under the mild and humane name of the Penitentiary
> system. The writer...has witnessed the sufferings of the
> men in these dark dungeons, into which he was shown
> by a torch-light where...[in] the cold and damp of
> winter with insufficient covering...[the prisoners were]
> in chains. If this is not killing by inches, what is....This
> is one way of...making the whole number of prisoners
> very small, in proportion to the population. (p. 814).

In 1835 the Society noted that Virginia laws appeared to be designed with
a realization that long prison sentences were the same as executions:
"the crimes of burglary, robbery, and rape, which are in many of the
states punished with death, are punished with confinement in the
Penitentiary in Virginia..." (p. 887). The 1833 report concluded with
these words: It

> was not customary to let visitors see...the prisoners
> in the solitary cells...moral and religious instruction
> is allowed, but not provided, [because] no more
> Christians and Christian ministers should be found
> from Richmond, and Petersburg, and Hampden

41

Sidney, communicating ...instruction...within the walls
of the Penitentiary. (p. 815—see 1844 entry). ⌒⌒

At the Maryland Penitentiary no chaplain was employed, but 211 convicts were allowed to spend a few hours before Sunday service in a school staffed by "ten volunteers from the city." "Sixty eight [of the students] are white, and one hundred and forty-three colored." (BPDS, 1972, vol. #2, pp. 618-620). ⌒⌒

Methodist preachers maintained a Sabbath school at the Kentucky Penitentiary. The students spent two hours in school on Sunday morning, and two more in the afternoon (BPDS, 1972, vol. #2, p. 618—see 1829 entry).

> Nearly all the prisoners are scholars....The super-
> intendent of the Prison has the care of the school. The
> teachers are such gentlemen as are employed by him.
> Some of the prisoners are very much pleased, and
> others displeased with the school. (p. 620). ⌒⌒

1834 — Sixty-eight children criminals between the ages of nine and eighteen arrived in Australia. They were all drunk. "On the ship they had broken into a six dozen crate of wine and shared it with the adult convicts on board." "By 1842 there were 716 lads...and a jumble of barracks, workrooms and schoolrooms had grown up to shelter them." Throughout the 1830s and '40s visitors could see "a colony of ragged pale-faced lads," "climbing among the rocks and hiding or disappearing from...sight like land-crabs." They were known as the Point Puer boys. Eventually there were about 2,000 youngsters who were transported as criminals. The governor wrote that

> the utmost care should be taken to enforce upon their
> minds the disgraceful condition in which they are
> placed, whilst every effort should be made to eradicate
> their corrupt habits. He did not want to see too much
> time wasted in 'instructing the boys in reading and
> writing.' They needed practical skills, which would
> make useful assigned servants of them. (Hughes, 1987,
> p. 409).

The students' schedule was regimented.

> Up at 5:00 a.m., fold hammocks, assembly, Bible reading
> and prayer; breakfast at 7:00, hygiene inspection,
> muster, and classes in practical trades like joinery or
> bootmaking from 8:00 to 12:00. At midday, ablutions
> and another inspection; at 12:30, dinner; from 1:30
> to 5:00, more apprentice work; wash and inspection

again, and supper at 5:30; muster for school at 6:15; then school lessons for an hour, followed by evening prayers and Scripture reading, and bed at 7:30. Later the time for schoolwork in the evening was increased to two hours; it made little difference, however, as most of the boys were by then too fatigued to learn anything much. (pp. 409-410).

By 1837 vocational instruction in the following trades was offered: "baking, shoemaking, carpentry, tailoring, gardening, nail-making and blacksmithery. Enrollment ...was limited," so a waiting list procedure was used.

There is no question that [the students] received a trades education as good as (and probably better than) any they could have hoped to get in England in the 1830's. But their intellectual schooling was rudimentary. In 1842, some boys who had been there two or three years had difficulty reading words of one syllable; their arithmetic was no better. The only readers the pupils had were Bibles, supplied by a Wesleyan mission, and there were a few spelling-books and primers, but never enough; for eight hundred pupils there was 'one very small blackboard seldom used; and not even a map of the world. The state of religious instruction was not much better... (pp. 410-411).

The likelihood of producing good little Christians at such a place was slight...The Point Puer boys had no reason to like their jailers; and although conditions there were at least no worse than an English orphanage or ragged-school, they were little better and its inmates loathed them....In 1843 one overseer, Hugh McGine, was murdered by a pair of fourteen-year-olds... (pp. 411-412).

The disciplinary record of one stunted boy, Thomas Willetts, has survived. He was transported at age 16 in 1834 for stealing some stockings and garden vegetables. During five years at Point Puer and Port Arthur he received "a total of 35 lashes from the full cat-o'-nine tails, 183 strokes of the cane on his butt and 19 sentences of solitary confinement." (pp. 411-413). In another report on the same subject, Clay later wrote that

In Van Diemen's Land [Tasmania, the large island southeast of Australia]...Point Puer [was] set up in 1834 on a narrow strip of land opposite Port Arthur [a major adult prison]. There juveniles were taught to

1834
(cont'd.)
read and write and to learn a trade as tailor, shoemaker, carpenter, boat-builder, mason or gardener for future use in Australia....few ever returned to Britain. Many... were orphans or victims of circumstances before they went out, deserted by parents, uneducated, homeless, friendless and unable to earn an honest living. (Clay, 2001, p. 41). △

1835 — **Louis Dwight** (see entry for 1825) wrote that convict "J.M." was "intemperate" and "quarrelsome" when convicted, but "humble and penitent" after discharge. Dwight's friends thought he was "a bit strange for attempting to introduce any reform measures into such an immense mass of wretchedness" as the Massachusetts Penitentiary. Dwight was responsible for most of the programs "for [the prisoners'] relief." He believed that interpersonal cognitive skills could help improve their "miserable and degraded" condition. (Sullivan, 1975, p. 38). △

1836 — The Auburn chaplain acknowledged the advantage of a well organized education program. He reported that the teachers there had a "conscientious regard for the rules of the Prison" (BPDS, 1972, vol. #3, p. 49—see entries for 1827 and 1843). △

The chaplain of the District of Columbia Penitentiary wrote "I have been materially aided in the school by some of the prisoners, who have been selected by the warden as monitors." He was pleased that "Some of the most unpromising subjects have acquired so perfect a knowledge of the art of reading, as to be able to peruse the Scriptures with comfort and advantage." (BPDS, 1972, vol. #3, p. 49). By 1841 the warden could report that "Of the prisoners, 31 could read when admitted, and 23 have since learned to read through the instrumentality of the school" (BPDS, 1972, vol. #4, p. 36). △

1837 — "The teacher, **Mr. Hyde**, has done a great and good work in the school [the Boston Farm School] during the last six months" (BPDS, 1972, vol. #3, p. 155; emphasis added). The School was located "on a beautiful island, of 120 acres, in the Boston harbor....The school-room is in the second story of the east wing. It occupies the whole story, and therefore can be well lighted." The room was 60 feet by 36 feet by 12 feet, with nine large windows, but it should have had a better ventilation system. One hundred and six boys used it. A Boston Prison Discipline Society field representative found that "the air was not good when we entered the room." Mr. Hyde ran a well organized class: "I do not recollect that even a look was required from the teacher to secure good behavior for the time being. Correct deportment was a matter of habit." There were courses in reading, spelling, arithmetic, geography, singing, and speaking. (p. 154). The students "Attend school from 9 to 12, from 2 to 5, and from dark till prayer-time....Among farmers, the winter season is the time for school; so it is at the Farm School." (p. 155). △

1837 (cont'd.) In England, public attention focused on the horrors of the government's criminal justice policy, especially in regard to the harsh conditions experienced by transported juveniles. A Select Committee of the Parliament met on the transportation problem (Hughes, 1987, p. 313).

1839 — The separate women's prison building was opened at New York's Sing Sing Prison.

> Male staff administered the women's department but matrons served in it...overcrowding, inadequate hospital and nursery facilities, and disciplinary problems, which culminated in an 1843 riot, plagued the institution. A brief redemption occurred after... the [1844] appointment of **Eliza W. Farnham**....[who] believed in rehabilitation instead of punishment. She... set up a library and a school...her secular methods provoked state officials....They...forced her to retract her programs...Farnham left Sing Sing in 1848. (Freedman,1981, p. 48; bold emphasis added).

The chairman of the New Jersey Penitentiary inspectors committee publicly thanked "the clergy of Trenton, who, without intermission, as without remuneration, have labored for the moral and religious instruction of the convicts" (BPDS, 1972, vol. #3, p. 441). In 1841 the inspectors noted "a deficiency of moral and religious books in the Prison." A legislative committee recommended that this need should be addressed because it would help to "improve their morals." A bill to appropriate $100 for library books was introduced. (BPDS, 1972, vol. #4, pp. 151-152).

Alexander Maconochie's book, *Australiana: Thoughts on Convict Management*, was published in London (Murton, 1976, p. 195). The London Society for the Improvement of Prison Discipline (the leading English prison reform organization—see 1816 entry) was interested in a report by Maconochie regarding the state of the British Pacific penal colonies (Barry, 1958, p. 17). The French so admired the British penal structure that they "construct[ed their] own Pacific convict colony, a hellish one, in the New Hebrides" (Hughes, 1987, p. 582). By the mid 1830s, however, the English were disgusted with the brutality of their transportation system. This was the context when Maconochie—a geographer (Barry, 1958, p. 13), and naval captain (p. 8)—arrived in Van Dieman's Land (Tasmania) in 1837, to serve as private secretary to Sir John Franklin, a mid-level colonial administrator (p. 14). He immediately fell out of favor with the ruling group of prison managers, who identified him as "a liberal, a philosophical radical with fantastic notions of 'the <u>rights</u> of convicts.' They were quite right in considering Maconochie as an enemy." (p. 28; emphasis in original). Except for

1837   the prison managers, "Maconochie was held in high esteem among
(cont'd.) the residents of the colony" (p. 58). In the long awaited report to the
         London Society, Maconochie wrote that the convict system

> is cruel, uncertain, prodigal; ineffectual either for
> reform or example; can only be maintained in some
> degree of vigour by extreme severity....It defeats, in
> consequence, its own most important objects; instead
> of reforming it degrades humanity, vitiates all under
> its influence, multiplies petty business, postpones that
> which is of higher interest, retards improvement, and
> is, in many instances, even the direct occasion of vice
> and crime. (Maconochie, in Barry, 1958, p. 47).

Maconochie cleared the finished report with his hierarchical superiors—
from his immediate supervisor all the way up to the Cabinet, in
London—before sending it to the London Society. Without its author's
knowledge or permission, the report was forwarded to a Select
Committee of Parliament studying transportation. "The Committee
accepted completely Maconochie's fundamental propositions." (Barry,
1958, p. 62). It was covered extensively in the English press. "In
September, 1838, when English newspapers reached the colony, [Sir
Franklin] lost no time in dismissing Maconochie." (p. 56). Unemployed,
Maconochie prepared guidelines and procedures to improve prison
discipline (p. 59).

1840 — **Alexander Maconochie** was assigned superintendent of the British
       penal colony at Norfolk Island (Murton, 1976, p. 15).

> Norfolk, an island of 13 square miles situated in the
> South Pacific midway between New Caledonia and
> North New Zealand...was discovered by Capt. James
> Cook in 1774 and served as a British penal colony from
> 1788 to 1855. In 1856, it was settled by 187 'Bounty'
> descendants who left Pitcairn Island, their first home.
> (Scott, 1984, p. 2).

Like the great prison reformer John Howard before him, Maconochie had
been held by the French as a prisoner of war. This experience helped him
reach a new threshold of understanding, rejecting standard institutional
management practices. Maconochie is credited with introducing "the
mark system" (classification, honor system, progressive housing), the
indeterminate sentence, and parole. (Murton, 1976, p. 15). "He built
schools" (Eriksson, 1976, p. 87).

> Maconochie's proposals rested on two fundamental
> beliefs. The first was that brutality and cruelty debase
> not only the person subjected to them, but also the

society which deliberately uses or tolerates them for purposes of social control....The second was that the treatment of a wrongdoer during his sentence of imprisonment should be designed to make him fit to be released into society again, purged of the tendencies that led to his offense, and strengthened in his ability to withstand temptation to offend again. (Barry, 1958, p. 72).

1840 (cont'd.)

When Maconochie arrived at the island, it had the reputation of being the most brutal of the penal colonies. Convicts often attacked officers just to end their miseries: "each man who heard his condemnation to death went down on his knees, with dry eyes, and thanked God." (Ullathorne, in Barry, 1958, p. 91). In retrospect during

the relative peace and security of Alexander Maconochie's administration on Norfolk Island, [author Thomas] Cook speculated that the [pre-Maconochie penal] System meant to encourage sodomy, using the perpetual threat of rape or humiliation as one of the automatic punishments for the unwitting convict. In this he was wrong, but one can understand why he thought it. Until Maconochie took over Norfolk Island in 1840, not one commandant in the System had shown the least concern for the rehabilitation of his prisoners. They acted purely as agents of repression, as guardians of the pit. And if the men in the pit had ways of degrading one another, why trouble to stop them? (Hughes, 1958, p. 270; emphasis in original).

Maconochie changed all this. He solicited and obtained funds from governor Gipps to buy musical instruments and start a library (Barry, 1958, p. 84). Soon after his arrival, on May 25, 1840, he organized a massive celebration to observe Queen Victoria's birthday. All the prisoners were let out for picnic feasts with extra rations of fresh meats and vegetables, sporting events, an afternoon play, a twenty-one gun salute and diluted rum toast in honor of the Queen, musical performances, and evening fireworks. At nightfall, all the convicts returned voluntarily to their cells. Maconochie's purpose was "to disarm their resentments against their native land," and to begin the process of exposure to temptation prior to release. (Barry, 1958, pp. 103-105).

He had not come as their torturer, one of the prisoners reported him as saying; but he did not have the authority to extend the Mark System to them as Old Hands [doubly convicted felons]. He could only try it with the new arrivals. Nevertheless, 'he felt no hesitation in saying that he should find little difficulty

47

in obtaining such an authority, and that he would venture therefore to place us under that System with the English prisoners....The cheers which emanated from the Prisoners were most deafening. From that instant all crime disappeared. The Old Hands from that moment were a different race of beings. The notion, the erroneous notion that had been engendered in their minds by a course of harsh and cruel treatment under which they had for many years been compelled to groan, was almost entirely eradicated when they found themselves received as <u>men</u> by their Philanthropic Ruler.' At once, old feelings of patriotism stirred in the convicts: 'No sooner did they rightly comprehend the purport of his message from our Most Gracious Queen,—that Sovereign who had been forgotten by them as having any dominion over the land of their Captivity—that land in which so much blood had been spilt,—than Her Majesty reigned in their hearts and they all appeared to labor cheerfully in the one large field of Reformation.' Maconochie was a zealot, but an acute one. He saw that in this terrible place the sense of a chain of authority leading back to England and its monarch had been ruptured; the men had given up hope because they believed themselves abandoned by their homeland. There was nobody beyond the prison to whom they could appeal. By reinstating the Queen as an icon, with all her imagery of youth, femininity and maternal concern, Maconochie showed great insight into their predicament....Dutifully, [Maconochie] penned a report to Gipps announcing that he would not obey his orders to keep the old and new prisoners under separate systems... (Hughes, 1987, pp. 502-503; emphasis in original).

"When the news of this extraordinary happening reached the [Australian] colonies, the reaction varied from shocked astonishment to vigorous disapproval, and from derisive mirth to hostile indignation..." (Barry, 1958, pp. 103-105). "The free were fearful of the bond, and fear and pity are incompatables, for men cannot pity those they have oppressed" (Barry, 1958, p. 108). This set the stage for Maconochie's dismissal; in fact, governor Gipps obtained authorization to do precisely that—but he could not find a suitable replacement. In the meantime, Maconochie implemented his program. He started a band and a choir; established "adult schools;" rewarded inmates for reading aloud to interested men in the hospital and gaol; gave every convict land for a small garden, and encouraged them to sell any surplus foodstuffs on the free market; authorized headstones on inmate graves; encouraged worship and helped found churches; built separate cottages to relieve overcrowding;

1840 (cont'd.) started a police force to protect private property; opened the doors to anyone who wanted to observe disciplinary proceedings; did away with corporal punishments almost entirely; encouraged prisoners to take ideas and complaints directly to him, instead of through the official channel of intermediaries; and "in every way sought to impress in them confidence in my [Maconochie's] desire to act right, and without passion, in regard to them." (pp. 112-115).

In a special Supplement to the *Sydney Herald* on Wednesday, July 1, 1840 entitled "Fete [celebration, fair] at Norfolk Island," the thinking of the free Australian population to Maconochie's program can be discerned. In part, the editorial stated that

> The interests of this Colony are deeply involved in this solemn mummery; and it must be exposed. In the name of the Colonials we protest against such proceedings, and against the repetition of this mockery of law, justice, and order. We protest against such excitements to insubordination so long as there are convicts assigned to settlers in this colony. Had her Majesty's Secretary for the Colonies witnessed the gloom and depression that pervaded the minds of some of the most humane, liberal, and honorable men in the Colony when the proceedings of that day were published, he would have dismissed the perpetrator [Maconochie] from the office he prostitutes to purposes detrimental to Colonial prosperity, loyalty, and peace. The employers of convicts apprehend in such acts, the suspension of their authority, and of obedience and order on the part of their assigned servants. They apprehend the worst consequences when information is communicated in the interior as to the altered state of Norfolk Island, the fear of which, to use the words of the Reverend Apologist of the system, Father MacEnroe, 'was worse than death to delinquents.' Settlers apprehend that the small portion of subordination, restraint, and discipline now existing over incorrigible and irreclaimable men, is at an end. The festivities and allurements of Norfolk Island, by placing them in a better than assigned service, will act as a Bonus to crime. The lives and prosperities of the settlers will now be completely at the mercy of ruffians, who prefer the perpetration of crime, with the chance of escape, to that quiet, demeanor that has raised thousands of their class to affluence and comparative respectability. From the date of Captain Maconochie's first address penal discipline was abandoned. This fete has put

an end to the distinction between crime and good conduct, and their consequences; and has given a dignified <u>finale</u> to the system both as to the convict population, and the military men employed in it. There is another view of the question, what effect will such statements have on the mass of prisoners in this Colony who are guiltless when contrasted with the convict of that Island to whom such indulgences have been extended? and what effect will they produce on this the thousands of starving men in England restrained from crime, not by moral obligations, but by the fear of penal servitude? In regard to the first, it offers a premium to every prisoner who will submit to a second transportation, to quit Colonial masters, labour, clothing, and homely fare, with bush solitude, in order to enjoy delectable 'climate and fruits' 'cricket matches' '<u>Hogsheads of Lemonade with libations of Rum</u>,' plays, idleness, speeches, bands of music, and multitudinous marks at Queenstown. In regard to the second, they will have no dread to join the revellers at Norfolk Island, indulging in plays and punch, who by crime have not incurred, but escaped from labour, sheep farming and daily toil. A man regardless of crime and starving in England will find his way to Norfolk Island, where his felon chains will be knocked off and he will be 'free to traverse the Island all day long.' But is that a state to be tolerated, in which the <u>reward of subordination is conferred on the criminal and turbulent</u>? It is monstrous injustice to every well behaved Convict in this Colony, who, while he is submissive and inoffensive, is neglected. It is such a man once convicted of whom there is a hope, who should be treated to plays, horse races, washerwomen, donkeys for handcarts, bands of music, and punch, all paid for at the expense of industrious <u>Britons</u>, who furnish the taxes for such absurdities by the sweat of their browe....We advise the Colonists to petition <u>en masse</u> against this monstrous abuse and abortion. Petition against the return thousands of marksmen from Norfolk Island, and against the transmission of cargoes from England. In this way peevish, petulant, and morose declaimers will be brought to their senses, when they vomit nonesenses or absurdities, falsehoods or fictions, to the disgrace of the Colony, and the detriment of its interests. <u>Recall all convicts and ticket-of-leave holders [parolees] into Government, keep your reformed libertines in the gaol of Norfolk Island, and forbid the importation of felons</u>. Britain will then be taught, without much loss as to this Colony with a desire to do her justice, and relieve her from the most contemptible outrage ever perpetuated upon her. Too many Norfolk Island felons have been allowed to revisit Sydney [on mainland Australia], through the Governor's mistaken leniency. Men in no respect altered, but for the worse, who should never have been permitted to set feet on our shores, to pollute her society, have returned to degrade her people. The Colonists have it in their power to prevent this infection, by petitionioning against it, and urging their petitions for a House of Assembly, or an extension of the Council. At all events, it is hoped that an end will be put to Captain Maconochie's system when these accounts are brought before the Secretary of State, as insulting to the Colonists, promoting insubordination, encouraging the military and the convicts, and laying a train for the embarrassment of future administrators, which may probably require more expense and energy to reduce than the sister colony of Canada, enveloped in the flames of discontent, insubordination, and civil war. (Sydney Herald, 1840, p. 1; emphases in original).

Soon thereafter Governor Gipps visited the Island: "Notwithstanding that my arrival at Norfolk Island was altogether unexpected, I found good order everywhere to prevail, and the demeanour of the prisoners to be respectful and quiet" (Gipps, in Barry, 1958, p. 140—see entries for 1842 and 1846). 〰

Early in his 1840-1844 role as superintendent of the Norfolk Island penal colony, Captain Alexander Maconochie requested permission to have some female and juvenile convicts sent there. Maconochie's thinking was that their presence would soften the convicts, and help justify his rehabilitation programs. Australian Governor Gipps denied the request (Clay, 2001, pp. 99, 134-135). Why did the Governor decline? In 1788 Philip King originally settled Norfolk Island with a population of nine male and six female convicts (see entry in "Introduction"). Soon thereafter he "promised that any 'partiality or reciprocal affection' between male and female convicts on the island would be tolerated." "True to King's expectations, convicts started pairing off...and children were born, six within two years." (p. 106). By 1800

morale was low, skilled labor short and buildings falling down. The settlement was also awash with illegitimate children, over 200 of them (nearly a fifth of the island's population), mostly illiterate and wild. The schoolmaster had been put in gaol [jail] for debt, and the missionary on the island was thought by one and all to be 'very unfit for a minister.' (pp. 109-110).

Long before Maconochie arrived on the island these women and children had been shipped to Australia. Though Gipps apparently did not consider how proper management might have improved upon the former experience at a "co-ed" penal colony, the Governor had reason to be cautious about Maconochie's 1840 recommendation. 🔺

Near Tours, France, jurist **Frederick Auguste Demetz** founded Mettray, a family substitute institution for juveniles. "Demetz had been deeply impressed by an American reformatory in Boston." Before opening Mettray, "Demetz trained 27 assistants for...seven months." (Eriksson, 1976, p. 102). The institution was known as a school and employed teachers. Its curriculum consisted of "religion, philosophy, physics, chemistry, mathematics, French, Latin, Greek, German, English, writing, book-keeping, drawing, and music..." (p. 122). Mettray students were "from more or less wealthy social backgrounds," and they "left it reformed" (p. 123—see 1900 entry). 🔺

Sing Sing's **Warden Seymour** established the first prison library that contained more than Bibles, religious tracts, and other inspirational material (McKelvey, 1977, p. 57). This event, though it may seem innocuous today, contributed to a gradual secularization of correctional education 🔺

The "Gaol Regulations" for the provincial jail of Upper Canada at Kingston provided "instruction in reading and writing" (Roberts, 1973, p. 40). Today the cluster of institutions around Kingston is one focus of Canadian correctional education activity. 🔺

Most of the chaplains—who were at the center of correctional education during this period—were volunteers. For example, at the Hartford, Connecticut County Prison, **Reverend Mr. Gallaudet** served as chaplain, without compensation (BPDS, 1972, vol. #3, p. 440). 🔺

Reverend Thomas Larcombe served as a chaplain at Pennsylvania's Eastern Penitentiary. He reported that some prisoners showed "satisfactory proof of reform," and "seemed to be awakened to a just perception of their past criminality..." (BPDS, 1972, vol. 3, p. 441—see 1842 entry). 🔺

Throughout the United States, a good education was still an anomaly. "...[W]hite adult literacy was about 90 percent" (Tyack, 1974, p. 66). 🔺

1840   In New York City and Boston the police force, a new social
(cont'd.) institution, was expanding—a response to growing public concerns
about urban environments.

> Conservative citizens worried about ethnic and religious
> riots, feared outbursts of social disorder and crime,
> and became despondent about traditional methods
> of social control. As informal mechanisms of shaping
> behavior broke down, cities created functionaries—
> men behind badges—to keep disorderly elements in
> line. The creation of efficient and uniformed police
> paralleled the movement to standardize [local public]
> schooling. Both were in part responses to the influx of
> the immigrant poor. (Tyack, 1974, p. 33).

By 1869 the local school-based systems for enforcing order were very
much in place. A

> principal, Mr. Dutton, took [Marian Dogherty, a new
> teacher] to her classroom with its fifty-six desks bolted
> to the floor and extra, movable ones in the rear, its 'high
> platform where the teacher sat.' The platform, she
> thought, 'was her throne and helped to fix her above
> the rest of the world in the minds of the children. If
> they desired to converse with her, they must step up;
> when they returned to their own quarters, they must
> step down.' As the Jewish and Italian girls marched in,
> faces shining from soap and dresses stiff with starch,
> they were models of deportment on that first day of
> school. 'Even the janitor seemed to them a celestial
> being, for when he shuffled in and banged the furniture
> about, an awe rested on their innocent faces, because
> he was a part of that great system that held them in
> its benign but awful hand.' The hierarchical order
> seemed fixed and immutable; a student, chastised for
> her temper, later wrote a theme for Miss Dogherty: 'I
> must not slam the door when I am mad, nor answer
> back the teacher. Teachers are sometimes aggravating,
> but we must put up with them because the city pays
> them to be like that.' (p. 255). ◠

1841— Georgia Penitentiary keeper **Charles H. Nelson, Esq.** reported that

> Sunday schools have this year been instituted, and
> directed by charitable individuals, without cost, other
> than such books as were required of me, which were
> promptly furnished, under a ready hope that their

1841
(cont'd.)

labors would bring the returning sinner home (BPDS, 1972, vol. #4, p. 154). 🐾

Boston was a flurry of activity. **John Augustus** introduced the idea of probation, for the first time ever, by "convincing the court to release a man being sentenced on a drunk charge to his care....By 1858 he had bailed out almost 2,000 men and women." (Murton, 1976, p. 10). Classes were started at the Boston House of Correction (McKelvey, 1977, p. 57). The Boston Prison Discipline Society issued a description of another nearby correctional education program:

> In the House of Correction at South Boston, a day school has been taught by the clerk, two hours each day, during several years past, for a class of young convicts, in the common branches of knowledge, in a room carefully fitted up for that purpose, and great good has resulted from it (BPDS, 1972, vol. #4, p. 37). 🐾

New York **Governor Seward** said that he "would have the school room in the prison fitted as carefully as the solitary cell and workshop, and although attendance there cannot be so frequent we would have it quite as regular" (Klein, in Wallack, 1939, p. 10). Apparently the need for schoolrooms was a focus of attention that year. A Boston Prison Discipline Society paper included a statement that the chaplain at Wethersfield Prison had emphasized the schoolroom problem, as well. (BPDS, 1972, vol. # 4, p. 37). 🐾

At the Norfolk Island penal colony Captain **Alexander Maconochie** was pressing ahead with his reformatory plans. He

> cared not a fig for the colonists' prejudices [against his innovative program on Norfolk Island—see 1840 entry]. He pressed ahead with his plans for cultural and moral reform....summed up in a shopping list he forwarded to [governor] Gipps. By past penal standards, it was outlandish. He wanted books, for instance—an encyclopedia, magazines on engineering, craft and farming, cookbooks for brewers and bakers; these would help teach the men trades they had never learned, or else forgotten. He asked for a copy of *Robinson Crusoe*, to instill 'energy, hopefulness in difficulty, regard & affection for our brethren in savage life, &c.' He wanted the convicts to read travel and exploration books, starting with Cook's Voyages, because 'the whole white race in this hemisphere wants softening towards its aboriginal inhabitants.' Hoping 'to invest country and home with agreeable

images and recollections [which] are too much wanting in the individual experience of our lower and criminal classes,' he sent for books on English history and popular national poetry—Robert Burns, George Crabbe, the sentimental sketches of English village life by Mary Mitford, a set of Walter Scott's Waverley Novels to encourage national pride in Scottish convicts, and the works of Rousseau-tinged woman novelist Maria Edgeworth, such as the satirical *Castle Rackrent* (1800), to do the same for Irish ones. He also stocked this prisoners' library with moral and religious works some, as he put it himself, of 'controversial divinity,' for he wanted the prisoners to think and argue together, not rot in their cells: 'Polemical discussions are sometimes inconvenient; but I do not dread them, for they are nearly always, I think, improving. Wherever a taste for them prevails, as in Scotland, Switzerland &c, it is always found accompanied by other good qualities; while on the contrary, where they are despised, as in France, or crushed, as in Spain, the national character seems to suffer....I would have no fear [of controversies], even in a prison.' He included the works of Shakespeare in his island library, for their nobility; had his doubts about the reformative power of theater ('the English drama is often licentious, but substantially its tendency is moral'); and felt that theatrical training could help convicts overcome their passions. Such had been his purpose on the Queen's Birthday [see 1840 entry]. Music would be the main therapy....Music was an 'eminently social occupation.' It taught collaboration and disciplined obedience. It rested on strict order and subordination, and if 'national and plaintive' in character, kept its hearers affable and patriotic. 'It is sometimes thought to lead to drinking... but this, when true at all, applies to <u>rude</u> rather than scientific music....He put in a request for trumpet, fifes, horns, cymbals and two 'seraphines' (reed accordions with keyboard and bellows, invented in the 1830s and popular in small parishes that could not afford full organs). He spent 46 £ of the government's money on a large stock of music-paper: old, infirm and crippled prisoners would be set to copy the scores out. (Hughes, 1987, pp. 506-507; emphasis in original). ⌒

1842 — **Alexander Maconochie**'s Norfolk Island Penal Colony became a center for transported (exiled) prisoners with life sentences from the Irish prison system (Eriksson, 1976, p. 90—see 1863 note). He later offered this outline of his tenure there:

I was four years in charge of Norfolk Island, with from 1500 to 2000 prisoners on it during most of the time, of whom two-thirds were always doubly convicted men, many of them of the worst previous characters. I never had more than 160 soldiers in garrison, instead of from 200 to 300 since kept there; and I never once called on those that I had for other than routine duty. I had only five inferior free officers engaged in maintaining the discipline of the establishment, instead of from forty to fifty who have since been attached to it. And my Police was composed of men selected by me from the general body of the prisoners, furnished only with short painted staves—instead of a large free and probationer force, armed with cutlasses, and in some cases pistols, that has since been maintained. (Maconochie, in Barry, 1958, p. 166—see 1844 entry). ⌒

In England, the Pennsylvania system of prison discipline (see Introduction) was widely implemented.

...individual religious instruction [was allowed], without the corrupting influence of inmate discussion... the authorities could congratulate themselves upon the knowledge that during sentences of two or three years no prisoner would have seen the face of another; and this by virtue of solitary confinement, the use of individual exercise grounds and chapel partitions (still seen in relic at Lincoln), and wearing of masks. (Banks, 1958, p. 18). ⌒

At Massachusetts State Prison, the warden was confident that the public wanted to hear about the progress of correctional education from year to year. **Jared Curtis** (see entries for 1826, 1832, and 1840) described the reformation of inebriates as a "holy cause." The school facilities there were in good condition: "The appearance of the school has never exhibited so much of cheering promise as at the present time." Curtis quoted Jesus: "I was in Prison, and ye came unto me." He was experimenting with a revised schedule for teacher service: "A new, and, it is believed, much improved, organization has recently taken place in this school, by which competent teachers have been secured to take charge of the several classes, steadily and for the season." This contrasted with the traditional rotating schedule pattern. (BPDS, 1972, vol. #4, p. 144—see 1845 entry). ⌒

Reverend Charles Cleveland, chaplain at the South Boston House of Correction, implemented the same improvement as Curtis (see immediately preceding entry). "Experience has proved that the

1842   system of dependence on permanent teachers has several and important
(cont'd.) advantages over that of alternation." He reported some of the results:

> One man recited at a hearing, 173 verses [from the
> Bible], and another, 138—a female, 176; another,
> 127, and another, 88...the total number of verses
> committed was 5,857. In the female Sabbath school,
> the number of pupils in attendance has averaged 100.
> Ladies, members of various city churches, have been
> conveyed over, at the expense of the city, to engage
> in the good work of instruction. Sixteen of the last
> eighteen Sabbaths, the same eleven teachers, the
> required number, were present. (BPDS, 1972, vol. #4,
> p. 145—see 1841 entry). ☁

Alarmed that Sing Sing financial agent David L. Seymour
neglected correctional education in his annual report, the Boston Prison
Discipline Society wrote

> It would be entirely within his province to show
> what effect it has upon the financial department.
> Are cheerful obedience, submission to authority,
> contentment, industry, and good-will, produced? If so,
> how far are the favorable pecuniary results connected
> with moral and religious instruction?... (BPDS, 1972,
> vol. #4, p. 148).

Chaplain John Luckey's report indicated that the school had
doubled in enrollment, which was voluntary.

> I venture the opinion that no patriot, no
> philanthropist, and surely no Christian, can witness
> these operations for one Sabbath, without being fully
> satisfied of their powerful influence in reforming
> the convict. Other and paramount indications of
> reform might be given; such as the great reduction
> of stripes [floggings], with as much or more labor
> performed than formerly; the apparent cheerfulness
> with which the prisoners toil; the ready and willing
> obedience they render; and the affectionate regard
> with which they uniformly speak of their keepers in
> general, and the principal keeper and the agent in
> particular. (p. 148—see 1843 entry). ☁

A joint select committee of the Mississippi legislature
recommended that a Sabbath school should be established at Jackson
Penitentiary.

1842
(cont'd.)

Many of the convicts might be taught reading, and the useful branches of literature and sciences, in addition to moral and religious instruction; and the Christian and the benevolent portion of the community...would, no doubt, cheerfully lend their gratuitous assistance in the promotion of so laudable an object. If a small sum, say one hundred dollars, were appropriated in the purchase of suitable school books, or histories, for the use of the institution, such a library would, no doubt, soon be greatly augmented by the voluntary contributions of the humane and the benevolent. (BPDS, 1972, vol. #4, p. 154). ⌂

Mr. Thomas Larcombe (see 1840 entry), the moral instructor at Pennsylvania's Eastern Penitentiary, was discouraged about working among students who were often

so depraved as to take pleasure in deceiving, or hope to compass some private or selfish purpose by false professions. These, and other causes, often produce doubt where there are appearances of real good having been effected. My position, therefore, is like that of a husbandman who cultivates a sterile soil, in the hope of a future and distant reward. The effects of moral and religious instruction have not been so encouraging during the past year as in the two years preceding; at least, an equal amount of good impression has not been observable. (BPDS, 1972, vol. # 4, p. 152).

Larcombe reported that the school's influence was "visible in promoting quietness and order, and the general good deportment of the prisoners." He "returned [to the free community]...twelve persons...now engaged in honest occupations, and respected in society...unharmed by temptation." (p. 152).

Of the number discharged, 74 could read and write, 9 of whom learned in Prison; 69 could read, 28 of whom learned in Prison; and 22 could not read. Of 126 committed in the same period, 2 had a good education, 67 could read and write, 26 could read only, and 31 could not read. (BPDS, 1972, vol. #4, p. 153—see 1845 entry). ⌂

Charles Dickens devoted a chapter in *American Notes* to his visit at Pennsylvania's Eastern Penitentiary, "Philadelphia, and its Solitary Prison." (See Introduction.)

Every facility was afforded me, that the utmost courtesy could suggest. Nothing was concealed or hidden from my view, and every piece of information that I sought, was openly and frankly given. The perfect order of the building cannot be praised too highly, and of the excellent motives of all who are immediately concerned in the administration of the system, there can be no kind of question. (Dickens, 1957/1842, p. 100).

Each prisoner's

name, and crime, and term of suffering are unknown, even to the officer who delivers him his daily food. There is a number over his cell-door, and in a book, of which the governor [warden] of the prison has one copy, and the moral instructor another; this is the index of his history. Beyond these pages the prison has no record of his existence... (p. 101).

Over the head and face of every prisoner who comes into this melancholy house, a black hood is drawn; and in this dark shroud, an emblem of the curtain dropped between him and the living world, he is led to the cell from which he never again comes forth, until his whole term of imprisonment has expired. (p. 100).

Every cell has double doors; the outer one of sturdy oak, the other of grated iron, wherein there is a trap through which his food is handed. He has a Bible, and a slate and pencil, and, under certain restrictions, has sometimes other books, provided for the purpose, and pen and ink and paper. His razor, plate, and can, and basin, hang upon the wall, or shine upon the little shelf. Fresh water is laid on in every cell, and he can draw it at his pleasure. During the day, his bedstead turns up against the wall, and leaves more space for him to work in. His loom, or bench, or wheel, is there; and there he labours, sleeps and wakes, and counts the seasons as they change, and grows old. (p. 101).

"Some reddened at the sight of visitors, and some turned very pale" (p. 103).

On the haggard face of every man among these prisoners, the same expression sat. I know not what to liken it to. It had something of that strained attention which we see upon the faces of the blind and deaf, mingled with a kind of horror, as though they had all been secretly terrified. In every little chamber that I entered, and at every grate through which I looked, I seemed to see the same appalling countenance. It lives in my memory, with fascination of a remarkable picture. Parade before my eyes, a hundred men, with one among them newly released from this solitary suffering, and I would point him out. (pp. 108-109).

"...the criminals who had been there long, were deaf" (p. 109). "If his period of confinement has been very long, the prospect of release bewilders and confuses him" (p. 108). Dickens asked an employee exactly how the men behaved at time of release.

'Well, it's not so much a trembling,' was the answer— 'though they do quiver—as a complete derangement of the nervous system. They can't sign their names to the book; sometimes can't even hold the pen; look about 'em without appearing to know why, or where they are; and sometimes get up and sit down again, twenty times in a minute. This is when they're in the office, where they are taken with the hood on, as they were brought in. When they get outside the gate, they stop, and look first one way and then the other; not knowing which to take. Sometimes they stagger as if they were drunk, and sometimes are forced to lean against the fence, they're so bad;—but they clear off in course of time.' (pp. 105-106).

Dickens wrote a summary of his experience in visiting the Prison: "It is my fixed opinion that those who have undergone this punishment, MUST pass into society again morally unhealthy and diseased." (p. 109; emphasis in original). "That it is a singularly unequal punishment, and affects the worst man least, there is no doubt" (p. 110). About 75 years later, **Thomas Mott Osborne** wrote about the results of Dickens' narrative.

No portion of the 'American Notes' aroused more wrath than this attack by Dickens upon Philadelphia's cherished institution. The Inspectors of the Western Penitentiary, in their report for 1843, referred scornfully to the great author as an 'itinerant book-maker;' and the Inspectors of the Eastern Penitentiary, after taking a year longer to get their breath, reported that 'they feel it a duty again to offer the convictions of their judgment, in favour of the superior benefits and advantages which result from the practical operations of the Pennsylvanian system of prison

1842 (cont'd.)	discipline; all the bearings of this system upon the prisoner are incontrovertibly beneficial'....Dickens was fundamentally right, as we now know; his broad and sympathetic interest in humanity had given him an insight denied to the worthy and respectable gentlemen who served on the Board of Inspectors, to whom it doubtless seemed little short of sacrilege to have their peace of mind disturbed, by questioning the excellence of the institution they served so conscientiously. 'We know by the light of modern experience,' writes Major Griffiths, 'that solitary imprisonment prolonged beyond certain limits is impossible except at terrible cost. The price is that the prison becomes the antechamber to the madhouse, or leads even to the tomb'....my only excuse for dwelling so long upon this...subject is that <u>solitary confinement still persists</u>... (Osborne, 1975/1916, pp. 102-103; emphasis in original—see entry for 1846).

Of course, solitary confinement continues to exist, in Special Housing Units (SHUs) and super maximum security facilities all across the country. ⌂

1843 —	The [Auburn Prison] agent...furnished two dozen of Colburn's mental arithmetic, which are very useful to men deprived of the use of slates and other means of mathematical instruction....There is also a lack of library books....We have a tolerable supply of tracts on hand, but they are mostly of the same impression with those which have been given out....If we had a few thousand pages more, of a new variety, it would add much to the reading interest of the place...during the dull hours of solitude...[and establish] such moral principles in the mind as would greatly promote their individual happiness and reformation. (BPDS, 1972, vol. #4, p. 389).

On the same subject, an 1844 report revealed that

> The Bible is the standard work for the perusal of these men, and some of them read no other book. I very much regret that some of them are compelled to use the old, worn-out books, unfit for further use in any place, especially in the dark cells....The Book of Common Prayer is frequently sought after by the convicts; but I have distributed all that were on hand, and frequent applications are made for more. (p. 389).

1843   In 1841 the chaplain had requested an extension of the school schedule,
(cont'd.) "the blessed results" of which would "influence... their families and
        society..." He said that most of the prisoners needed the school, and
        the fact "That a few educated men find their way into prison, does not
        disprove this statement." (Chenault, 1949-1951, p. 8). This was verified
        in a needs assessment by **Chaplain Thomas Townsend** in 1842, which
        said, in part, "they not only are unable to read or write, but, in some
        cases, cannot even count [to] ten correctly." Townsend was convinced
        that the correctional school was the last hope for many convicts. "Here,
        or nowhere, these neglected and unfortunate youth must be instructed
        in the first principles of education, their minds elevated, and they thus
        prepare to become better sons, better husbands, better parents, better
        citizens." (BPDS, 1972, vol. #4, p. 151—see 1847 entry). 🔺

        Enrollment at Sing Sing had reached "About one-half of the
        whole number in the male department...and all in the female." The
        school was closed, as indicated in the following report, presumably
        from **Chaplain John Luckey** (see 1842 entry):

> In both prisons [the male and female departments]
> convicts alone were teachers. Several hundred were
> assembled in the chapel, and divided into classes of
> about ten each. Only one or two keepers were present,
> and it was of course impossible for them to know
> the subjects the convicts conversed upon under the
> pretense of teaching and learning. Several instances
> were detected in which forbidden topics were
> discussed; and there is reason to believe that an escape,
> which was nearly successful, was planned in the school
> between a teacher and his pupil. The employment of
> such teachers was forbidden, and the schools, much
> to the regret of the board were abandoned for want of
> teachers. (Chenault, 1949-1951, p. 4).

One year earlier, the agent and principal keeper had asked the chaplain
"to employ the 'better sort' of convicts as teachers, or abandon the
school." (p. 4). Another problem had also surfaced in 1842:

> our confidence in the professions of reform made by
> convicts while in Prison, has been somewhat shaken,
> within the last two years, by the return of two or three
> of this class to their former criminal course since their
> discharge. (BPDS, 1972, vol. #4, p. 149).

Luckey added that he had "on file a number of letters from others of this
class, living in various parts of the country, as also from their friends,
advising me of their continued reform." (p. 149). By 1844 things were
looking up. The library was reorganized and started up again.

1843
(cont'd.)

On the Sabbath day you can scarcely pass one cell in one hundred without seeing its inmate ardently engaged in reading his library book. Consequently this indulgence, in feasting their minds...was so favorably received, that all noises hitherto indulged in by them, such as whistling, singing, talking, and thumping of their bunks and furniture, has almost entirely ceased. (Chenault, 1949-1951, p. 5).

In 1845 a new schedule was implemented, with students involved in lessons for one-half to three-quarters of an hour each morning. By 1846 the curriculum consisted of history, astronomy, geography, physiology and physical education (with an emphasis "upon health, moral purity, and happiness"), in addition to the three Rs. Enrollment was at 60-70, in two classes. (p. 5—see 1847 entry). ⌂

1844 — The correctional education advocacy work of the Boston Prison Discipline Society began meeting widespread success. The Richmond (Virginia) Penitentiary school experimented with a grading system (McKelvey, 1977, p. 37—see 1826 and 1833 entries). At Eastern Penitentiary, in Pennsylvania, a secular teacher was hired and a library was started (Roberts, 1971, p. 4). "In the Vermont State Prison, the warden, assisted by his sons, and the officers of the Prison, devotes considerable time, on the afternoon of the Sabbath, to the instruction of the prisoners'" (BPDS, 1972, vol. #4, p. 387—see 1833 entry). The State Prison inspectors in Rhode Island recommended

that provision be made by law for the employment of a suitable religious instructor, to be compensated by the state. The present mode of leaving the instruction of the convicts to the benevolence of individuals, is not satisfactory in its results, and, it is feared, may have an unfavorable affect on the discipline of the Prison. (p. 388). ⌂

New York City's police force was founded. Many feared "it would become...indifferent to public influence...functioning against the people" despite "assurances that [it] would function as the people's police." (Geary, 1975, p. 373). ⌂

Ohio Penitentiary Chaplain **Reverend S.T. Mills** reported that there were 50 to 70 students in the Sunday school, including many who "entered...entirely illiterate, [and] are now able to read the Bible intelligently." He wrote that "...there has been too much indifference manifested to the subject of moral and religious instruction in this institution; but the remedy, in a great measure, depends on future legislation" (BPDS, 1972, vol. #4, p. 504). By 1847 a position for a "moral and religious instructor" was assigned to the institution. Included in

1844   the duties was responsibility to "see that each convict that can read
(cont'd.) is furnished with a Bible or Testament....[and] To see that the Sabbath
School is properly attended and supplied, as far as practicable, with
suitable teachers and books." (Hicks, 1925, pp. 419-420). The curriculum
included reading, writing, spelling, geography, arithmetic, and history
(*History*..., 1891, p. 41). ⌁

Alexander Maconochie was fired from his assignment
as Norfolk Island Penal Colony superintendent. He had initiated
meaningful prison reform, including schools for inmates, and his
programs had been judged successful—even in the letter that informed
him of dismissal. (Murton, 1976, p. 200—see entries for 1839, 1840, 1842,
1846, 1860, 1870, and 1958). ⌁

1845 — Few institutions offered instruction in the Three Rs. Most correctional
education programs were Sabbath schools: the part-time, visiting
chaplain at the cell door in the evening with a Bible and a lantern,
teaching basic reading. (Wallack, 1939, p. 18). ⌁

At Philadelphia's Cherry Hill Prison **Chaplain Larcombe**
"was given an assistant in the person of one **Mr. Willis**, an overseer
who served as a teacher." Earlier chaplains had been assisted by the
city's Catholic and Jewish clergymen in the effort to provide moral and
religious instruction. "The chaplain was obliged to pursue his spiritual
counseling on an individual basis, passing from cell to cell." Larcombe
"taught basic subjects to the illiterate prisoners as well, for during the
first decade religious and educational subjects went hand in hand."
(Teeters and Shearer, 1957, p. 152; emphasis added). Swedish feminist,
social worker **Fredika Bremer** visited Cherry Hill in 1850. She wrote
that "The library was large and contained, in addition to religious
books, scientific treatises, travel books and literary works, selected with
discrimination." (Eriksson, 1976, p. 71—see 1845 entry). ⌁

The New York Prison Association held its first annual meeting
(Rule, 1920, p. 137—see entries for 1846 and 1854). In subsequent decades
this organization would become even more active in correctional
education than the Boston Prison Discipline Society. ⌁

New York State's Clinton Prison was opened: "...we have no
Sabbath school for the want of a suitable place to conduct it in." By 1846
the warden reported

so large a portion of the convicts [were] thrown out of
employment [because of a legal provision which tied
up the prison's funds, that] it was thought advisable to
convert one of the prison halls into a school room, where
the assistant keepers should instruct those under their
charge in reading, writing and arithmetic....Those not

1845
(cont'd.)

requiring instruction are allowed to spend their leisure hours in reading. Many of [the students] are zealously engaged in their studies, and those especially who were previously unable to read, express the warmest gratitude for the privilege enjoyed. It is hoped that one object of our penitentiary system may be thus attained, in the moral and mental culture of the convict's mind. (Chenault, 1949-1951, p. 6—see entries for 1846, 1847, and 1863). ⌂

Eventually more attention was directed to the issue of reading materials for prisoners. The library at the Massachusetts State Prison was funded by

an appropriation of $100 a year from the earnings of the convicts, though it was not supported by the convicts. Books of a religious or moral nature might be taken out and returned by the prisoners weekly. Many of the convicts owned their own books... (Lewis, O.F., 1967, p. 167).

During the 1820s the "over-stint" (wages for overtime) had provided money that was often used "for the purchase of 'infidel books.'" The library had been started with a donation of $50 from the warden, apparently to eliminate this effect of the over-stint. (p. 167—see 1833 entry). ⌂

1846 — New York State prison authorities were allowed to spend $100 from the library fund on books for convicts. By 1847 this arrangement was expanded to an annual basis, thus supplying the prisoners' need for "books, maps, and stationery." (Wallack, 1939, p. 4). **Chaplain Abram Haff**, at Clinton Prison, wrote about correctional education, and the lack thereof, in the annual prison report:

We have no Sabbath school, for the want of a suitable place to conduct it in. The Bible and Book of Common Prayer, are the books containing the most permanent reading which the convicts have, and those are read, I trust, with pleasure and profit...the Bible is the only book furnished by the State....I would suggest some additional permanent reading....But we find that a simple belief in the doctrines of religion alone, does not always make men honest; not even sufficiently so, to keep them out of our State prisons; while we frequently meet with men of sterling integrity, who are wholly destitute of religious faith. (Clinton, 1846, p. 30).

1846   Haff offered a student learning needs assessment.
(cont'd.)

> Of the number here confined, there are 1 in 15 who
> cannot read. 1 in 4 who cannot write. 7 in 8 who
> had Christian parents. 1 in 3 who have belonged to
> a Christian church. 1 in 4 who came here through
> intemperance. 1 in 13 who came here through gambling.
> 1 in 3 who came here through keeping bad company.
> (pp. 30-31).

The Prison Association of New York (PANY) described the "growing sense of the importance of [correctional education]." The PANY report stated that increasing attention "is given to moral and religious instruction," and that therefore "an exceeding weight of responsibility rests upon every state, in this regard...to provide proper instruction, and set apart a portion of each day for that purpose" as "one of the most important elements of reformation." (PANY, 1846, p. 104). ⚞

Back in England after leaving Norfolk Island in the South Pacific, **Alexander Maconochie** launched an extensive career in writing and lobbying for prison reform (Barry, 1958, p. 184), often in partnership with **Matthew Davenport Hill**, general reformer and Birmingham judge. Hill had connections with U.S. penologist **E.C. Wines** (p. 189), through Sing Sing warden **Gaylord Hubbell**, who visited England in 1863 (p. 230—see 1870 entry). Maconochie served as governor of Birmingham Prison from 1849-1851 (pp. 196-208). He was called before Parliament several times to offer expert testimony on prisons and prison reform issues (p. 190). ⚞

Charles Dickens ran into former penal colony superintendent Alexander Maconochie at a Ragged School conference in England—a meeting of juvenile correctional educators. A week later the famous author invited Maconochie to dinner. "Dickens had always been interested in penal issues, ever since the time of his father's stay in Marshalsea debtors' prison. In 1842 [see entry] he had visited the Eastern Penitentiary at Philadelphia..." Dickens eventually

> incorporated Maconochie's mark [reformatory] system
> into the running of Urania Cottage, the 'Home for
> Homeless Women' he set up with **Angela Burdett-
> Coutts** in Lime Grove, Shepherd's Bush [England].
> It was named after Aphrodite Urania, the pure
> goddess of love. Its method of operation was based on
> Maconochie's, as Dickens explained: 'I do not know
> of any plan, so well conceived, or so firmly grounded
> in a knowledge of human nature...as what is called
> Captain Maconochie's...' The girls were to be 'tempted
> to virtue,' not 'dragged, driven, or frightened'....Every

girl was required to keep a duplicate copy of her daily mark-paper [itemized behavioral record]. This had a dual function. 'Besides the probability of its producing some moral effect upon her, it would be a lesson in arithmetic in which she could not fail to have a personal interest.' (Clay, 2001, pp. 256-259; bold emphasis added). ⌒

1847 — Section 61 of the New York State legal code provided for the appointment of two instructors at each State prison (Auburn, Sing Sing, and Clinton— and the law was made applicable to institutions that were constructed later), as advocated by the New York Prison Association. The resultant program was structured much like chaplain-organized Sabbath schools, with the emphasis on basic reading in a cell study setting. The new teachers were hired as a distinct class of prison officers. (Reagen and Stoughton, 1973, p. 37). **Terry Angle** later pointed out that these were common, or elementary, school teachers—as opposed to religious and moral teachers (Angle, 1982, p. 5). They were appointed by the board of inspectors of each prison (Chenault, 1949-1951, p. 6). The law provided that

> it shall be the duty of such instructors with, and under the supervision of the Chaplain to give instruction in the useful branches of an English education to such convicts as, in the judgment of the Warden or the Chaplain, may require the same and be benefited by it; such instruction shall be given for not less than one hour and a half daily, Sunday excepted, between the hours of six and nine in the evening (Wallack, 1939, p. 18).

The law required that

> The chaplain shall make a quarterly report to the inspectors, stating the number of convicts that shall have been instructed during the last quarter, the branches of education in which they shall have been instructed, the textbook used in such instruction, and the progress made by the convicts, and to note especially any cases in which an unusual progress had been made by a convict (Chenault, 1949-1951, p. 8).

In 1848 an Auburn teacher wrote of his students' "eagerness to learn." At Sing Sing, "two [teachers] were procured for the male prison, and a little after, one for the female..." Correctional education had a "tendency...to elevate their minds, and lift them above the groveling position which they occupied previous to their commitment." By 1850, all of the six new positions were filled. (Chenault, 1949-1951,

1847　　p. 6). "At Auburn Prison 198 convicts, or 1 in 2-1/2, of the whole
(cont'd.)　number, have been taught....At the female prison 35 convicts, or 1 in 2
of the whole number, have received instruction...the instructress, who
is an experienced teacher [was hired as a] matron." (Chenault, 1949-
1951, p. 7). There were no more important changes in the New York
correctional education laws until 1925 (Chenault, 1949-1951, p. 8—see
1874 entry). 📐

By today's standards, the costs of correctional education
seem minimal. The estimated expense of supporting a correctional
teacher, "including chaplain's duties," was $1,000 per year (PANY,
1847, p. 30). 📐

The New York Prison Association launched an advocacy
role for correctional education, and made information available for
public consumption. The Association announced that less than 1% of
penitentiary expenditures were directed to education-related services
(Lewis, D., 1965, pp. 215-251). 📐

The first state-run juvenile institution was constructed in
Westborough, Massachusetts (Angle, 1982, p. 5). During the next few
decades Massachusetts juvenile facilities served as models that other
jurisdictions sought to replicate. 📐

Chaplain Campbell, recently appointed at Sing Sing, enlisted
the assistance of "several young gentlemen residing in [the] village" as
teachers. He wrote "Ignorance is a fruitful source of crime; therefore, the
State wisely provides for the instruction of the young." However, the
daily morning schedule of approximately one half hour's instruction
"has been interrupted for almost the entire year now past." Campbell
reported that few convicts had previously been employed. Then he was
told, "We cannot have schools, or take any portion of time (excepting
the Sabbath) for moral instruction, because it interferes with the claims
of the contractors." "Such arrangements," he wrote, "are detrimental
to the main objects of the prison system...both as regards the good
government of the prison and the prevention of crime, and consequently
the protection of society..." The female annex also had new industrial
contracts, and "all general instruction...was abandoned....Only the
evening classes for teaching reading, writing, etc., were continued."
Campbell described his situation:

> The demands of it, the teaching of the convicts to read
> and write, the distribution and supervision of the
> library, the proper supply of books, etc., are enough
> to tax the whole time and strength of one man, and
> one therefore, whose time must necessarily be drawn
> very largely upon for the performance of other duties,
> can devote but a very limited portion of it, even to the

1847   superintendence of, much less to personal labor in this
(cont'd.) department. (Chenault, 1949-1951, p. 5).

As if these problems were not enough, the following selected contraband list suggests some of the institutional constraints he faced:

> newspapers, story books...*Burglar's Companion, History of Buccaneers, Comic Almanac, Family Almanac*...songs, maps, *Treatise on Surveying*, pictures, chalk, writing desk...five quires of writing paper...*Farmer's Instructor*.... lice and bedbugs...pocket-books...*The Murderer*, slate and pencil, paintings...*French Grammar, Chronological Dictionary*...*Lives of Females*, letters and songs, *Latin Grammar, Latin Exercises, Ainsworth's Dictionary, Assembly Report Document No. 2...Domestic Medicines.* (p. 5).

In the days before compulsory school attendance, interest in the reformation of delinquents spread throughout the Eastern U.S. For example, in this year a municipal institution for juveniles was established in New Orleans (Abbott, 1968 vol. #2, pp. 323-328).

1848 — The original state reform school in the United States was opened in Massachusetts (Abbott, 1968 vol. #2, pp. 323-328). Although the pace of activity seems slow by modern standards, a movement for juvenile institutions was under way.

Zebulon Brockway was hired as a clerk at Connecticut's Wethersfield Prison, by Amos Pilsbury's brother-in-law, Warden **Leonard Wells**. Brockway served in the capacity of clerk for two years, encountering many stories about Amos Pilsbury's exemplary leadership at Wethersfield. (Brockway, 1969/1912, p. 40—see 1851 entry).

During the late 1840s the Sing Sing Women's Prison School experienced severe disruption because stubborn program supporters, obsessed with their differences, proved unable to unite. Traditionally, the School was supported by the chaplain and the chief matron, but in this case they argued over phrenology, the "science" of biological crime determinants. Phrenologists held that "born criminals" could be identified by the contours of their skulls, but that educational activities could sometimes alter criminal tendencies through brain exercises. Sing Sing's Women's Prison matron **Eliza Farnham** believed in phrenology, but chaplain **John Luckey** believed it would lead to moral relativism. Luckey said Farnham's approach could be used to justify wickedness and diminish personal accountability for transgressions. Farnham used an array of correctional education programs to combat the despondency of institutional life, and to help women develop educational aspirations. Like Luckey, she wanted to

1848   expand educational opportunities, but they clashed repeatedly over
(cont'd.) the phrenology issue. "By July, 1848 the situation had become so bad
        that either Mrs. Farnham or the chaplain had to go. In a showdown
        before the board of inspectors... Luckey was relieved of his job." But
        Luckey and his friends continued their outspoken criticism of School
        management, while prison leaders watched. The Luckey group said
        that (a) some teachers rejected the divinity of Christ, (b) secular texts
        were used instead of the Scriptures, (c) unorthodox women's fashions
        were discussed, (d) some Dickens stories were actually read aloud in
        class, and (e) Farnham had inculcated the students to the point that they
        would rather read novels than perform domestic labor. In 1847 a State
        Senate committee had been convened to investigate. Unconvinced of
        the need to improve or expand School services, the committee called
        for a return to "old fashioned wisdom." Some committee members
        equated Farnham's "misguided philanthropy" with "insurrection,
        incendiarism, robbery, and all the evils most fatal to society and
        detrimental to law and order..." Farnham left the institution in 1848,
        just as the "great reform period at Sing Sing was coming to an end."
        (Lewis, D., 1965, pp. 215-251). ⌒

1849 — **Colin Arnott Browning, M.D.** was a staff surgeon with the Royal British
        Navy who served on transportation ships to Australia. Transportation
        was the exile of criminals to that remote continent. During his second
        voyage to Australia, in 1834 on the ship *Arab*, he organized a school.
        During his third voyage, on the *Elphinstone*, he refined the system.
        During his fourth voyage, in 1840 on the *Margaret*, he applied the
        principles already proven to female convicts. By his fifth voyage,
        on the *Earl Grey*, 264 convicts were enrolled in the floating school.
        And "still more abundant blessing attended my sixth, seventh, and
        eighth voyages in the *Theresa*, the *Pestonjee Bomonjee*, and *Hashemy*"
        (Browning, in Carpenter, 1969/1864, vol. #1, p. 284). It was in 1849 at
        the completion of his eighth voyage, on the *Hashemy*, that Dr. Browning
        received greatest acclaim.

> It may be worthy of remark that, on review and
> comparison of my eight voyages, I find the amount
> of reformation among the prisoners strikingly to
> correspond with the degree of diligence and zeal with
> which the Gospel, in its Divine simplicity, was brought
> to bear, from the hour of embarkation, upon their
> understandings and hearts. During my first voyage,
> there was less of Christian instruction, and much less
> of apparent improvement. As experience grew, and
> practical Christianity was from the beginning relied
> upon, coercion in any form became less and less called
> for; and, during my last three voyages, not only were
> no lashes inflicted, but not a fetter was used, nor a
> prisoner placed in confinement, or under the charge of

1849
(cont'd.)

a sentry. (Browning, in Carpenter, 1969/1864, vol. #1, p. 284; emphases in original).

Browning gave an encouraging address to the convicts immediately after embarkation, focusing on the problems of their previous lives and their prospects for the future. The next day the population was organized into three divisions, under three captains and several petty officers, all elected by the convicts themselves. As soon as this was accomplished Browning had the prisoners' irons, "their badges of disgrace," removed. All this was preparation for organizing the school.

> The whole of the people are now to be formed into schools, according to their degrees of knowledge. To each school a teacher is appointed, and over the whole a General Inspector. The teachers are chosen with great care from amongst those who appear to combine with the greatest scholarship the best abilities, the most amiable disposition, and the greatest degree of moral integrity. The peculiar tact necessary to communicate instruction with success, has, with few exceptions, to be acquired. (Browning, in Carpenter, 1969/1864, vol. #1, p. 286; emphasis in original).

Then he addressed them a second time, emphasizing their duty to each other and as citizens. "A very short time suffices to familiarise the people with the daily routine..." (Browning, in Carpenter, 1969/1864, vol. #1, p. 287; emphasis in original). He described the results as "delightful and interesting."

> Much...depends on the character of the schoolmaster. The difference in the effects produced on the same class of pupils by teachers of different degrees of skill and zeal, is great, and shews the value of efficient instructors, and their vast influence on the acquirement of useful knowledge, and therefore on the future character and destinies of men. The pupils of a dull and indolent teacher betray, in a marvellous degree, the unhappy characteristics of their master; and the spirit and life of the ardent and industrious schoolmaster are as visibly imbibed by the pupils committed to his care.... All that I can do myself personally, is occasionally to instruct them how to proceed, and to lecture them seriously on the momentous character of their duties. Charged as is the Surgeon-Superintendent with 'the entire management of the prisoners,' and the whole of the medical duties of the transport, unassisted, all he can daily attempt is an occasional, and often hasty visit to the schools, the influence of which is

perhaps increased by its being always <u>expected</u> by the people...However brief and rapid these visits are, they help to maintain a constant intercourse between himself and the schools; they afford him an opportunity of making observations both on teachers and pupils, giving them a word of direction, reproof, or encouragement! and of manifesting interest in the people and the work in which they are engaged. (Browning, in Carpenter, 1969/1864, vol. #1, pp. 287-288; emphases in original).

A system of courts to address disciplinary infractions on the ship was organized under the school. Four judges were appointed by the prisoner who was "chief captain and inspector of schools," and a fifth who was the inmate clerk who worked for Browning. The most severe punishment allowed was "<u>probation,</u> under close observation, ...dismissed for the present with the assurance that his next offence will be subject to a more serious punishment, and make it necessary to bring him before the Surgeon-Superintendent." (Browning, in Carpenter, 1969/1864, vol. #1, p. 288; emphasis in original). Browning reported that this system worked well.

A perception of truth, and conviction of right and wrong, influence the minds of the prisoners unmixed with any impressions produced by my immediate presence and authority. Another beneficial tendency of the working of this court, is to lead the people to sit in judgment upon themselves, and to form a just estimate of their own character and conduct. (Browning, in Carpenter, 1969/1864, vol. #1, p. 289).

As the minds of the people become enlightened, the esteem of my approbation, and dread of incurring my displeasure, increase. Instead of the mere apprehension of punishment, both affection and gratitude soon begin to exert a happy influence; they perceive and feel that I am their <u>friend;</u> that my sole aim is their improvement and happiness; that nothing pleases and delights me so much as <u>real</u> reformation in principle and behaviour; that nothing causes me greater pain and disappointment than their continuance in immoral and irregular habits, except, indeed, <u>hypocritical pretensions</u> to a change of character which does not manifest itself in their temper and conduct... (Browning, in Carpenter, 1969/1864, p. 289; emphases in original).

1849   Carpenter wrote that
(cont'd.)

> In the School Dr. B. did not confine himself to dry lessons, but gave simple lectures on natural history, natural philosophy, and other subjects calculated to raise and elevate their minds. Most especially, however, did he devote his efforts to make the men under his care fully acquainted with the Bible, and to direct their minds to the teachings and truths it contains. He also gave them much definite instruction on moral subjects, which might be useful to them in after life. He chiefly aimed, however, to lead them to a true change of heart... (Carpenter, 1969/1864, vol. #1, p. 289).

> A voyage spent under such influences, and with such earnest and well-directed effort to benefit the Convicts, could not but produce the best possible effect on them. On their arrival at the place of their destination, an officer of the army came on board, who was also a justice of the peace. He was much struck, and highly delighted with the appearance of the people. (Carpenter, 1969/1864, vol. #1, p. 290).

The volume ends with several impressive testimonies to the benefit of organizing schools like Dr. Browning's on transport ships. ⚕

1850 — Gold was discovered in Victoria, Australia.

> The gold rush transformed Australia's destiny. Before it, people could scarcely be induced to settle there. Now a stampede rose from every quarter of the globe. In less than a decade, the country took in 600,000 new faces, more than doubling its population. The bulk of that growth was in Victoria, where the richest goldfields were. Melbourne became larger than Sydney and for a time was probably the richest city in the world per head of population. But the real effort of gold was to put an end to transportation. When it was realized in London that transportation was seen as an opportunity rather than a punishment, that convicts <u>desired</u> to be sent to Australia, the notion of keeping the country a prison became unsustainable. A few boatloads of convicts were sent to Western Australia until 1868 (they would find gold there as well, in equally gratifying quantities) but essentially the gold rush of the 1850s marked the end of Australia as a concentration camp and its beginning as a nation. (Bryson, 2000, p. 81; emphasis in original). ⚕

1850
(cont'd.) In Massachusetts jails, women made up 19.5% of the population, but in the penitentiaries women amounted to only 3.6%. In New York penitentiaries women made up 5.6% of the population. In 1831 **Beaumont** and **de Tocqueville** had reported that 1/12 of the incarcerated U.S. population was female; in 1838 New York secretary of state John Dix found that in England 1/5 of the population was female, but in New York the fraction was 1/16. In 1843 another New York secretary of state reported that the proportion had increased to 1/14. (Freedman, 1981, pp. 11-12—see 1860 entry). ⌒

Problems regarding urban crime concerned nearly everyone. British reformer **Mary Carpenter** quoted a New York City police chief about

> a deplorable and growing evil existing in that community of vagrant, idle, and vicious children of both sexes, who infest the public thoroughfares, hotels, docks, etc....In my opinion, some method by which these children could be compelled to attend our schools regularly, or be apprenticed to some suitable occupation, would tend, in time, more to improve the morals of the community, prevent crime, and relieve the city from the onerous burden of expenses for the Almshouses and Penitentiary, than any other conservative or philanthropic movement with which I am at present acquainted. (Carpenter, in Dell'Apa, 1973b, p. 11—see entries for 1851 and 1872). ⌒

In the U.S., because of the inequality that originated with racially-based slavery, the question of access to educational opportunity was central.

> In a case that served as precedent for the doctrine of 'separate but equal' that persisted for more than a century, Judge Lemuel Shaw decided...that the [Boston] school committee had the right under its 'powers of general superintendence' to classify black children... (Tyack, 1974, p. 114).

A group of Boston African Americans had petitioned for desegregated schools in 1846. "During the nineteenth century no group in the United States had a greater faith in the equalizing power of schooling or a clearer understanding of the democratic promise of public education than did black Americans." (p. 110). In New York

> there were an estimated 11,000 Negro children in the state, [but] the municipalities requested only $396 in 1849. These 'colored schools' were independent of the

<table>
<tr><td>1850
(cont'd.)</td><td>regular school system, administered by the village trustees rather than by the school committees; the state superintendent of common schools suspected that funds intended for black children went instead to the white public schools. (p. 112).</td></tr>
</table>

In 1853 "colored free schools" were implemented in New York City, thus removing African American common schooling from under the control of White philanthropists and transferring it to the City board of education. In 1857 a pattern of board spending was identified in City schools—"one cent per Negro child and sixteen dollars per white child for sites and school buildings, even though there were 25 percent more black children attending school in proportion to their total population than white." (p. 119). In 1873 the City ended mandatory segregation, and for 22 years thereafter "no black teachers were hired" (p. 117). In 1863 (the year of Lincoln's Emancipation Proclamation) Chicago passed a "Black School Law," requiring segregated education. By 1874 African Americans in 26 separate Illinois counties attended segregated schools. (pp. 115-116). The African American school system in Washington, D.C. began in 1862, with a three member White board appointed by the Secretary of the Interior. By 1869 two of the board members were African American, and in 1873 Congress expanded the African American board to nine members appointed by the governor of the District. (p. 120). Segregation advanced according to local patterns in each community. "The Negro community in Indianapolis made great sacrifices to provide private schools for their children in the 1860's before the city opened public education to them." The superintendent of schools wrote of his admiration of these schools in 1866. In 1897 an African American General Assembly member introduced a bill to abolish all discrimination on grounds of race, but 30 teachers signed a petition against it on the grounds that such action would "be detrimental to the colored people of the State" and might eliminate African Americans from 53 teaching positions, out of a total of 585. (pp. 116-117). Another pattern of segregation can be traced in St. Louis.

> The state constitution in 1865 required the city to educate Negroes; in 1866, St. Louis' white board of schools took over responsibility for a separate system of black schools. Radical Republicans on the central school board wished to build schools for Negro students, appealing to the fact that blacks were taxpayers and that the law and sentiment of the community approved schooling as 'common justice to the colored people.' But Democrats ridiculed the idea of 'extravagant school houses for the education of Negroes' and said that if the Radicals 'like to associate with niggerdom, as would seem to be the case, let them

1850
(cont'd.)

go to them, but not at the expense of the white men.' In the 1866 election the Democrats won most city offices, including all the eligible school positions. (p. 121).

In 1868 the African American community built a school at its own expense. (p. 121). That was the same year that the 14th Amendment was ratified, to guarantee equal protection under the laws (p. 119).

In 1878 the Colored Educational Association requested the board to name the schools after prominent blacks like Toussaint L'Ouverture, Alexandre Dumas, and Crispus Attucks. The board refused, suggesting instead that they be named for white 'men who have distinguished themselves in the cause of the colored race.' (p. 122).

Only in 1890 were the names changed. (p. 122). In California, legal changes also affected school segregation. "In 1874 the California court affirmed that separate but equal schools for Negroes did not violate the Fourteenth Amendment....San Francisco abandoned its segregated black schools in 1875, largely because the separate schools were costly and unpopular with the Negro community." (p. 115). But "Chinese and Japanese pupils met gross discrimination and cruelty—in 1906 they were segregated in special schools in San Francisco and were assaulted by roving gangs of toughs—yet they also generally did well in school." (pp. 247-248—see entries for 1819, 1930, and 1954). ⌂

"The Convict Prisons [in England]...employed civilian teachers. But in the other prisons there were warder/schoolmasters." (Forster, 1981, p. 11). ⌂

Terry Angle later wrote of correctional education during this period. "For the most part, schools and libraries were in favour with the wardens because of their disciplinary value." (Angle, 1982, p. 5). ⌂

1851 — New York's Auburn Prison inspectors reported on

the subject of lighting the halls more perfectly at night, so as to enable all convicts to read until the usual hour of retiring to bed....If [the early evening] could be employed by them in reading, and pursuing their regular studies, it would be a great benefit to the convict, as well as advantageous to the discipline of the prison. The men would be more contented, and less liable to be engaged in forming plans of escape, and concocting mischief...without legislative aid, it will be difficult, if not impossible, to accomplish... improvement. (Chenault, 1949-1951, pp. 7-8).

1851　　But nothing was done, and in 1871 the chaplain was still "calling for
(cont'd.) sufficient gas light, that each prisoner may see to read in his cell two
　　　　hours each evening..." The chaplain at Clinton Prison reported the
　　　　same problem in 1872.

> Only the ground floor and middle gallery cells are now
> sufficiently lighted to admit of reading in them; and
> then only as the book is held to the grates of the cell
> door; and this only when the cell is opposite the lamp
> suspended near the wall of the prison. (pp. 8-9).

In 1875 the Sing Sing chaplain summarized the situation at his facility.
"I have reason to believe that the teachers have been as diligent, faithful
and successful as could be expected under so defective a system of
teaching." (pp. 7-15). ⌒

Zebulon Brockway became deputy warden of the Albany
County Penitentiary (see 1867 entry), serving directly under **Amos
Pilsbury**. Brockway was 24 years old. (Brockway, 1969/1912, p.
43). Pilsbury sponsored his "apprenticeship," and facilitated his
appointment to the superintendency of the Albany Municipal and
County Almshouse in 1853 (Brockway, 1969/1912 p. 53—see 1853
entry). ⌒

Mary Carpenter's book on *Reformatory Schools* was published.
See 1850 entry. She coined the phrase "reformatory school movement."
(Carpenter, 1872, p. 105). The book was about alternative education,
especially Sunday schools, in mid 19th century England. The target
population consisted of children from the "perishing classes...[poor,
and] living by plunder...and...the dangerous classes...the scum of the
populace." (Carpenter, 1970/1851, p. 99). Many were "wholly and
entirely without friends and relations of any kind...some have parents
who encourage them [in crime]" (p. 15). Boys under age 15 were
sometimes transported to Australia (p. 16—see 1853 entry). Carpenter
was concerned that, in response to one teacher's question "Who is Jesus
Christ? there were upwards of 100 [young students] entirely ignorant"
(p. 26). Many teachers classified learners according to how well they
could recite or write the Lord's Prayer (pp. 22-23). She discovered that
"the mere mechanical power of reading and writing, unaccompanied
by sound moral, industrial, and religious training, really prepares the
ill-disposed for greater audacity in crime" (p. 27).

> In 1781 the Sunday [or ragged] School was first founded
> by **Robert Raikes** at Gloucester...who...was trained
> for his work by a long practiced habit of visiting the
> Bridewell [an historic jail], and endeavoring to impart
> Christian principles, with instruction in reading
> and writing, to the unhappy inmates... this may be

considered the first Ragged School. (pp. 111-112; bold emphasis added; underline emphasis in original).

> [Raikes] selected for the purpose a Sunday which from time immemorial had been devoted to a festival that would have disgraced the most heathenish nations. Drunkenness, and every species of clamor, noise, and disorder, formerly filled the town on that occasion. On the day selected for the [first Sunday school celebration, in 1786] it was filled with the usual crowds who attended the feast; but instead of repairing to the alehouses, as heretofore, they all hastened to the church, which was filled in such a manner as I never remember to have seen in any church in this country before; the galleries, the aisles were thronged like a playhouse. Drawn up in a rank round the churchyard, appeared the children belonging to the different Schools, to the number of three hundred and thirty-one. The gentlemen walked round to view them; it was a sight truly interesting and truly affecting. Young people, lately more neglected than the cattle in the field, ignorant, profane, filthy, clamorous, impatient of every restraint, courteous in conversation and in behaviour, free from that vileness which marks the wretched vulgar. The inhabitants of the town bear testimony to this change in their manners. (pp. 114-115).

In 1844 a Ragged School Union was established (p. 61). By 1850 "the increase in the number of Ragged Schools throughout the [London] metropolis, since 1844, has been 62; of Ragged School teachers 852; of Ragged School pupils, 15,249." (p. 127). Carpenter reported that the best teachers were full of religious zeal, but "it is needful also to know how to teach, and how to adapt one's language and manner to these children, so as to make oneself really intelligible to them" (p. 122). "Female teachers are often found to possess peculiar power of subduing by force of gentleness the very wildest..." (p. 123). A typical facility was

> partitioned off on either side, into small boxes or compartments, in each of which there is a class of scholars, presided over by a teacher. There are classes also in the middle of the room, divided from one another by screens. On a kind of platform at the upper end sits the superintendent... (p. 33).

> The system of teaching boys en masse is a very excellent and convenient system to a certain extent. Arithmetic, reading, &c., may be taught by means of a piece of

1851	chalk and a large black board; history, whether sacred
(cont'd.)	or otherwise, may be implanted by a single teacher
	addressing a large class... (p. 137).

> As the greater number cannot read, the master recites each verse to them, while they follow him gently; frequently he stops to explain the verse, to lead them to realize the meaning of it, and to apply it to their own circumstances; for he endeavours to gain as much knowledge as possible of them, and frequently brings the events passing in their little world home to their consciences in a forcible manner; then their voices rise with true harmony, and none can doubt that these holy words are borne by the sweet strains deeply into their hearts.... (pp. 139-140).

Some schools provided vocational education (pp. 166-167), special activities—such as an "anti-slavery bazaar" (p. 167), and health education (p. 168). Most teachers were volunteers, although "qualified and therefore...fairly paid teacher[s]" were needed (p. 155). Students "from 13 to 15 years of age...who both understand and practice good methods of instruction" often served as teacher aides (p. 201). Statistics revealed unaddressed educational needs: "20,000 children, who...'are estimated to be still destitute of any means of instruction in Liverpool" (p. 251). Carpenter advocated ragged schools, free day schools, and "industrial feeding schools" (which meant exactly as the name implied), supported by government taxes and compulsory attendance laws (p. 38). Otherwise, "The only School provided in Great Britain by the State for her children, is—THE GAOL!" (p. 260; emphasis in original—see 1823 entry). ⌒

1853 — The colonists in Western Australia refused to accept any more transported British prisoners, so Parliament passed an act to end the practice (Carpenter, 1872, p. 2). As a result, prisons became a focus of increased attention. One judge, as late as 1851, said that he often passed "sentence of transportation upon a boy under 15 years of age, if he is a very hardened offender, and has been convicted frequently before." (Carpenter, 1970/1851, p. 16). Several years earlier, Parkhurst Prison for juveniles was established, to eliminate the transporting of youngsters, but "it appears the judges are not aware of the order," and the practice was maintained (p. 294—see 1830 entry on Parkurst, and 1863 entry for information about impacts from the end of transportation in Ireland). ⌒

Zebulon Brockway became superintendent of the Monroe County Penitentiary, in Rochester, New York (Brockway, 1969/1912, p. 58). He served in this capacity until 1861, and his comments reflected the professional orientation he and his colleagues shared.

1853   It was a "time of special emotional awakening—the importance of
(cont'd.) the welfare of the prisoners assumed enlarged proportions; not less
        regard for the material objects of management, but increased interest
        in the essential immaterial, spiritual things and relations." (p. 66—
        see 1857 entry). 🐾

1854 — Several women left the New York Prison Association to establish the
        Women's Prison Association (WPA). They experienced initial frustration
        in their efforts to raise funds for a separate women's prison. In 1861,
        however, the WPA received a financial contribution from New York
        City. (Freedman, 1981, p. 34—see 1860 entry). 🐾

        At Pennsylvania's Cherry Hill Prison, **Abram Boyer** was
        appointed full-time teacher. "He immediately supplanted the 'three
        Rs' with courses in bookkeeping, phonography [phonetic spelling]
        and mathematics.' In addition he offered instruction in Spanish and
        German for those who cared and were able to absorb them." (Teeters
        and Shearer, 1957, p. 159). Boyer had 71 students

            to which of each I give a lesson once in seven or eight
            days....Through the 1850s several publishers made
            relatively large contributions to the library of volumes
            which were primarily of a religious nature. However,
            there were many dealing with adventure, travel, and
            biography. (p. 160). 🐾

        In his book, *Chapters on Prisons and Prisoners and the Prevention
        of Crime*, published in London, **Joseph Kingsmill** wrote about the
        correctional education mission. "To discipline and improve the
        intellectual capacities of the prisoner, by education, books, and every
        available means, is a high duty of a chaplain, and a most interesting
        one" (Kingsmill, 1854,p. 335—see entries for 1837 and 1899). 🐾

        An Englishman in Germany named **George Combe** wrote of
        an important innovation at Munich Prison. Combe's report appeared
        in the *Illustrated News*, caught **Matthew Davenport Hill**'s attention
        (see entries for 1846, 1860, 1863, and 1872), and was reprinted in
        his *Repression of Crime*. The report attracted such attention that
        Mary Carpenter (see entries for 1850, 1851, and 1872) inserted it in
        her 1864 book *Our Convicts*, in the chapter "Principles of Convict
        Treatment." Highlights from Combe's letter appear in the following
        lines. "I have found...an unexpected illustration of the power of the
        moral sentiments to govern and reform criminals, without using the
        lash or any severe punishments..." The bars on the windows were
        especially flimsy, the 600 hardened Bavarian criminals had access
        to all sorts of tools in the shops, and there was only a handful of
        officers.

| 1854 (cont'd.) | ...yet the culprits do not break the prison; they obey cheerfully, they work diligently; and there is an air of mental calmness about them that is truly extraordinary....How has all been accomplished? by the genius of one man [the warden], **Herr Von Obermaier**! (p. 92; bold emphasis added; exclamation emphasis in original). |

At reception each prisoner was interviewed by Von Obermaier, asked about his family, and urged to reform himself for their sake.

> I use persuasion with the offender—punish him [only] by withholding part of his food, or depriving him of some other enjoyment—and he generally gives up his misconduct. When the general spirit of the men is directed towards virtue, an individual finds it extremely difficult to persevere in vice in the face of their condemnation....If once...the prison is pervaded by a sound public opinion, and the desire of improvement has gained the ascendancy, then the reformed penitents...become such powerful instruments of further improvement that complete security in every department, and for every individual is established....without the lash, the solitary cell, the treadmill, the crank-wheel, pious visitors, or any of the other appliances regarded as indispensable elements of prison discipline. (Combe, in Carpenter, 1864/1969, v. 1, pp. 92-95). ⌒

1855 — **Corder's** book, *Life of Elizabeth Fry: Compiled from her Journal*, was published in Philadelphia. An Englishwoman, Fry was an exemplar for Quakers on both sides of the Atlantic. Corder's book emphasized the need for what would be called "networking" today—liaising between prisoners and audiences interested in prison reform and correctional education. (Corder, 1855—see 1817 entry). ⌒

1856 — The first State Industrial School for Girls was opened in Lancaster, Massachusetts. The legislature originally intended to establish a women's prison. The School for Girls used indeterminate sentences and conditional pardon and release. It had inmate employment and a cottage housing system—the first institution in the United States to use cottages instead of cells or dormitories. (Freedman, 1981,p. 56—see 1868 entry). ⌒

1857 — The earliest reference to a magic lantern show at an institution was by **J. E. Carpenter**, in a biography of England's **Mary Carpenter**. After dinner on Christmas Eve, 1857, the 200 Ragged School children at Carpenter's Bristol institutions—Kingswood was the boys' facility and Red Lodge was the girls'—were treated to the high tech show funded, in part, by **Lady Byron**. The Kingswood hall was decorated with evergreens for the occasion. We have no record about the theme of the pictures displayed that night, but it is likely that they focused on traditional Christmas themes. In addition, the playground was expanded for the Holidays, and Mary Carpenter gave gifts to each student. (Carpenter, J.E., 1974/1881, p. 186). 🝙

Mountjoy Prison, in Dublin, Ireland, was in the system implemented by **Sir Walter Crofton**, the Englishman who restructured the Irish Prison System after the Great Potato Famine, on the model established by **Alexander Maconochie** in the South Pacific, 1840-1844. Mountjoy was part of the first full scale European replication of Maconochie's Reformatory Prison Discipline. For many in the U.S., the terms "Irish System" and "Reformatory Prison Discipline" were synonomous. In February, 1855, Crofton appointed **Edward McGauren** as head schoolmaster at Mountjoy. The following selections from the schoolmaster's journal reveal some of McGauren's everyday experiences in the classroom from the years 1857 and 1864.

> 8th July, [18]'57. Senior section of juveniles at school— Moral Lecture, Science of Common Things, and Competitive Examination. Warden McDonnell in charge. I have seen enough to feel quite satisfied that to reform a prisoner it is not only necessary to teach him right from wrong but to make him love what is right and to detest what is wrong—that this is not possible while the convict remains in a gloomy, sullen, or embittered mood. And that, as this is the general state in which our prisoners are received, it is indispensable to use persuasive, instead of coercive measures to work him into a reconciled and cheerful state of mind, so that the mind will admit impressions which otherwise it would not receive. I am far from wishing it to be understood that coercive measures are in all cases unnecessary, but I wish it to be distinctly understood that <u>in all cases</u> persuasive measures are essential in the <u>beginning</u> of the convict's incarceration. There is generally a spleen (sic) the Officer and the prisoner arising from various causes. Very often the prisoner fancies that the officer's principal business in the prison is to annoy and thwart him; and very often I fear does the officer make it his business to vex and irritate the prisoner. Very often again the prisoner's manner and bearing are disrespectful and annoying unknown to himself; and very often is the officer's manner and tone of voice wanting in that sweetness which makes us feel anything unoppressive. It is not alone necessary for

the officer to abstain from harshness either in voice or manner, he must do more. He must pay attention to his face—he must wear an agreeable smile, a pleasant face and tune his voice into a winning softness, so that these untutored appearances of good will and brotherly love may be reciprocated <u>through sympathy</u> by the prisoners. For the purpose of establishing this sort of feeling between officer and prisoner I would recommend that the officers should be lectured at least twice a week on the proper treatment and management of prisoners. (Mountjoy Prison, 1866, p. 7; emphases in original).

...at these lectures extracts from the most approved authors...[on] Reformatory and Prisons Discipline be read and fully explained. I would most strongly recommend at least as regards the juveniles that all misconduct reports against prisoners be submitted to me for the purpose of dealing with them as I have so successfully dealt with all those coming through the schoolmaster since my appointment—of course still to continue to hand over to the juveniles for punishment such as appeared to me to deserve it. I would then have an opportunity of setting permanently, without human suffering and without the least danger of permitting a dangerous laxity of discipline,—any little differences between officers and prisoners. I am convinced that fully 90 per cent of the annoyances officers receive from prisoners arise from the unfortunate ill feeling between them- and which is only made the greater by punishment." (p. 8).

....24th Nov. 1857. Messrs Woods and Doyle complain of the cold of the school room. Whether the school room is to be partitioned into small apartments or not, some sort of adequate heating apparatus is urgently required in it as no man could teach efficiently for four consecutive hours in such a temperature on a cold winter's day. (p. 23).

25th. Instructed one of Mr. Doyle's classes in the School room. Without raising my voice beyond its natural pitch or increasing its loudness I found that it attracted the attention of the prisoners in Mr. Wood's class which was at the time under his instruction in the room. The experiment so far I fear will prove a failure. (p. 23).

1857
(cont'd.)

2nd Dec. 1857. Evening School as usual. For more than an hour after commencing business the noise of the supper and the ringing of trays completely prevented me from proceeding....Governor [warden] introduced a plan of school class with the adult prisoners which I regard as an inconvenient method [of] teaching; but a greater objection is, that it is at variance with a justly recognized principle in discipline—'no person to interfere with the arrangement of the school, except the schoolmaster or school inspector, so long as such school arrangements offer no obstruction to the maintenance of the discipline of the prison.' (p. 27).

April 7th 1864. Sir, I must respectfully beg to call your attention to the fact, that the last portion of the pens for the use of the prisoners, have been issued; hence, in the course of a few days, the writing of the prisoners must be suspended unless the Requisition on her Majesty's Stationary Office, dated Feb. 15Th '64, happens to be supplied in this particular in the mean time.... Stationary run short pens. (p. 32).

Dr. Carolyn Eggleston located the above handwritten 1857-1866 teacher's journal in 2000, while she was engaged in historical research in Dublin. ◢◣

1860 — After 1860, women who had gained a foothold in public charities demanded policy changes in prison systems. "Three principles guided them: the separation of women prisoners from men; the provision of differential, feminine care; and control over women's prisons by female staff and management." (Freedman, 1981, p. 46). "After 1840 women joined the ranks of the criminal class in America" (p. 13). In 1842 the proportion of females in the Massachusetts system rose to 20%, and by 1864 it reached a high of 37.2%. During the 1860s "Women's conviction rates for crimes against property rose...ten times as fast as men's." As "the Civil War removed male wage earners from many families, women may have had a greater need to resort to crimes..." (pp. 13-14). Also during the 1860s, "**Elizabeth Chance**...discovered in her visits to Rhode Island institutions that prisons held classes for men but not for women and that female inmates were offered neither exercise nor mental occupation while incarcerated" (p. 48; bold emphasis added). ◢◣

In England, **Alexander Maconochie** died. However, his ideas would live on in Ireland (see 1863 entry) and North America (see entries for 1846 and 1870). Ireland's **Sir Walter Crofton** "was avowedly a disciple of Maconochie" (Barry, 1958, p. 212). Crofton was "A prison disciplinarian of Captain Maconochie's school who was destined to improve, develop, and in fact, almost perfect his master's theories"

1860   (Clay, in Barry, 1958, p. 213). When Maconochie left the Birmingham
(cont'd.) Prison warden assignment in 1851, **Matthew Davenport Hill** held a
meeting at which Maconochie summarized his prison reform work: He
had pursued "the noblest missionary cause that could be conceived.
To raise the fallen—to rescue the lost—a higher and more interesting
enterprise could not be devised." (Hill, in Barry, 1958, p. 209—see
1870 entry). ⌒

The public "schools of most of the cities and large towns [in the
United States] were graded. By 1870 the pendulum had swung from no
system to nothing but system." (Tyack, 1974, p. 45). **Henry Barnard** had
started the rush to divide instruction according to grade levels in 1838,
when he

> first gave his lecture 'Gradation of Public Schools, with
> Special Reference to Cities and Large Villages,' which
> he would repeat in more than fifty cities across the
> country during the next two decades. He maintained
> that a classroom containing students of widely varying
> ages and attainment was not only inefficient but also
> inhumane. (p. 44).

"In 1862, **[William Harvey] Wells** published *A Graded Course of
Instruction with Instructions to Teachers*, which not only outlined specific
items to be covered in each subject at each grade level (see 1874 entry),
but also prescribed the proper teaching methods" (p. 46; emphasis
added). By 1909 the U.S. Government defined "a 'retarded' pupil as
'one who is 2 or more years older than the normal age for his grade'
(using six years as the normal age for first graders)" (p. 242). "In October
1917, 10,000 parents and children rioted in Jewish neighborhoods in
New York to protest the introduction of the 'Gary Plan' [gradation] into
the city's schools, for they believed that it would condemn youth to
blue-collar occupations and prevent upward mobility" (p. 250). Studies
done in 1909, 1919, and 1931 indicated that "the ethnic differences in
school performance persisted over time." Performance was calculated
according to grade level attainment. (p. 243). ⌒

1861 — With the beginning of the Civil War, "...prisoners were engaged in
making products needed by the Northern forces and thus the American
industrial prison was born" (Murton, 1976, p. 25). **Zebulon Brockway**
described the Michigan Law of 1861 as "the first legislation in America
which discriminates, for the purpose of prison treatment, between felons
of sixteen to twenty-one years of age and older criminals" (Brockway,
1969/1912, p. 68). Brockway established an industrial system at the
Detroit House of Correction, where he had been invited to serve as the
first superintendent. He emphasized prisoner reformation through the
use of grades. (Davis, 1978, p. 10). Brockway also began what might
be called a personal conversion to science, which he described as "the

1861   birth of more scientific methods of reformatory treatment of prisoners
(cont'd.) in America" (p. 84—see 1854 entry). He later reported that "The
          dismissal...of...old doctrines...cleared the field of our endeavor and
          opened wide to science that which had been dominated by sentiment
          alone" (p. 85). ⌒

                Correctional education issues were discussed extensively at the
          Birmingham, England Educational Conference (Carpenter, 1872, p. 91).
          Correctional educators **Matthew Davenport Hill** and **Mary Carpenter**
          were active in and around Birmingham. ⌒

1862 — The Detroit House of Correction and prisons in Wisconsin, Ohio, and
          New Hampshire had weekday correctional education programs. Prayer
          meetings were also held regularly. (McKelvey, 1977, pp. 75-76). ⌒

                Dr. E.C. [Enoch] Wines became secretary of the New York Prison
          Association. He was very supportive of Massachusetts State Prison
          warden **Gideon Haynes'** efforts to expand correctional education.
          (Wallack, 1939, p. 10). ⌒

1863 — **Sir Walter Crofton** announced that there had not been a flogging at the
          prisons he managed in three and a half years "thanks to his systematic
          treatment" program (Eriksson, 1976, p. 94). Crofton, the architect of
          the Irish reformatory/prison system, established "three principles for
          long-term convicts:

                    [a] Long-term prisoners are better and more effectively
                    treated in small groups and by convincing them
                    throughout their stay in prison that any improvement
                    in their situation depends entirely on their own ability
                    to utilize qualities that differ radically from those that
                    landed them in prison. [b] By allowing prisoners to
                    work in a more natural situation before their release
                    than is possible in ordinary prisons, the public can be
                    taught to accept them and thereby lessen the difficulties
                    encountered by ex-convicts. [c] [Law enforcement]
                    Devices that render professional crime more risky will
                    certainly serve as crime deterrents. (p. 95).

          An Englishman, Crofton had been commissioned in 1853, along with
          three others, to investigate Irish prisons (p. 91). Crofton's system had
          been implemented in 1855, based upon his "belief in the existence of a
          'criminal class' which had to be controlled and absorbed and gradually
          reinstated in society as a whole" (p. 92). By 1862 he had presented a
          paper on his four progressive treatment phases. Lusk, near Dublin, was
          the site of Crofton's first open, or minimum security, institution. The
          staff there were told that they should:

1863
(cont'd.)

[a] convince the prisoner of their faith in him and give him credit for progress that he had achieved and that had been documented by marks earned; and

[b] ...convince the public there is good reason to believe that a prisoner who is soon to return to freedom, where he will either succeed or fail, is capable of handling a job. (p. 94).

Lusk had a very low escape rate. A Lusk teacher named **Mr. Organ** "took upon himself the task of finding work for the conditionally discharged. He went from one employer to the other time after time to persuade them to hire an ex-convict." (p. 95). Crofton hired a female superintendent for the women's section of Mountjoy Prison, and an all-female staff, except for the doorkeeper. Attacks on the new system began in 1862, "launched by a Presbyterian chaplain at Lusk." Crofton had already retired by the time the assault became full-blown (p. 96— see 1872 entry). 🞄

An act to regulate correctional education was introduced in the English Parliament. It was "for the Amendment of the Law relating to the Religious Instruction of Prisoners in County and Borough Prisons in England and Scotland" (Statutory Provisions, 1887). 🞄

Prison managers in the U.S. were learning about the new reformatory procedures and concerned that their economic and political commitments to the Auburn system of prison discipline constrained their ability to implement the new methods.

Men who combined great abilities with philanthropic enthusiasm were ready to take up once again the thankless task of achieving a better system. In 1863 **Gaylord B. Hubbell**, Warden of Sing Sing, undertook at his own expense a thorough investigation of English and Irish penal management and returned to the United States of America an ardent advocate of the system used by **Sir Walter Crofton** in the Irish prisons. He had been greatly influenced by **Matthew D.** and **Frederick Hill** [see 1860 entry], whose labours and opinions were a significant factor, too, in the development of the views of the **Rev. Dr. Enoch Cobb Wines**, the secretary of the New York Prison Association, and of the Association's vice president, **Dr. Theodore W. Dwight**, the first head of Columbia Law School. In a report to the New York Legislature in 1867, Dwight and Wines recommended the adoption of the Irish system in the prisons of the State of New York. **Frederick Benjamin Sanborn**, secretary of the State board of Charities in Massachusetts, had, in 1864, strongly urged a trial of the system in the penal institutions of that State. In 1868, **Zebulon R. Brockway**, then superintendent of the House of Correction in Detroit, Michigan, delivered an address to the New York Prison Association, advocating indeterminate sentences. In 1869 the New York Legislature authorized the establishment of a reformatory at Elmira, and in 1876 the Elmira reformatory was opened, with Brockway as its superintendent. Through the enthusiasm of Enoch Wines an event of great significance in the development of penology occurred in 1870, when on 12 October, the first meeting of the National Prison Association was held in Cincinnati. Matthew Davenport Hill and Sir Walter Crofton submitted papers to the Congress and Brockway read an arresting paper, *The Ideal of a True Prison System for a State*. He contended that punishment should not be the aim, but merely an instrument, of penal policy, that the protection of society should be achieved by the prevention of crime and the reformation of the criminal. The purpose of reformation was to transform individuals who were social dangers and liabilities into acceptable and useful citizens. To achieve it, sentences should be indeterminate, and the penal system should provide for a graduated progress from a house of reception, through an industrial reformatory, to an indeterminate reformatory, envisaged as a co-operative settlement. The Congress at Cincinnati adopted a Declaration of Principles, which have since been the fundamental principles of the American Prison Association [now known as the American Correctional Association]. The Declaration is probably the best known statement of the concepts that are the framework and the inspiration of modern penology. Almost everything of general as distinct from local significance in that Declaration will be found in [**Alexander**] **Maconochie**'s writings [see 1837 entry]. But not only are its sentiments his; studded through the Declaration will be found his very language... (Barry, 1958, pp. 230-231; emphases added—see entries for 1870 and 1872).

In the United States, prison reformers emphasized the importance of correctional education, and the need for reform. The chaplain at New York State's Clinton Prison

estimated that if the teacher lost no time on his rounds, seven minutes a week could be devoted to each pupil. A similar estimate in 1876 cut the time to six minutes per pupil. Further reports in 1871 and 1873 indicated that a pupil could be seen by his teachers no more than two or three evenings a week, and then only for a period of from five to ten minutes....[The] Auburn chaplain...[in] 1876 complained that the teachers 'labor under serious disadvantages, being obliged to instruct each inmate separately, and that through the grating of the cell door.' A Sing Sing report for 1856 declared, 'We have endeavored to make our calls as frequent as possible which have been once in about every ten days. Our time of teaching has been as prescribed by law: we teach five days in the week, from one and a quarter hours to one and three quarter hours each evening. (Chenault, 1949-1951, p. 7).

Chenault later reported that

except for a brief interval at Clinton, none of the [New York State] prisons permitted the grouping of inmates in classes....In some instances [the teacher] was permitted to unlock the cell and go in to impart his instruction; more frequently, however, he was required to stay outside on the bleak gallery and talk to the inmate through the heavy lattice of the cell. (p. 7).

New York State anticipated an increased number of offenders as a result of crimes by returning veterans at the end of the Civil War. **A.B. Tappen** proposed a special institution for young offenders who were not confined for excessively violent crimes. (Gaither, 1982, p. 20).

1864 — The town of Elmira, New York had already hosted a Union army training camp, but in 1864 a prisoner of war camp for Confederate soldiers was added. There was a great deal of controversy over the treatment of Confederate soldiers at the prison camp. Amid complaints about poor food, water, and sewage problems were accusations of refusal to treat the Confederate sick. Eventually a separate physician for the Confederate prisoners was appointed. **William Wey**, who later served on the Elmira Reformatory Board of Managers, was one of the physicians associated with the prisoner of war camp. The camp was closed in 1865, but questions about treatment continued into the next century. Elmira Reformatory, another institution that opened in 1876, was built on the site of the Civil War prisoner of war camp, and Elmira inmates actually used the remaining facilities while building the Reformatory. (Holmes, 1912—see entry for 1876).

In 1864 **Mary Carpenter**'s book *Our Convicts* was published. In part, she reported **Matthew Davenport Hill**'s papers on prison reform in Spain.

In the city of Valencia there has long been a penitentiary gaol [jail], under the government of **Colonel Montesinos**, a gentleman who has made for himself a European reputation, by his skill in the treatment of his prisoners. He acted upon them by urging them to self-reformation. He excited them to industry, by allowing them a small portion of their earnings for their own immediate expenditure, under due regulations to prevent abuse. He enabled them to raise their position, stage after stage, by their perseverance in good conduct. When they had acquired his confidence, he entrusted them with commissions, which carried them beyond the walls of their prison; relying on his moral influence which he had acquired over them to prevent their desertion. And, finally, he discharged them before the expiration of their sentences, when he had satisfied himself that they deserved to do well, had acquired habits of patient labour, so much of skill in some useful occupation as would ensure employment, the inestimable faculty of self-denial, the power of saying 'No' to the tempter, and, in short, such a general control over the infirmities of their minds and hearts as should enable them to deserve and maintain the liberty which they had earned. His success was answerable to the wisdom and zeal of his administration. Instances of relapse but rarely occurred, and the Spanish Government, rightly judging that talent like this ought to have the widest scope, appointed him Inspector-General of all the prisons in Spain. It so happened, however, that the legislature of that country was minded to establish a new criminal code, and (for what reason I know not) held it advisable to convert sentences of imprisonment for long terms of years, which prevail on the Continent, into incarceration for life. This was done; but, unhappily, this was not the only, nor the most pernicious change. In the chapters of the new code, which relate to the management of prisons, governors [wardens] are prohibited from offering those encouragements to the prisoners which had raised them step by step until they were fitted for the enjoyment of liberty; and they also make it imperative that every sentence of imprisonment shall be fulfilled to the last hour. Prisons, which had been models of order and cleanliness, of cheerful industry, and of praiseworthy demeanour in general, now exhibit a painful contrast to that happy state of things; they have become the scenes of indolence, disorder and filth; and the prisoners are either reduced to despair, or urged upon plots for escape, which, in a multitude of instances, were followed by success. (Carpenter, 1864/1969, vol. #1, pp. 89-90; bold emphasis added).

Colonel Montesinos assigned no armed force to supplement the guards during the 20 years of his tenure at the prison, and often allowed up to 400 men to work outside the walls without officers. There "were never either plots nor desertions. For each hundred persons are required an overseer, chosen from among retired sergeants in the army, four 'cabos primeros' and four 'cabos segudnos,' selected from the prisoners." (p. 90).

> Colonel Montesinos is not now at the head of the prison of Valencia, having relinquished his office. By the system which he established, the prisoner was made aware that by behaving well, by applying himself to the acquisition of some art or trade, and by good moral conduct, he would ameliorate his present treatment and improve his future position; and the desired result had been obtained of diminishing to two per cent the annual re-commitments, which had formerly amounted to thirty-five per cent. (p. 91; emphasis in original).

However, when the criminal code was changed,

> unconsoled by the hope of improving their lot, Colonel M. observed that the convicts lost their energy, a feeling of despair spread among them, and their ardour in acquiring a trade abated; indeed, that they continued to work at all was the result of discipline and consequent subordination, but they laboured without zeal, without any love of work, and without the hearty goodwill they had exhibited before the introduction of the new penal code. Finding no means by which he could counteract this terrible evil, which utterly destroyed his system, Colonel M. resigned his appointment. He had, moreover, another reason, namely, that the promulgation of the said code was followed by the appointment of incompetent persons as officers, who, faulty in character, and having other unfavourable qualities, could not produce good results. (p. 91; emphasis in original).

> The same material organization remains in the prison of Valencia, but the spirit of his internal arrangements has disappeared since the Colonel departed, to such a degree that in the workshops scarcely any work is

1864
(cont'd.)
done, and what is accomplished is badly performed; the remarkable cleanliness and order which was formerly observed has disappeared; desertions, then so exceedingly rare, were of those who worked outside the walls, now amount to a most disgraceful number, so that there have been as many as 43 convicts at once under heavy punishment for attempts to escape. There have been no imitators in Spain of the penal system of Colonel Montesinos, but as Inspector-General of all prisons in the kingdom, he established therein his system, which produced more or less favourable results, according to the character and disposition of their respective governors. Some improvement however was visible in all; workshops were introduced which were profitable to the treasury, and above all, the moral benefit to the convicts was very apparent. That the good results were not more universal was owing to an impediment, which, in spite of his utmost efforts, the Colonel was never wholly able to overcome. It arose thus:—When reorganising any establishment, he laid down a plan in accordance with his penal system, and himself put it in execution. During his stay there all went well, and every thing got into its proper place, but as soon as he went away, the imperfect regulations which the General Board of Prisons did not care to reform were brought back into force, and confusion again prevailed. Nevertheless, the doctrines of Colonel Montesinos remained, and gradually, with much labour on his part, regained their former ascendancy. The effects they produced were always good in a greater or less degree, and brought some revenue to the Treasury. (pp. 91-92). ⚹

1865 — Instructors in New York, Pennsylvania, Connecticut, and New Hampshire used the cell study method; Ohio's chaplains conducted classes on three evenings each week; Sabbath schools were used in other systems (McKelvey, 1977, p. 57). New York State's annual combined appropriations for teachers, chaplains, and books amounted to approximately $5,500 (p. 107). ⚹

1866 — Finland's Act on the Enforcement of Sentences "stipulated that prisoners were to receive elementary education. But "Beginning in 1889, prisoners were obliged to work while serving their sentences, and education was not set on equal terms with work. (Nordic Council of Ministers, 2005, p. 47—see 1942 entry). ⚹

1867 — Massachusetts State Prison warden **Gideon Haynes** convinced the State legislature to appropriate $1,000 for textbooks and a good

1867   library. Classes for illiterates were organized on a semi-weekly basis.
(cont'd.) (McKelvey, 1977, p. 69). The textbooks were for illiterates. Haynes also
established educational lectures, which were held several times each
month. (Wallack, 1939, p. 10). ⌒

The focus on correctional education enhanced the perception
that education was valuable, and institutional education systems
required attention. In his *History of the Albany Penitentiary*, **David Dyer**
wrote that

> No secular instruction is imparted to the prisoners here,
> an omission which we grieve to record. Nevertheless,
> all prisoners who so desire, are furnished with spelling
> books, and quite a number, especially of the colored
> convicts, learn to read, and take great pleasure in
> learning. The prison library contains some seven
> hundred volumes. Books of a general religious tone and
> character predominate; next comes history, biography,
> etc. There are a few scientific books. The privilege of
> the library is greatly prized, and the books are much
> read. The books are exchanged every Sabbath morning.
> (Dyer, 1867, p. 266—see 1851 entry). ⌒

Dr. Miller's *A Treatise on the Cause of Exhausted Vitality, or, Abuses
of the Sexual Function* appeared. In the 19th century masturbation was
thought to be associated with debauchery and criminality.

> The habit of self-abuse is practiced amongst girls as
> well as boys. Previous to the age of puberty the effects
> are very similar in both sexes, momentary excitement,
> followed by depression of spirits, and irritability,
> induced by the exhaustion of the nervous system.
> After having indulged in this habit for a time, the child
> loses its bright and happy look; it becomes pale with a
> greenish tint, the eyes are sunken, and surrounded by
> dark rings; the vermillion of the lips is faded, the limbs
> are attenuated, the muscles soft and flabby, and both
> in form and feature the child has the appearance of
> being old and worn out. Gradually, so gradually that
> the parents do not notice it, the mind becomes dull,
> the power of comprehension is diminished, the child
> sits listless, seemingly absorbed in thought, and is
> startled whenever suddenly addressed; all its motions
> are slow and heavy; it seeks solitude, that its vicious
> propensities may be indulged; it is obstinate, peevish,
> and irritable; shuns the plays it formerly loved, and
> becomes morose and taciturn. And these conditions
> may continue to the end of life, even though the habit

had long been abandoned....Dr Acton, in his excellent work on the sexual organs, in noting the outward signs of self-abuse in the boy who is guilty of this sin, describes 'his frame weak and stunted, the muscles underdeveloped, the eye sunken and heavy, the complexion sallow and pasty, the face often covered with pimples of acne, the hands cramped and cold, and the skin moist. The boy shuns the society of others, creeps about alone, and joins with repugnance the amusements of his schoolfellows...becomes careless in dress and manners, and uncleanly in person; his intellect is often of the lowest class, and, if his evil habits are persisted in, he may end in becoming a driveling idiot or a peevish valetudinarian.'....it will surely lead to misery, ruin, and death: 'Every indulgence of the sexual desire by children who have not attained their growth, is an unmitigated evil; an illicit pleasure, to be bitterly repented of in after years.' [Adults are afflicted by similar symptoms]....Women are...weakened...by the excessive excitation of the nervous system....In hospitals and lunatic asylums there are more women than men suffering from the effects of this terrible scourge. (Miller, 1867, pp. 43-45).

...[T]he effects of self-abuse are quite as apparent upon the mind as upon the body [in adults of both sexes]; and derangements here are often the first intimation received by friends that something is wrong in the beloved one. The sufferer from this vice becomes listless, inattentive, indifferent; there is an inability to concentrate the mind, or apply it with any degree of vigor; want of interest in friends; loss of self-control; failure of memory, and difficulty of conducting conversation; the reasoning is disconnected, and oftentimes the mental powers entirely fail; the victim becomes diffident, bashful, and ashamed, and seldom looks people in the face; his love of books is lost, history becomes a blank...the beauties of art are passed unheeded....he is at the mercy of the tempest-tost waves, in constant danger of being ingulfed, and except by some almost miraculous intervention, he must assuredly be lost. (pp. 41-42).

If "self-abuse" was evil and associated with criminality, many believed it was the duty of the institutional staff to stop it. The staff at New York State's Elmira Reformatory identified several common medical problems in 1890-1891: "physical degeneration, general debility, masturbatic deterioration, physical and mental dullness and

1867 	inertia..." (Eggleston, 1989, p. 140). Indeed, one of the charges raised
(cont'd.) 	against Elmira superintendent Zebulon Brockway in 1894 was that "an
inmate had rings put around his penis...a common medical procedure
to cure masturbation" (Eggleston, 1989, p. 195). ⌒⌒

1868 — Interest in the new reformatory methods was keen among many North
American prison managers. **Dr. E.C. Wines** began planning the first
American Prison Congress (Wallack, 1939, p. 11). ⌒⌒

       Mr. Ruth, who succeeded Mr. Larcombe as moral instructor
at Pennsylvania's Cherry Hill Prison, reported that he "visited
approximately 600 prisoners about once a month which called for 20
to 25 visits a day, exclusive of Sunday. This totals about three visits
per hour." The chaplain supervised all instruction. (Teeters and Shearer,
1957, p. 156). About 25% of the total population received an average of
four secular lessons per week (p. 157). ⌒⌒

       Zebulon Brockway had visited the State Industrial Schools
for Girls in Lancaster, Massachusetts in 1867 (see 1856 entry). In 1868
he established the Women's House of Shelter as an adjunct to the
Detroit House of Correction (Brockway, 1969/1912, p. 106—see 1869
entry). ⌒⌒

1869 — **Brockway** hired **Miss Emma A. Hall** to begin the school at the House of
Shelter. He described her as "the pioneer of educators in comprehensive
effective effort among adult prisoners in America..." (Brockway,
1969/1912, p. 110). Hall left her job as a Detroit public school teacher to
become a matron. The House of Shelter was the first institution where
females had full authority over other females. Hall established a merit
system, offered training in marketable skills, and fostered strong social
bonds among the inmates. She worked with approximately 30 female
students, in surroundings which were described as "commodious and
well furnished." (Freedman, 1981, p. 50). Enrollment in her classes
increased steadily (Brockway, 1969/1912, p. 110—see 1873 entry). ⌒⌒

       Brockway started a school at the Detroit House of Correction;
219 of the 385 inmates were enrolled. Attendance was obligatory, and
included Saturday lectures. Prisoners were allowed to have lights in
the cells for study. "Intellectual and industrial" tasks were addressed in
evening classes twice each week. (Roberts, 1971, p. 6). **Lucien Rule** later
wrote that

       The Sunday School was started long ago by **Robert
Raikes** [see 1851 entry] to educate and uplift the
besotted, ignorant multitude and their children;
and Zebulon R. Brockway, founder of the American
Reformatory System, began his great movement
with a Social Sunday School in Detroit that cleaned

1869
(cont'd.)

up a whole area of the submerged poor and taught the churches to roll up their sleeves and get down to business....The Reformatory audience is the most critical and sensitive audience in the world to insincerity or cant, and they are merciless on a man who does not mean what he says; but the confidence of these young men is the most precious gift... (Rule, 1920, p. 136; emphasis added).

Rule described the

reformatory agencies that Mr. Brockway employed: [a] The primary school held three evenings each week. [b] The weekly lecture of scientific cast. [c] The singing exercise on Sabbath morning. [d] The pungent and plain presentation of religious truth on the same day. [e] The prayer meetings held for the men on Sunday afternoon, and for the women on regular week days, in the evening after work hours. [f] The personal visitation and private interview of each prisoner with the chaplain. [g] A well selected and carefully distributed library of fresh, readable books. (p. 138). 〆

Brockway helped to draft New York State's new Indeterminate Sentence Law. This work eventually resulted in the establishment of Elmira Reformatory (Brockway, 1969/1912, p. 126—see 1861 Detroit entry). 〆

The Indiana legislature passed an act to establish a Female Prison and Reformatory Institution for Women (Freedman, 1981, p. 51). Separate facilities for females were still very unusual. 〆

1870 — The decade of the 1870s was in some ways a time of ferment. In 1870 New York feminists joined forces to advocate the establishment of separate prisons for women, managed by women (Freedman, p. 1981, 37—see 1854 entry). 〆

Max Grunhut later wrote that while compulsory public school attendance was operative in most communities, and "made itself gradually felt with the new generation, every third prisoner was illiterate." (Grunhut, 1973/1948, p. 231). "About 20,000 of the 38,000 prisoners in the United States were practically illiterate, and certainly less than 8,000 of these were under some instruction in prisons" (Fisher, in Ryan and Sivern, 1970, p. 187). 〆

Over the years, New York State prisons had spent a cumulative total of $20,000 on books for prisoners. The law required that a catalogue of these books must be maintained, yet no such record existed. (Wallack, 1939, p. 5). 〆

1870   **Enoch Wines, Amos Pilsbury,** and **Zebulon Brockway**
(cont'd.) were the guiding lights of the Cincinnati National Prison Congress. This event marks the beginning of the American Prison Association (known now as the American Correctional Association), which was organized to professionalize prison management and develop a basis for the humane treatment of convicts. The Congress served as a great advocacy forum for reformatories, which were conceived to protect young offenders from the corrupting influence of hardened criminals. "**Crofton**'s skillfully organized Irish progressive system [see entries for 1863 and 1872] came into the limelight and **Maconochie**'s Australian experiments [see entries for 1839, 1840, 1842, 1844, 1846, and 1860] stirred the imaginations." (Eriksson, 1976, p. 98; bold emphasis added). "At this convention **Governor Rutherford B. Hayes** [who later served as the 19th U.S. president] welcomed the 130-odd wardens, chaplains, judges and humanitarians" (Gaither, 1982, p. 20; bold emphasis added). Reformatory supporters pressed for more educational programs, since education was linked to self-improvement and reformation. The reformatory movement flourished between 1870 and 1900 (Barnes and Teeters, 1959, pp. 417-439). One of the themes of the Declaration of Principles, which the delegates adopted as a "manifesto" expression of their aspirations and beliefs, is the importance of correctional education:

> [Principle] X. Education is a vital force in the reformation of fallen men and women. Its tendency is to quicken the intellect, inspire self-respect, excite to higher aims, and afford a healthful substitute for low and vicious amusements. Education is therefore, a matter of primary importance in prisons, and should be carried to the utmost extent consistent with the other purposes of such institutions. (Wines, E.C., 1871, p. 542—see 1863 entry).

The Congress "was the starting shot for the reformatory movement in the United States. Brockway deserves the honor of having pulled the trigger. His ideas were revolutionary for the time..." (Eriksson, 1976, p. 99). ⌒

       Brockway hired **Professor H.S. Tarbell** to direct the Detroit House of Correction School (Gehring, 1982, p. 4). Tarbell later described the teacher's role in correctional education:

> The most important element in the whole arrangement is a suitable teacher....He must be a painstaking, consistent, steadfast man, of so much character and scholarship as to secure the respect and confidence of the prisoners. There must be no sham, no mere assumption about him for [of] all shrewd observers of men and motives, of all lynx-eyed detectors of hum-

bug and affectation, the inmates of our prisons are the sharpest. (Tarbell, in Wallack, 1939, pp. 7-8). ⌒

Professor Tarbell gave a speech on "The Prison School" at Cincinnati. He reported on an 1869 correctional education needs assessment at the Detroit House of Correction: 65% of the inmates "could not write numbers consisting of two figures," and 74% "could not give the ordinary combinations of the multiplication table." He suggested that "the object of the prison school" is

> To give to the inmates...higher thoughts, increased acquisitions, and desires for a better life....The methods employed cannot be wholly, or even mainly, those used with most success in the case of the children of our public schools....On the other hand, the instruction adapted to the college is equally unsuited to them, for while there are...mainly characteristics and development... there is only the <u>knowledge</u> of the child...instruction [should take place] <u>every</u> evening....The necessity of small classes and numerous teachers [is evident] from the construction and changing membership of these classes...they cannot be handled as such absolute units as the classes in our public schools, but much individual work must be done, and each prisoner receive such aid as he personally and immediately needs. Still, an approach to the proper unity of a class should be made... (Tarbell, in Wines, E.C., 1871, pp. 193-196; underline emphases in original).

Regarding the intellectual ability of inmate students, Tarbell said "The judgment and reasoning power of such men, schooled by necessity and adventure, are frequently sharp; and they cut straight through sham, pretense, semblance or assumption." He recommended that

> The schoolroom must be more attractive than the cell, and its work more desirable than sleep or solitary musings....These men do not enter the school hungering after knowledge. It becomes the labor of the school to create the appetite it supplies. (Tarbell, in Wines, E.C., 1871, pp. 197-200).

He reported that "Prison managers, who are quick to discern the moral influences at work among the men, have stated that the school pays in the more ready work and easier discipline of the men." He found that student learning progress at the Detroit House of Correction was

> at least <u>twice</u> the progress...made [by] children pursuing the same branches at the same point of advancement

1870 (cont'd.)	make in the same number of months in our public schools. There are several things which give the prison school, in some respects, an advantage over the public school. The secluded life, tending to induce reflection; the desire of the mind for active exertion...the greater force of character and mental grasp, from the increased age of the pupils; the sense of the value of knowledge, and the feeling that it is now or never with them...the new hope infused into the men...the awakening of their faculties to a relish for purer delights, and the fitting them for a better society... (pp. 197-202; emphasis in original). ⌓

1871 — Attendance at the Detroit House of Correction School now reached 291, or approximately 75% of the average total population (Brockway, 1969/1912, p. 101). **Professor Tarbell** presented 30 special evening educational lectures that year (p. 102). The lecture program had started in 1870, when **Professor D.P Mayhew** (see entries for 1878 and 1888) taught a "remarkable and useful...course...on psychological topics." (p. 103). ⌓

1872 — The first International Prison Congress was held in London, England (Brockway, 1969/1912, p. 135). **Zebulon Brockway** told the assembled delegation that "The prison school should be carried on for the high and holy purpose of forming aright character. Everything must bend to this." (Wallack, 1939, p. 9). He explained his orientation regarding the administration of correctional education:

> The educational effort in prisons, if made efficient for reformation, must be well and thoroughly organized. No slate-and-pencil arrangement, with the teacher at the cell-door occasionally, but a veritable school congregated, graded, and divided into classes....The higher branches of study should be introduced, and inducements offered to young, capable men to prepare themselves for particular spheres of activity, even the learned professions... (Wallack, 1939, p. 7).

Sir Walter Crofton also attended the conference. By this time his Irish reformatory and prison "system was imitated almost all over the world, particularly in Europe." It was a major topic of conversation at the London conference. Crofton had been "one of the commissioners of the English prison administration" from 1866 to 1868, "and he was among the leaders at the international penitentiary congress....He again served as head of Ireland's prison administration for the period 1877 to 1878, after which he retired." (Eriksson, 1976, pp. 96-97—see 1897 entry). ⌓

1872   After the 1870 Congress the field of correctional education
(cont'd.) entered into a profound lull in North America, protracted because of
state legislators' reluctance to end the productive Auburn system and
embark on a program of reformatories modeled on those of Maconochie
and Crofton. **Zebulon Brockway** resigned from his position as Detroit
House of Correction superintendent, and went into private business
(Brockway, 1969/1912, p. 151). 🕮

   Mary Carpenter's book, on **Sir Walter Crofton's** Irish
reformatory system was published—see 1863 entry. Acknowledging the
relevant contributions of John Howard (see Introduction), Elizabeth Fry
(see 1832 entry), Alexander Maconochie (see 1837 entry), and Matthew
Davenport Hill (the book was dedicated to him—see 1846 entry) in
the preface, Carpenter explained that the volume was prepared at the
request of **E.C. Wines** (Carpenter, 1872, p. vii).

> The Crofton system of convict treatment has been
> proved to have fulfilled all the objects of punishment.
> It gives suffering for evil doing, and encouragement to
> self-improvement; it rouses the offender to independent
> action, under the control of law and duty, it excites in
> him a feeling of goodwill towards those under whose
> control he is placed, by showing him that they are
> pursuing a course which will tend to his good, and that
> they are acting from a sense of duty. It finally restores
> him to society. It is thus Reformatory Prison Discipline.
> (p. 125).

"May all unite in this great work!" (p. 131; emphasis in original). "It is
the law both of God and man that sin should be followed by suffering—
that what a man soweth that he must reap." (p. xii). However,

> the will of the individual should be brought into such a
> condition as to wish to reform, and to exert itself to that
> end, in cooperation with the persons who are set over
> him....No fear of punishment, no hope of advantage,
> can produce a change of heart. (p. xi; emphasis in
> original).

Crofton's system had three progressive stages, each with its own
routine and diet. The first stage consisted of "Separate imprisonment in
a cellular prison at Mountjoy, Dublin, for the first eight or nine months
of the sentence," dependent upon "the conduct of the convict." These
prisoners had "the advantage of much time devoted to...religious
and secular instruction." (Crofton, in Carpenter, 1872, pp. 5-6). They
also experienced "omission of meat from the dietary for the first four
months" (Crofton, in Carpenter, 1872, p. 14).

The peculiar feature of the Irish Convict System in the second stage, is the institution of marks to govern the classification [patterned after Maconochie's model]. This is a minute and intelligible monthly record of the power of the convict to govern himself...a certain number of marks are required to be obtained by the convict before he can be promoted from one class to another....There are four classes in the second stage... school instruction and lectures take place in the evening. (Crofton, in Carpenter, 1872, pp. 6-10).

"In [the third] stage there are no marks....Individualization is the ruling principle...the convict is cooperating in his own amendment....The mind of the convict is in alliance with the minds of those placed over him. (Crofton, in Carpenter, 1872, pp. 10-12). As in Maconochie's system (see 1840 entry), "exposure to the ordinary temptations and trials of the world" were used to advantage (Carpenter, 1872, p. 24). Third stage prisoners were assigned to minimum security institutions, or served "comparatively as freemen, though under surveillance" (p. 25). Parole was implemented under the auspices of the local police (pp. 44-66), and follow-up and placement services were operational (p. 51). Second stage correctional education programs were most extensive. Crofton knew that "it was not sufficient to establish schoolmasters in the gaols, unless they took other measures both to stimulate the teachers and to rouse to exertion their very ignorant scholars." "96.2 percent were almost without any education at all." He recommended that the prison schools "should be placed under the Inspectors of the National Board of Education." (p. 27). Carpenter described the change in management to the Crofton system with words such as "buoyant state of mind," "cheerfulness,"

improved state of feeling...they apply themselves to their laborious occupations...a striking contrast to the listlessness, sullenness and gloom, so commonly exhibited by the ordinary convict in similar circumstances. In the school, the earnestness and vivacity with which they engage in their studies after the fatigue of the day, and the anxiety they evince to acquire information and excel one another, afford still more satisfactory evidence of mental and moral improvement... (pp. 30-31).

In her chapter on "Prevention" Carpenter explained an incident encountered by a teacher, which reflects on the characteristics of the target population: "When, some years ago, I gave a lesson to a Ragged [Sunday] School in this district on the destruction of Sodom, the wickedness and riot described in the Scripture narrative appeared to the children merely a portraiture of familiar scenes..." (p. 92).

1873 — The situation in Detroit shifted when Brockway left. **Emma Hall** retired from her role as matron/instructor at the Detroit House of Shelter (Brockway, 1969/1912, p. 110). ⌒

       E.C. Wines and **Zebulon Brockway** worked with the U.S. War Department to plan a military prison at Rock Island, Illinois. Congress failed to appropriate the funds, however, and the institution was not built. Brockway was appointed as a permanent member of the Michigan Prison Commission. (Brockway, 1969/1912, p. 149). ⌒

       Chaplain Hosea Quinby reported on *The Prison Chaplaincy* and its relationship to correctional education at New Hampshire State Penitentiary. He had established a cultural program. "...[L]ectures from outside gentlemen, with three readings by lady elocutionists, and a number of drill exercises in singing. A gentleman also gave us a number of lessons in penmanship." The average Sabbath school enrollment was 86. Nearly 200 volumes were added to the library, in addition to a new library catalogue, repair of the general book collection, "two large blackboards for drill exercises in arithmetic...a set of charts on penmanship, [and] a set...of outline maps in geography...expending in all $260.45." Quinby described the school situation in these words:

> all our pupils had to perform their daily tasks at manual labor from early morn till night;...their cells are not the most advantageous rooms for study;...what they obtained they had to gain in these pent up places, in the odds and ends of their time, as best they could. Then, again, we could have our school only when the guards could be spared from their common prison duties. Still, with all the drawbacks, a number of the inmates made commendable proficiency... (Quinby, 1873, pp. 50-51). ⌒

       Attention to the need for reformatory prison discipline intensified. The U.S. Government established a reformatory in Indiana (Wallack, 1939, p. 21). ⌒

       In its 28th annual report, the Prison Association of New York described the previous educational condition of the 1,161 prisoners that it aided each month: 145 could neither read nor write, 224 could read only, 426 could read and write somewhat, and 66 were well-educated. The report included this statement:

> That education should form a part of any system of prison discipline which seeks the reformation of convicts, is apparent...and its importance is the more manifest when we take into consideration the fact that a large proportion of the inmates of our prisons are

young men who need such instruction. (PANY, 1873, pp. 145-146—see entries for 1845, 1847, and 1854). ⌂

1874 — The New York State law that provided two civilian instructors at each institution (see 1847 entry) was amended so that there would be four instructors at Auburn, four at Sing Sing, and two at Clinton (Wallack, 1939, p. 6). Chenault later reported that "the teachers...continued to work under the same disadvantageous conditions with even a greater paucity of educational materials" (Chenault, 1949-1951, p. 15). ⌂

The national Conference on Charities and Correction was founded, as a professional association of social workers (Freedman, 1981, p. 39). Over the years this conference served as a focal point for correctional education professionalization. ⌂

The Indiana Women's Prison opened in Indianapolis (Freedman, 1981, p. 46). It had a school wing and a library (Freedman, 1981, p. 69—see 1869 entry). ⌂

Samuel King, Portland, Oregon's first superintendent of public schools, "developed a uniform curriculum...and then tested the children at the end of the year to discover if they had been 'thoroughly drilled in the work assigned'" (Tyack, 1974, p. 47). "Incensed and anxious, the teachers joined irate parents to force King's resignation in 1877" (p. 48).

In 1890, eighty-two of the largest cities reported the amount of time devoted during the eight years of elementary education to the various branches of the [local school] curriculum. The average amount of total instruction per child was 7,000 hours, meaning that in a given year the typical student spent four and a half hours a day for 200 days in study or recitation during school hours. Of that total amount of time, children averaged 516 hours in spelling; 1,188 in reading; 500 in geography; 1,190 in arithmetic; 300 in grammar or 'language lessons'; 150 in history; 169 in physiology (in sixty-six cities); 167 in 'morals and manners,' largely in oral lessons (in twenty-seven cities); and 176 in natural science (in thirty-nine cities). In addition, singing and physical education normally rounded out the course of study (physical education—probably mostly as 'recess'—occupied about 2,000 hours in the average sixty-three cities reporting it). Although new subjects and methods of instruction were added to the school curriculum during the latter half of the nineteenth century—such as vocal music, physical training, drawing, physiology, and instruction in

1874
(cont'd.)

science through 'object lessons'—textbooks remained
the central source of information and authority in the
curriculum. (pp. 46-47).

In 1902, **John Dewey** warned that "it is easy to fall into the habit of
regarding the mechanics of school organization and administration
as something comparatively external and indifferent to educational
purposes and ideals" (p. 197). By 1913, a study of Portland, Oregon's
schools revealed "a rigidly prescribed, mechanical system, poorly
adapted to the needs of either the children or the community" and "a
uniformity that is almost appalling....The curriculum was 'vivisected
with mechanical accuracy into fifty-four dead pieces." (p. 192). ⌂

1875 — Interest began to shift again to needed correctional education
improvements. A January 18th New York Times article indicated "that
the Society for the Reformation of Juvenile Delinquents [apparently
in New York State] received $7,468.61 for the purposes of educating
detainees" (Angle, 1982, p. 6). ⌂

Period Two: 1876-1900

1876 — The "pioneer reformatory for adult males" was opened at Elmira, New York (Chenault, 1949-1951, p. 9). Although many juvenile institutions and the Detroit Houses of Correction and Shelter were operated like reformatories, the reformatory movement is generally considered to have started at the 1870 Cincinnati Conference (see entry for that year), and Elmira is cited as the first adult reformatory institution. (See 1873 Indiana entry.) The offer to serve as Elmira superintendent came to **Zebulon Brockway** in a telegram "from **Louis D. Pilsbury**, son of Amos Pilsbury with whom I [Brockway] had been associated in the early fifties, who was one of the newly appointed board of managers of the reformatory, and who at the same time was the superintendent of state prisons of New York." (Brockway, 1969/1912, p. 155; emphasis added). Brockway accepted this invitation the following day (p. 156). Louis Pilsbury was the Board president. He was also the greatest living advocate of the Auburn system of prison management (p. 169—see 1816 entry). The "Reformatory...was separate from the Prison Department at this time and under its own Board of Managers" (Chenault, 1949-1951, p. 8—see 1927 entry). Brockway later wrote that "The unique characteristic of this period [at Elmira] was the educational idea of it all" (Brockway, 1969/1912, p. 242). In an 1883 report to the legislature, the Board of Managers described the institution's mission: "The Reformatory is a training school with varying appliances to meet the necessities of illiterates as well as those who have already enjoyed the advantages of education to a certain extent" (p. 243). Brockway sought to permeate the entire Elmira setting with a school-like atmosphere. This would diminish hostility between convicts and officers by allowing the staff to function more like teachers than overseers. To accomplish it he implemented the first progressive housing program in the country, and had guards grade inmates in conduct and demonstrated attitudes. The New York State Indeterminate Sentence Law that created the Elmira Reformatory, which Brockway himself had written (see 1869 entry), was complete with instructions regarding institutional management.The Act not only provided indeterminate sentences; it also established criteria by which inmates would move through the program and a client age range of 16-30. The only amendment the State legislature adopted was a clause mandating that indeterminate sentences could not exceed the maximum sentence provided for the relevant offense. (McKelvey, 1977, p. 132). A hundred years later, **Tom Murton** wrote about the adult reformatory movement, of which Elmira was an initial North American experiment: "The reformatory movement was really the first effort to retrain inmates" (Murton, 1976, p. 57). Brockway soon used specialized services from Elmira Women's College to establish a "school of letters" and a vocational trade school (Roberts, 1971, p. 7—see 1878 entry). The library was started with a core of books, magazines, and "selected expurgated newspapers" (Brockway, 1969/1912, p. 244). Newspapers were considered contraband at the time. Mr. White, secretary of the summer school, wrote that

1876
(cont'd.) The Librarian, an educated prisoner, reported on the library, its needs, the plan for distributing books, the awakened new taste and wish for reading, and he gives duplicates of three library cards from the three school divisions [academic, vocational, and summer] which show the effective use of the library. (p. 241). ⌒

British imperialism—through the combination of colonization and the transportation of criminals to help accomplish that aspiration—signaled terrible effects for indigenous peoples in many nations. In the Van Diemen's Land penal colony

> The government arranged a funeral procession for the last Tasmanian on May 11, 1876. Huge crowds lined the pavements to watch her small, almost square coffin roll by; they followed it to the cemetery, and saw it lowered into a grave. It was empty. Fearing some unseemly public disturbance, the government had buried her corpse in a vault of the Protestant Chapel in the Hobart Penitentiary the night before... (Hughes, 1987, p. 424—see 1830 entry). ⌒

Cesare Lombroso's book *L'Uomo Deliquente* was published. In 1916, **Thomas Mott Osborne** described Lombroso as "The man who seems to have been responsible for a great deal of the nonsense which has been written and talked under the name of penology." Osborne quoted Major Griffiths, who said that Lombroso set forth the idea of

> 'a criminal type, the instinctive or born criminal, a creature who had come into the world predestined to evil deeds, and who could surely be recognized by certain stigmata, certain facial, physical, even moral birthmarks, the possession of which, presumably ineradicable, foredoomed him to the commission of crime.' Lombroso's theories were hailed as the foundation of a new science—criminology... (Osborne, 1975/1916, pp. 23-24).

These criminologists "talk and write glibly of 'the criminal type,'—having in mind certain retreating foreheads and chins, furtive eyes, large, flapping ears, and the style of nose and mouth they personally most dislike." But Osborne quoted **Dr. Charles Goring,** a physician at England's Parkhurst Prison, who summarized the relevant research:

> we have exhaustively compared... criminals, as a class, with the law-abiding public. From these comparisons, NO EVIDENCE HAS EMERGED CONFIRMING THE EXISTENCE OF A PHYSICAL CRIMINAL

| 1876 | TYPE, SUCH AS LOMBROSO AND HIS DISCIPLES |
| (cont'd.) | HAVE DESCRIBED. Our data do show that physical |

differences exist between different kinds of criminals; precisely as they exist between different kinds of law-abiding people. But, when an allowance is made for a certain range of probable variation, and when they are reduced to a common standard of age, stature, intelligence and class, etc., these differences tend entirely to disappear...THERE IS NO SUCH THING AS A PHYSICAL CRIMINAL TYPE. (Goring, in Osborne, 1975/1916, pp. 25-26; emphases in original).

Osborne conceded that "there is a 'prison type'" (Osborne, 1975/1916, p. 27). "But to talk of any large proportion of convicts being mentally deficient is the sheerest nonsense. I have sometimes found myself wondering how a batch of wardens would themselves come off in a rigid, scientific test of mental attainments." (p. 226—see entries for 1895 and 1976). ⌒

1877 — The U.S. Government established a reformatory in Massachusetts (Wallack, 1939, p. 21). Also, the Massachusetts State Reformatory Prison for Women in Framingham was opened, with "private rooms" instead of cells (Freedman, 1981, p. 68—see 1880 entry). ⌒

During a retrospective moment in 1912, **Zebulon Brockway** characterized and explained the threshold of professional awareness that he personally experienced in 1877. He admitted that "excessive reliance was placed on mere common schooling as in itself a reformatory agency." (Brockway, 1969/1912, p. 174). ⌒

New York correctional educators were paid according to separate scales—men were salaried at $300/year; women at $200/year. Classes met from 6:00-9:00 PM. (Wallack, 1939, pp. 6-7). Chenault later reported that

a superintendent of prisons superseded the Board of Inspectors, mainly because of political differences, and poor financial management by the Board, led to a Constitutional amendment and the appointment of a superintendent—a move expected to eliminate the evil of politics and to permit the operation of the prisons on a sound basis. (Chenault, 1949-1951, p. 15—see 1889 entry). ⌒

Enoch Wines reported that most of the prisons in the North had libraries, but that the books were donations. A custom to provide $25-$200 annually for library budgets developed in many institutions. In New York State a catalogue of about 1,000 appropriate prison library

1877   titles was prepared. (McKelvey, 1977, p. 108—see entries for 1862, 1868,
(cont'd.) and 1873). ⌂

1878 — Reconstruction of the former Confederacy had ended. The South
       Carolina legislature repealed a law authorizing a school for inmates
       within the Department of Corrections (Miller, 1978, p. 236—see 1981
       entry). ⌂

       Brockway hired **Dr. D.R. Ford**, of Elmira Women's College, to
offer courses in physical geography and natural science for advanced
Elmira students (Brockway, 1969/1912, p. 225). Brockway also hired
D.P. Mayhew, of Michigan State Normal School (see entry for 1871), and
assigned him as moral education director. Classes in Bible teachings,
ethics, and psychology soon began. Later **Charles Collin** taught ethics
and economics, and **Professor J.R. Monks** lectured on history and
literature. Grades were used to record student progress, but inmates
were free to select which courses, if any, they would pursue. (McKelvey,
1977, p. 133). ⌂

       Citing Barnard's edition of the 1878 *American Journal of
Education*, Angle pieced together (in 1982) information on correctional
education

              at 51 reform schools across the country. Control of the
              schools vary. Some were state run, others privately
              operated, some were associated with church groups,
              while others were overseen by either municipalities
              or trustees. By this time the schools took in children
              of all ages between 5 and 21, although the most
              common age range seemed to be 7 or 8 to 16. A variety
              of types of study took place. Geography, reading,
              writing, spelling, and arithmetic were taught in all
              reformatories. Grammar and history were taught
              in most, and some schools went as far as to offer
              music, drawing, philosophy, algebra, and geometry.
              Industries too, were in operation in all the facilities
              included in the report. The most common were
              sewing, shoemaking, tailoring, farming, housework,
              gardening, and cane seating; no doubt reflecting the
              common trades of the era. The [institutions] were
              fairly large. Barnard reported on the 1876 population,
              and the following sampling was typical: New Jersey
              State Reform School For Boys—264 boys; New Jersey
              State Reform School For Girls—30 girls; Pennsylvania
              Reform   School—345   total;   Providence   Reform
              School—182 boys, 36 girls; Vermont Reform School—
              133 total. (Angle, 1982, p. 6). ⌂

1878
(cont'd.)   "An anonymous writer in *Harpers*...reported that 'women teachers are often preferred by [local public school] superintendents because they are more willing to comply with established regulations and less likely to ride headstrong hobbies.'" Women were described as "unambitious, frugal, and filial." They had more "'access to the heart' of little children because of their 'peculiar faculties.'" (Tyack, 1974, p. 60).

> Statistics on teachers are approximations at best, but it appears that the percentages of woman teachers in the United States increased from 59 percent in 1870 to 70 percent in 1900 to 86 percent in 1920. Women teachers clearly predominated in cities. In 1885 in fourteen representative cities, women outnumbered men ten to one. By 1905 only 2 percent of teachers in elementary schools were men, as reported in a careful study of 467 cities done for the NEA [National Education Association] by Carroll Wright. By contrast, 38 percent of the elementary school principals were men. In the high schools, which generally paid more and were more prestigious than the elementary schools, 94 percent of the principals and 38 percent of the teachers were men. (p. 61).

In 1880 Mary Abigail Dodge wrote of "The Degradation of the Teacher."

> Here were women teachers, she said, forced to obey, paid less than men for the same work and often barred from advancement because of their sex, bullied by superintendents and school board members who were their intellectual and social inferiors....The men get the money and the credit; the women do all the important work for a mere pittance. (p. 63).

In 1901 the only women state superintendents of instruction were in Idaho and Colorado, and "women county superintendents appeared most frequently in states on the plains and far West." (p. 65). By 1911 Lotus D. Coffman simply reported that women were willing to work as teachers for less than men (p. 61—see 1905 entry). ⌒

A new Prison Commission was established in the U.K. Its management included the diverse education programs that had been established at the various institutions. The Commission had

> inherited 113 local authority prisons in England and Wales fifty schoolmasters were numbered in the legacy. Unfortunately we know little about them...but what

109

1878
(cont'd.)

we do know is that the office of prison schoolmaster statutorily originated in Robert Peel's Parliamentary Gaol Act of 1823. Two of its clauses related to education. One required provision to be made in all the institutions to which the Act applied 'for the instruction of prisoners of both sexes in reading and writing... under such rules and regulations and to such extent and to such prisoners as to the visiting justices may seem expedient.' The other required the authorities, as expedient, to appoint schoolmasters, arrange their conditions of service, fix their salaries and pay them out of the rates [taxes]. (Forster, 1981, p. 27—see 1823 entry). ⌒

1879 — **Brockway** assigned **Dr. Ford** to the role of school principal at Elmira Reformatory. Elementary classes were conducted by six public school principals and three attorneys. School subjects included geometry, bookkeeping, human physiology, and sanitary science. Classes met six evenings each week. (McKelvey, 1977, p. 133). Income from prison labor at the Reformatory paid almost the entire cost of running the institution. (Brockway, 1969/1912, p. 226). ⌒

The Canadian Justice Minister issued a *Report of Penitentiarie*. It included "Rules and Regulations for School" (Weir, in Roberts, 1973, p. 41). ⌒

Massachusetts legislators passed the Indenture Law. Female inmates who displayed "fitness of service" were placed in conditional post-release employment as domestics. During the next 25 years, approximately 1,500 women (about 25% of the female inmate population) were placed in these assignments; the State considered the system highly effective. (Freedman, 1981, p. 92). ⌒

1880 — **Eliza Mosher**, a Quaker who had served as prison physician at the Women's Reformatory in Framingham, Massachusetts (Freedman, 1981, p. 72), was appointed as institutional superintendent (p. 73). She worked closely with chaplain **Sarah Pierce** to develop rehabilitative programs for inmates—establishing a merit grading system, offering "individual teaching and training," and inviting students from nearby colleges to assist in education, recreation, and visitation (pp. 72-73). Among the foreign-born, Dr. Mosher found "the highest incidence of syphilis, alcoholism, insanity, illiteracy, and recidivism in the prison, with a recommitment rate of over 70%." (p. 83—see 1882 entry). ⌒

Dr. Luke Blackburn, "a widely known physician" (Rule, 1920, p. 141), "organized a Sabbath school [at the old Kentucky Prison at Frankfort] and selected eight or ten of the best prisoners as teachers. He met them once or twice a week in a teachers training class...but...found

1880   that the prisoners did not respect fellow-convict teachers." Blackburn
(cont'd.) went on to become State governor, and then came back to reorganize
        the school.

> **Mrs. Blackburn** herself was the teacher of the largest class. The governor's sister, **Mrs. Judge Morris**, taught the Catholics in the prison. The men said that whereas Sunday was formerly the longest and dullest day of the week, it was now the best and sweetest of all. **Dr. Gober**, the prison physician, was also interested in the Sunday school work, taking a conspicuous part in the class exercises and lending every assistance possible. There were three classes among the women prisoners...**Chaplain Tharp** catalogued the books, bought five hundred song-books and two hundred quarterlies. Mrs. Blackburn solicited money to help buy literature and books that were needed, and Christian people responded liberally. Reading matter was forwarded from a prison supply house in Chicago, and Chaplain Tharp revived the circulating library system....The men were pitifully anxious to overcome their ignorance....The chaplain wanted blackboards and slates and books...as provided by law. He [offered]...instruction in spelling, reading and writing; English grammar and geography; history, physiology and the laws of health. He also asked [for] a reading room...where the prisoners might enjoy an hour of self-improvement." (Rule, 1920, p. 146; emphases added—see 1883 entry). ⌂

Researchers were gathering data on the effects of the emerging local schooling movement, and its relation to other problems of life in the U.S. One modern study by Selwyn Troen helped

> determine which white children actually went to public schools in 1880 in St. Louis. During the four years from eight through eleven, schooling reached almost nine out of ten children, while only a tiny number were working. By contrast, from the age of fourteen fewer than one half attended school, and many moved directly into the work force. The earlier a child left school, the likelier it was that he entered an unskilled job: 88 percent of those who went to work at twelve were unskilled or semiskilled, whereas by age sixteen 47 percent were in those categories, and 21 percent in white-collar positions. More girls than boys stayed in school after age ten, and fewer girls had jobs....Attendance in school from ages thirteen through

111

1880	sixteen increased from 31.7 percent for the children
(cont'd.)	of unskilled workers to 80 percent for the sons and
	daughters of professional fathers. As Troen observes,

1880
(cont'd.)
sixteen increased from 31.7 percent for the children of unskilled workers to 80 percent for the sons and daughters of professional fathers. As Troen observes, 'it made little difference whether the father of a child at eight or twelve was a physician or a boatman; for most children it made all the difference a few years later.' In St. Louis the drop-out age and years of attendance varied little from 1860 to 1908. (Tyack, 1974, p. 67).

In 1939 Newton Edwards warned that education had become "...an instrument of social stratification and of regional and racial inequality" (p. 272). "Researchers documented that educational attainment and credentials were becoming increasingly important in employment and found shocking differentials in educational finance [between school districts]." (p. 273). ⌂

1881 — Professor **J.E. Carpenter**'s definitive biography of **Mary Carpenter** began with this sentiment: "This book is chiefly written as a record of work for workers" (Carpenter, J.E., 1974/1881, p. v). Mary Carpenter was born in 1807. Her father was a minister. In 1817 the family moved from Exeter to Bristol, England. Bristol remained her home base throughout the rest of her life. As a child Mary taught Sunday school. In 1829 she started a school for girls in which her mother served as superintendent (pp. 1-28). As a young woman, Mary sought to imitate the work of John Howard (see below). Much later, in 1866, she wrote recommendations that Howard should have considered in his influential report, including "instruction by a trained and efficient teacher" (p. 258). In 1833 Mary Carpenter was converted to the cause of social activism by Dr. Tuckerman, a North American minister who focused on work among the Boston poor (p. 34). In 1836 she had what today would be called a religious epiphany that impacted her profoundly. She felt she knew God's intention for her life work (pp. 45-46). By 1846 Carpenter was deeply involved in the effort to end slavery in the U.S., an effort that consumed much of her time for the next two decades. Later she was deeply concerned about the failure of John Brown's guerrilla initiative (p. 208). In early 1861 she felt connected to the troubles that were brewing in the United States, which soon erupted into the Civil War. Carpenter contributed to Antislavery Bazaars that were organized in England to help fund abolitionist efforts. She was devastated at the news of Lincoln's assassination, and favored the radical Republican cause during Reconstruction (p. 243). In 1846 Carpenter established her first Ragged School in a rented building—organized like a residential Sunday school—with an enrollment of about 200. Like the antislavery effort, the Ragged School theme endured until the end of her life. Ragged Schools extended literacy to the poor, so they could read the Bible and cope in the world. Soon there was a Night School, as well. (pp. 76-90). J.E. Carpenter later wrote of alternative education "the field was altogether new..." (p. 91). By 1849 Carpenter was networking, writing, publishing,

1881 and organizing a nationwide Ragged School movement. It was through
(cont'd.) this work that she came into contact with **Matthew Davenport Hill**, the
recorder (judge) in Birmingham who later played such a pivotal role in
getting word of Maconochie's South Pacific penal reforms to Crofton
in Ireland. With Hill, Carpenter prepared many of the papers reviewed
by the Parliamentary Committee of Inquiry on Juvenile Delinquency.
She bought the site of her next Ragged School, Kingswood, in 1850. To
avoid spending money on herself, so she could save it for the program,
Carpenter walked nearly four miles to her Ragged School every day.
In 1852 Carpenter's aspiration was simple: "Let me only humbly and
earnestly go on with the work in which I have been abundantly 'blessed'"
(p. 131). By 1853 she was doing international research to identify models
that reduced delinquency and recidivism. In 1873 she visited several
prisons in Europe, including Neufchatel (p. 313). The struggle for equal
rights for women increasingly demanded her attention. Carpenter was
regularly in touch with **Lady Byron**, who funded a house called Red
Lodge for girls as an adjunct to one of Carpenter's Ragged Schools
(p. 164). The Kingswood and Red Lodge students summarized their
gratitude: "We were lost—we are found!" (p. 174; emphasis in original).
Soon Carpenter focused her attention on the Red Lodge work, and
in 1857 she moved to a house across the street from the institution,
purchased for that purpose by Lady Byron. In 1858 Carpenter started
another institution in the Park Row section of Bristol, not far from
Red Lodge. A Birmingham conference that Carpenter helped plan in
1851 led directly to her work on free day schools, industrial feeding
schools, and reformatory schools. The scope of this effort was gradually
bringing her in contact with staff from convict prisons. Carpenter
worked with members of Parliament to introduce bills for reformatory
school funding. She spoke with **Alexander Maconochie** during an
1854 visit to Parkhurst Prison, on the Isle of Wight (p. 162). By 1858 an
Oxford professor characterized Mary Carpenter as "a person who lives
under high moral 'excitement'" (p. 199; emphasis in original). In 1859
she wrote and published a pamphlet entitled "The Claims of Ragged
Schools to Pecuniary Educational Aid from the Annual Parliamentary
Grant, as an Integral Part of the Educational Movement of the Country"
(Carpenter, J.E., 1974/1881, p. 204). That year a minister friend wrote
to Carpenter: "If Jesus of Nazareth were to come back and be the Jesus
of London, I think...He would be a new Revolution of Institutions,
applying his universal justice....You are doing this work—the work of
humanity." (pp. 207-208). Carpenter met **Walter Crofton** at a January,
1861 conference in Birmingham that focused on education, welfare,
and neglected children (p. 225). They had great respect for each other's
work. She corresponded with Crofton, who spoke highly of her books.
Carpenter stopped at Crofton's house for dinner in the summer of 1875,
just because she was in London and could not imagine being so close
without visiting. (p. 346). Garibaldi's struggle in Italy captured Mary
Carpenter's imagination. (pp. 230-231). Indeed, when Garibaldi visited
Bristol in 1864, she would have been crushed by the pressing crowd

1881   of supporters if Matthew Davenport Hill had not rescued her (p. 238).
(cont'd.) Another event in her life during 1864 was that the Pope condemned
         Mary Carpenter's books (p. 242 n.). The plight of Indian women was
         a compelling concern to her. In 1866 Carpenter traveled to the Indian
         subcontinent for the first time, and in 1868 the government funded
         her plan for a normal school to license Indian women who wanted to
         become teachers (p. 283). In "1870 Carpenter established the National
         Indian Association in England to promote India and bring future Indian
         leaders to England to be educated....The Indian Association 'helped
         brilliant young Indian leaders...[including] Mohandas K. Gandhi to find
         lodging, tuition, and connections in England.'" (Gehring and Bowers,
         2003, p. 117). She returned to India in 1875 and took note of the progress
         in that country's correctional education (Carpenter, J.E., 1974/1881, pp.
         344-345). On the way, Carpenter was excited when her ship passed
         through the new Suez Canal. When she arrived in India for this second
         visit, Carpenter was greeted as a hero. (pp. 349-350). In Calcutta she
         advised the Secretary to the Indian Government of her recommendations
         for Indian prison reform. Her recommendations are properly seen as
         an update of **John Howard**'s original recommendations, forged in the
         context of her research on "what works?" These recommendations
         resulted from a lifetime of study:

I.   That all prisoners should sleep in separation during the whole term
      of their imprisonment [see Pennsylvania and Auburn Systems
      above].

II.   That education should be given daily by competent Native teachers,
      with moral instruction.

III. That a first stage in all imprisonment should be passed in separation
      from other prisoners, day and night, with unskilled labour, penal
      dietary, and instruction [see Crofton above].

IV.   That there should be a system of marks for conduct, labour, and
      education, with gratuities for extra work, enabling the prisoner by
      his own exertion to rise to greater privileges, and to obtain remission
      of sentence [see Norfolk Island above]. (p. 369).

As a result of these initiatives, a prison reform/education conference
was held in Calcutta in 1877 (p. 370). In 1867 John Stuart Mill helped
persuade Carpenter of the importance of the women's vote (p. 338).
Carpenter was in regular correspondence with Queen Victoria (p. 281
n.); they often presented together at conferences, and sent flowers to
each other to celebrate holidays. Carpenter also corresponded with
Florence Nightingale (p. 302). In 1872 Carpenter wrote to E.C. Wines,
who worked closely with Zebulon Brockway, later superintendent of
Elmira Reformatory (see above). She recommended that Wines and U.S.
prison managers carefully scrutinize Crofton's system in Ireland, to see

1881   if it might meet the needs Wines had articulated for prison reform in the
(cont'd.) U.S. (pp. 307-308). On a trip to North America in 1873 Carpenter spent
        time with many abolitionists: Wells, Garrison (p. 321), Lucretia Mott
        (p. 331), General Howard, and Frederick Douglass (p. 323). She visited
        Sumner and Agassiz (p. 336). In 1874 Carpenter wrote to the secretary
        of the Prison Association of New York, to express concern about "the
        dreadful state of the Prisons" in the U.S. (p. 327 n.). Likewise, she was
        astonished at the poor state of the Canadian prisons around Montreal
        and Kingston (pp. 324-325). In 1874 and 1875 Carpenter worked with
        a number of politicians for a "Bill to provide the proper Education by
        School Boards of Neglected Children." In this she enjoyed the support
        of the Right Hon. W.E. Forster, who wrote "The evil is clear enough,
        and I do not doubt that for it your plan will be to a great extent a
        remedy. In fact your experience proves this..." (Forster, in Carpenter,
        J.E., 1974/1881, p. 340). Mary Carpenter died in 1877. J.E. Carpenter
        gave excellent summaries of her legislative initiatives, and of her own
        institutional work, on pp. 373-377 in his biography. ◢

1882 — The school at Elmira Reformatory had its first summer session (Roberts,
        1971, p. 8). **Dr. Ford** listed the courses that were offered: "ethics, geometry,
        elements of psychology, and health, single entry bookkeeping, United
        States history, elements of physics, psychology, elements of political
        economy, and geography." (Brockway, 1969/1912, p. 240). ◢

        Clara Barton, the nurse of Civil War fame who led the
        International Red Cross, replaced Eliza Mosher as Massachusetts'
        Framingham Reformatory for Women superintendent. Governor
        Butler (formerly a Union general) resolved that if Barton did not take
        the position, he would not offer it to another woman. At the insistence
        of women reformers, she assumed the post until 1884. (Freedman, 1981,
        pp. 74-75). ◢

        There were many purposes for the local schools, and some
        of them diverged from our current, official purposes. This year one
        educator declared

                'If we were to define the public school as an instrument
                for disintegrating mobs, we would indicate one of its
                most important purposes'....Mob violence exploded
                again and again in American cities of the nineteenth
                century, sparked by religious, racial, ethnic, and class
                conflict: the burning of the Charlestown (Massachusetts)
                convent and the anti-Irish riot in 1834; 'Bloody Monday'
                in Louisville in 1855, when Know-Nothing partisans
                tried to bar immigrants from the polls; the Draft Riot
                in New York in 1863 in which mobs brutally killed
                blacks and burned and looted buildings; the violent
                railroad strike of 1877 which spread city to city from

Baltimore to San Francisco, leaving in its wake scores killed, hundreds wounded, and charred, gutted trains and buildings; the Pullman strike in Chicago in 1894 that pitted federal troops against a crowd of 10,000; and many others....In 1894, confronting industrial turmoil and Populist excitement, the NEA resolved at its annual meeting that 'we deem it our highest duty to pronounce enthusiastically, and with unanimous voice, for supremacy of law and the maintenance of social and political order.' Massachusetts governor Edward Everett warned that the militia had to be made dependable through proper schooling. His fears were not groundless; quite often militia members called out to quell riots fraternized with the mobs instead. (Tyack, 1974, pp. 74-75). ⚎

1883 — **Brockway** brought **Professor N.A. Wells** from Syracuse University to Elmira Reformatory, to teach an industrial arts course "for the inmates who...had little interest in education" (Brockway, 1969/1912, p. 243). These classes, designed for "dullards," had an enrollment of 50 students and ten capable inmate "monitors." The first course was on terra-cotta modeling, and it was so successful that a second 13-week session was planned for the following summer. Eventually, content in the areas of plumbing, telegraphy, tailoring, and printing were included, in a year-round schedule. (McKelvey, 1977, p. 134). Brockway reported that the terra-cotta program lasted only 11 weeks. He described the 50 students as the "primary class," and the ten helpers as the "advanced class." Instruction was "given orally and without printed patterns, except that the advanced pupils made portraits in hammered copper from photographs." (Brockway, 1969/1912, p. 243). Brockway wrote that "This industrial art school experiment...was declared to be a model much in advance of any educational organization in our free society." The teachers discarded many of the textbooks and developed their own instructional materials. (p. 245). ⚎

Brockway bought a printing press and began an inmate-managed educational newspaper. It was called the *Summary* because it functioned as a digest of the events reported in daily newspapers, which were contraband at the Reformatory. This was the first prison newspaper of its type. (McKelvey, 1977, p. 134). In 1887 *The Prison Mirror* inmate newspaper was started at Minnesota's Stillwater Prison (Brisbane, 1984, p. A6). ⚎

The school at Elmira Reformatory had many programs. In **Charles Collin**'s Elmira Reformatory ethics class,

The attention...that year was directed to the lawful and unlawful, or what a man may do as determined

116

1883
(cont'd.)

by rules and principles drawn from the Scriptures and from the laws of society and from equity and natural reason. These topics, under the remarkable guidance of the instructor, in free discussion, became absorbing and interesting to the men. (Brockway, 1969/1912, p. 247).

The school secretary, an inmate, wrote of these Sunday classes: "The main questions were uttered as from a strictly intellectual, non-religious point of view, but the religious bearings which were naturally suggested as the discussion progressed were not wholly ignored though never intruded." (p. 248). Brockway wrote that he was rarely absent from the sessions (p. 249). They demonstrated an inclination to search for truth, and Brockway's leadership provided a liberal measure of academic freedom, or freedom of inquiry (pp. 247-248). Collin wrote that he

took positions confidently and abandoned them freely. Some called me a socialist and a communist, but they soon found that names did not trouble me in my search after substance, and that I was desirous to follow only my intellect wherever it might lead me, wholly regardless of my landing place. (p. 245).

Class membership soon rose to 500 (Rule, 1920, p. 140). ⌒

One important education program, trade and industrial education, had diverse roots and activities.

In 1883 the manual-training idea had not found expression to any great extent in American education, for it is commonly assumed that the early forms of manual training arose from the Centennial Exposition in 1876. But a few quotations will show that the thought that all industrial work in reform schools must have an educational aspect, in fact must have the educational as its chief end, was beginning to be felt. (Snedden, 1907, p. 74).

The author of this observation, **David Snedden**, went on to discuss agricultural education at the Connecticut Boys School, domestic education at the Connecticut Industrial School for Girls, a variety of industrial trades training at the Illinois State Reform School, and other examples from juvenile institutions in Iowa, Maine, Maryland, Massachusetts, Minnesota, New Jersey, New York, Ohio, Vermont, Wisconsin, etc. (Snedden, 1907, pp. 75-82). ⌒

Reverend H.H. Kavanaugh was appointed chaplain at the old Kentucky Prison, filling the vacancy left by chaplain Tharp's resignation.

1883   Kavanaugh was resident chaplain, salaried at $1,200 a year. He was
(cont'd.) able to mobilize resources for correctional education, just as governor
         Blackburn and chaplain Tharp had done earlier.

> His son, Mr. Frank Kavanaugh, of the Kentucky State
> Library [said]...that Chaplain Kavanaugh gradually
> became so absorbed in the noble service he was
> rendering the prisoners that he resolved to devote
> every hour of every day possible to the work. **Warden
> Todd**, in his annual report, highly commended the
> chaplain and approved most heartily the splendid
> Sunday school work. The warden said that all the
> prisoners respected the chaplain. Every local pastor
> in Frankfort was asked to [help]...including also
> the Catholic and negro priests and preachers....The
> Sunday school went forward by leaps and bounds. The
> teachers from outside were retained....The library was
> enlarged and more used than ever; but the Legislature
> had been tardy as usual in providing school books and
> school rooms for the instruction of the prisoners. But
> in spite of this handicap, Warden Todd and Chaplain
> Kavanaugh used the chapel hall as a school house.
> They both insisted that convicts should not be treated
> like dumb animals, but as human beings. (Rule, 1920,
> p. 147; emphasis added). ⌒

Chaplain Waterbury managed the school at Massachusetts
Penitentiary between 1879 and 1883, and subscribed to many of
Louis Dwight's views. Waterbury gave each student "a Bible and a
weekly religious newspaper, all of which 'compelled an inmate to be
intelligent.'" (Sullivan, 1975, p. 52). ⌒

1884 — **Professor J.R. Monks** succeeded Mr. Collin as the Elmira ethics
       instructor. He served in that capacity until his death in 1895. Monks
       reported on the changing sense of professional identity among the
       instructors: "On the whole the character of our scholastic regime is less
       that of a common school than an academy or college, the maturer age of
       the pupils and the enforced decorum operating to this end." (Brockway,
       1969/1912, p. 263). ⌒

Elmira Reformatory was attracting international attention as
the showcase institution in the United States.

> Elmira was a truly unique institution and it acquired
> an international reputation. **William Tallack**, in an
> address to the Congress of Prisons held in Rome in 1884,
> reported that the innovative methods were working.
> He noted that the inmates appeared stimulated and

<table>
<tr><td>1884
(cont'd.)</td><td>inspired to learn, and that they were studying reading, writing, and calculus. (Angle, 1982, p. 6; emphasis added). ⚑</td></tr>
</table>

The New York superintendent of prisons "directed the officers in charge of the several prisons" to establish night schools "for the convicts who are illiterate, to teach them the rudiment of our common school education." The order was implemented at Sing Sing and Auburn, but at Clinton Prison "the warden did not deem it expedient to open the night school in a common school-room, where the convict scholars could congregate, on account of the peculiar character of the prisoners." Chenault later reported that "Teaching in the cells was continued until it was again proven to be very unsatisfactory, and regular organized classroom instruction at Clinton did not begin until 1889. (Chenault, 1949-1951, p. 8). ⚑

Ellen Johnson succeeded Clara Barton as Framingham Women's Reformatory superintendent. Johnson emphasized "training for self-control" and insisted that the prisoner

> must learn to do right without compulsion or she will cease to do right when the compelling force is gone.... No lesson is more important than that which teaches respect for the law, and dread of its wrath. At the same time, it is a fundamental point in our theory that every criminal can be won by gentleness and patience. (Freedman, 1981, p. 76—see 1900 entry). ⚑

Freedman later constructed an inmate profile for this period indicating that approximately 20% of Massachusetts' female state prisoners were illiterate, as well as 25% of those in Indiana, and 15% in New York. She reported that most of these "inmates had some formal education before the age of fourteen." (Freedman, 1981, p. 82). ⚑

A new reformatory was established at Concord, Massachusetts (Freedman, 1981, p. 49). Penal historians later characterized the 1880-1900 period as the rise of the reformatory. ⚑

1885 — Approximately 75% of the total prison population in the United States was engaged in productive labor. (Reagen and Stoughton, 1976, p. 59—see entries for 1940 and 1973). ⚑

Brockway did away with regular chaplain services and substituted presentations by able guest speakers. There were 36 visiting presenters this year. The format provided intellectual stimulation for officers as well as inmates, and served to promote good relations with the surrounding community. (McKelvey, 1977, p. 134).

1885
(cont'd.)

The prison school secretary reported that he could see a change in the intellectual tone of the entire institution; that the improvement in manners and deportment was so marked, that he hoped it would become a regular requirement for every inmate to receive careful attention to his reading; and that he would be gently but positively compelled to undergo this class instruction and supervision in his reading so as to raise him from the 'Diamond Dick' grade of fiction to the love of real human literature. He believed that every prison library should be utilized for the profitable employment of the prisoner's evening hours with good books. (Rule, 1920, p. 139).

The Elmira English Literature class was made obligatory, and attendance increased from 60 students to about 500. They were "subject to examinations that would affect the grade standing and progress toward release." (Brockway, 1969/1912, p. 273—see 1886 entry). "Passing along the corridors and galleries when the prisoners were in their cells in the evenings, fully 90 per cent of the entire prison population might be seen engaged in study..." (p. 274). 🐾

Reverend Josiah Strong claimed that "lack of religion in the common school was one of the curses of the 'rabble-ruled' cities" (Tyack, 1974, p. 105). Others declared that the problem was merely "the kind of religious instruction offered in the classroom" that caused problems (p. 17). Regardless of which view matched the facts, school administrators demonstrated an ability to accommodate provincial orientations—even as late as the 1930s, 98% of school district superintendents were native-born, 90% were of "White, Anglo-Saxon, Protestant" extraction, and 85% were raised in rural areas or small towns (p. 233). They responded to needs identified by people like themselves, and "tended to glorify the sturdy virtues of a departed rural tradition. They took their values for granted as self-evidently true—not subject to legitimate debate." In the 1880s there was a concerted drive to eliminate foreign language instruction from elementary school curricula. (p. 109). All of the states had some form of "temperance instruction" by 1901 (p. 105). One superintendent valued conformity and patriotism to the extent that in 1917 he "recommended firing any teacher whose sympathies" were in doubt (p. 234). 🐾

1886 — **Brockway** had a special building constructed at Elmira Reformatory to house trade school programs. He encouraged **Dr. Hamilton Wey**, a visiting physician, to organize a special class for 12 "low-grade intractable convicts," with "intensive physical training along the lines of the recently imported Swedish [massage] technique." This special education program included early morning instruction, planned and measured diets, "steam or hot-water baths with

1886　rubbing and kneading of muscles by an expert trainer," and focused
(cont'd.) physical drills and calisthenics. After several months the program
was discontinued because Dr. Wey moved to other assignments, but
Brockway and Wey both noted that ten of the 12 special students
"were ready to take an active part in the normal institutional life."
(McKelvey, 1977, p. 134). 🙢

The Elmira Reformatory library was enlarged "...by an
expenditure of $500 from the prison funds; and by large additions
of English classical authors, the gift of Mr. Valentine Lawson. The
whole collection of books was scientifically catalogued, classified, and
shelved..." (Brockway, 1969/1912, p. 238). 🙢

At the National Conference of Charities and Correction (see
1874 entry), **Charles Collin** (see 1878 and 1883 entries) presented a
paper entitled "Moral Education in Prisons" to the Committee on Labor
in Prisons and Reformatories. Articles such as "Papers on Penology"
and "Education as a Factor in Prison Reform" appeared frequently in
national journals and magazines, and visiting North American and
foreign groups toured Elmira Reformatory regularly. The "Elmira
System" was becoming well known. New reformatories were opened
in Pennsylvania and Ohio (Brockway, 1969/1912, p. 283). 🙢

Philanthropic interest in libraries was beginning to peak. In the
decades that followed this interest would be a great assist to correctional
educators.

Though tax-supported public libraries first appeared in
the United States in the mid-19th century, their spread
began decades later, thanks to industrial magnate
Andrew Carnegie. After working his way from bobbin
boy at a textile mill to owner of the world's largest
steel company, Carnegie saw libraries as a way to help
self-motivated individuals benefit society by bettering
themselves. For 30 years following 1886, his vast
wealth funded the building of nearly 1,700 libraries
in more than 1,400 American cities and towns. To get
a Carnegie grant, a community first had to show the
need for a library, provide a site, and agree to support
the library with annual taxes totaling 10 percent of the
grant. (Dodge, 2005, p. 74).

The American Library Association's "initial role [was] as 'guardians
of public morals' in the decades after its founding in 1876. Many
librarians at the time scorned popular novels for their morbid influence
on readers." (p. 75—see 1902 entry). 🙢

1887 — A country newspaper in upstate New York ran a series of anti-prison industry articles which prompted an investigation of Elmira Reformatory (Brockway, 1969/1912, p. 286—see 1888 entry). The first New York House of Refuge for Women opened at Hudson (Freedman, 1981, p. 46). It "was not a prison...but an educational institution" (p. 86). At one point a few years later, the school at Hudson was temporarily closed, for lack of teachers (p. 71). New York State's second House of Refuge for Women, at Albion, opened in 1893 (p. 46). It promised to "give such moral and religious training as will induce to form good character and such training in domestic work as will eventually enable them to find employment, secure good homes and be self-supporting." (p. 89). The third, the Bedford Hills Reformatory, was completed in 1901 (p. 46). "...[W]omens prisons were intended to retrain women through sympathetic female staff, prayer, education, and domesticity" (p. 90). ⌂

1888 — The Canadian Penitentiary Act put schoolmasters under the supervision of the chaplains (Weir, in Roberts, 1973, p. 41). This decision maintained the relation between church and state and delayed the secularization of the institutional schools. ⌂

In a Prison Sunday sermon on "The Restoration of the Criminal" in Springfield, Illinois, **F.H. Wines** said that

> Every well-managed prison should be to some extent a school...instruction should be given to all who need it, both in literature and in the knowledge of trades. No man who enters prison unable to make an honest livelihood should be allowed to leave it, until he is capable of supporting himself by his own exertions. (Wines, F.H., 1888, p. 10—see 1981 entry).

He said that a library is essential, and that convicts need "instruction as to their social relations, responsibilities, and obligations"—that school is the best place to get "better thoughts." (p. 10). Wines also said that "...reformatory work in a prison must be work with individuals; and adapted to their individual needs. For this each prisoner requires to be thoroughly studied, personally known, and personally touched." (p. 11). ⌂

New York's Yates Law brought State prison industries to an end. It was a response to agitation by businessmen who did not want to compete with prison labor. (Reagen and Stoughton, 1976, p. 41—see 1887 entry). The Yates Law was preceded by "Constant friction and quarreling among the inspectors, mainly because of political differences and poor financial management by the Board," which led to "a Constitutional amendment and the appointment of a [statewide] superintendent," in 1877. During "the 1880's a

1888   crisis in prison labor absorbed most of the time and effort of prison
(cont'd.) administrators." (Chenault, 1949-1951, p. 15). Several hours after the
        Yates Law was implemented, **Zebulon Brockway** began a military
        training department which drilled companies of Elmira Reformatory
        inmates each day. The physical education department, which had
        previously delivered services only to "abnormals," was expanded to
        include calisthenics for the entire population. Brockway transformed
        the fife and drum corps into an enlarged brass band. (McKelvey, 1977,
        p. 136). The military drills occupied the inmates from five to eight
        hours each day (Brockway, 1969/1912, p. 290). A new prison law was
        passed in 1889, which "gave some recognition to vocational training"
        (Chenault, 1949-1951, p. 8), and provided that prison industries would
        be coordinated by the vocational education department (McKelvey,
        1977, p. 136). 🔺

        An Elmira Reformatory follow-up survey revealed that "78.5
per cent [of the ex-offenders] lived self-supporting and orderly lives....
Some of the replies received from the men themselves complained
bitterly of what they felt to be the cruelty of the inquiry." (Brockway,
1969/1912, p. 297). **Professor Ford** was assisted by **Professor D.P.
Mayhew** (see entries for 1871 and 1878), who became Elmira's "resident
moral [social education] instructor" (p. 229). Mayhew

            succeeded in bringing in orderly mental processes
            among pupils who were frivolous and scatter-
            brained...work similar to that so admirably done with
            the prisoners at the Detroit House of Correction....
            His lectures were on physiology, ethics, and Biblical-
            spiritual interpretation. The experiment proved
            valuable, but not so successful as his similar work
            at Detroit had been [see 1878 entry]. The difference
            should be attributed to Professor Mayhew's advanced
            age, increased deafness, and clearly to the fact that the
            Elmira prisoners were more absorbed in earning merit
            marks in the other departments as well. (p. 230).

The strong professional identification that Professor Ford felt with the
public schools is revealed from his writing: "The best of order and a
growing desire for a plain common school education is now the marked
feature of the reformatory school. It is wonderful, in most cases how it
revives and brightens latent manhood." (p. 231). 🔺

        New classes for "dullards" were organized, under the
leadership of **Dr. Hamilton Wey**, the Elmira Reformatory physician. He
also published several articles about this special education program,
which was based on what had been learned during the 1886 experiment.
(Brockway, 1969/1912, p. 296). 🔺

1889 — New York State law was amended to require instruction for prisoners "in the trades and manufactures prosecuted in such prison or in other industrial occupations." The same law required individualized educational records for each inmate file. (Wallack, Kendall, and Briggs, 1939, p. 7). It was drafted by **Charles Collin**, the former Elmira ethics instructor, and emphasized the importance of correctional education. ⌒

Elmira Reformatory was expanded to include "a lecture hall with seating capacity for 600, and a school building of three stories containing 28 modern class rooms, a trade class in the basement, and a drawing class room." (Brockway, 1969/1912, p. 300). The new gymnasium was completed this year, with marble rooms for hot baths and massage (Brockway, 1969/1912, p. 302). It had been designed immediately after the Yates Law was passed (McKelvey, 1977, p. 126— see 1888 entry). **Dr. Hamilton Wey** used the new baths and massage rooms for "specific scientific physical renovation, to improve defectives and dullards in their moral habitudes." About 10% of the institution's 1,500 inmates were involved in this latest special education experiment; without it, the staff thought that the targeted students would remain incorrigible. Part of the plan involved 56 separate bodily measurements for each student, recorded monthly. (Brockway, 1969/1912, p. 302). **Brockway** expressed the view that "by means of prison science, most of the prisoners committed to the reformatory could and would be so changed in their habits and tastes as to become suitable inhabitants of a free community. The work of forming and reforming human character was felt to be a very exalted sphere of action but not beyond the realm of science." (p. 306). ⌒

F.H. Wines wrote that, after labor, education is the best tool "to lift the criminal to the level of a higher life....The prison which furnishes no education, even to convicts so densely stupid and ignorant as these, can accomplish nothing whatever in the direction of their reformation." (Wines, F.H., 1889, pp. 23-25). However, he also recognized the need

> to elevate the character of prison officials, and to imbue them with a nobler spirit and a more unselfish aim. It has been said that, to reform the prisoner, you must begin by reforming the warden; but it is equally true that, to reform the warden, you must sometimes begin by reforming the commissioners by whom he is appointed; and, to reform the commissioners, it might sometimes be well to begin by reforming the governor. We might even go a step further, and say that, to reform the governor, it is necessary to reform the people by whom he is nominated and elected. (p. 27—see 1890 entry). ⌒

124

1889   In Sweden, "Uppsala county prison [had] employed a person
(cont'd.) skilled in carpentry to teach vocational skills" since 1874. By 1889 an
          institutional annual report included the following:

> As long as mechanical, monotonous work from which
> they [prisoners] can learn very little is all they are
> offered, it will be easy for their thoughts and lively
> imaginations to be occupied with demoralizing ideas.
> (Nordic Council of Ministers, 2005, pp. 97-98—see 1950
> entry). ⌒

1890 — New York State first introduced capital punishment by electrocution
       (Murton, 1976, p. 5).

> In the 1880s [Thomas] Edison and George Westinghouse
> were battling for control of the new electric power
> industry. Edison hoped to market his direct current
> (DC) system, while Westinghouse championed
> alternating current (AC). They engaged in a bitter press
> dispute, with Edison declaring that AC was unreliable,
> unsafe, even deadly. In 1887, the New York Legislature
> assigned a commission to investigate alternatives
> to hanging as a means of execution. Edison saw an
> opportunity to defeat his competitor and offered the
> use of his West Orange, N.J. lab to an engineer, Harold
> Brown, to experiment with alternating current. Brown
> electrocuted more than 50 stray cats and dogs, and
> when the New York officials said his results with small
> animals might not be applicable to humans, he killed a
> horse and a cow. The officials were convinced. At New
> York's Auburn State Prison on Aug. 6, 1890, William
> Kemmler, a convicted ax murder, became the first victim
> of an electric chair. Powered by alternating current, the
> chair proved Edison's assertion that Westinghouse's
> system could indeed be deadly. (Wallace, Wallechinsky,
> and Wallace, 1982, p. 17).

Of course, in the long run AC advocates prevailed: AC powers all our
residential, industrial, and business endeavors. ⌒

          A friend offered New York City resident **William George** "an
old building that he had been thinking somewhat of demolishing" for
use as a summer camp site (George, 1911, p. 11). George "had the good
fortune to be born and reared upon a farm" (p. 1). Several days before
the house offer, he chanced upon a City child and talked with him about
the country. The boy mentioned several of his friends, and asked "Why
don't you take a lot of them up to the country with you this summer?"
Almost without thinking, George burst out "I'll do that very thing" and

125

1890   "from that impulsive decision started the inception of the idea which
(cont'd.) was destined to develop into the Junior Republic." (p. 7—see 1895
          entry). That year he took "about forty boys and ten girls" upstate for
          a "Fresh Air" camp (pp. 8-9). In 1891 he took two separate parties to
          the same site, for a total of about 100 boys and 25 girls (p. 13). By 1894
          George decided to make the camp residents work for their food and
          clothing, paying them in token money (pp. 56-57)—and started a camp
          bank, police force, and jail (p. 61). ⌒

          The National Prison Congress was sponsored by **Dr. F.H.
          Wines**. In a lecture on "Twenty Year's Growth of the American Prison
          System," Wines pointed to Elmira Reformatory as the best example in
          the country (Brockway, 1969/1912, p. 133). ⌒

          "In the half century following 1890...there was a vast influx into
          urban [public] schools of youth who previously might have gone to
          work or roamed the streets, pushed into the classroom by child labor
          laws and compulsory attendance..." (Tyack, 1974, p. 186).

          > The state superintendent in California wrote that
          > citizens should support compulsory education 'to save
          > themselves from the rapidly increasing herd of non-
          > producers...to save themselves from the wretches who
          > prey upon society like wild beasts.' For such children,
          > the state should establish 'labor schools, school ships,
          > industrial and technical schools' so that children can
          > be taught not only how to read but also 'how to work.'
          > (p. 69).

          > As David Rothman has shown, the nineteenth century
          > was an age of institutionalization when agencies
          > separated the insane into asylums, the poor into
          > almshouses, the criminal into prisons. Fear of disorder,
          > of contamination, of the crumbling of familiar social
          > forms such as the family, prompted reformers to create
          > institutions which could bring order into the lives of
          > deviant persons and, perchance, heal the society itself
          > by the force of example. (p. 72).

          > In 1909 Ellwood Cubberley expressed a point of view
          > common among WASP [White, Anglo-Saxon, Protestant]
          > educators when he declared that the 'new immigrants'
          > from southeastern Europe were 'illiterate, docile, often
          > lacking in initiative, and almost wholly without the
          > Anglo-Saxon conceptions of righteousness, liberty, law,
          > order, public decency, and government.' (p. 132).

1890   In 1889 a Boston school committee member declared that
(cont'd.)

> 'many of these children come from homes of vice and
> crime. In their blood are generations of iniquity....They
> hate restraint or obedience to law. They know nothing
> of the feelings which are inherited by those who were
> born on our shores.' 'It is largely through immigration
> that the number of ignorant, vagrant and criminal
> youth has recently multiplied to an extent truly
> alarming in some of our cities,' wrote the secretary of
> the Connecticut board of education. 'Their depravity
> is sometimes defiant and their resistance to moral
> suasion is obstinate.' Clearly, to wean such children
> from their corrupt homes and neighborhoods, to train
> them in industry, temperance, and obedience, would
> require systematic effort. (p. 75).

Who was to blame?

> From Joseph Tuckerman in Boston in the 1830's
> to Jocob Riis in New York in the 1890's, reformers
> chastised society for neglect of the children who
> learned from the school of the streets 'disobedience to
> parents, prevarication, falsehood, obscenity, profanity,
> lewdness, intemperance, petty thievery, larceny,
> burglary, robbery, and murder.' If family discipline and
> the traditional village restraints broke down, then the
> school must fill the moral vacuum. (p. 68).

Adele Shaw wrote

> If it hopes to Americanize a school population chiefly
> of foreign parentage...the school system 'must use
> abnormal means....To educate the children of our
> adoption we must at the same time educate their
> families, and in a measure the public school must be to
> them family as well as school... (p. 231).

But "Many teachers and administrators did not want the unwilling
pupils which coercion would bring to their classrooms, even though
police and downtown merchants might want to get children off the
streets and curb hooliganism." A Massachusetts superintendent
complained in 1870 that such children disrupted graded schools:

> 'without any habits of study, unused to school order
> with discipline, coming by compulsion and not by
> choice, with no prospects of remaining longer than
> the law requires, and joining classes for which they

1890
(cont'd.)
had no real fitness...[these children were disqualified] for membership.' When Chicago made some effort to enforce an 1889 law on compulsory attendance, Superintendent Howland said that 3,528 of the former truants were 'subject for reform schools.' (p. 70).

The schools were as regimented as any prison.

> The proper way to read in the public school in the year 1899 was to say, 'Page 35, Chapter 4,' and holding the book in the right hand, with the toes pointing at an angle of forty-five degrees, the head held straight and high, the eyes looking directly ahead, the pupil would lift up his voice and struggle in loud, unnatural tones. (pp. 255-256).

This was the origin of the phrase "to toe the line"—there was actually a line painted on the floor where the students were required to stand when reciting.

> The young...were taken away from the rest of society for a portion of their lives and separated in schools. Like inmates of the poorhouse, they were expected to learn 'order, regularity, industry and temperance,' and 'to obey and respect' their superiors. As in some of the asylums, reformatories, and refuges, they were assorted in large groups 'under a central administration' and followed an exact schedule and military routine....In retrospect one may claim that urban education in the nineteenth century did more to industrialize humanity than to humanize industry. (p. 72).

"Typical school administrators were mere 'drill sergeants' and described average city school bureaucracy as 'a combination of the cotton mill and the railroad with the model State-prison'" (pp. 81-82).

> A black principal in New York, William Bulkey, observed that 'if a boy...wants to learn a trade he must commit a crime,' for only in a reformatory could a black child acquire a manual skill since in business he 'runs up against a stone wall.' (p. 222).

"Sociologist **David Snedden**...admired the experiments possible in reform schools, for there the experts had a preselected population over whom they had virtually total social control." (p. 191; emphasis added). The role of the schools to select or deselect students for future roles interested one professor: "Supposedly the function of the schools was to create intelligence rather than to discover it, but given the importance

1890   of heredity...schools mainly winnowed out the 'incompetents' and
(cont'd.) rewarded the 'competent...'" (p. 206). Despite this awesome and
overarching function, the local public schools could not even respond
well to everyday routine challenges. In 1916 Ayres reported that

> in hardly a city in the country can the school
> authorities tell how many pupils begin school each
> year, or how fast they advance, or what proportion
> finish or why they fall out or where or why they lose
> time. (p. 201).

Nevertheless, there was "A kind of survival of the fittest in which the
academic proletariate was lumpen [unemployable] at the bottom and
the talented rose" (p. 202). "...Ayres mostly blamed educational systems
which taught children to fail" (p. 201). The combined influence of these
conditions reminded many that the local public schools existed, in the
main, to occupy the time of a surplus adolescent population.

> Twentieth-century educators would be faced with the
> full implications of preventive detention. It would not
> come as a surprise to find that the reform school and
> its curriculum would strike some educators as the best
> model for the reformulation of the common school for
> the new kinds of students entering urban classrooms.
> (p. 71).

Later, during the 1960s, one reform organization adopted a slogan that
expresses the sentiment of these observations: prisons are maximum
security factories, and factories are minimum security prisons. ⌒

1891 — Elmira Reformatory parolees were encouraged to use the institution as
an "asylum whenever urgent need occasioned" (Brockway, 1969/1912,
p. 325). The record suggests there were more inmates to use this
provision than 21st century readers might assume. ⌒

Since the Civil War the number of Federal prisoners had been
gradually increasing. The "three prison act [McNeil Island, Atlanta, and
Leavenworth]...made a start toward the acquisition of its own housing
for...federal prisoners" but problems continued regarding the lack of
strong central control and a highly politicized personnel system (Keve,
1984, pp. 163-164). ⌒

The American Prison Association conference was held in
Pittsburgh. Mr. Pettigrove, of Massachusetts, reported there that ex-
convicts who neglect to communicate during parole had "in every
case...grown careless about writing because they were doing so well"
(Brockway, 1969/1912, p. 326). ⌒

1892 — Experiments in the provision of educational services for students with disabilities continued under Brockway's leadership. A scientific dietary experiment was conducted at Elmira Reformatory (Brockway, 1969/1912, p. 327).

1893 — The inmate editors of Elmira Reformatory's *Summary* newspaper printed the first scientific study of prison diets (Wallack, 1939, p. 137—see entry for 1892). In the *Elmira Reformatory Yearbook*, it was reported that "Sixty eight per cent [of the inmates] were on admission practically illiterate; 75 per cent were without a regular and remunerative occupation; 92 per cent were reared without the restraints and benefits of good home surroundings" (Brockway, 1969/1912, p. 214).

A 250 X 300 foot military drill hall was constructed at Elmira Reformatory (Brockway, 1969/1912, p. 345). Two new classes were added at the school: Natural history for low achieving students, and nature studies for more advanced students. Another special education class "for selected dullards" was supervised cooperatively by the school director, the physician, and the institutional superintendent. These students were known as "the kindergartners;" the program included hot and cold baths, "brain education," and specially fitted clothing; perfect cleanliness was the rule. (Brockway, 1969/1912, pp. 346-347).

1894 — **Charles Warner** presented a paper on "The Elmira System" in Saratoga, before the American Social Science Association. In part, he said that "To rectify the bodies, to develop and train abnormal minds*—this is glorious work....[and] daily we get a little more light, and the area of darkness withdraws." (Brockway, 1969/1912, p. 338).

*Note: Brockway later asserted that "mushy sentimentalists, speaking pathologically, were suffering with 'a fatty degeneration of the heart.'" He went on to report the Warner speech with different words: "To reform diseased bodies and crooked minds is the work of experts; it is scientific work." (Rule, 1920, p. 140)

In England, the Gladstone Committee addressed prison reform issues. Prison Commission chairman **Colonel Edmund Sir du Cane** (who was also chairman of the Directors of Convict Prisons) "held undisputed sway over his domain." (Banks, 1958, p. 19). Essentially, the Gladstone Committee recommended "that the prison system should both deter and reform" (Forster, 1981, p. 8).

As early as 1822 the **Rev. John Clay** made protest: '...the chaplain is not in the right place amid whips, cranks, treadmills, and other instruments of bodily pain, and he feels that the message of mercy with which he is charged cannot be effectively delivered to

130

the prisoner when everything about him savours of spite and vindictiveness.' (Clay, in Banks, 1958, p. 19; emphasis added—note: in 2001 a book on Maconochie appeared, authored by another John Clay).

In 1836 the first prison inspections took place. The trend toward consolidation and reform began in 1865, when "an Act of Parliament sought to standardize and control the various county and other local jails..." Compulsory education was implemented in 1870, under the chaplains. (Banks, 1958, p. 21—see entries for 1823 and 1832). By 1877 convict and local institutions were consolidated under the Home Office, but still "the punishment of hard, dull, useless, uninteresting, monotonous labour...[was] yielding gradually to 'useful' tasks under extended cellular confinement." (Banks, 1958, p. 19). **Evelyn Ruggles-Brise** (see 1901 entry) succeeded du Cane in the mid 1890s, and extended this work, based on the idea that

> prison discipline and treatment should be more effectually designed to maintain, stimulate, or awaken the higher susceptibilities of prisoners, to develop their moral instincts, to train them in ordinary industrial habits, and whenever possible, to turn them out of prison better men and women physically and morally than when they came in. (Fox, in Banks, 1958, pp. 20-21).

The Act of 1898 was built on these principles—and it shaped English correctional education for the next 50 years (Banks, 1958, p. 21—see 1910 entry). ⌖

1895 — The John Howard Association of London was an influential prison reform organization. In 1895 the Association published material labeling the "Elmira System" a "palace prison" (Brockway, 1969/1912, p. 341). ⌖

William R. George founded the George Junior Republic in Freeville, New York. It was an outdoor juvenile institution located on 350 acres, serving 100 boys and 50 girls, aged 14-21. George believed that

> the delinquent children in his care...have the right to a happy childhood and a good upbringing;...they should be taught a trade and trained to be good citizens.... He proceeded to create a small 'republic,' which was actually modeled on the United States government... nothing should be free of charge—everything should be paid for in work. After a few years of experimentation, George entrusted almost the entire responsibility for

his republic to the boys and girls. It has been claimed that this marked the end of the originally high rate of escapes. George himself took a 'back seat' as a senior advisor... (Eriksson, 1976, p. 134).

George's model served as the prototype for **Thomas Mott Osborne's** Mutual Welfare League—see 1913 entry. ⌒

Elmira Reformatory school director **Monks** died. See 1884 entry. His personnel system had been based on the principle that "the best of teachers should be assigned to instruct the dullest pupils." (Brockway, 1969/1912, p. 350). ⌒

Cesare Lombroso's book *The Female Criminal* was published. One aspect of the book was that Lombroso attributed criminal tendencies to women by virtue of biological characteristics (Freedman, 1981, p. 112—see entries for 1876, 1906, and 1976). ⌒

"After an unsuccessful lawsuit...a black [local public school] teacher, Mrs. Susie Frazier, won an appointment to teach on a white faculty in the city [New York]." A few years before, New York Governor Grover Cleveland spoke out against segregation, and "the state decided in 1884 to close the last black schools." (Tyack, 1974, p. 120). In 1874 the African American community in St. Louis began to press for African American teachers in their neighborhood schools. "In the first three years after the introduction of black teachers, the numbers of pupils rose 35 percent (1878) 20 percent (1879), and 27 percent (1880)." (p. 122). In a 1940 nationwide survey, Doxey Wilkerson "found that in twenty-eight cities in his sample with fewer than 7,000, however, only four employed black teachers" (pp. 225-226). Tyack later wrote that "There was no shortage of trained black teachers—teaching was one of the favorite career choices of black high school girls, and there were many training programs for black teachers in both North and South." (p. 225). ⌒

1896 —

Thirty-six trades and branches of trades were taught to the resident population of 1,500 [at Elmira Reformatory]....Of the 329 men paroled that year, 324 went to the trade or employment acquired or arranged at the reformatory; four had trades on admission to the reformatory,; only one was discharged without trades training. (Brockway, 1969/1912, p. 359).

Mr. Clark, a graduate of Cornell University's Mechanical Engineering Department, was the trade school director. (p. 359). ⌒

Another special education program was started at Elmira Reformatory, this one for a trial period of six months. The students "were either exceptionally stupid or deficient in a single faculty such

1896   as the arithmetical, or they were incapable of the ordinary prudential
(cont'd.) self-regulation of their demeanor." Individualized attention was the
focus of this program, which was designed by **Professor Bates**. It was
a comprehensive effort, involving physical, manual, and technical
instruction. (Brockway, 1969/1912, p. 360). ⌒

> At the George Junior Republic, where the juvenile citizens voted
democratically on important issues, several girls decided to participate
as full citizens. "Don't take those votes" said an elected boy official

> > 'don't you know women ain't allowed to vote?' A
> > lively argument pro and con ensued on the spot, when
> > one of the girls said: 'Why, of course, we can vote,—the
> > tax collector made us pay some of the first money we
> > earned last night to run the government and pay the
> > officers, and if we pay money for the government I
> > guess we're going to have something to say about it.'
> > (George, 1911, p. 76).

"In course of time the Republic girls finally secured the franchise;
through a two-third vote of the male citizens it became a part of their
special constitution." (p. 77). At the George Junior Republic "the courts
and sessions of the legislature were held in the afternoon; the prisoners,
dressed in striped bed-ticking, were escorted to a stone pile where with
light sledge-hammers they broke stone for the road construction."
(p. 89). The institution's first years were rather lean, and food donations
from nearby farmers played an important role in the diet.

> > ...[T]he bill of fare was not elaborate. One of the boys,
> > who is now a lawyer in the city of Cleveland, acted
> > as cook. We had tomatoes and potatoes for breakfast,
> > and potatoes and tomatoes for dinner and a hash of the
> > same for supper... (p. 101).

News of George's youth institution experiment spread quickly, and
"scores of visitors came each day to see the colony in operation."
(p. 99). The Republic developed all the features of a normal town: a
hotel, industries—especially "the somewhat famous 'Junior Republic
Ginger and Chocolate Wafers'" (p. 209)—political parties, town
meetings, a newspaper—the *Junior Republic Citizen*, etc. (p. 217).

> > In the fall of '96 we established a school in the Republic
> > for the primary and grammar grades. Previous to
> > this the young citizens had attended school in the
> > village of Freeville. The school had to have its pioneer
> > experience, also. One of the old barns was remodeled
> > and fitted up with second hand benches, old tables,
> > chairs and atlases. Second hand books, very much the

1896
(cont'd.)

worse for wear and written by authors both good and bad, completed the outfit. In this ramshackle building some of the most notable Junior Republic citizens were educated. (p. 160).

Most of the residents spent one-half of each day in school, one-half day at work (p. 211).

There are two sessions each day from eight till twelve A.M. and from one to five P.M. At the present time [1911] there are eight teachers, including the principal. The school is thoroughly organized and is conducted on the same lines as a high school outside. The citizens have practically nothing to say about the conduct of the school or its discipline. The Republic receives $100 a year from the State for the services of each teacher; the Junior Republic Association pays the balance of the expense for the support of the school with the exception of the money paid by the two or three tax-payers within the district. Probably the Junior Republic School District has the smallest number of tax-payers of any school district within the State. Students may be prepared in this school for entrance to the leading colleges and universities. Each year the list of Republic citizens who enter college is increasing... (p. 307).

"**Thomas Mott Osborne** (see 1913 entry), mayor of Auburn, New York, served as a Republic Supreme Court Justice" (p. 287—emphasis added). Osborne was "President of the National Association of Junior Republics, and also the President of the George Junior Republic Association of New York." George quoted one resident:

'Uncle Tom [Osborne] is all right. He's just like one of the boys. It's funny, but if there is a fellow in jail or who is awfully tough, he is just Uncle Tom's kind.' Probably no other man understands Republic principles better than 'Uncle Tom.' (pp. 206-207—see 1911 entry). ⌂

1897 — **Sir Walter Crofton** died, at age 82 (Eriksson, 1976, p. 97—see entries for 1863 and 1872). Crofton's work in the Irish prison system had built on the innovations begun by Maconochie in the South Pacific, and influenced Brockway's program at Elmira Reformatory. ⌂

"Officers of the U.S. penitentiary [service] had been placed under classified service." The Civil Service Commission was established by Congress during president Chester Arthur's term, in 1883 (Keve, 1984, pp. 140-141). ⌂

1897   Important reforms were being experienced in various European
(cont'd.) nations. In 1897 attention was directed especially to those in Germany.

> In Germany the Principles of 1897 provided that in
> institutions for juveniles the prisoners should have
> lessons 'in the subjects taught in elementary schools.'
> Adult prisoners under thirty with terms exceeding
> three months were eligible 'as far as they were still in
> need of the same instruction.' As a rule the prison school
> consisted of a lower and higher course, followed by a
> continuation school. Equipment and methods were
> those used in elementary schools. Before the First World
> War wider aims were ruled out, owing to the view that
> lessons for adults were psychologically objectionable
> and lectures incompatible with prison discipline. The
> post-war reforms affected the scope and aims of prison
> education. According to the Prussian Prison Regulations
> of 1923 the object of the prison school was to 'lift the
> prisoners morally, stimulate them mentally, and fill the
> gaps of their knowledge.' The teaching of young prisoners
> should be adapted to the curricula of continuation and
> vocational schools. A Prison School Order of 1924 gave
> warning against the constant alternation of question and
> answer in the teaching of new subjects and the repeating
> of old ones, and recommended discussions, debates,
> and papers as means of a directed self-instruction. The
> principal subjects were personal and civil life, German,
> arithmetic, industrial, commercial, or agricultural
> vocational courses, domestic science and needlework,
> drawing, hygiene, gymnastics, and singing. Special
> courses of one to two hours a week up to six months
> could be offered to qualified prisoners. The realization
> of such schemes suffered from the small number of
> teachers available. As a rule, during the twenties, there
> was one teacher for every 100 to 150 prisoners. Prisoners
> used to have about two hours [of instruction] a week.
> Progressive reformers wished to extend this to an hour
> a day. Most regulations emphasized the importance of
> this service by the provision that the time for lessons
> should be set aside from ordinary working hours. Only
> Thuringia and Brunswick followed the English pattern
> in that they instituted an evening school after a full
> interrupted working day. (Grunhut, 1973/1948, pp. 232-
> 233).

1898 — **Zebulon Brockway** had become famous for his work at Elmira
      Reformatory. In 1898 he was elected president of the American Prison
      Congress (Wallack, 1939, p.9).

1898   The educational profession was still poorly defined, even in the
(cont'd.) public schools. For example, professors in the new field of educational
administration discovered how "scanty" their literature was. A

> few works in the slowly emerging field of psychology;
> and a handful of books by experienced educators
> recounting professional folklore; a few writings
> of European educational theorists, supplemented
> here and there by the works of an American...
> hardly the basis for scientific expertise. (Tyack,
> 1974, pp. 135-136).

One work, by William T. Harris, was entitled *The Theory of Education in
the United States of America* "represented...a consensus of educational
leaders," but it was only a small pamphlet and had been published in
1874 (pp. 49-50). In most jurisdictions (New York became an exception
in 1885, when its tenure system was implemented) teachers faced "the
insecurity of annual reelection" (p. 104).

> Teachers testified that worry over making ends meet
> and providing for the future added immeasurably to
> their nervous burden. Hear their voices: 'The strain is
> so great and the salary allows no sum for recuperation.
> There is no line of work which so drains vitality.' 'If I
> could get something else that would pay better, I would
> give up teaching in spite of the fact that I love the
> work, but after teaching ten years most of us are unfit
> for anything else. We give the best years of our lives to
> the work and how few live to enjoy the pension!' 'I am
> so worn out from teaching sixty pupils that most of my
> money goes for medicine and trips for my health.'
> (p. 259; emphasis in original).

The average national teacher turnover rate for 1919 was 20% (p. 268).
It was generally—and gradually—acknowledged that "only educators
were proper guardians of the educational function" (p. 146), but the
ebb and flow of other professional influences can be clearly identified.
"Increasingly, leading schoolmen in the latter nineteenth century
talked more in terms borrowed from business and social science and
less in [the] evangelical rhetoric [of educational reform]" (pp. 75-
76). Tyack reported later that during the 1890-1940 period, "teachers
and administrators often came under the spell of the individualistic
orientation of the psychologists who dominated educational thought."
(p. 181—see entries for 1957 and 1973). ◠

> Increasingly, North Americans were looking to the local public
> schools to deliver the promises of democracy—and some of the trends
> supported this view.

1898
(cont'd.)

As U.S. Commissioner of Education and the leading schoolman of the era, William T. Harris had reason for pride as he looked back...on the accomplishments of American educators since 1870. In those twenty-eight years, he reported, the number of pupils in public schools increased from less than 7,000,000 to 15,000,000; 71 of 100 persons between five and eighteen years were enrolled in some school as compared with 61 in 1870; and expenditures jumped from $63,000,000 per year to $199,000,000 (a rise from $1.64 per capita of total population to $2.67). The typical young American of 1898 could expect to receive five years of schooling. Of 100 students in educational institutions 95 were in elementary schools, 4 in secondary, and 1 in a post-secondary school. (Tyack, 1974, p. 66).

However, as early as 1842

in a Fourth of July oration, Horace Mann declared that elsewhere the experiment had always failed 'through an incapacity in the people to enjoy liberty without abusing it.' Politics after the Civil War seemed to many educators to confirm Mann's warnings. In 1880 a rationale for public education in Portland stressed that 'the self-government of the government of the people (see entries for 1895, 1907, and 1913) is still on trial,' and that amid the sweeping waves of immigration only the common school could train 'every child in our own tongue and habits of thought, and principles of government and aims of life.' One might trust 'parental instinct' to educate an individual child, but the state required homogeneity; 'the right of preservation of a body politic' took precedence over all other rights. (p. 75).

In 1902 one New York school principal wrote that

'education will solve every problem of our national life, even that of assimilating our foreign element.... Ignorance is the mother of anarchy, poverty and crime. The nation has a right to demand intelligence and virtue of every citizen, and to obtain these by force if necessary.' He went on to claim that a 'pupil's very association with intellectual and honorable men and women [in school] tends to inspire toward higher standards of living.' (p. 232). ◢

1899 — "The first 'juvenile court' in America was established in Illinois."

> The 1890's [also] saw the introduction of a new
> Indiana law which made county boards of education
> responsible for educating those children who became
> public wards....The implication of both of these new
> laws was that children were no longer to be dealt
> with as criminals. By 1900 there were 65 reformatories
> housing 19,410 children and according to three French
> gentlemen they were getting satisfactory results. In
> a report to the International Congress of Assistance,
> held in France in 1889, they refer to the 'unique and
> revolutionary' reformatory system in the United States
> and England. They claimed that the industrial schools
> they found were doing an excellent job. Nonetheless an
> editorial in the *Charities Record* of 1901 was still calling
> for 'better equipment' and more 'first-rate teachers'
> in the juvenile reformatories across the land. (Angle,
> 1982, p. 6). ⬙

"Where riots and outrages occurred it was often found that the discipline had been peculiarly severe. About 1899 riots and outbreaks occurred in various girls' schools in Colorado, Iowa, New York and New Jersey." The New Jersey Charity Aid Association studied the matter, and recommended (a) diminished use of corporal punishment, with scrupulous records maintained, (b) individualized discipline, (c) deprivation of privileges as the best punishment, (d) merit systems, (e) diminished use of "unnatural or constrained physical postures as punishment," (f) "No male assistants should be used in punishing girls," (g) if solitary confinement is used, it should be "of a mild character," and (h) better recreational opportunities, "to counteract tendencies toward obscenity." (Snedden, 1907, p. 148). ⬙

Brockway implemented two new educational programs at Elmira Reformatory. One was a special education venture for "degenerates and motiveless men;" the other was a prerelease "class," to cultivate personal economy in prisoners who were nearing their conditional release. (Brockway, 1969/1912, p. 363). The prerelease effort was available to the 150 best behaved inmates, about 10% of the population. They ate their meals café style, at small tables with white table cloths, and selected their dishes from a menu, at an average cost of five cents per day. Their food was better than the usual fare. (p. 364). The program involved decision-making and nutrition. These men ate off better crockery than the others, and dressed in blue clothes for their evening meal. (p. 367). "The first set of 10 were deficient generally.... The second set of men was composed of undersized, ill-developed weaklings...the third set of 10 men were strong, physically and of fair intelligence. They failed chiefly in demeanor." (pp. 366-368). ⬙

1899   In England, Her Majesty's Secretary of State issued *Rules for*
(cont'd.) *the Government of Local Prisons* under the authority of the Prison Act of
1898.

No prisoner shall be compelled to attend...any religious instruction given by the chaplain, minister, or religious instructor....The chaplain shall conform to the rules and regulations of the prison....A prison minister shall have access to the catalogue of books to be issued to prisoners, and no book to which he makes objection shall be issued to any prisoner of his persuasion....No books or printed papers shall be admitted into any prison for circulation among the prisoners unless approved by the Commissioners; and no books or printed papers intended for the religious instruction of prisoners belonging to the Established Church shall be admitted without the concurrence of the chaplain....Each prisoner shall be furnished with a Bible and prayer books, such as is approved for the denomination to which he belongs....Every unconvicted juvenile prisoner shall be daily instructed by the schoolmaster for one hour....Any boy whose ignorance makes it impossible to instruct him shall be read to by the schoolmaster from books specially selected by the chaplain....The chaplain shall select a special set of books to form a library for the use of unconvicted juvenile prisoners, picture books being provided for those who cannot read. (Secretary of State, 1899, pp. 18-52—see 1919 entry). 🕭

The Elmira Reformatory manual training department was discontinued by the Board of Managers, a result of what Brockway described as a "trifling fault...not germane to his [department head **Professor Bates'**] general usefulness." A breach developed between the new board and Brockway. (Brockway, 1969/1912, p. 370). 🕭

The superintendent of public instruction in East Orange, New Jersey "persuaded the board to 'experiment' with an 'ungraded' class of 'backward colored pupils.'" African American leaders, outraged at this blatant Jim Crow action, organized protests and boycotts, but were unable to influence decision-makers. One board member explained:

teachers and parents felt that Negroes had 'different temperaments.' When asked why there were no whites in the special classes, one principal replied that there were no backward whites in his school. From there it was a clear path to an 'ideal state school code' written by a leading northern educator in 1914, praising the

1899
(cont'd.)

unifying force of the common school, and noting that at the same time the state might set up separate schools for 'defective, delinquent, or...negro' children. Not surprisingly, the Alabama state superintendent asked him to come south the next year to rewrite the state's school law. (Tyack, 1974, p. 124).

To have been born black was normally to have been labeled a failure—an inferiority all too often justified by a bogus science—as millions of Negro children learned in school systems which were consciously or unwittingly racist. Black Americans arrived in northern cities in large numbers at a time when centralization had undermined ward school politics, when educators were increasingly empowered to make classifications of pupils according to their notion of what was best for the client, when the results of biased tests were commonly accepted as proof of native ability, when those in control of schooling generally agreed that the function of schools was to sort and train students to fit into the existing order, and when much writing in education and social science tended to portray black citizens as a 'social problem,' linked in research and library classification schemes with delinquency, prostitution, and disease—when they were considered at all. Sociologists often saw blacks as cripples. (p. 217).

In Cleveland, for example, 25 percent of the children assigned to 'special classes' for defective children in 1923 were black, even though in theory mental retardation was equally common among whites. Likewise, 50 percent of all work permits issued to Negro girls in that city were marked 'retarded,' signifying that the students had not 'passed the seventh grade by reason of mental retardation.' By contrast, only 4 percent of all native-born white children received 'retarded' work permits. (p. 220). ◢

1900 — **Zebulon Brockway** resigned from his role as Elmira Reformatory superintendent (Brockway, 1969/1912, p. 370). Elmira had

one of the pioneer trade schools in the country. Brockway had developed an educational program far beyond that which existed in any other adult prison. Gradually other prisons adopted the model and they in turn began to be designated as reformatories. (Angle, 1982, p. 6).

140

1900   Brockway was elected mayor of the town of Elmira, New York, and
(cont'd.) served for a two year term (Brockway, 1969/1912, p. 377). ⌂

The adult reformatory movement, which had its first expressions in the U.S. at the 1870 Cincinnati congress and the establishment of Elmira in 1876, had grown strong; there were now reformatory institutions all across the country. (Barnes and Teeters, 1959, p. 377). One dimension of the movement was the proliferation of indeterminate sentences. "Beginning around 1900, indeterminate sentences—'two to five' or 'ten to 20'—became common." (Angle, 1982, p. 40). ⌂

Distinctive patterns of management for female prisoners were developed in Indiana: "womanly sympathy, familial discipline, and domestic training" (Freedman, 1981, p. 57). Officials soon regretted the lack of libraries and schoolrooms in the new institutions (p. 70). In general, women's reformatories were not under female control (p. 71). Prayer and education became major institutional features, and training often emphasized domesticity. "While inmates were taught to value traditional feminine ideals of purity and submissiveness, this training often defeated the concurrent goal of teaching women to be self-sufficient." (p. 105). ⌂

The history of English colonization had included indenturing servants to the American colonies before the Revolution, then sending convicts to Australia until transportation became politically unpopular in the mid 19th century, and shipping orphans to Canada around the turn of the 20th century—orphan trains. These strategies boosted global profits and "solved" domestic problems by exporting England's urban poor.

> Those who considered ...placing out [orphans] were well aware of established forms for assisting the poor.... England's 'Ragged Schools' [19th century juvenile facilities]...were based on...reform rather than the simple incarceration of children....the British system of 'transportation' [of criminals]...as far back as the early 1700s....the country's less desirable citizens were shipped to North America, Capetown, and Australia.... a new component...[was] added. Along with convicts, the poor, particularly women and children, were... resettled....The frontiers of the Empire needed labor, and in some cases prospective wives for male settlers. Transportation ...[was] a way to supply that demand... (Holt, 1992, pp. 45-46).

The orphan train procedure was duplicated in the U.S. during the late 19th century to help populate the American West. Available orphans were shipped wholesale from large Eastern cities, deposited on train

141

1900
(cont'd.) station platforms, and picked up by farmers or merchants who needed cheap labor—usually for the cost of food and clothes. ⌇

Modern observers of the juvenile justice systems assume a complex constellation of social and legal causes for crime. However, "Back in 1900, when the first juvenile courts were established in Chicago and Denver, it did seem as if the final answer to the problem had been found..." (Oursler and Oursler, 1949, p. 127). ⌇

Although not yet a focus of correctional education attention, libraries were always seen as important. "A prominent Philadelphian, **Edward T. Stotesbury**, made a donation of $1,000 for the purpose of replenishing the library" at Cherry Hill Prison (Teeters and Shearer, 1959, p. 160; emphasis added—see 1854 entry). ⌇

Frances Morton succeeded Ellen Johnson as Framingham Women's Reformatory superintendent. She focused on authority and discipline and ended recreational hours, telling the women that "they would do better to use the time learning to sew." (Freedman, 1981, p. 97). ⌇

In France reforms in juvenile facilities took center stage. The Mettray family substitute institution

> had become almost military...the institutional population consisted of 325 boys sentenced for crimes, 99 who had been remanded for reformative treatment (correction paternelle), and 25 who had been handed over...by affluent parents....Each week the 'families' had a good conduct competition, the winner being the one with the fewest penalties. The reward was an extra meal with meat and the best placing at institutional festivities. Fourteen different trades could be practiced, but the majority of pupils (a total of 253) did farm work. (Eriksson, 1976, p. 123—see entry for 1840 and 1937). ⌇

Approximately 6.4% of all 17-year olds in the U.S. graduated from high school, or 94,883. In 1890 this figure had only been 3.5%, or 43,731; in 1870, 16,000. (Tyack, 1974, p. 57). In 1860 one writer found that the parents of high school students in his town did not include any "factory operatives, ordinary laborers, or Irish." In 1880 another writer reported that "only 31.7 percent of the children of unskilled workers in St. Louis were in school from ages thirteen to sixteen, compared with 64.1 percent for white-collar workers and 80 percent for professional families." (p. 58). Secondary enrollments consisted mostly of girls— 57.6% of the pupils and 64.8% of the graduates were female. An 1893 National Education Association (NEA) statement

1900
(cont'd.)

declared that the function of high schools was 'to prepare for the duties of life that small proportion of all children in the country...who show themselves able to profit by an education prolonged to the eighteenth year, and whose parents are able to support them while they remain so long at school. (p. 45).

Tyack's summary parallels the NEA's: "most schoolmen before 1900 regarded the high school as a minority institution designed for the bright child whose parents were willing and able to forego her or his labor." (p. 58). As early as 1870 the U.S. commissioner of education had declared that "the pattern of eight years of elementary school had become the norm..." (p. 45). "The general tendency of American cities is to carry all of their children through the fifth grade, to take one half of them to the eighth grade and one in ten through high school." (Ayres, in Tyack, 1974, p. 200). The extension of secondary opportunities to most school children would only be realized in the late 1930s and early 1940s—later for incarcerated students. ⌒

More than two thirds of the funds for local public schools came directly from local tax bases. Fully 79% of local expenditures was directed to education, up from 47% in 1850. This trend had begun with a "common school revival of the 1840's and 1850's— second, perhaps, only to [a similar revival in] Germany." (Tyack, 1974, p. 66). "In making educational facilities available, in sending their children to school mostly without effective governmental compulsion, and in underwriting the opportunity costs, most Americans demonstrated their faith in the value of formal education." (p. 68).

The costs of city schools in 1910 were twice as high as in 1900, three times higher than 1890. From 1890 to 1918 there was, on average, more than one new high school built for every day of the year. Attendance in high schools increased during that period from 202,963 to 1,645,171, an increase of 711 percent while the total population increased only 68 percent. The curve of secondary school enrollment and graduation continued to soar: in 1920, 61.6 percent of those fourteen to seventeen were enrolled, and high school graduates represented 16.8 percent of youths seventeen years old; in 1930, the figures were 73.1 percent and 29 percent; in 1940, 79.4 percent and 50.8 percent....From 1900 to 1920 educators became less ambivalent about coercion [in relation to the compulsory attendance laws] than they had often been during the nineteenth century. (pp. 183-184).

143

1900
(cont'd.)

Boston had implemented a compulsory attendance law in 1852 (p. 69); Chicago in 1889 (p. 70). In 1885 16 states had compulsory attendance laws, but by 1900 that number had grown to 31 (p. 71). "They seem to have been sponsored largely by labor unions eager to prevent competition from child labor, by philanthropists eager to 'save the child,' and by politicians who saw compulsory attendance as a partisan issue." (p. 71). "In terms of foregone income of students aged ten to fifteen [the net loss was estimated to have] jumped from $24,800,000 in 1860 to $213,900,000 in 1900" (pp. 66-67). The inspector who administered the 1893 Illinois child labor law reported that school principals made a common practice of expelling children at age 11 (p. 70). In 1909 Helen Todd asked 500 Chicago children

> 'If your father had a good job and you didn't have to work, which would you rather do—go to school or work in a factory?' Of these 500, 412 said they preferred the factory. Bewildered, Todd jotted down their reasons: [a] "Because it's easier to work in a factory than 'tis to learn in school.' [b] 'They ain't always pickin' on you because you don't know things in a factory.' [c] 'The children don't holler at ye and call ye a Christ-killer in a factory.' [d] "They're good to you at home when you earn money.' [e] 'What ye learn in school ain't no good. Ye git paid just as much in the factory if ye never was there.' (pp. 177-178).

Enforcement of the compulsory attendance law in Chicago was described as "practically hopeless," and Chicago, New York City, San Francisco, and Philadelphia all shared a common problem—if all the children who were obliged to attend ever did attend there would only be a fraction of the required seats, schoolrooms, and teachers (p. 71). But by 1960 "over 46,000,000 students were in school, constituting about 99.5 percent of the children aged seven to thirteen years, 90.3 percent of youth aged fourteen to seventeen, and 38.4 percent of those aged eighteen and nineteen" (p. 269). ◠

1901 — In England, Prison Director **E. Ruggles-Brise** (see 1894 entry) wrote a summary of events at the prison congresses of Paris (1895) and Brussels (1900), for the Home Department's secretary of state.

> No one can deny, that the creation of schools and libraries in prisons was a very happy idea. Their object, be it understood, is not to make prison life pleasant but to make it profitable. Their object is three-fold: [a] to prevent prisoners from brooding over their condition and nursing thoughts of anger, revenge, and discontent; [b] to elevate their minds; [c] to increase their knowledge. (Ruggles-Brise, 1901, p. 34).

He reported on three resolutions adopted by the congresses:

> [a] Schools should be organized for all classes of prisoners, both illiterate and those possessing a certain education. They should be so organized as not only to supply the elements of education to those who are in need of it, but also an instruction with a moral tendency, which, without conflicting with religious beliefs, should be permeated with the spirit of religion, an indispensable means of reform. [b] Libraries should be organized on the same lines, and with the same double object—instruction and reform. The duty of providing the necessary books, rests, in the first instance, with the Government, but the co-operation of private individuals or societies is desirable, especially with the view of procuring foreign books for foreigners. [c] A special weekly publication for the use and benefit of prisoners is to be recommended. (pp. 34-35). ⌒

1902 — New libraries were opened at Minnesota's St. Cloud Reformatory and the Red Wing Training School for Juveniles. Stillwater Prison, also in Minnesota, had a library collection of 4,000 volumes—despite an 1884 fire. The collection there had grown from 300 volumes in 1868 to 900 in 1878. Losses from the fire were replaced, in part, with $150 from the inmate newspaper and a $250 personal loan from the warden. (MacCormick, in Roberts, 1973, p. 318). As early as 1853—two years after the Prison was established—the legislature required that

> 'visitors' fees shall be applied for the purchase of books for the use of the prison...'These fees, 'not exceeding twenty-five cents,' grew to so large a sum during the next fifty years that in 1903-04 the Board of Control

1902
(cont'd.)

changed this ruling and less money was available thereafter. (Jones, 1938, p. 174—see 1938 entry). ⌒

In England the Borstal system was emerging. Rooted in innovations by Maconochie in the South Pacific, and Crofton in Ireland—but most directly on New York's Elmira model—services to confined wards were becoming systematized.

> What was to become the borstal [juvenile institution] system began in the old convict prison in the village of Borstal, near Rochester in Kent, in 1902. Associated labour [the Auburn system—see 1816 entry] introduced at the end of the century was the beginning of the end of the separate system [the Pennsylvania system—see entries in Introduction and 1842], which was formally, and finally, ended in 1930. And immediately after the Gladstone Report [submitted in 1898—see 1894 entry], there was a Departmental Inquiry into Prison Education....In 1919 warders were renamed officers. In 1930, in a famous episode, a group of borstal boys set out from the closed borstal at Feltham, and marched, in stages, to Lowdham Grange, which became the first open [minimum security] institution in the penal system. (Forster, 1981, p. 9). ⌒

1903 — Four hours of compulsory school attendance were required each week in Canadian prisons (Weir, in Roberts, 1973, p. 41). Soon, urban school reformers in the United States would focus attention on the compulsory attendance regulations in many North American institutions. ⌒

In Norway, the 1903 Prison Act "established that individuals under the age of 18 should always have education while in prison." Consistent statistics on prison literacy began in 1918. (Nordic Council of Ministers, 2005, p. 68). ⌒

1904 — New York State superintendent of prisons **Cornelius V. Collins** asked commissioner of education **Dr. Andrew S. Draper** to establish a system of schools in the prisons. Draper was "much interested in the subject," and accepted the challenge. (Chenault, 1949-1951, p. 8). By 1910 New York State boasted this description of its correctional education program in the institution *Handbook*:

> The schools in the State prisons have been organized by the State Superintendent of Prisons [see 1877 entry] to fit the peculiar conditions and needs of the prison population. The curriculum of the prison schools differs from that of the ordinary common school in that it is made to apply to adult illiterates, in order

146

to carry them along to a point where their reasoning faculties will enable them better to direct their hands to mechanical endeavors. The very large proportion of foreign-born inmates in the State prisons makes it further more necessary to adjust the course of study to include the elements of the English language and some instruction as to the government of the country and the duties of citizenship. At each prison a suitable number of well-lighted schoolrooms are provided, and a head teacher is engaged to instruct and supervise the convict teachers in their duties. Approximately 1,500 men in the prisons now attend school an hour and a half every day except Sundays and holidays. The progress made by these adult scholars is remarkable. The results in a reformative way from the schools are more potent than from any other agency, except perhaps from the industrial training, which, accompanying the schools, forms a co-ordinate branch of the scholastic training." (p. 9). ▵

Thomas Mott Osborne was asked to speak before "the annual meeting of the National Prison Association, held that year in the city of Albany...[He] made an address on 'The True Foundation of Prison Reform....'" Osborne reported that

Outside the walls a man must choose between work and idleness,—between honesty and crime. Why not let him teach himself these lessons before he comes out? Such things are best learned by experience. Some can acquire their lesson by the experience of others; but most men in prison under the present system cannot do that. They are in prison for the very reason that they cannot do that. But every one who is not an absolute fool can learn by experience, and the bulk of men in prison certainly are not fools. (Osborne, 1975/1916, pp. 152-153).

Osborne first became acquainted with the George Junior Republic (see 1895 entry) in 1896.

When William R. George, the founder and superintendent, first suggested that the same principles which were working so successfully with young boys and girls might work with equal success in a prison, the idea seemed preposterous; but subsequent reflection made me think that he was right. (pp. 153-154—see 1913 entry). ▵

1904
(cont'd.)
David Snedden reported in 1907 on the children committed to the New York Juvenile Asylum in 1904: "Seventy-four boys and 52 girls could not read; 19 boys and 3 girls could read only; 10 boys and 2 girls could read and write; 484 boys and 114 girls could read, write, and cipher." **Frank Dell'Apa** explained these statistics in 1973:

> In short, nearly 17 percent were illiterate. There were many behavioral problems, and the progress of education in reformatories lagged seriously. Although it was many years before the development of modern testing and diagnostic techniques, it was clear to most educators at the time that the learning problems of institutionalized children were not in general caused by retardation. (Dell'Apa, 1973b, p. 15). 🔺

New York public school superintendent **Julia Richman**'s report on drop outs and immigrants was released.

> She realized that many of these students had 'developed a street shrewdness which makes it absurd to give...training designed for the baby mind.' The best teachers should be assigned to special classes for these students...to detect the reasons for retardation and to find appropriate remedies. (Tyack, 1974, p. 203). 🔺

1905 — At the International Prison Congress in Budapest, guidelines were established for adolescent and adult correctional education programs. "Education, secular and religious, will be compulsory; lessons of patriotism and of moral conduct will be impressed." (Topping, 1929, p. 41). 🔺

> The National Education Association reported on the different salary scales by gender, in 467 city school systems. Female elementary teachers earned an average of $650/year, males $1,161; female elementary principals $970, males $1,542; female high school teachers $903, males $1,303. As early as 1861 "St. Louis paid male principals $800 and female principals $400, while in 1904 New York paid a maximum salary of $2,400 to male high school teachers, $1,900 to female" (Tyack, 1974, p. 62). "The employment of women appears to correlate highly with the pace of bureaucratization" (p. 61). So did struggles to fight the inequities that resulted.

> In San Francisco **Kate Kennedy**, a suffragist, teacher, and member of the Knights of Labor, lobbied successfully with her sister colleagues for a legislative act in 1870 that awarded women the same pay as men for equal work. **Margaret Haley** in Chicago and **Grace Strachan** in New York were strategists for massive leagues of

1905 (cont'd.)	women teachers and won justice that had been denied them when they had no power. After women received the vote in 1920, within a decade ten states passed laws providing equal pay for equal work....Equal pay for women no more eliminated the sexism in schools than desegregation destroyed racism in the armed forces, but in both instances the response of the organizations illustrated that the bureaucratic form could lend itself to the righting of specific injustices quite as much as to the perpetuation of the inequities of the larger society. (p. 65; emphases added).

The New York law was secured in 1911, after a protracted struggle. Around the country and in all occupations, only 18.7% of female workers received equal pay for equal work in 1904; by 1924 that figure had risen to 79.7%. (p. 267). ⚿

1906 — Intelligence tests were pioneered, thus providing "a tool for correlating mentality and crime" (Freedman, 1981, p. 110). Over the subsequent decades much attention would be directed to the perceived differences in intelligence between criminals and the population at large. ⚿

The Elmira Reformatory Board of Managers was renamed "State Board of Managers of Reformatories;" responsibility for the Eastern New York State Reformatory at Napanoch was added to the Board's duties (Allen, 1927, p. 6). Napanoch, also known as Eastern, was intended to be organized along the same lines as Elmira (see 1876 entry). ⚿

1907 — **Katharine Bement Davis**, superintendent of New York State's Bedford Hills Women's Reformatory, implemented lessons in self-government. She emphasized the "importance of women in...a democracy [even] though they take no part in actual government." In this she alluded to the fact that women were not permitted to vote—the nineteenth amendment to the Constitution, which provided women's suffrage in 1920, had not yet been implemented. Davis had studied at the University of Chicago, with Thorsten Veblen. (Freedman, 1981, pp. 132-133). John Dewey was also at the University of Chicago, "developing his progressive philosophy and practice of teaching at his famous Laboratory School" (Tyack, 1974, p. 178). At Bedford Hills, classes were offered in academic, industrial, and recreational subjects, physiology and sex hygiene. A staff member was assigned to manage "out-door work." Davis wrote that "Our efforts are to fit girls for life and not to pass examinations." Classes in machine knitting and hat making began in 1903, and by 1904 typing and stenography were offered. At that time these were male-dominated careers. Soon, courses in carpentry, cobbling, painting, and book binding were included in the industrial education curriculum. (Freedman, 1981, pp. 132-133). ⚿

1907   In his book *Administration and Educational Work of American*
(cont'd.) *Juvenile Reform Schools*, **David S. Snedden** wrote

> The juvenile reform school has not sprung from
> our public school system but has grown partly in
> connection with charity and philanthropy, and partly
> in connection with the departments of justice and
> penology....The educational work of juvenile reform
> schools has had few points of contact with the general
> system of public and private education of this country.
> The problems to be worked out have been so special
> and peculiar as to make it impossible for the workers
> to find in the public school system much of suggestion.
> (Dell'Apa, 1973b, pp. 9-10).

Snedden found that

> what is commonly termed physical education...
> [originated with] gymnasium work and military
> drill, because workers in the institution feel that the
> entire round of physical education is a vastly bigger
> subject than any series of specific exercises, and is
> largely connected with the wider subjects of nurture,
> cleanliness, regular physical work, and regular rest...
> (Snedden, 1907, p. 64).

"The problem that confronts the institution is to make [military
education] an effective means of education without allowing the
exercises to fall into distaste." The military education program was
considered very successful at the Michigan School for Girls. (p. 146).
Snedden reported that the "system of alternation [between vocational
and academic education] is commended highly and the belief expressed
that the public schools will eventually find it to their advantage to adopt
the same system." Basic skills instruction was also recommended,
because of student deficiencies in the Three Rs, and because "these
subjects lend themselves most readily to the disciplinary atmosphere of
the institution." (p. 158). Snedden discussed the George Junior Republic
(see 1895 entry), and another similar institution, Thompson's Island
Farm School of Boston.

> The Cottage Row [at Thompson's Island] is a series of
> small buildings begun by the boys in 1888 and since
> owned by a boy's corporation. Here trades are practiced
> and a full-fledged business system is maintained. Self-
> government is maintained, a band and boys' trading
> establishment is carried on, and in other respects the
> Cottage Row is made effective as a means of discipline
> and training in moral independence. (p. 144).

1907　In general, Snedden recommended that public schools replicate
(cont'd.)　many aspects of reform school education programming because (a)
correctional education courses were relevant, especially with regard
to industrial education, and (b) reform school student classification
systems were much more useful than those of the public schools
(Snedden, 1907, pp. 202-203). There was great interest among urban
school reformers like Snedden in the results of compulsory education
in juvenile institutions. ⌒

The U.S. attorney general instructed the McNeil Island Federal
Penitentiary administration "to acquire the necessary equipment and
begin taking fingerprints as the official new identification system."
The fingerprint technique had been known for decades, but not often
practiced.

> The generally used method for systematic identification
> of criminals had been the set of elaborate physical
> measurements developed by Alphonse Bertillon of
> the French police. Prisons in this country, including
> McNeil Island, were well aware of the Bertillon system,
> but using it regularly was another matter. It required
> equipment, staff training, and a fair amount of time
> in taking and recording the measurements of each
> person...it was...Mark Twain who did much to bring
> fingerprinting into the popular consciousness and
> acceptance. In 1894 he published *Pudd'nhead Wilson*, a
> novel which primarily dealt with some touchy racial
> issues. But it was also a detective story, and a major
> element in the plot was the hobby pursued by the
> central character who liked to collect 'fingermarks' on
> glass slides. (Keve, 1984, p. 147).

In 1894, fingerprinting had been a major topic at the first annual
convention of the National Chiefs of Police Union, in St. Louis. Soon
after the convention, former Chicago police chief Robert McClaughry
became warden at the new Leavenworth Federal Penitentiary. "During
October 1904, McClaughry and Sergeant Ferrier and the warden's
son, William McClaughry, systematically recorded the fingerprints
of all the inmates at Leavenworth, providing thereby the basis for a
Justice Department identification file of all federal prisoners." By 1903
the New York State prison system was beginning to use fingerprints."
(pp. 147-148). ⌒

Burlington City, Iowa librarian **Miriam E. Carey** was appointed
"Supervising Librarian" for the Iowa State Board of Control, in charge
of institutional libraries. She had been working since 1903 to have the
post established—the year she got the Board of Control to declare: "We
seek to provide each institution with a good working library suited to

1907   the needs of its inmates." The supervising librarian position had been
(cont'd.) created in 1905, through a joint effort by institutional superintendents
and the State Board of Control. (MacCormick, in Roberts, 1973, p. 319).
In 1907 Carey presented a paper on institution libraries to the Minnesota
Library Association, and by 1908 she was asked to relocate in that state
(Jones, 1938, p. 176—see 1909 entry). ⌒⌒

The average attendance at Minnesota's Stillwater Prison
school was 164, of which 48 were compelled to attend and 116 attended
voluntarily. There were 14 classes, with a program that corresponded to
the State's primary and grammar school system. Correctional education
was under the supervision of the Stillwater City superintendent of
public instruction. In his 1909 book about convict life at the Prison,
W.C. Heilbron wrote that "The prison that now neglects suitable
educational facilities for the instruction of its inmates is considered
behind the times." The Stillwater Prison school operated eight months
each year. "To the ambitious man there is plenty of opportunity for self-
improvement." (Heilbron, 1909, pp. 78-79). ⌒⌒

Suerken, Gehring, and Stewart later wrote that the distinguishing
feature of a correctional school district is that

the state department of education (state education
agency) recognizes it as a local education agency.
This recognition is based on staff qualifications and
adherence to state education laws and regulations. In
turn, recognition brings all the rights, privileges, and
duties of a local education agency. (Suerken, Gehring,
and Stewart, 1987, p. 84).

These conditions were satisfied with State of New Jersey legislation—
Chapter 65, Section 8, Laws of 1907—introduced by Assemblyman
John Groel, which required that correctional school rooms should be
provided and supervised "by a board to be known as the State Prison
School Board." (Norcott, 1979, pp. 76-77). The Act was implemented in
1909, accompanied with $2,500 for start-up costs. It gave the new School
Board authority to (a) establish school rules, subject to approval by the
prison Board of Inspectors, (b) appoint teachers and fix their salaries
and terms of employment, (c) purchase textbooks, equipment, and
supplies, and (d) prescribe the curriculum, equivalent to that provided
by elementary schools around the State. Teachers were required to
hold New Jersey certification; the head teacher could not be an inmate;
any inmate could be enrolled, with the Keeper's written permission;
operational funds were provided directly from the State Treasury. The
school district was required to submit its annual report and all proposed
curriculum changes to the State Board of Education. (Norcutt, 1979—
see entries for 1919, 1923, and 1969). ⌒⌒

1908 — The Elmira *Reformatory Yearbook* included this information on the 8,000 prisoners who had been incarcerated there since 1876:

> 25 percent gave evidence of previous physical injuries and disabilities; 22.7 percent were either ill or bore symptoms of disqualifying illnesses; 12.8 percent had defective eyesight, 5.4 percent defective hearing, and 57.8 percent had defective teeth; 19.9 percent were tuberculous and 43.7 percent were afflicted with some form of venereal disease. (Brockway, 1969/1912, p. 217).

"The examiner...reported...37.4 percent as the ratio of prisoners received whom he adjudged to be mentally defective" (p. 218). 🌄

The social composition of public schools was in transition. The U.S. Immigration Commission reported that 43 percent of all urban teachers were second-generation immigrants—"but almost six-sevenths of those came from the British Isles, Germany, and Canada (non-French)." (Tyack, 1974, p. 233). The Commission "counted more than sixty nationalities and discovered that 58 percent of all students had fathers who were born abroad." (p. 230). What Tyack called "Anglo-conformity," "assimilation," and "Americanization" of the immigrant were typical, and many school textbooks were "aimed" at foreigners. He reported that for some teachers, "nothing less would satisfy them than assaulting all forms of cultural difference, than creating a sense of shame at being 'foreign.'" (p. 235). In New York City

> From 1899 to 1914 there was a 60 percent increase in school enrollment. In September 1897, 500 children clamored to gain admission to P.S. [Public School #] 75 but were turned away; the building, built for 1,500 pupils, already contained 2,000. On a single day after the arrival of a steamer as many as 125 new children would apply to P.S. 110. In 1905 the *New York Times* estimated that from 60,000 to 75,000 children were denied admission to school for lack of space... (p. 230).

By 1913 the U.S. Commissioner of Education

> observed that 'for the enrichment of our national life as well as for the happiness and welfare of individuals we must respect their ideals and preserve and strengthen all of the best of their Old World life they bring with them. We must not attempt to destroy and remake— we can only transform. Racial and national virtues must not be thoughtlessly exchanged for American vices. (pp. 238-239).

1908
(cont'd.)

John Daniels, a sociologist who traveled all over the nation studying biculturalism, wrote in 1920 that 'if you ask ten immigrants who have been in America long enough to rear families what American institution is most effective in making the immigrant part and parcel of American life, nine will reply 'the public school.' (p. 241).

Some educators "believed that the 'new immigrants' were genetically inferior and hence beyond the power of the environment. Some believed that schooling could not overcome the terrible effects of poverty" (p. 232). Although not new immigrants, some educators afforded African American students the same treatment that foreigners received.

In 1928 a Cincinnati principal, Mary Holloway, studied how to relate her junior high school to a black community characterized by 'low economic status... crowded living conditions, false standards of conduct, and general lack of intelligence.' One important task, she thought, was proper guidance about sex, since over half the girls first learned the facts of life from friends, meaning that 'but a small minority have a sane, healthy attitude toward the subject because of a lack of scientific knowledge and terminology on the part of the informants.' (p. 219).

Cincinnati superintendent of schools Dyer told the education staff "Up here on the hill, in a wealthy suburban district...is a grammar school. Its organization, administration and course of study must necessarily differ from that other school, located in the heart of the factory district." (p. 195). Tyack later put some of these events into a larger perspective. So

hopeful were Americans that education could provide equality of opportunity—an equal chance at the main chance of wealth—that only a handful perceived the problem stated by **Merle Curti** in 1935: 'Above all the privileged classes expected the free public school to increase wealth, secure their property, and prevent revolution, while the lower classes thought that popular education would break down class barriers, lift them into the ranks of the rich and bring about, in short, substantial equality.' Curti doubted that the schools could do both tasks. (pp. 87-88; emphasis added—see 1947 entry). 🔺

1909 — **Katharine Bement Davis** completed an eight year study of more than 600 prostitutes at Bedford Hills Reformatory for Women. She reported

154

1909 that 15% were feeble minded and that "degenerate strains appeared
(cont'd.) in the heredity of 20%." She also pointed out that 50% were not fully
literate, and that most were from large, urban families. (Freedman, 1981,
p. 117). During the next few years, **Jean Weidensall** studied Bedford
Hills inmates for her book, *Mentality of the Criminal Woman*. Weidensall
found that incarcerated women had more conflicts than most females
while in school, less formal education, and fewer motivations to work.
She also found that career prostitutes had no "unusual gift or impelling
sex impulse." (p. 119). Weidensall was a graduate of the University of
Chicago (p. 118—see 1907 entry). ⌒

    Miriam Carey became the "Institutional Organizer" of the
Minnesota Public Library Commission. She also served as chairperson
of the American Library Association Committee on Hospital and
Institution Libraries. (MacCormick, in Roberts, 1973, p. 319—see 1913
entry). Her annual report of the 14 Minnesota institutional libraries
was the first complete record of correctional education library progress
in any state. Carey's job was "to pay regular visits to each library,
establish records, introduce a uniform system of classification, provide
statistics by means of charging systems as well as records, and stimulate
reading by the selection of books suitable to each institution." (Jones,
1938, p. 176). ⌒

    Based on the model that had been established at Elmira
Reformatory, some institutional schools gradually acquired facilities
intended for educational purposes. For example, in 1909 a building at
Philadelphia's Cherry Hill Prison was "set aside for school purposes"
(Teeters and Shearer, 1957, p. 160). ⌒

1910 — Attention was focused on remedies to alleviate the prostitution
problem during a nationwide "white slave scare" (Freedman, 1981,
p. 118). Across the U.S., many expressed concern for the welfare of
prostitutes. ⌒

    Jessie Donaldson Hodder became superintendent of
Massachusetts' Framingham Women's Reformatory. See entries for
1880, 1882, and 1900. She had served as the matron at the Lancaster State
Industrial School for Girls (see entries for 1856 and 1868) and a counselor
for unwed mothers. Hodder "brought a new education and scientific
spirit to bear" at Framingham, and sought to replace moral reform with
academic and occupational training. (Freedman, 1981, pp. 135-136). In
1913 she hired **Dr. Edith Spaulding** to serve as the resident Framingham
physician. Spaulding's work supported the views expressed by the
Bedford Hills Laboratory for Social Hygiene (see 1911 entry), "that low
intelligence alone did not cause crime." Instead, it was related to "a
network of causes and effects, mental, physical, and social, interwoven
and interactive." (p. 119). Spaulding found that environmental factors
such as parental death, incest, poverty, prostitution or alcoholism in

1910   the home, lack of parental supervision, and hereditary handicaps
(cont'd.) played significant roles (p. 120). By 1915 Hodder expanded the school
to include physical fitness programs, but her requests for vocational
education funds and a gymnasium were consistently rejected. Together,
Jessie Hodder and **Katharine Bement Davis** advised the site selection
committee for the Connecticut State Reformatory. (p. 136—see 1931
entry).

   The International Prison Congress was held in Washington,
D.C. (Brockway, 1969/1912, p. 135). The participants studied three
prison management systems that developed from three institutions in
New York State: Auburn Prison, Elmira Reformatory, and the George
Junior Republic (Holl, 1971, p. 223). The Congress formally sanctioned
the indeterminate sentence system (Brockway, 1969/1912, p. 135).

   The New Jersey legislature established a female correctional
institution. Named Clinton Farms, it opened in 1913. By 1914 each
cottage was managed by an elected inmate government, and classes
were held in domestic science, institutional sewing, and "outdoor
farmwork." In 1930 a beauty school was added. (Freedman, 1981,
p. 137).

   In England, correctional education was usually offered in the
cells, for a quarter of an hour at a time, two to three times per week.
Classes were only allowed in convict prisons. Previous Home Secretaries
had recommended lectures, debates, and discussions. **Winston
Churchill**, who had been imprisoned as a Boer War reporter and now
served as Home Secretary, also recommended concerts. (Banks, 1958,
pp. 21-22—see entries for 1919, 1923, and 1927).

1911 — A survey on prostitution revealed that "the barometer of crime rises as
that of prosperity falls, and this is particularly true as regards the crimes
of women." **Kate Richards O'Hare**, who later became a prisoner herself,
emphasized the "vicious results of women's economic dependency."
(Freedman, 1981, p. 124). **John D. Rockefeller** chaired a grand jury
investigating prostitution.

> The millionaire moralist wanted to eliminate the social
> evil and decided to create an Institute, the Bureau
> of Social Hygiene, to study the problem. Impressed
> by a pamphlet **[Katharine Bement] Davis** wrote...
> Rockefeller invited her to join the board of his bureau.
> At Davis' suggestion Rockefeller chose Bedford Hills as
> the home of the Bureau's Laboratory of Social Hygiene.
> (Freedman, 1981, p. 117).

He purchased 81 acres of farmland and leased the land and its
buildings to the women's reformatory for five years. "During those

years the laboratory employed a staff of up to twenty women social scientists." **Jean Weidensall**—Davis had hired her as the Reformatory psychologist—became the Laboratory manager. (pp. 117-118; emphasis added—see entries for 1912 and 1916). ⚈

William George's first book was published, *The Junior Republic: Its History and Ideals*. The Introduction was written by **Thomas Mott Osborne** (see 1913 entry), who insisted that "a good book needs no introduction," (Osborne, in George, 1911, p. vii), but that "Mr. George is learning new things all the time."

> Mr. George had really discovered...a new application of a very old principle—nothing less than <u>Democracy</u> itself applied to a very puzzling problem—with results that were wonderfully, startlingly successful...'a laboratory experiment in Democracy'....I ask....Why should training in citizenship, the necessary function for every citizen in a Democracy, be confined to the children at the George Junior Republic? Why is it not desirable in the schools my children attend?...Mr. George opened my mind to the possibility of the same principle being used as a basis for an intelligent and <u>reforming </u>Prison System—a system which should be social sanitary drainage—not merely a moral cesspool. At first I laughed at the idea; then I saw the Truth... the Junior Republic is but one brilliant example of... the Democracy which is a political expression of the Golden Rule....I hope I may live to see the day when in every school and college in the land alongside of the standard of Scholarship may be raised the standard of Citizenship....Gladstone said: 'It is liberty alone that fits men for liberty.' (Osborne, in George, 1911, pp. ix-xii; emphases in original).

In his book, George explained the Republic way of life to a group of youngsters: you will

> accept frankly existing conditions and you will meet and grapple with them, as if you were at the age of twenty-one, instead of being a few years younger. You will not learn by theory, but by actual experience to meet the problems. There will be no 'isms' tolerated in your little commonwealth, except straight out and out, unadulterated 'Americanism.' (George, 1911, pp. 191-192).

By this time there were several institutions built on George's model, "the Carter Republic at Redington, Pa., and the National Republic at

Annapolis Junction, Maryland, this latter supported by the people of Baltimore and Washington" and one in Litchfield, Connecticut (p. 316). George's book contains a manual for starting new Republics. In 1908 "the National Association of Junior Republics was formed in New York City." George aspired to assist in the

> establishment of at least one Junior Republic within every state of our union which should be open to all boys and girls who were physically and mentally sound from all classes of society, preference, however, to be given to those who most needed its benefits. (p. 137).

Central to "the great art of running the Republic was not to run it at all" (p. 318—see 1895 entry). ⌒

Immigrants flooded into the U.S. "Ethnic succession" applied when the condition in which the most recently arrived immigrants were considered the most retarded, and were most criminal.

> Joseph Van Denburg reported that [public] secondary students in New York whose fathers were born in the United States, Russia, England, and Germany contributed disproportionately large numbers to the high school population, while children of Irish and Italian fathers were poorly represented. Studies during the 1920's also showed substantially higher high school retention rates for the same groups than for children of Irish, Italian, and Polish parents. (Tyack, 1974, p. 244).

In 1909 Leonard Ayer's book *Laggards in Our Schools* presented an analysis of what we now call the drop out problem (p. 200). In part, Ayer reported on immigrant faith in schooling:

> ...nationwide there were forty-four illiterate native white children of native parents compared with only nine per 1000 among the white children of immigrants. Likewise, 72 percent of second generation children and 69 percent of foreign-born children aged five to fourteen were in school in comparison with 65 percent of children of native parentage. Much of the national discrepancy, of course, resulted from minimal schooling of southern whites, but in most northern cities the attendance of immigrants' children equaled or excelled that of the native born. (p. 242).

> By 1950 the second generation of white immigrants not only ranked higher in occupational prestige than

the first generation but they had more than their proportionate share of white-collar jobs in the entire labor force. It could be argued, then, that through his children the immigrant shared in the American dream of success. (pp. 244-245). ⌒

1912 — After 1912 the notion of a female criminal type came into disrepute, and the interplay of social forces was emphasized. Studies by sociology authors **Frances Kellor** and **Jean Weidensall** (see 1911 entry) supported this view. Many female sociologists argued that traditional "women's work" was an incentive to crime (Freedman, 1981, p. 121—see 1895 entry). ⌒

    Zebulon Brockway's book *Fifty Years of Prison Service* was published. Much of it focused on educational innovations at the Detroit House of Correction, the Detroit House of Shelter, and Elmira Reformatory. Brockway wrote that "The best behaved prisoner is often the worst citizen" (Brockway, 1969/1912, p. 406), and "I should rate the prisoners as non-moral rather than immoral" (p. 222). He wrote that "Prisoners came imbued with the idea that they were imprisoned for punishment, and this idea, until it could be removed, provided a hindrance to their interest and progress in the means adopted for reformation..." (p. 167). Brockway said that inmates must have the opportunity to fail, as well as to succeed—"a certain range of personal responsibility and goal-setting ability" (Brockway, 1969/1912, p. 310). **Tom Murton** developed this theme in his 1976 book *The Dilemma of Prison Reform*. **Thomas Mott Osborne** (see 1913 entry) met with Brockway while he was superintendent of Elmira Reformatory (Osborne, 1924a, p. 2), and later became a great prison reformer himself. In his lecture on "The Ideal of A Prison System," at the Cincinnati Prison Congress of 1870, Brockway had said that "In administering a prison, the intellectual education of all classes must take more prominent place, and the education of adult prisoners must not be neglected." (Brockway, 1969/1912, p. 407). **Austin MacCormick** picked up on this phrase—as well as a number of central ideas that Brockway had discussed, in his 1931 book *The Education of Adult Prisoners*. ⌒

    A chance situation emotionally impacted a man who, as a result, changed his life to become a major prison reform and correctional education contributor.

    One day in 1912, while confined to his home by illness, [**Thomas Mott Osborne**] read **Donald Lowrie**'s *My Life in Prison*. This book stirred Osborne to his depths. It crystallized all of his previous experience and reflections. The problem became a matter of increasing moment in his life and ultimately came to dominate all of his public career. After that, every time he appeared

159

in public to deliver an address he chose to speak about prisons and prison problems. His unusual gift of speech had made him much sought after as a lecturer, and his continuous stirring of public discussion contributed to raising the whole question of prison reform in the State of New York. When William Sulzer became governor in 1913 he announced that he would attempt the reorganization of the state penal system, and Osborne suggested that he appoint a prison commission. The governor countered by offering Osborne the chairmanship of the commission. So it came about that Thomas Mott Osborne, rich in experience, possessed of broad sympathy and profoundly concerned with basic questions of penal administration, was given the official opportunity to do what he could about it. (Tannenbaum, 1933, p. 63; emphasis added—see 1913 entry). ⌒

In the January, 1912 *Outlook*, **Theodore Roosevelt** wrote

I recently visited the Junior Republic....I had expected to be pleased and interested but my interest and pleasure far outran my expectations....Mr. George's theory is that any boy or girl, man or woman, of sufficient strength of character can be taught, or to speak more accurately, can teach himself or herself, that good citizenship is the only kind of citizenship worth having even from the individual's own standpoint. The place is a manufactory of citizens, men and women, and I do not know any place better worth visiting nor any place better calculated to produce in the mind of the visitor a healthy modesty about drawing conclusions too rapidly from any set of observations.... (in George, 1937, p. 41).

Elsewhere, Roosevelt wrote

You [George] are doing the very things I am trying to uphold: The dignity of labor, the principles of right and wrong, and the splendid, energetic way in which you set about it has won my respect and esteem. This makes for what we are trying to do, in teaching each man self-support and to work for decent government. (George, 1937, pp. 56-57). ⌒

A book by **William George** and **L.B. Stowe** appeared, *Citizens Made and Remade*. In part, George confirmed that "The art of running a Junior Republic is not to run it at all" (George and Stowe, 1912, p.

1912   117—see 1895 entry). "In these communities [Junior Republics] youth
(cont'd.) learn to govern themselves by governing themselves, learn to support
         themselves by supporting themselves. In short, they learn to live by
         living..." (p. 182). ⌒

         During the decade after 1912, 56 cities established departments
to monitor local public school teacher certification (Tyack, 1974, p. 186).
"In 1900 only two states had specialized credentials; by 1930 almost
all states had elaborate certification laws" (p. 185). In 1885 "normal
departments" in high schools provided teacher training (p. 58). "Less
than half of the teachers in 1947 had completed a college education..." (p.
274). By 1966 "93.4 percent of all public school teachers had bachelor's
degrees or higher" (p. 269). ⌒

1913 — **Thomas Mott Osborne**, former mayor of Auburn, New York and
         chairman of the State Commission on Prison Reform (see 1912 entry),
         disguised himself as Inmate Tom Brown to learn first hand about
         conditions at Auburn Prison (Chamberlain, 1935).

> The voluntary imprisonment received nation-wide
> attention and brought the whole question of the
> improvement in our penal system to the surface as
> it had never been before. Osborne became a national
> figure and the prison problem a matter of wide interest
> and discussion. That alone would have justified the
> week spent behind the prison walls. But it gave Mr.
> Osborne something more immediate to his purpose—
> the confidence of the prisoners....Something new,
> something different, was about to take place and the
> prisoners felt that whatever was to come their part in
> the matter would be significant and important. The
> very prison atmosphere seemed charged with plan
> and purpose... (Tannenbaum, 1933, pp. 69-71).

Within a few weeks Osborne had facilitated the implementation of the
Mutual Welfare League, an inmate-run organization which governed
most prison activities, with the consent of the warden. The League
was based on the George Junior Republic model, with which Osborne
was involved as a board member (see 1895 entry). Homosexual rapes,
assaults, and the drug traffic diminished substantially at Auburn
after the League was established, and prison industries production
increased dramatically. Osborne, who already had a national reputation
as the reform politician who revolted against New York's Tammany
Hall, now focused on the prison reform movement. His emphasis on
deterrence plus rehabilitation was expressed by a school of thought that
he called the New Penology. Osborne sought to transform correctional
institutions into education-oriented operations, where inmates learned
about (a) democracy, (b) earning their own way, (c) cooperation,

1913   and (d) responsibility, through practical application on a daily basis.
(cont'd.) (Chamberlain, 1935). ⚊

Osborne was not alone in his unusual procedure for implementing prison reform. Several women also embarked on the same strategy.

> In November 1913, **Madeline Zabriskie Doty**, a member of the New York State Commission on Prison Reform, together with **Elizabeth C. Watson**, voluntarily spent a week in confinement at Auburn Prison—Women's Division. Their identity was unknown to either staff or inmates. Both were committed... as Maggie Martin and Lizzie Watson. Supposedly each had been sentenced to serve 18 to 30 months for forgery. (Baker, 1985, p. 20; emphasis added).

Their joint report revealed rather extreme conditions, and resulted in some improvements. (p. 20). At a subsequent meeting Doty and the prisoners decided to establish the Daily Endeavor League, "its color emblem a blue bow." A charter was prepared, representatives were voted in from each housing unit, and a president was elected. "Participation in the League turned the interest of the women toward the improvement of conditions from their prior sole concern with personal woes. A reign of good behavior resulted...Sunday...recreation ....Correspondence and visiting rules were liberalized..." (p. 20). ⚊

Warden John Leonard founded Maryland Penitentiary's first formal education program. Directed by the chaplain, the school had three parts: (a) for male illiterates, (b) for female illiterates, and (c) a correspondence school. By 1918 it included an auto mechanics course. (Roberts, 1971, p. 9). ⚊

Miriam Carey was promoted to supervisor of Minnesota institutional libraries (MacCormick, in Roberts, 1973, p. 319—see 1928 entry). In Minnesota, and in corrections throughout the U.S., Carey would later be known as the founder of an important dynasty of professional leaders in the prison library movement. ⚊

1914 — **Katharine Bement Davis** left Bedford Hills Reformatory to become the New York City Commissioner of Correction (Freedman, 1981, p. 117). During her tenure at the Women's Reformatory, Davis had steadfastly refused to segregate the institution according to race (p. 139). ⚊

Thomas Mott Osborne (see 1913 entry) was appointed warden of New York State's Sing Sing Prison (Chamberlain, 1935). "Sing Sing had but recently been through a series of one of its periodic disturbances, riots, and fires. The [former] warden was charged with

162

1914   graft and was forced to resign..." (Tannenbaum, 1933, p. 104). Regarding
(cont'd.) his appointment as warden, Osborne later wrote: "Had I been offered
        the presidency of China, I should not have been much more surprised"
        (Osborne, 1975/1916, p. 205). A Mutual Welfare League chapter was
        started there, based on the Auburn Prison model (Chamberlain, 1935).
        Osborne helped to establish an educational unit at Sing Sing, known as
        the Mutual Welfare Institute. It was

> initiated by an inmate who succeeded in enrolling
> between 80 and 90 percent of the inmates. Subject
> matter was limitless: if a prisoner could teach the
> desired subject to another who wished it, the class
> was authorized. The students erected a special school
> building to house the overflow of classes. The school
> staff met regularly to discuss educational policy and
> methods. (Murton, 1976, p. 205).

Osborne's own account of school enrollment differed from Murton's.
He reported that "a third of the entire population is enrolled" in evening
classes. However, he also reported that

> Even if the prisoner has not been a member of one or
> more of the evening classes...he has been intellectually
> stimulated by the new system. The politics of the League,
> the hearings before the two courts...arouse endless
> discussion. The meetings of the Board of Delegates...
> give valuable exercise always to mind, as well as
> sometimes to lungs. It is really true...that men are too
> busy and interested to plan escape or to let their minds
> dwell upon evil... (Osborne, 1975/1916, p. 225). ⌒

The San Quentin Department of Education was established.

> The University of California sent several of its professors
> to the prison to study the possibilities of developing a
> program of education. At first a sporadic and rather
> ineffective lectureship was established and certain
> professors came and went. This was arranged on a
> week-end visiting scheme, and as usual the professors
> were impressed by the prisoners' attentiveness, but
> so far as we know little resulted. Shortly thereafter
> the University of California provided the prison with
> the correspondence course facilities of the University.
> Students at the prison who were interested in studying
> University of California correspondence courses were
> permitted to enroll without cost. Lessons written by
> the prisoners were returned to the University, where
> they were graded (Shuder, in MacCormick, 1938, p.1).

1914   In 1933, as a result of the Depression budget shortfalls at the University,
(cont'd.) the Prison assumed responsibility for the program with a staff of inmate
        "assistant readers." It "worked out splendidly," and was reported in
        the 1938 issue of *Correctional Education*. (p. 1—see 1938 entry). ⌂

1915 — **Austin MacCormick** committed himself to Maine State Prison as a
        "forger," in order to "learn the prison business." Only the warden knew
        that he had not been actually sentenced (Wright, 1980, p. 61). ⌂

        Many of the concerns we have regarding intelligence testing
        and standardized tests in general had not yet developed. **William
        Healy**, editor of the new *Journal of Delinquency*, wrote

        > The entrance of psychology into the field of delinquency
        > problems is a thoroughly accomplished fact. From this
        > most satisfactory advance in psychological effort there
        > can be no retreat...it is clear that much will be gained
        > for a long time from trying a variety of methods of
        > approach to the problems, for instance by inventing
        > and standardizing new tests and systems of tests for
        > mentality of all grades. There is much, also, to be
        > hoped from the development of research along many
        > other lines than the mere giving of intelligence tests
        > to delinquents and the making of mental diagnoses.
        > (Dell'Apa, 1973b, p. 16). ⌂

        The "multi-factor" approach to criminality became popular,
        as some criminologists studied "criminals' family lives, educations,
        and economic conditions. Nevertheless, the concept of the defective
        delinquent remained powerful, and hard-core biological determinism
        waned only after the 1920's." (Freedman, 1981, p. 111). ⌂

        The library work that began with Miriam Carey in Iowa and
        Minnesota was gradually being replicated by interested states across
        the nation. In 1915 the American Library Association published the first
        edition of the *Manual for Institution Libraries* (MacCormick, in Roberts,
        1973, p. 319). ⌂

        The first prison correspondence course program was founded
        at California's San Quentin Prison (Wallack, 1939, p. 278—see 1914
        entry). Correspondence courses and distance learning later became
        a topic of continuing interest in correctional education delivery
        systems. ⌂

1916 — The Bureau of Social Hygiene at Bedford Hills Women's Reformatory
        was expanded. It now included a psychopathic delinquent women's
        hospital (Freedman, 1981, p. 119—see 1916 entry). ⌂

In his book *Society and Prisons*, **Thomas Mott Osborne** discussed the failure of various prison discipline systems: reformatories and earlier, the Pennsylvania and Auburn prison discipline systems.

> ...[R]eformatories have been deficient in only one thing—reform....No system for the punishment of criminals which leaves wholly out of consideration that the beings who are to be punished are human will ever be successful; and this is precisely where the reformatory system has come to grief. (Osborne, 1975/1916, p. 115).

The Pennsylvania

> system had approached the problem from the mental side; aiming to solve it by making men <u>think</u> right. The other system [Auburn] had approached the problem from the physical side; aiming to solve it by making men <u>act</u> right. Both failed because the problem of crime is primarily neither a mental nor a physical problem but a moral one. No man can be reformed except his conscience be quickened; unless there be established, either consciously or unconsciously, natural and healthy relations between the criminal and society—between the sinner and God. The successful prison system must approach the problem from the spiritual side; aiming to solve it by making men <u>feel</u> right...[T]hose who have watched most carefully the origin and development of the [Mutual Welfare] League feel that its substance is basic and eternal. They believe that the true foundation of a new and successful penology has at last been found. (pp. 185-186; emphases in original).

Comparing prisons and schools, Osborne wrote:

> no system that does not differentiate—no system that does not allow for the careful consideration, development and training of individuality, taking into full account each man's personal needs, is a fit system of education for a prison any more than it is for a school or college. (p. 222).

Osborne identified central questions about criminal justice: "Are you looking for immediate or for permanent results? Do you believe in discipline or in training? Do you wish to produce good <u>prisoners</u> or to prepare good <u>citizens</u>?" (p. 212; emphasis in original—see 1912 entry). "The lectures that make up *Society and Prisons* were delivered

1916   at Yale University as the 1916 Dodge lectures on the responsibilities of
(cont'd.) citizenship" (Giallombardo, in Osborne, 1975/1916, p. viii).

> Osborne disposes effectively on the concept of the
> criminal type that was a feature of popular superstition
> and academic criminology. He makes it clear that
> there is no such person as 'the criminal.' The criminal
> is essentially a human being, although there is, he
> maintains, a prison type that is created by prison
> conditions. (Giallombardo, in Osborne, 1975/1916, p.
> ix—see entries for 1876 and 1976).

> ...[T]here is a 'prison type',—the more shame to us who
> are responsible for it. Forth from our penal institutions
> year after year, have come large numbers of men,
> broken in health and spirit, white-faced with the
> 'prison pallor,' husky in voice—hoarse from disuse,
> with restless, shifty eyes and the timidity of beaten
> dogs. But these are creatures whom we ourselves have
> fashioned; the finished product of our prison system.
> (Osborne, 1975/1916, p. 50).

Regarding deterrence: "less depends upon the severity of a punishment
than upon the certainty of its infliction" (p. 71). Regarding correctional
officers, Osborne cited

> The brutality which is a perfectly natural consequence
> of the system. The nervous condition of the men, caused
> by the silence [of Auburn system prison management],
> the monotony and the espionage, carries with it an
> equally nervous condition of the guards. 'We stand on
> a volcano,' said one of the officers of Dartmoor prison
> to a writer from the London Times. 'If our convicts
> here had opportunity to combine and could trust one
> another, the place would be wrecked in an hour.' This
> nervousness of the guard makes him irritable and
> severe. He is afraid; and his fear engenders brutality;
> and brutality breeds revenge; the feeling of revenge
> and hatred for the prison authorities brings about more
> nervousness and greater fear; and so the vicious circle
> is complete. Every generation or so there is a revelation
> of prison tortures; and a scandalized community forces
> the legislature to pass a law forbidding some special
> form of punishment that the diabolical ingenuity of
> man has invented; only to have some new cruelty
> devised to take its place. (pp. 150-151).

<table>
<tr>
<td>1916
(cont'd.)</td>
<td>The underlying principles of [Osborne's] theory of prison reform center about the organization of inmate labor: [a] willing and efficient labor must be the foundation of a correctional system that insists it is preparing offenders to return to society; [b] in order for a man to work willingly, he must work voluntarily; [c] an inmate should receive a full day's pay for a full day's work; and [d] if the prisoner receives full pay, he should pay for his own treatment. In short, to be truly effective, prison labor must not only be voluntary, but 'fully remunerated.' The latter would make it possible for many inmates to support their families while in prison. These principles are the basis of Osborne's scheme of prison reform. There is to be no punishment except the deprivation of liberty; the prison's function is to reform, and it is to operate on democratic principles. The 'operation of the theory' was achieved through the Mutual Welfare League. (Giallombardo, in Osborne, 1975/1916, p. x).</td>
</tr>
</table>

Regarding the League, Osborne wrote "...the thing works...the thing works....In Auburn prison for more than two years, in Sing Sing prison for more than a year, the new system has been in operation and the thing works....it works" (Osborne, 1975/1916, pp. 222-233; emphases in original—see 1921 entry).

> It is not merely that vice has been materially diminished,—the matter goes far deeper than that; the very standards of conduct have undergone reconstruction. One of the men, as he was about to leave Sing Sing at the expiration of his term, came to say good-bye to the warden. 'Do you realize what it is that the League has done here?' said he. 'Let me tell you. It has started the men discussing the right and wrong of things, every day, from one end of the yard to the other.' If this be true,—if a prison can contain a sort of large class in social ethics—freely and naturally discussing the right and wrong of everyday happenings, is not that the most important thing of all? Because therein lies precisely that exercise of the conscience—just that practice in discrimination between right and wrong, between wise and foolish, that is necessary for those who have committed sin and need to cleanse their souls and patiently form new standards. (p. 229).

"Osborne's success with the Mutual Welfare League was largely due to his genius for developing personal relationships" (Giallombardo, in Osborne, 1975/1916, p. xiii). "The [League] delegates were filled

1916   with an enthusiasm which bore an almost religious character. They
(cont'd.) were pioneers of prison democracy...'it was up to them to show that
       they could behave themselves and act like gentlemen.'" (Osborne,
       1975/1916, p. 167). Osborne called it a "new movement" (p. 203), and
       "a new and genuinely scientific penology" (p. 15). Near the end of the
       book, Osborne wrote "he who asserts the impossibility of reform in any
       man forgets history and denies his religion." (p. 235). ☁

1917 — Support for eradicating the causes of prostitution, which began with
       the 1910 "white slave scare," now waned. With U.S. involvement
       in World War I, attention shifted toward protecting soldiers from
       venereal disease, and a new repression against prostitutes became
       the hallmark of public policy. (Freedman, 1981, p. 147—see entries for
       1919 and 1920). ☁

       Thomas Mott Osborne became warden of the U.S. Naval
Prison at Portsmouth, New Hampshire, with **Austin MacCormick** as
his assistant. Osborne came to Portsmouth directly from Sing Sing;
MacCormick directly from his role as instructor at Bowdoin College.
Osborne repeated his 1913 Tom Brown act, "enlisting" in the Navy and
becoming a "deserter." (Wright, 1980, p. 61). Austin MacCormick did
the same, and used the name "John Austin" (Callan, 1981). Tannenbaum
later reported that another man was also involved in the

> week as voluntary prisoners at the naval prison. Here
> he [Osborne] found the old system in full swing, with
> shaved heads, huge yellow and red numbers that
> disfigured the clothing of the prisoners, poor food and
> oppressive espionage. He himself was searched some
> fifteen times a day. In his report to the Secretary of the
> Navy he mentioned 'the inevitable tendency to treat
> prisoners as if they were not possessed of ordinary
> feelings....This lack of decent consideration causes
> certain of the sentries to speak to the prisoners in a
> most over-bearing and insulting manner—often being
> language which no man but a helpless prisoner could
> endure'....While awaiting orders to take command
> of the Naval Prison he wrote to the Secretary of the
> Navy: 'The purpose of my going to Portsmouth, as I
> understand it, is to work out a fundamental change in
> the purpose of the prison. It has been a prison; you wish
> me to make it a school. It has been a scrap heap; you
> wish me to make it one of humanity's repair shops.'
> That is what he proceeded to do on a scale never before
> attempted. In the time that Osborne was in charge of
> the prison he handled approximately 6,000 prisoners—
> without any guards within the prison enclosure...
> (Tannenbaum, 1933, p. 279).

1917   Under Osborne and MacCormick, the Portsmouth Naval Prison had
(cont'd.) a Mutual Welfare League, and no walls—but an excellent reputation
for effectively reforming Navy prisoners. **Franklin Delano Roosevelt**
(see 1933 entry), undersecretary of the Navy, supported Osborne in
this work, largely because rehabilitated inmates were needed for the
World War I effort (Chamberlain, 1935). Later Roosevelt, as president,
"drafted" MacCormick to manage military prisons in the Philippines
during World War II, and awarded him a special Presidential Medal of
Merit for his outstanding service. (Wright, 1980, p. 60). The following
story, in which Osborne was the Commandant and MacCormick was
the absent Executive officer, is relevant to the general organizational
climate of the Naval Prison during World War I.

> After the Mutual Welfare League had been in operation
> at the Portsmouth Naval Prison for over two years, my
> Executive Officer left for a few month's sea duty; and
> in his place Lieutenant C., an officer of long experience
> in the service, reported for duty at the prison. During
> the first day he looked about; found upwards of 2000
> prisoners, most of them living in barracks outside
> the prison—with no bolts or bars and no wall about
> the grounds; saw a number of prisoners go down to
> their work in the Navy Yard, accompanied by a few
> marine guards; saw the rest going about their duties at
> the prison without any guards at all; saw the working
> parties return and the guards march away to the
> marine barracks; saw the third-class prisoners entirely
> under the charge of their fellow prisoners of the first-
> class; saw, in short, an unguarded prison run by the
> prisoners. At the end of his first day, Lieutenant C. came
> into my office looking pale and disturbed. 'Commander
> Osborne,' he broke out, 'I can't stay here.' I looked up
> from my desk. 'What's the trouble?' 'I can't stay here,'
> he repeated; 'I'm scared to death. Why don't these men
> all run away? I would.' Now, don't get excited about
> it,' said I; 'sit down.' He did so; and as he dropped
> into a chair, he fairly groaned. 'I don't understand it.'
> 'Well,' said I, 'Lieutenant, I will tell you something.
> Please don't give me away; for this is a secret. <u>I don't
> understand it either</u>. I've been trying to understand it
> for six years—ever since I got into this prison game;
> and I haven't succeeded yet. However, don't let it
> worry you; it is not necessary that either of us should
> understand it. We know, as a fact, that they do not run
> away; and experience proves that we can proceed with
> perfect security upon that fact. Now you may explain
> it any way you like, but I may as well tell you that I
> shan't care a snap of my fingers for your theory; and

my theories are of no particular value or interest to you or any one else. Not only that; I have not a single theory or idea about this prison game that I am not ready to alter or throw away the moment it bumps up against a fact. We are learning new facts every day here; because we are dealing with real, live human beings—the most interesting things in the world. The Lieutenant seemed somewhat comforted; but as he glanced out of the window, the troubled look came again into his face. 'But you haven't any wall here, or even a fence!' 'No,' said I; 'we haven't; and I'll tell you why. When those barracks were built, they had a beautiful plan all mapped out with a high and heavy steel fence which could be electrified and protected by barbed wire; and this was to go on the water-side as well as the land-side and spoil that fine view, that does us all good to look at. I went to the Commandant and said: 'Admiral, for heaven's sake don't let them put up that monstrosity. If we have a fence that is hard to climb, of course my boys will all want to climb it. Put up a light wire fence that any fool can get over, and I'll see that they don't get over it.' So they put up that chicken-wire stuff that you see. 'Do you know what I have said several times at mass-meetings to these fellows here?' I continued. 'I have told them: "Of course you know and I know that it's dead easy to get away from this place. I should be ashamed of any one of you who couldn't escape from here.' But I always added: 'I should be ashamed of any one of you who did.' Do you know what is the number of escapes we have had here? Eight, out of over six thousand prisoners! And only think how easy it is! And we have had none at all since our last marine guards went over-seas and the prisoner police have been on the job. More than that, Lieutenant—' But all that is another story. If more people had seen the Mutual Welfare League in operation at the Naval Prison during the years 1917-21... (Osborne, 1924b, pp. 44-49; emphases in original). ⚯

George Ordahl reported the following facts in an article entitled "Mental Defectives and Juvenile Court," which appeared in the *Journal of Delinquency*:

[a] 25 percent of the minor dependents, 45 percent of the minor delinquents, and 75 percent of the adult delinquents examined for this study are feeble-minded. [b] If the feeble-minded and borderline group are combined then 45 percent of the minor dependents

and 60 percent of the minor delinquents are below average-normal intelligence. [c] In both the minor and major delinquent groups 60 percent of the parents, so far as data were available, are either alcoholic, immoral, feeble-minded, or insane. [d] The chief offenses of the boys are truancy, and offenses against property. That of the girls is immorality. [e] Boys below 14 years of age, judging from this study, apparently become delinquent because of a lack of proper home control; boys above this age because they have not the necessary intelligence to make needed adjustments. [f] The girls examined apparently became delinquent because they lacked the necessary intelligence or mental balance to control their impulsive tendencies. (Dell'Apa, 1973b, p. 17).

The U.S. Congress passed the Smith Hughes Act, to help fund vocational education (Smith, Aker, and Kidd, 1970, p. 474). Passage resulted from the tenacious efforts of a coalition which included philanthropist/industrialists, the National Association of Manufacturers, and chambers of commerce.

By 1910 the movement had won broad support, with endorsements from the NEA [National Education Association] and the American Federation of Labor (which had long been suspicious of the trade schools as sources of scab labor, but which apparently joined the movement in the hope of sharing in its control and improving the earnings of skilled labor). (Tyack, 1974, p. 189).

Industrial schools had been advocated by John Philbrick as early as 1861, for "a class of children, more or less numerous, which is too low down in the depths of vice, crime, and poverty, to be reached by the benefits of a system of public education." (pp. 69-70—see 1883 entry). In 1916 a Massachusetts principal prescribed vocational education for the "ne'er-do-well," but Tyack later suggested that other terms were often used to describe the vocational education student—"laggard," "slow learner," "retarded," "reluctant." "Hand-minded," and more recently, "disadvantaged." Normally, only 10% of local public school students were involved in vocational education, but educators were increasingly convinced "that the primary goal of schooling was to prepare youth for the job market..." (p. 190). Originally, the Smith-Hughes Act was not applicable to correctional education (MacCormick, 1931, p. 105). The process of opening up Federal vocational education funds for correctional education was initiated by Congress in 1963—see entry. In 1968 the Act was amended to include services to disadvantaged offenders. For years it was called

1917   the Vocational Education Act (Shearin, 1981), but it is now known as
(cont'd.) the Carl Perkins Act. ⚬

The Bolshevik Revolution had profound effects. For example, all of the incarcerated juveniles at a youth camp in the Ukraine simply ran away (Makarenko, 1973, vol. 1, p. 7). ⚬

1918 — Neither **Rockefeller** nor New York State continued to fund the Laboratory for Social Hygiene. That laboratory had been established at Bedford Hills Women's Reformatory in 1911 (Freedman, 1981, p. 141). ⚬

General W. St. Pierre Hughes, executive officer of the Canadian Penitentiary Branch, included a correctional education recommendation among his list of 15 areas for improvement: "#4. That a duly qualified, competent, certified school teacher be appointed to each of the six penitentiaries." The recommendations were published in 1919 and 1920. (Topping, 1929, p. 41). ⚬

Gradually, the innovations that had been implemented at showcase reformatories during previous years were now impacting correctional education around the country. For example, in 1918 the Maryland Penitentiary school was expanded to include elementary and secondary academic studies, automobile mechanics, and scientific agriculture (Roberts, 1973, p. 7). ⚬

Even in states with corrections systems dominated by contract labor arrangements, diversification was under way. A Virginia law authorized inmate instructors at the State Penitentiary (Virginia Code Commission, 1981). ⚬

After a political upheaval, the Prussian government recognized prisoners' rights to buy and read newspapers. During World War I, the Belgian prison paper *L'Effort vers le bien* was very successful. The German Principles of 1923 allowed inmates to buy approved newspapers at their own expense. In England newspapers were sometimes provided for recreation rooms, especially where progressive housing programs were in place. At the 1885 Rome International Prison Congress, the Spanish delegate had suggested that "an international prison weekly should be created, *Le Dimanche*." The pioneer summary sheet of outside news was Elmira Reformatory's *Summary*—see 1883 entry. "From the prisoner's point of view, however, no substitute can compete with the 'real thing.'" (Grunhut, 1973/1948, p. 244). ⚬

Things were changing, becoming more consolidated, in the local school systems. Important decisions, with lasting impacts, were being made.

| 1918 | A group of...[public school] educational leaders |
| (cont'd.) | formed the 'Cleveland Conference,' which agreed... |

that the time was ripe for 'a radical reorganization' of schooling and concluded that changes would 'go on in the haphazard fashion which has characterized our school history unless some group gets together and undertakes in a cooperative way to coordinate reforms. (Tyack, 1974, p. 1878).

School boards were getting smaller (p. 127), and their membership was steadily shifting to the ranks of the middle and upper classes (p. 141). Superintendents were acquiring more power within their organizations (pp. 144-145), and the number of system-wide support staff was increasing rapidly (p. 185). Uniform curricula received great emphasis (p. 45), and teachers were supposed to behave as little soldiers in a grand line/staff hierarchy of educational employees (p. 257).

Grass roots politics of education in the ward system could be defined as corruption or parochialism. Practically unchecked power to classify students and to differentiate the curriculum could be defined as the legitimate province of the professional expert. A shift of the method of selection of school boards to favor the upper-middle and upper classes could be explained as a means of getting 'better' public officials. The slogan 'get the schools out of politics' could disguise effective disfranchisement of dissenters. The quoted opinions of 'experts' could be used to squelch opposition. (p. 133).

"'Accountability' was a word they sometimes used to describe their goal; 'bureaucracy' was a negative label they pinned on features of the system they wished to change." (p. 167). The "application of scientific method" and "the professional training of school executives" were emphasized by George Strayer, of Teachers College, Columbia University.

By 1930 almost all influential schoolmen had become converts. The results were everywhere apparent: 'better organization of the administrative and supervisory employees into line and staff categories; the differentiation of the 'traditional elementary school and senior high school' into institutions like junior high schools, vocational schools, and junior colleges that 'provide unique opportunities for boys and girls who vary greatly in their ability to acquire skill and knowledge'; grouping of pupils by scientific tests; the expansion of high schools with multiple tracks until they enrolled 50 percent of students of high school

1918
(cont'd.)
age; extensive revision of the curriculum; the keeping of detailed records on students, from IQ's to physical history and vocational and recreational interests; and rapid upgrading of the standards of training for all professional personnel. The principle underlying such progress was 'recognition of individual differences' and consequent attempt 'to adjust our schools to the needs and capacities of those who are registered in them (p. 182). 𝄌

1919 — New York governor **Alfred E. Smith** directed superintendent of prisons Charles F. Rattigan to appoint a committee "to carry out a survey of all the institutions under this department." Rattigan assigned the chairmanship to **Adolph Lewisohn,** and the committee members were "Leaders in the fields of education, psychiatry, vocational training, medicine, administrators of correctional systems and institutions, representatives of manufacturers, labor organization leaders, jurists, and chaplains designated by the heads of the church organizations..." This was the first of three major citizen committees that would influence New York State correctional education in the 1920s and '30s. It was described as "the first [committee] ever to be appointed by the administrative head of the prison system, and never before had such a corps of experts in the several fields been called upon to assist." (Chenault, 1949-1951, p. 10). 𝄌

New Jersey's correctional school district (see entry for 1907) had developed a record of success. The Prison library was improved and expanded, with new collections in the Italian, Hungarian, and Polish languages; a night school was established, followed in 1919 by a day school with AM and PM, one and one-half hour sessions; correspondence courses were increased—especially in the summer months, during school vacation; enrollments rose, an effect of a new School recruitment program; a fully certified head teacher and two "sub-teachers" were hired, in addition to the moral instructors provided by previous legislation; the curriculum was gradually secularized, and included reading, writing, geography, arithmetic, citizenship, United States history, hygiene, and cultural programs; Americanization classes flourished; classroom space was expanded and a School office established; an educational diagnostic program was implemented by the new Psychology Department; a vocational education program was founded—using industrial sheet metal and machine shops; school assignments became as obligatory for inmates as work assignments; the separate cell study program was maintained. No disciplinary problems related to the School were reported. (Norcott, 1979). A psychology department was also established at the New Jersey State Prison in 1919, to help gather diagnostic information on prospective students. As part of a major literacy emphasis, daytime school assignments were authorized for the first time, and the library was expanded and

1919 improved. "Perhaps most importantly, the Education Department had
(cont'd.) evolved into an organized, progressive delivery system." (pp. 89-93—
see entry for 1969). ⌒

In *State v. Heitman*, a Kansas court permitted separate
sentencing policies according to gender. The decision was based on
the ideas that male and female crimes were two different problems,
and women were more reformable and could therefore benefit from
maximum sentences. (Freedman, 1981, p. 148). ⌒

Roman Catholic **Father Edward Joseph Flanagan**'s Boys Town,
outside Omaha, Nebraska established its

> ...first magazine—the *Boy's Town Home Journal*. It was
> printed by a shop in Omaha, but was written and
> edited by Father Flanagan and his boys. It was no great
> journalistic achievement, but it narrated events of the
> home, recorded gifts, and specialized on the back-yard
> sports. The *Journal* is no longer published, but today
> [1949] at Boys Town they print its direct descendant,
> the *Boy's Town Times,* a more professional job of editing,
> and produced on their own power presses. (Oursler
> and Oursler, 1949, p. 167). (See entries for 1929, 1934,
> 1948, and 1949.) ⌒

In England, 74 prison officers who went on strike with the
police were dismissed. The officers did not win bargaining rights until
1938. (Forster, 1981, p. 10). Notebooks and pencils "were first issued to
prisoners" (Banks, 1958, p. 25).

> After the First World War conspicuous efforts were
> made to work out an educational policy for English
> prisons. Local Educational Authorities were asked to
> lend certified teachers for elementary and continuation
> classes in institutions for young prisoners. Lectures,
> which the Departmental Committee of 1896 had
> tentatively recommended for the benefit of a few
> prisoners, were arranged on the initiative of the
> chaplains. In larger prisons the men were assembled,
> under the presidency of the chaplain, for debates and
> discussions. An important departure occurred in 1923,
> when, under the auspices of the Board of Education,
> the Adult Education Scheme was put into operation.
> Before the Second World War 400 men and women
> volunteered as teachers for evening classes after the
> hours of associated work. The subjects were educational
> in the wide sense of the word, including academic
> topics such as history, mathematics, and languages,

<table>
<tr>
<td>1919
(cont'd.)</td>
<td>vocational subjects such as shorthand, book-keeping, and needlework, and general subjects such as play-reading, music, and Bible study. In 1926-7 more than 10,000 prisoners were reached by this scheme. Local educational advisors co-operated with the Governors [wardens] in enlisting voluntary teachers and arranging classes. From time to time the teachers were invited to general conferences at the Home Office. (Grunhut, 1973/1948, p. 232).</td>
</tr>
</table>

"Much of the credit belongs personally to...**C.O.G. Douie**." Only 23 years old, he became the education advisor to many institutions. (Forster, 1981, p. 34). In 1922 experimental classes were held at Dorchester Prison "without the presence of a uniformed officer" (Banks, 1958, p. 28). "Unfortunately the war put a temporary end to...[the whole adult education] scheme" (Grunhut, 1973/1948, p. 232). 🐾

1920 — **Adolph Lewisohn** had hundreds of inmates interviewed, as input for his report—see 1919 entry. The document "covered more than 400 printed pages, including chapters on 'vocational training' and 'educational work in prison.'" (Chenault, 1949-1951, p. 10). Chenault later reported that "the prison school" system in New York State changed "little between 1850 and 1920," with the exception of the improvements implemented at Elmira Reformatory (p. 9). The following list presents some of Lewisohn's major findings: (a) Regarding vocational training, the committee was "impressed with the magnitude of the problem..." because "there was no such training in evidence in any prison." (b) Educational work was labeled

> a very minor affair...one would naturally expect that the school work would be one of the most important activities in these institutions. In fact one would think that educational work would take precedence over all other functions of a prison except possibly the productive work, or at least that production and training through education would be so closely related that it would be difficult to tell which was considered the more important. (p. 10).

(c) On the contrary, Lewisohn found that only "One paid teacher is provided for...each prison" (see 1847 and 1874 entries). (d) "His salary is about one-half of what a similar position involving equal possibilities would pay." (e) A "teacher is expected to work from eleven to eleven and one-half months a year with little or no opportunity to attend, and then only at his own expense, those meetings in which improvements in educational methods are considered." (f) He has "no expert supervisor to whom he is responsible, nor any course of study or teaching procedure to follow other than the assistance of a visiting inspector from the State

1920   Educational Department who has no authority to suggest or direct."
(cont'd.) (p. 10). The visiting inspector was **Dr. Hill**, who

> stood out strongly for placing education above
> production and has not approved of continuing the
> school work to the evenings. He states in common with
> some of the teachers that the men come to the evening
> school 'fatigued.' Observation...forces a smile at the
> word 'fatigued' [because it understates the situation].
> (p. 11).

> [(g) A] teacher has as his assistants only inmates who
> are often assigned to him because there is no other work
> open to them...the only inmate previously trained as a
> teacher, now in Auburn, has been 'promoted' to be a
> butler. (p. 11).

(h) "[If] an inmate is very much needed in the shops, he is not expected
to attend school. On the other hand, if he is not good anywhere else
around the prison he is sent to school." (i) The "books used are out-of-
date."

> [(j)] It seems hardly possible to believe that the State
> imprisons an illiterate for a term of years and then
> allows that man to be paroled without reference to his
> ability to read and write and understand the simplest
> English expressions, and yet such is a fact. (p. 11).

(k) The "books and...methods [are] intended for children." (l) The
convicts received compulsory attendance like

> patients unwillingly taking a hypodermic injection of
> some unwished serum. The guards sit or stand nearby
> to see that the full dose is received....Compulsory
> attendance is always possible and compulsory
> attention may be imposed by the guards, but no one
> can make to order compulsory thinking and mental
> growth. (p. 11).

In general, Lewisohn found that "Obviously the greatest force for good
in prison is education—education from every angle..." and that "prison
reform is an educational problem." He reported, however, that "Every
condition which should make prison education stagnant, uninspired,
unprogressive, exists today." (p. 11). The Adolph Lewisohn committee
recommended that "If they [prisoners] are excused [from work
assignments] they should be paid a wage while at school equivalent to
what they would earn in the shop..." In addition, the report included
this suggestion:

177

1920
(cont'd.)
The State should require every prisoner to read, write and speak our language before discharge. If the State is to compel, it must furnish opportunity for compliance.... The proper kind of teaching to illiterates will awaken their mind and spirit and lay a foundation for training and the broader elements of education. (p. 12).

Despite all of the committee's work and specific findings, "very few of the recommendations—and none pertaining to the educational program—received early favorable action." (p. 12—see entries for 1925 and 1930). ⚎

From 1918 to 1920 the U.S. Congress had appropriated over $400,000 for "construction, enlargement, repair, or equipment of reformatories...for...delinquent women and girls." Forty-three institutions were assisted through these funds. (Freedman, 1981, p. 147—see 1917 entry). ⚎

Few observers were conscious of the long history of prison system failure. But socialist organizer **Kate Richards O'Hare** (see 1911 entry) advocated that "Every existing prison should be abandoned as soon as possible, replaced with hospitals and prison farms and small industries." (Freedman, 1981, p. 146). ⚎

New evidence was emerging to counteract myths that had developed regarding the intelligence of criminals and prisoners. World War I mass intelligence testing helped to discredit notions which associated low IQ scores with potential deviancy (Freedman, 1981, p. 116). ⚎

"Mordecai Plummer introduced the use of inmate guards in the New Castle Workhouse in Delaware....This 'Plummer System' was abandoned in 1933 because of exploitation by inmate guards." It was adopted by other states, however, including Arkansas, Mississippi, Louisiana, (Murton, 1976, p. 192) and Texas. ⚎

Anton S. Makarenko was assigned by the chief of a local department of education to establish a new school for juvenile delinquents in the Ukraine. (Makarenko, 1973, vol. 1, p. 1). He began reading books on education (Makarenko, 1973, vol. 1, p. 19—see entries for 1917 and 1921). ⚎

1921 — As civil war raged around him, **Makarenko** established the Gorky Colony in the Ukraine. It was an agricultural camp, but none of the staff or inmates had any real knowledge of agriculture. The boys had to struggle to stay clothed and fed. Makarenko hired a number of teachers, and focused on developing a sense of community among the residents. There were many initial problems with nearby peasants

1921 and farmers. (Makarenko, 1973, vol. 1, p. 94). Problems soon plagued
(cont'd.) Gorky Colony: a typhoid epidemic, the death of a newborn infant, and
a hostile citizenry in the surrounding villages. By the end of the year,
however, some gifted students were sent to the "Rabfak" school, for
higher education. (vol. 1, p. 189). 🝗

The Virginia Penitentiary Board of Directors received letters
from American Federation of Labor president **Samuel Gompers**, and
prison reformer **Thomas Mott Osborne**—see 1913 entry. Gompers
wrote that

> The citizens of Virginia are to be congratulated on the
> evolution of the contract system in the penal institutions
> of the State and the introduction of the State-use
> system. The State-use system has been most strongly
> advocated by the organizations of labor. Thirty States
> have the system and the reports from all are that it has
> been most advantageous. The State-use system is the
> only honest system that can be followed in justice to
> free labor. (Virginia, 1922, p. 4).

Osborne's letter reviewed the findings that he made during a visit to
Richmond Penitentiary and Powhatan Prison Farm, and congratulated
the Board on "a most enlightened prison policy"—the establishment of
a prison government. The Board had developed that policy after "very
helpful conferences with Mr. Osborne during his stay in Richmond." In
the Board's words, the new policy would help

> the old idea that a prison is a place of torture and
> slavery [to] give way to the truer idea that it is a place
> of correction, where the inmate should be given every
> assistance to redeem himself. This does not mean that
> crime will be condoned nor criminals coddled. It means
> simply that your Board of Directors recognizes that
> reformative methods in the prison will beget greater
> returns for society than punitive methods. Furthermore
> it means that the new prison policy in Virginia will be
> to help the convict help himself; so that the convict
> who, relatively speaking, helps himself most will get
> the most help from the State; that upon release he may
> prove to be an asset for the State rather than a liability.
> (p. 9).

While Osborne found the new policy to be progressive, he noted that

> the foundation under your admirable reforms seems
> to me not yet a solid one—one upon which you can
> confidently proceed to complete your structure....If

we expect these men to be honest and useful citizens
when they are released from prison, we must certainly
give them a chance to form and practice, while they are
behind the walls, those qualities which are necessary
for good citizenship....The thing can be done, because
it has been done. I am not presenting a theory but
stating the facts of experience. I refer, of course to the
Mutual Welfare League, some of the remarkable results
of which I have told you. What you need here, in your
Penitentiary, Farm and Road Camps, in order to get
the greatest results from the work you have done and
are planning to do, is to have your prisoners form a
Mutual Welfare League. (pp. 9-10—see 1916 entry).

Also this year, religious director **R.V. Lancaster** reported that "Already
more than three thousand books have been donated to the library..."
(p. 23). But the real news was from the Education Department,
which was directed by **Clyde Busby**. "The educational work at The
Penitentiary had its beginning in September, 1920, when **Dr. J.A.C.
Chandler**, president of the College of William and Mary, at the request
of the Governor, appeared before the Penitentiary Board. He was asked
to recommend an educational program..." The report began with these
words: "In order to understand more fully the plan of procedure as
discussed in this report, it seems appropriate at the outset to refer
briefly to some of the principles prevailing in prison reform..." (p. 24;
emphasis added). The prison reform/correctional education link was
discussed in general terms. "In addition...there is a dullard to whom
society must likewise give special consideration. It happens too often
that he violates, or is used by others to violate, the laws of society
through ignorance." On another issue "The State must see to it that
children have the fundamentals of an elementary education if they can
take it, whether the parents wish it or not." (p. 25—see 1972 entry). A
very comprehensive 16 page correctional education needs assessment
followed. "The median education of the 182 white inmates is that of a
fifth grade in our elementary schools, and the median education of the
402 negro inmates is that of a second grade in our elementary schools."
(p. 30). The

first school...organized at the Penitentiary...had in it
two classes of approximately fifteen white men in each,
under an instructor who was a prison inmate. [See
1918 entry.] One class had men of 8 and 9 years and
the other men of 10 and 11 years mentality. Attendance
in these classes was entirely optional; in fact, it was
conditioned on good conduct. These classes were soon
followed by two other classes for negro inmates, with
optional attendance. The two groups of white men, as
originally organized, are still attending instruction. The

1921
(cont'd.)
negro classes have been reclassified. As an indication of the respect and appreciation of the men for this work, no violation of the rules has occurred in these classes... (p. 4).

The report concluded with a series of recommendations regarding methods to secure, improve, and expand the benefits of correctional education. It was submitted by **K.J. Hoke**, educational advisor. (p. 4). In its 1914 report, the Board had referred to Hoke, who was then the assistant superintendent of Richmond public schools in charge of educational programs for backward children (p. 22). ⧠

"Berlinda Davison studied the [local public] schooling of blacks in the San Francisco Bay region." She noted that intelligence test scores were often used to fuel mischaracterizations. "In the teachers' comments explaining the failure of the black children, again and again the phrase 'low mental level' cropped up, nudging 'laziness' and 'indifference' as favorite labels." Davison found "The number of years of education had little correlation with the type of work the black men pursued, and skilled workers were rarely able to follow their trades because of discrimination in unions." (Tyack, 1974, pp. 218-219). ⧠

1922 — **Thomas Mott Osborne** founded the National Society of Penal Information to carry on Mutual Welfare League prison reform work in the world outside the prisons (Callan, 1981, p. 1). The Society had been founded as the "outside branch" of the League, mostly to help in the fund raising for Osborne's legal defense. Now it was renamed. In 1931 the Society published **Austin MacCormick**'s book *The Education of Adult Prisoners*. It was later renamed again to become The Osborne Association, Inc. MacCormick served as executive director for decades. ⧠

Solzhenitsyn later reported that there had been an "absence of a criminal code or any system of criminal law whatsoever before 1922" since the 1917 revolution in what had become the Soviet Union. (1974, p. 32). Conditions in that regard were analogous to those of revolutionary France—see 1792 entry. For example, in 1919, in connection with the "pseudo plots" of the "National Center" and the "Military Plot," there were "big hauls" into the Soviet prisons.

...in Moscow, Petrograd, and other cities on the basis of lists—in other words, free people were simply arrested and executed immediately, and right and left those elements of the intelligentsia considered close to the Cadets were taken into prison. (What does the term 'close to the Cadets' mean? Not monarchist and not socialist [as opposed to communist]: in other words, all scientific circles, all university circles, all

181

(cont'd.) artistic, literary, yes, and, of course, all engineering circles. Except for the extremist writers, except for the theologians and theoreticians of socialism, all the rest of the intelligentsia, 80 percent of it, was 'close to the Cadets.') In that category, for example, Lenin placed the writer Korolenko—'a pitiful petty bourgeois, imprisoned in bourgeois prejudices.' He considered it was 'not amiss' for such 'talents' to spend a few weeks in prison. From Gorky's protests we learn of individual groups that were arrested. On September 15, 1919, Lenin replied to him: 'It is clear to us that there were some mistakes.' But: 'What a misfortune, just think about it! What injustice!' And he advised Gorky 'not to waste [his] energy whimpering over rotten intellectuals.' (pp. 31-32; emphases in original).

These conditions continued. In 1933 "Comrade Molotov said...'We do not see our task as being mass repressions'".... But by 1934-1935

one-quarter of Leningrad was purged—cleaned out— .... Let this estimate be disproved by those who have the exact statistics and are willing to publish them. (To be sure, this wave took in much more than Leningrad alone. It had a substantial impact on the rest of the country in a form that was consistent though chaotic: the firing from the civil service of all those still left there whose fathers had been priests, all former noble-women, and all persons having relatives abroad.) Among such lashing waves as this, certain modest, changeless wavelets always got lost: they were little heard of, but they, too, kept flowing on and on (pp. 58-59; emphasis in original).

through the Soviet prison system.

As early as 1921 interrogations usually took place at night. At that time, too, they shone automobile lights in the prisoner's face (the Ryazan Cheka [secret police]—Stelmakh). And at the Lubyanka [Prison] in 1926 (according to the testimony of Berta Gandal) they made use of the hot-air heating system to fill the cell first with icy-cold and then with stinking hot air. And there was an airtight cork-lined cell in which there was no ventilation and they cooked the prisoners. The poet Klyuyev was apparently confined in such a cell and Berta Gandal also. A participant in the Yaroslal uprising of 1918, Vasily Aleksandrovich Kasyanov, described how the heat in such a cell was turned up until your blood began to ooze through your pores. When they saw this happening through the peephole, they would put the prisoner on a stretcher and take him off to sign his confession. The 'hot' and 'salty' methods of the 'gold' period are well known. And in Georgia in 1926 they used lighted cigarettes to burn the hands of prisoners under interrogation. In Metekhl Prison they pushed prisoners into a cesspool in the dark. (p. 98).

...it seems strange today to read in the recollections of former zeks [government investigators] that 'torture was permitted from the spring of 1938 on.' There were never any spiritual or moral barriers which could have held the Organs [government representatives] back from torture. In the early postwar years, in the *Cheka Weekly, The Red Sword,* and *Red Terror,* the admissibility of torture from a Marxist point of view was openly debated. Judging by the subsequent course of events, the answer deduced was positive, though not universally so....In the years 1937-1938... interrogators were allowed to use violence and torture on an unlimited basis, at their own discretion, and in accordance with the demands of their work quotas and the amount of time they were given. The types of torture used were not regulated and every kind of ingenuity was permitted, no matter what....Then, from the end of the war and throughout the postwar years, certain categories of prisoners were established by decree for whom a broad range of torture was automatically permitted... (p. 99).

In 1937, and again in 1945 authorities perceived that

there were virtues to...[the overcrowded prison] arrangement...which more than made up for its flaws. The overcrowding of the cells not only took the place of the tightly confined solitary 'box' but also assumed the character of a first class <u>torture</u> in itself...one that was particularly useful because it continued for whole days and weeks—with no effort on the part of the interrogators. The prisoners tortured the prisoners! The jailers pushed so many prisoners into the cell that not every one had even a piece of the floor; some were sitting on others' feet, and people walked on people and couldn't even move about at all. Thus, in Kishinev KPZ's—Cells for Preliminary Detention—in 1945, they pushed <u>eighteen</u> prisoners into a cell designed for the solitary confinement of one person; in Lugansk in 1937 it was <u>fifteen</u>. And in 1938 Ivanov-Razuminik found <u>one hundred forty</u> prisoners in a standard Butyrki cell intended for twenty-five—with toilets so overburdened that prisoners were taken to the toilet only once a day, sometimes at night... (pp. 124-125; emphases in original). ⌒

Gorky Colony, now a co-educational institution, acquired a large nationalized agricultural estate. Social education became the main focus of programs there. The Colony grew quickly, as refugees, thieves, and waifs streamed in. **Makarenko** hired skilled craftsmen as vocational instructors, and townsfolk soon looked to the institution for services from blacksmiths, wheel-wrights, and carpenters. The population had successfully overcome a rash of anti-Semitism among its members, and thievery in town by runaways. Makarenko began a program of confiscating illegal stills belonging to farmers surrounding the Colony, because a number of inmates had developed drinking problems. (Makarenko, 1973, vol. 1, p. 166). ⌒

John Dewey's work was attracting nationwide attention. He feared that the public schools were becoming

a vast filtering system...unaware of its own biases: 'we welcome a procedure which under the title of science sinks the individual in a numerical class; judges him with reference to capacity to fit into a limited number of vocations ranked according to present business standards; assigns him to a predestined niche and thereby does whatever education can do to perpetuate the present order. (Tyack, 1974, p. 198).

His fears were well founded.

In 1908 Edward T. Thorndike had aroused the alarm of citizens and the ire of superintendents with his study 'The Elimination of Pupils from School,' which concluded that almost half the pupils entering school did not reach the eighth grade. (p. 200).

Army experiments with intelligence testing during World War I gave the testing movement new vigor (p. 204).

In 1925 the U.S. Bureau of Education told how 215 cities used intelligence tests....The group IQ tests were most heavily used in the elementary grades, and there primarily for administrative purposes...to classify students....Cities employed individual intelligence

1922
(cont'd.)
tests largely to diagnose serious learning problems and to sort out subnormal children. (p. 208).

"Intelligence tests often were unintentionally biased against certain groups" (p. 189).

Challenges like the Americanization of immigrants abounded, to be sure, but the strategies to respond to them were to be found in 'science,' in administrative efficiency, and professional specialization. For leading schoolmen it was mostly an age of confidence inspired by a dream of social efficiency. (p. 180).

Low scores of southeastern Europeans on the army tests confirmed WASP [White, Anglo Saxon, Protestant] belief in the immigrants' inferiority and gave powerful arguments to those Congressmen who voted to discriminate against them in the immigration restriction laws of the 1920's. The tests appeared to give scientific validation to garden-variety social prejudice. (p. 205).

"Nature-nurture controversies might pepper the scientific periodicals and magazines of the intelligentsia, but schoolmen found IQ tests [an] invaluable means of channeling children; by the very act of channeling pupils, they helped to make the IQ prophecies self-fulfilling." (p. 180). Journalist Walter Lippmann wrote that

If...the impression takes root that these tests really measure intelligence, that they constitute a sort of last judgment on the child's capacity, that they reveal scientifically his predestined ability, then it would be a thousand times better if all the intelligence testers and all their questionnaires were sunk without warning in the Sargasso sea. (p. 214).

The Chicago Federation of Labor issued a report in 1924, which included this statement:

the alleged 'mental levels,' representing natural ability, it will be seen, correspond in a most startling way to the social levels of the groups named. It is as though the relative social positions of each group are determined by an irresistible natural law. (pp. 214-215).

'Teachers, administrators, and supervisors...have received the adaptations of the [Army] group intelligence examination to school uses with open arms

185

1922
(cont'd.)

and all too often with uncritical acceptance of what has been made available.' Tests became a fiscal bonanza for their makers... (pp. 206-207). ⌂

1923 — **Makarenko**'s Gorky Colony moved to a new facility—the nationalized estate on which the juveniles had been working for nearly two years. The inmates adopted regimental dress and military exercise, and were the envy of the youngsters in town. Local farmers helped to correct the food crisis, and community relations improved. (Makarenko, 1973, vol. 1, p. 344). The wards implemented a new system of rotating work assignments which helped to improve morale (p. 355). Makarenko's advocacy of study and cooperative labor had ushered in a new political consciousness at the institution. A Komosal chapter—young peoples' developmental organization—was established there, to promote the Communist Party's efforts in the study of political economy. A political instructor was appointed to help facilitate this effort. (p. 390). **Rose Edwards** later wrote of the Makarenko colonies during this time.

> It was a period when political ideas relentlessly pressed ahead....when political revolutionaries ultimately brought about the full-scale annihilation of the ancient regime, and, charged with an unprecedented will for radical change, set out to accomplish their bold, far-reaching visions of total social transformation and the creation of a new Soviet man....Makarenko...identified with the prevailing...consciousness...believed that by destroying the 'old world' a new, ultimately ideal society would emerge. (Edwards, 1991, p. 19).

In modern terms, Makarenko's pedagogy "involved developing the whole person, a process Makarenko termed 'upbringing'.... moral education....to remold...character....[without] recipes or formulas." (p. 342). Ultimately, all of Soviet local education was modeled on Makarenko's ideas about correctional education for confined juveniles. At one point Makarenko

> told how he had acquired real pedagogical mastership only after having learned to say 'come here' in fifteen or twenty different tones of voice, and after he had learned to give his face and his posture twenty different nuances of expression (pp. 351-352).

He concluded that "many parents and teachers did not know how to speak to a child." Makarenko gave the following example.

> 'The other day a father came to me and said: 'I am communist, a worker. I have a good son. He does not obey me. I tell him something but he does not obey. I

say it for the second time—he does not obey. I say it for the third time—he does not obey. What shall I do with him?' I asked the father...to sit down and began a conversation with him. 'Now show me how you talk to your son.' 'Well, like this.' 'Try it once this way.' 'It does not work.' 'Try again.' I spent half an hour with him, and then he had learned how to give an order. It was merely a matter of voice. (p. 352).

Makarenko maintained that

mien [demeanor] should...be independent of the educator's mood. Never did he permit himself to wear a gloomy expression, even when he was worried or not well. Makarenko was of the opinion that the educator had to be lively and wide-awake, but genuinely angry when something was wicked, so that pupils would really feel the anger and not mistake it for pedagogical moralizing....he dismissed some educators because they grumped and pouted all the time. Grown people working with children had to know how to control their feelings and keep their worries to themselves. (p. 356).

As Makarenko put it,

A pupil apprehends your feelings and your thoughts not because he knows what is going on in your heart, but because he is watching you and listening to you. Watching a play we admire the actors on the stage, and their beautiful acting gives us aesthetic pleasure. Well, here the pupil is watching too, but the actors he is watching are educators and the impact has to be educative. (p. 355). 🐾

At a meeting in Washington, D.C., representatives from nationwide women's organizations recommended that the Federal government should establish a new female institution. Their plan was approved by Congress in 1924, and by 1927 Alderson Federal Correctional Institution was opened. Located in West Virginia on a 500-acre site, this cottage-style reformatory was managed by women and had buildings named for English women's prison reformer Elizabeth Fry, Katharine Bement Davis, Jane Addams, and other prison and social reformers. (Freedman, 1981, p. 146). **Mary Belle Harris** served as the first superintendent (p. 149). 🐾

Kate Richards O'Hare's book was published, about her incarceration for speaking out against U.S. involvement in World

1923   War I. See 1911 entry. *In Prison* contained excellent arguments for
(cont'd.) deinstitutionalization. Incarcerated at the Missouri State Prison in
        Jefferson City, O'Hare called herself "sometime Federal prisoner
        number 21669." In her chapter on "Prison Food, Clothing, Education,"
        she wrote about correctional education. "There were no provisions in
        our prison for educational or vocational training." (O'Hare, 1923, p. 93).
        "But, while all education that might be helpful and possibly curative
        was relentlessly shut out, education in the ways of vice and crime
        and degeneracy flourished" (p. 95). She could make that declaration
        because

> A few weeks after I entered I sent a formal request to
> Mr. W.R. Painter, chairman of the prison board, asking
> permission to open a night school. One of the girls
> who had finished the grade school offered to teach
> the beginners, and I tendered my services to teach the
> more advanced. The women were pathetically eager
> for the opportunity to attend school, but the prison
> board ignored the request, and the prison still has no
> school for the women prisoners. The work which the
> women do has no educational value and will not in the
> least help them to adjust themselves and their lives to
> accepted social standards. (p. 94).

The book provided useful information about specific events relevant to
prison health care during the period, the inadequacies of the criminal
justice system, and double standards that jeopardize females and the
poor. In 1933 **Frank Tannenbaum** wrote about the period between the
World Wars at the prison in which O'Hare was assigned.

> A prisoner writing from the State Prison at Jefferson
> City, Missouri, after describing conditions at the
> institution and after detailing the fact that convicts
> cut their fingers off to escape the hardship of contract
> labor says: 'Men are committing suicide in preference
> to doing three or four years of this particular kind of
> imprisonment.' (Tannenbaum, 1933, p. 27).

Thomas Mott Osborne [see 1913 entry], who had visited the
prison wrote to a correspondent as follows: "In fact, the thought
of Jefferson City is one of recurring horror to me, I have not the
slightest doubt of the accuracy of this information. But then, what
can we do?" (pp. 27-28). ᝣ

> A special Massachusetts legislative committee studied the
> relocation of the State Prison to Charlestown (Murton, 1976, p. 207—see
> 1927 entry). This initiative would eventually prompt a series of difficult
> events in Massachusetts. ᝣ

1923   "In England between 1923 and 1929, due to the generosity of
(cont'd.) the Carnegie [Corporation] Trustees, a special Prison Education Library
of several thousands of volumes was established, supplementing the
work of the voluntary teachers." (Grunhut, 1973/1948, p. 243—see
entries for 1886 and 1919). Carnegie funding for libraries would soon
contribute to a rethinking of the entire configuration of correctional
education services in the U.S.—see 1927 entry. ⌂

1924 — The principles of the New Penology were set forth in **Thomas Mott
Osborne**'s book *Prisons and Common Sense* (Osborne, 1924b). Another of
Osborne's books, *Within Prison Walls*, about his voluntary incarceration
as "Tom Brown," was also published (Osborne, 1924a). Later, Wallack,
Kendall, and Briggs picked up on some of the themes in this book and
entitled their own book, about New York State correctional education,
Education Within Prison Walls (Wallack, Kendall, and Briggs, 1939—see
1939 entry). ⌂

In Minnesota, prisoners in solitary confinement were not
allowed to have pencils. In Tennessee, convicts could be punished
for "...failure to make satisfactory progress...[in] school...inattention...
talking...soiling books...writing or receiving notes" (Tannenbaum, 1933,
pp. 15-17). ⌂

Makarenko's innovations in Soviet juvenile facilities had
become models that helped influence that nation's adult prisons.

The Soviet Union established the Bolchevo Colony
for youthful offenders...outside Moscow. There was
a staff of only five for a population that at one time
reached 2,000. There were no armed guards, there was
complete self-government, and the inmates could have
their wives with them. (Murton, 1976, p. 195—see 1935
entry). ⌂

Correctional libraries were being improved in many nations.
In "Thuringia [Germany], from 1924 the revenue from fines imposed
in connection with the remission of prison terms was set aside by the
Ministry of Justice for prisoner's welfare, including purchases for
prison libraries." (Grunhut, 1973/1948, p. 243). ⌂

A comparison of the U.S. Army draft population and the Illinois
inmate population revealed that inferior intelligence was found in 25%
of the Army group and 24.7% of the prison group (MacCormick, 1933,
p. 23). This should have been the last word on the IQ of prisoners issue,
but the dialogue about that subject has continued. ⌂

1925 — A University of California Extension Division was established at San
Quentin Prison (Morris, in Roberts, 1973, p. 18—see 1915 entry).

1925   This was an early and important benchmark that contributed to the
(cont'd.) subsequent postsecondary programs for inmates movement. ⌒

New York State law required that the average time devoted to
instruction should not be less than one and one half hours daily for
each inmate, although wardens could determine criteria for entrance
to school. In addition, the responsibility for correctional education was
taken from the superintendent for state prisons and transferred to the
commissioner of education. Only certified teachers could be employed
as correctional education practitioners, and a curriculum was required
for each institutional course. This same law also made the first New
York State reference to inmate teachers—but without requiring that they
be certified. (See 1918 Virginia entry.) By 1929 correctional education
was put back under the authority of the superintendent of state prisons
(Wallack, 1939, pp. 7-8). ⌒

1926 — **Thomas Mott Osborne** died of a heart attack (Chamberlain, 1935).

When the guards unlocked the cells in Auburn prison
on the 21st of October and announced that Tom
Brown was dead it was 'Like the low moaning wind
which presages the awful hurricane at sea.' The news
spread through the prison—Tom Brown is dead. The
prisoners had lost their best friend. (Tannenbaum,
1933, p. 288). ⌒

The new intelligence tests continued to prompt concern about
the relation between IQ and crime. In his book *The Delinquent Boy,* **John
Slawson** reported that

1) eight out of ten delinquents scored lower than non-
delinquents in tests of abstract verbal intelligence, 2)
there was no significant difference in scores on tests of
non-verbal intelligence and mechanical aptitude, [and]
3) there was no correlation between intelligence scores
and number of arrests or type of offense. (Dell'Apa,
1973b, p. 19). ⌒

1927 — **Austin MacCormick** was assigned to coordinate "a study of educational
and library work in American prisons and reformatories for adults."
See 1929 entry. The survey was sponsored by the American Association
for Adult Education and funded by the Carnegie Corporation. It was
a project of the outside chapter of the Mutual Welfare League, which
was known as the National Society of Penal information. (MacCormick,
1931, p. ix—see 1922 entry). ⌒

Howard Gill was appointed superintendent of the new
Massachusetts Prison, and given wide latitude in its construction.

1927   The facility opened in 1933 (Murton, 1976, p. 17), and would be called
(cont'd.) Norfolk (see 1928 entry). Gill had been a private business consultant
         (Murton, 1976, p. 193). "In 1925, Herbert Hoover's Department of
         Commerce contracted with Gill to study state prison industries
         programs. Gill toured penitentiaries across the country and discussed
         correctional theory with numerous penologists." (Serrill, 1982, p. 27).
         At least one of those discussions was with **Thomas Mott Osborne**—see
         1913 entry (Murton, 1976, p. 17). As superintendent, Gill's rules were
         "no escapes, no contraband," and his criteria for staff selection were
         that candidates for employment had to be "close to the earth, humane
         and willing to learn." Gill established a school (see 1931 entry), and
         improved industries and medical care at this relocated institution. He
         implemented and refined Thomas Mott Osborne's Mutual Welfare
         League structure. His version was called the Inmate Council. It was
         established to provide inmate participation instead of self-government.
         Gill's structure put inmates and guards as equals, under the warden's
         supervision—as opposed to Osborne's, which had guards under the
         warden and inmates. (pp. 193-211—see 1933 entry).

New York State's Elmira Reformatory (see 1876 entry) came
under the control of the commissioner of Correction. From 1876 to 1926
the Reformatory functioned with its own board of managers, with a
strong "emphasis on education, productive labor, the mark system, the
indeterminate sentence and parole." (Chenault, 1949-1951, p. 9). "During
the first two decades of the twentieth century, both in the Reformatory and
in the [State] prisons, there was a continuation of the outworn educational
practices inherited from previous administrations" (Chenault, 1949-1951,
p. 10). The 1927 *Elmira Hand Book* reveals that the mark system was still
very much as Maconochie had designed it in 1840 (Allen, 1927, p. 11).
The following vocational courses were offered:Barber, Bookbinder, Brass-
smith, Bricklayer, Machinist, Moulder, Paint-mixer, Plasterer, Cabinet-
maker, Carpenter, Clothing cutter, Electrician, Frescoer, Hard-wood
finisher, Horseshoer, House-painter, Iron-forger, Machine-wood-worker,
Plumber, Printer, Shoemaker, Sign-painter, Steam-fitter, Stenographer
and Typewriter, Tailor, Tinsmith, Upholsterer (pp. 16-17).

> There are six school days in each week, including
> Sunday. The school classes are apportioned as
> follows: Monday—Arithmetic, European history
> and current events; Tuesday—Arithmetic, civics and
> economics; Wednesday—Language, civics, geography
> and physiology; Thursday—Language, American
> history, and 'Special A' arithmetic; Friday—Language,
> literature, and 'Special A' arithmetic; Sunday—Ethics,
> question box and current topics. (Allen, 1927, p. 15).

The program also included military education (with an "awkward
squad" for new and disabled students), "special [vocational] training

1927   classes for mental defectives," a Music Department with a brass and
(cont'd.) reed band, and separate "special languages classes for the foreign-born
          and the native-born." (pp. 15-16). ⌒

          Reform was an important aspiration of this period. In England,
the Birmingham Prison chaplain reported that

> Educational classes, carefully arranged, are becoming,
> without question, a most valuable factor in Prison
> Reform. I am satisfied that they are being used by those
> who attend not merely as a break from the ordinary
> routine, but as an opportunity for improvement of
> mind... (Banks, 1958, p. 30).

In 1935 the Winchester Prison chaplain wrote that 12 "gramophone
recitals" were added to the evening lecture program/"Wireless
demonstration" series (p. 31). Banks described the adult education
scheme between the wars (see 1919 entry):

> A great, free, spontaneous growth of adult education
> had interpenetrated the prisons of the country. It was
> indeed a triumph for the power of voluntary effort,
> and, although surprisingly much of this volunteer
> aspect mercifully survives, its pristine glow, eclipsed
> during the years of war, was never rekindled in the
> tired country. (p. 35—see 1946 entry).

Prison Commission reports from 1923-1928 indicate a sequence of
special library grants from the Carnegie Corporation Trustees. In 1934
"a new post of Librarian Officer" was established (pp. 218-219). ⌒

1928 — In Massachusetts **Howard Gill**

> took the Norfolk [Prison superintendent] job...[H]e
> lost a battle to keep the institution small. The prison
> was designed for 1,200 inmates. But Gill did get
> [Massachusetts Correction commissioner Dr. Warren]
> Stearn's commitment that the new inmates would be
> introduced gradually, and that the Norfolk staff would
> have veto power over them. (Serrill, 1982, p. 30—see
> 1933 entry).

Gill established the Joint Committee on Construction at Massachusetts
Prison, with representatives from the Inmate Council and officers
(Murton, 1976, p. 210). Massachusetts' Norfolk Prison was named after
the Norfolk Island Penal Colony in the South Pacific, where Maconochie
became warden in 1840. ⌒

1928   **Perrie Jones** succeeded Miriam Carey as the manager of
(cont'd.) Minnesota's prototypic institutional library system (MacCormick, in
          Roberts, 1971, p. 325). In 1938 Jones wrote

> during Miss Carey's fifteen years as Supervisor....
> Foundations were laid for sound library procedure, the
> gospel of reading was persistently and tactfully spread
> throughout the institutions, appropriations for books
> and equipment were increased; in short, the library
> as a definite, professional department of institutional
> procedure in Minnesota had come to stay. (Jones, 1938,
> p. 176—see 1938 entry). ⚵

News of **Anton Makarenko**'s success became accessible
internationally, and **John Dewey** came to visit him. Believing that
"the Russians 'are more akin to the American people than to any other
people'" (Martin, 2002, p. 356), he came to the USSR in spite of official
scrutiny of his motivations by the Federal Bureau of Investigation (p.
351). Dewey's visit was in 1928, to "a children's Colony...on the estate
of a former Grand Duke" near Leningrad (Dykhuizen, 1973, p. 236).

> ...in Peterhof—up the Neva...The place marks the nearest
> approach of the White Armies to Leningrad [during the
> Civil War]; the buildings were more or less ruined in the
> warfare...not yet wholly restored, since the teachers and
> children must do the work; there is still need in some
> quarters for hot water and whitewash. Two-thirds of the
> children are former 'wild children,' orphans, refugees,
> etc., taken from the streets...I have never seen...such
> a large proportion of intelligently occupied children.
> They were not lined up for inspection. We...found
> them engaged in their various summer occupations,
> gardening, bee-keeping, repairing buildings, growing
> flowers in a conservatory (built and now managed
> by a group of particularly tough boys who began by
> destroying everything in sight), making simple tools
> and agricultural implements, etc....their manner and
> attitude is...what stays with me—I cannot convey it; I
> lack the necessary literary skill. But the net impression
> will always remain. If the children had come from
> the most advantageously situated families, the scene
> would have been a remarkable one, unprecedented...
> When their almost unimaginable earlier history and
> background were taken into account, the effect was
> to leave me with...admiration for the capacities of the
> people from which they sprang...an unshakable belief
> in what they can accomplish. (Dewey, 1929, pp. 27-29).

1928
(cont'd.)

This was one of Makarenko's schools, under the auspices of the Soviet Police. Dewey was so impressed that in 1933 he helped make a film about Makarenko's educational contributions, which was titled after Makarenko's main books, *The Road to Life*. In 1933 Dewey introduced a Soviet film about Makarenko's career, also titled *The Road to Life*, with the following words:

> Ten years ago, every traveler in Russia came back with stories of hordes of wild children who roamed the countryside and infested the streets. They were the orphans of soldiers killed in the war, of fathers and mothers who perished in the famine after the war. You will see a picture of their old road to life, a road of vagabondage, violence, thieving. You will also see their new road to...life, a road constructed by a brave band of Russian teachers. After methods of repression had failed, they gathered these children together in collective homes, they taught them cooperation, useful work, healthful recreation. Against great odds they succeeded. There are today no wild children in Russia. You will see a picture of great artistic beauty, of dramatic action and power. You will also see a record of a great historic episode. These boys are not professional actors. They were once wild children, they once lived in an actual collective. You will also see an educational lesson of the power of freedom, sympathy, work and play to redeem the juvenile delinquent; a lesson from which we too may learn. (in Bowen, 1965, p. 4).

John Schunck became director of the Maryland Penitentiary school. He invited Johns Hopkins University graduate students to assist in the operation, so that classes could be held four evenings each week. (Roberts, 1971, p. 9—see 1918 entry).

The conversation about inmate intelligence continued, ad nauseum. Over a ten year period at the Illinois Reformatory for Men, 13.7% of the inmates were found to have superior intelligence, 72% average intelligence, and 13.6% inferior intelligence (MacCormick, 1933, p. 23).

The Pennsylvania Department of Welfare issued an extensive and straightforward follow-up report on its Sleighton Farm juvenile institution, *Correctional Education and the Delinquent Girl*. Study variables included mental ability, marriage, sex life, community life, relationship of correctional education and future success/lack of success, occupation, etc. (Commonwealth of Pennsylvania, 1928).

1929 — **Austin MacCormick**'s survey of United States prison education was completed for the National Society of Penal Information. The report was published in 1931 as *The Education of Adult Prisoners*. MacCormick visited 110 institutions. His findings indicated that correctional education was afflicted by a lack of clear goals, funding inadequacy, wholesale replication of public school methods, and poor teaching. He advocated individualized instruction, an attitude-centered approach, broad-based curriculum, emphasis on student responsibility, social and cultural education, and correctional education as part of rehabilitative programming. This was the first national correctional education survey, and it was recognized as the definitive book on the field. It became the basis for improvements in correctional education during the following decades. The book is extremely readable. It was republished in 1976, and most of its chapters are still very relevant. MacCormick was appointed assistant director of the new U.S. Bureau of Prisons. (MacCormick, 1931, pp. ix-xiv). **Sanford Bates** was the director. MacCormick served in this capacity for four years (Encyclopedia Americana, 1979, vol. #18, p. 28).

In some ways parallel to **William George**'s earlier accomplishments at the Junior Republic, **Father Flanagan**'s initiatives at Boys Town were gathering form.

> Work on the new buildings...was begun in September of 1929....By the fall of 1930 the buildings were finished.... The governor, Arthur J. Weaver, made a speech in which he said the state of Nebraska was a better place now because of the home which **Father Flanagan** had founded there... (Oursler and Oursler, 1949, p. 236).

The school, which had its official origins "Around 1919 or 1920,...[was] conducted by the Sisters, [and] already, in its curricula and results, surpassed the requirements of Nebraska educational laws. Classes in those days were limited to grammar grades." (p. 186).

> The one really new addition to the educational program [in the early 1920s had been]...the 'trades school.' All they were able to begin with was a carpenter shop. The first trade at the home was that of Joseph, foster father of Jesus. Before long, under the tutelage of a master carpenter, teaching on part time and for the rest kept busy on jobs around the place, the boys were able to make tables and lamps and bookcases, all very much needed in the four temporary houses (p. 197).

By the late 1920s "There were...five new buildings, all brick structures and fireproof: a gymnasium with a swimming pool, a trades-school building, a faculty residence, a dry-cleaning plant, and a combination

1929 laundry and boilerhouse." (p. 236). "Each student is placed in one of
(cont'd.) three general programs—college preparatory, vocational, or farming.
Trades and farm students spent half of each day in their specialized
field. College-preparatory pupils devote full time to academic courses."
(p. 260). In 1949 Oursler and Oursler wrote that boys with disabilities
were not accepted into the institution because the facilities for their care
were not available (p. 254). For all the residents "physical punishment
was forbidden." (p. 157). At Boys Town delinquents were encouraged
to identify as students. "They... forgot that they were supposed to be
criminals." (p. 138). Flanagan focused the boys' attention on how they
could improve their future, rather than on the guilty past. To an inmate
he once said "Our only concern is what happens next and from here on
out: the future!....There is no punishment...Try to get it straight—realize
what I'm saying to you—you're beginning again!" (p. 137; emphasis in
original). Father Flanagan de-emphasized the role of poverty in juvenile
crime.

> Most of the judges were convinced the [Boys Town]
> effort was worth while, but some professional social
> workers found it hard to grasp. Poverty in their
> notebook had always been written down as the prime
> cause of delinquency. And now this priest was insisting
> that poverty, while it played a part, was not the major
> cause—in fact, his boys were living in poverty with him
> and learning from it. In a home run on a shoestring and
> a prayer, he was proving his point... (pp. 155-156).

Cultural activities were important at Boys Town. Father Flanagan
"started a band that went on a tour." The highlight of this trip was "a
climactic concert before the inmates of Leavenworth Penitentiary. If the
concert brought no huzzahs from critics, it did bring cheers from men
behind bars." (p. 165). Encouraged by this success, Flanagan wondered
"Why couldn't he put together a group of performers and take them
out on the road, a band of juvenile minstrels and vaudevillians, a
show dramatizing the story of the home and its needs? (pp. 203-207).
However, by the late 1920s and early '30s the

> tours of his troupes were abandoned. Music and
> singing were confined to activities around Boys Town
> itself. The band played at games and gave informal
> concerts, and there was a loosely formed choir, solely
> for chapel services. But Father had not given up the
> dream of a traveling choir... (p. 213).

The Boys Town band played for president Calvin Coolidge, composer
John Philip Sousa, baseball heroes Babe Ruth and Lou Gehrig, and actor
Tom Mix. (p. 230—see entries for 1934, 1948, and 1949). 🔁

1929   The Hawes-Cooper Act was passed by Congress to restrict
(cont'd.) competition to private enterprise by prison industries (Reagen and
          Stoughton, 1976, p. 58). This and other legislation enacted during the
          Great Depression made a lasting impact on how prison made goods
          could be sold. ⌒

          In his book *Canadian Penal Institutions*, **C.W. Topping** described
          the school at Kingston Penitentiary.

> Classes are held six days each week at the noon hour
> and for two hours five evenings each week. Stress is
> laid on the 'three Rs,' but eight inmates passed their
> high school entrance examinations and three completed
> some college entrance work in 1926. The noon school
> is chiefly for illiterates and uses the class system, while
> the evening school is carried on by consultation in
> the cells. There is also a local correspondence system,
> which is very effective; but outside correspondence
> schools have not gained much of a footing on account
> of the inability of inmates to raise the necessary fees.
> (Topping, 1929, p. 41).

The library contained approximately 13,000 volumes in "classical and
modern fiction, biology, chemistry, drama, ethics, logic," and a set of
Encyclopedia Britannica. (pp. 41-42). ⌒

          The Mutual Welfare League "collapsed" at Sing Sing Prison
(Murton, 1976, p. 17). A 1937 report described a "series of disastrous riots
within the prisons of New York State in 1929 and 1930" (MacCormick,
1937, p. 6). "After the riot in 1929 in Clinton Prison, New York State, 181
men were placed in solitary confinement and kept there for 18 months"
(Tannenbaum, 1933, p. 38—see 1842 entry).

> Afterwards, there was an awakening of the public
> conscience to the fact that something was fundamentally
> wrong with the penal system. It was realized further that
> the disorders were caused not only by physical faculties
> necessitating overcrowding and idleness, but also
> were brought about through the methods of treatment
> existent at that time. (MacCormick, 1937, p. 6).

In 1930 the Lewisohn Commission was established—see entry.

> The Commission soon recognized that the problem was
> something more than dealing with structural changes
> in antiquated buildings, or the replacement of certain
> incompetent members of the personnel or the granting
> of added privileges here and the strengthening of

1929
(cont'd.)

discipline there. The problem proved to be beyond that of mere punishment but was basically the establishment of a system of inmate rehabilitation. (p. 6).

Tannenbaum's view follows:

> The 1929 riot, rebellion, arson and murder in Auburn Prison give peculiar poignance to the struggle of the prisoners in that institution to maintain the [Mutual Welfare League] self-governing community. On the face of the evidence available, a direct and indirect attempt to undermine the powers of the League in Auburn Prison finally succeeded, after a period of years, in completely undermining its morale, destroying its power, and making it useless as an instrument of internal discipline and less than useless as an instrument for the shaping of character... (Tannenbaum, 1933, pp. 267-268). ⌂

1930 — The 60th Annual Prison Congress established a Standing Committee on Education, with **Austin MacCormick** as chairman (APA, 1930, p. 409). This event marked the origin of the Correctional Education Association. The words that established the Committee follow:

> Whereas, education in the broadest sense has been found to be one of the most effective measures in the rehabilitation and reformation of delinquents, and Whereas, a program of education would do much toward amelioration of idleness in our correctional and penal institutions and also in greatly reducing the disciplinary problem thereof, Be it Resolved, that a Committee on Education of the American Prison Association be authorized and a Chairman be appointed, for the purpose of promoting educational programs in institutions of that character. (p. 258; emphases in original—see 1946 entry).

Further, the APA Congress endorsed a resolution on adult basic education in jails and other institutions, which said, in part "...we pledge our best endeavors to aid this patriotic movement and we [endorse] the policy of regular organized class work in our jails and prisons to teach the illiterate inmates to read and write." (p. 259). The APA Congress also added recreational services to the text of Principle #10, which had been developed at the 1870 Congress to express advocacy for correctional education (Wallack, 1939, p. 11—see entries for 1870 and 1960). ⌒

"The Federal Bureau of Prisons was...organized...(see 1929 entry). [Director **Sanford**] **Bates** considered education as a prime functional component of the correctional process in federal prisons. As a result of his convictions, educational programs were given immediate recognition" (Gaither, 1982, p. 21; emphasis added). Several new Federal institutions were planned, each with school facilities, budgets for libraries, and trained supervisors of education. Assistant supervisors of education were appointed at the Atlanta, Georgia and Leavenworth, Kansas penitentiaries. The Reformatory for Women at Alderson, West Virginia was equipped and staffed for vocational instruction, in addition to the academic programs that were already operational. The U.S. Industrial Reformatory for Men at Chillicothe, Ohio was staffed by a supervisor of education, an assistant supervisor, four academic instructors, and ten vocational instructors (Roberts, 1971, p. 12). "In 1940 Mr. Bates states: 'The most hopeful trend in prison work in America today is the growing realization that a term in prison can be made into an educational experience'" (p. 21). ⌒

1930   The New York State legislature established the Commission
(cont'd.) to Investigate Prison Administration and Construction. Governor
Franklin D. Roosevelt appointed **Sam A. Lewisohn** chairman of the
Commission, and a pro-education statement of purpose was soon
developed.

> ...New York should develop a prison system which will
> protect society from the criminal and his evil deeds
> by endeavoring to reeducate and retrain the men and
> women in prison so that these men and women may
> be fitted upon release to become useful members of the
> community... (Wallack, 1939, pp. 9-10).

Sam Lewisohn was **Adolph Lewisohn**'s son (Chenault, 1949-1951, p.
12—see entries for 1919 and 1920). The Commission employed **Walter
Wallack**, from Teachers College, Columbia University, as Educational
Advisor in 1932, and stationed him at Elmira Reformatory (Wallack,
1939, pp. 9-10). Wallack recommended the establishment of a correctional
education commission, which Governor Lehman implemented in 1933
(New York, 1941). The 1929 prison riots led directly to the establishment
of this Commission—see entry.

> Following certain preliminary efforts the Commission
> considered a complete reorganization of the system of
> prison schools, believing that education, while not a
> panacea for the solution of the crime problem, is a major
> factor in any program of socialization. It found that
> 'there were no courses of study which met the needs
> of young men confined in abnormal surroundings for
> varying periods of time. These young delinquents had
> run away from all that the public schools had to offer
> them. For them the steady grind of the classroom was
> anathema.' (MacCormick, 1937, p. 6).

Simultaneously, **Austin MacCormick**'s criticism of the Elmira
correctional education program was circulated widely in a draft of
his book *The Education of Adult Prisoners*. "Here one finds illustrated
practically every fault that has been charged against reformatories
in general." MacCormick listed broad problems with the Elmira
physical plant, program, military discipline, compulsory school
attendance, teaching staff, and large classes, and then proceeded
to describe specific problems that he encountered during his visit
there (MacCormick, 1931, pp. 288-289). The Lewisohn Commission
preliminary report was submitted in December. The final report
was issued in 1931, with addenda released in 1932 (Chenault, 1949-
1951, p. 12). Commission funds were soon exhausted, but the State
Department of Correction established a new position for a Director
of Vocational Education, hired Wallack to fill it, and then stationed

1930
(cont'd.) him at Elmira (Wallack, 1939, p. 10). This position formed the core of the subsequent Division of Education in the Department of Correction (Kendall, 1981). The Division was the first correctional education bureau in a state department of corrections, and it served as a model for future statewide correctional education systems in other states. ◿

The Sing Sing school dropped its compulsory attendance policy for "prisoners possessing less than a sixth-grade education" (Wallack, 1940, p. 107). By 1940 it had adopted an adult education program with a comprehensive array of academic, vocational, and social education (p. 108). ◿

Criminologist **Ruth Cavan** found that correctional education had been greatly affected by three trends. They were (a) the rapid breakdown of prison industries, (b) the development of important prototypic models in the Federal Bureau of Prisons, and (c) increased attention to correctional education issues by psychiatrists and sociologists who focused on inmate's post-release adjustment to community life (Roberts, 1971, p. 11). ◿

A word association test of approximately 200 Cleveland local public school teachers "who taught in predominantly black schools" revealed negative noun and adjective responses to "the word 'Negro'.... Indeed, many blacks were profoundly ambivalent about having Negro children taught in mixed schools by white teachers." (Tyack, 1974, p. 228). In the mid-1930s a survey of 159 high schools nationwide revealed "few differences between the opinions of northern and southern schoolmen on key [race-oriented] issues" (p. 223). "Literacy among blacks increased from 42.9 percent in 1890 to 90 percent in 1940; Negro high school enrollment jumped from 19,242 in 1917-18 to 254,580 in 1939-40 (an increase from 1.6 percent of total black enrollment to 10.5 percent)" (p. 222). W.E.B. Du Bois' writings characterize various dimensions of African American participation in the public schools. In 1897 he "found that 85 percent of the Negro children [in St. Louis] aged six to thirteen attended school for at least part of the year. The illiteracy of black youth ten to twenty years old in that city was only 4 percent" (p. 123). In 1929 he rejected the idea that African American students were inferior:

> 'their retardation [not functioning at expected grade level] is due to wretched Southern school systems; their dullness comes from poor food and poor homes'....He pointed out that separate schools would inexorably become 'less well-housed, less well-supported, less well-equipped and less well-supervised than the average public school.' (p. 228).

1930 By 1935 Du Bois concluded that "race prejudice in the United States
(cont'd.) today is such that most Negroes cannot receive proper education in
white institutions." (p. 229). ⚎

1931 — **Austin MacCormick**'s book, *The Education of Adult Prisoners,* was
published (MacCormick, 1931). In part, MacCormick reported that 10-
25% of all adult reformatory prisoners were illiterate, and that 55-75%
had not attained the 6th grade academic level (MacCormick, 1931, p. 19).
He also found that inmates exhibited a higher incidence of emotional
disturbances and psychopathology than the free population in the
community at large (p. 15). On Adult Basic Education, as a substitute
for adult education in the traditional sense, MacCormick reported as
follows:

> A strictly utilitarian philosophy of education, which sees
> education always in terms of vocational advancement,
> is not valid for the prisoner just because he so often is
> an unskilled worker and needs vocational training. A
> broader philosophy...[is needed]....we are not dealing
> with 'the prisoner,' but with individual prisoners.
> (pp. 36-37).

On the need to expand into the cultural dimensions of adult education
MacCormick wrote:

> The term 'cultural education' is an unfortunate one; it
> is likely to be sniffed at by both prisoners and officials.
> It is difficult to think of a better term for education
> which is unrelated to vocational advancement, which
> does not aim at increasing one's pay, which has no
> utilitarian aim whatever, but which is entered into
> for intellectual or aesthetic satisfaction or for 'the
> enrichment of self....Driven by the monotony of the
> prison routine they turn to reading and study. It is safe
> to say that most prisoners with education read more in
> a month in prison than they read in six months in real
> life. (pp. 189-192).

On the human requirements that generate these classroom learning
needs, and the courage it takes to act on them, he wrote:

> Let any skeptic who wishes scoff at these proposals. In
> penal institutions, where life is drab and ugly, where
> beauty of sound and color and form and expression
> seldom enters, there is a desire for beauty. It is usually
> unconscious, unexpressed, uncritical, but it is real. To
> feed it is to strengthen one more of the finer impulses
> that move men upward. (p. 200).

1931   On the themes of correctional education that demand increased
(cont'd.) attention, MacCormick reported: "...the result hoped for from all the
         types of education which we offer the prisoner is social education;
         this is, in fact, what is hoped for from the whole program of the penal
         institution." (p. 204). ⌒

         At the 61st Annual Prison Congress, the new Committee on
         Education made its first report. It was extensive, and included data
         on the scope of correctional education and needed library services.
         (Wallack, 1939, p. 12). ⌒

         In 1925 **Dr. Miriam Van Waters'** *Youth in Conflict* book appeared.
         She had served as superintendent of Los Angeles Juvenile Hall during
         and immediately after World War I. (Rowles, 1962—see entries for 1931
         and 1948.) Van Waters was appointed superintendent of Massachusetts
         Reformatory for Women at Framingham. (Rowles, 1962). In 1938 her
         article appeared, "Incentive and Penalty in Education" (Van Waters,
         1938). It is exemplary. After World War II she wrote a United Nations
         report on specialized treatment for female offenders. Van Waters earned
         an excellent reputation as a reform-oriented superintendent who was
         especially supportive of cultural education in corrections. (See entry for
         1948.) ⌒

         During the construction of Massachusetts' Norfolk Prison (see
         entries for 1927 and 1928), superintendent **Howard Gill** had

              quickly established rapport with the small group of
              inmate workers, who were carefully chosen from the
              overcrowded Charlestown prison in Boston. He sent
              away the tough Charlestown guards who had been
              supervising the construction and hired other men who
              like himself had little or no background in prison work....
              Gill succeeded in establishing a prison community
              extraordinary for its time. Most rules were made and
              enforced by the inmates themselves....It was Gill who
              made [this construction site/institution] work...it
              was the personality of Gill that made the difference.
              He was warm, friendly, a natural father figure for the
              inmates. At the same time he was stern, authoritarian
              and absolutely confident in his own abilities and in the
              rightness of his ideas. He was dynamic, charismatic, and
              in the words of one observer, 'irrepressible.' He bubbled
              over with natural enthusiasm for every enterprise that
              he undertook....Gill's dominance of Norfolk made it
              very much like the 'therapeutic communities' of today.
              In such communities, as long as the charismatic leader
              is in charge, the program functions well. As soon as he
              falters, so does the program. (Serrill, 1982, p. 27).

1931   By 1931, with the wall completed (p. 28), Norfolk Prison was opened
(cont'd.) (p. 25).

> Security staffs were confined to the walls and towers
> and were not even allowed to talk to the inmates.
> Instead they were supervised in the housing units by
> 'house officers' and on the job by civilian foremen.
> The house officers were supposed to be their principal
> supervisors. These men, most of whom had little or
> no background in corrections, lived in the housing
> units with the inmates, assuring that their relationship
> would be as intimate as possible. (p. 28).

"Gill's strongest desire was to discover the secret to an offender's
criminality" through "casework that would pinpoint the exact cause of
a man's inclination to commit crimes." In 1982 Gill was still "working
on a book, based mostly on his Norfolk experience, describing a plan
of rehabilitation he calls 'clinical criminology;' in it he attempts to
categorize offenders according to their treatment needs." (p. 29—see
1889 entry). Toward this end Gill in the 1930s implemented elaborate
diagnostic, classification, and progressive housing systems at the
Prison (pp. 29-30). His plans called for "high school classes and courses
in auto mechanics—programs that were unavailable. Both the staff and
inmates began to regard the program as a sham." (p. 31). The institution
did have what Gill called "a decent routine," with time for reading, and
one of the first correctional movie theaters in the country. But "elaborate
diagnostic procedures led to recommendations for school, work and
training that could not be fulfilled." The only rehabilitative programs
"during Gill's tenure were a small, makeshift literacy program run by
an 'educational director' earning a guard's salary, plus counseling by
house officers and caseworkers and a few recreation programs."
(p. 30).

> 'In the hospital model [see 1976 entry] the doctor rules
> and...rules quite arbitrarily; he diagnoses and prescribes
> and the patient accepts and swallows. In a democratic
> community model...authority is to be shared,
> responsibility divided and autocracy prohibited—the
> goal is partnership, not docile obedience.' [Rothman,
> in Serrill, p. 31]. In the end, according to Rothman...
> neither model survived. Instead, Rothman believes,
> Norfolk evolved into a conventional prison in which
> brute force or the threat of it became the operating
> principle. (Serrill, 1982, p. 31).

In 1932 the Prison construction project was awarded to a private
contractor, thus eliminating most inmate jobs. "Throughout 1932 and
1933 the state prison population had been burgeoning....Stearns [the

1931   statewide commissioner who had given the Norfolk staff veto power
(cont'd.) over incoming inmates] resigned in early 1933....When Commissioner
Andrew Sayer refused to remove the disruptive inmates, it made a
difficult situation impossible." (p. 30). By 1933 "Gill and his staff
had to resort to solitary confinement on bread and water to control
the behavior of particularly recalcitrant inmates." (p. 31—see 1933
entry). ⌒

Framingham Women's Reformatory superintendent **Jessie
Hodder** died. She had been impeded from implementing many of the
reforms that she advocated since 1910. (Freedman, 1981, p. 150). ⌒

Although becoming more limited in scope, the education
programs in facilities for women were expanding in enrollment.
Approximately 50% of the inmates at the Alderson Federal
Reformatory for Women were enrolled in the school program
(Roberts, 1971, p. 12). ⌒

Governor Franklin Delano Roosevelt's respect for the work
of **Thomas Mott Osborne**'s earlier work, and for **Austin MacCormick**,
was gathering new importance.

> Things began to happen in New York State...and
> the fog over [correctional] education began to lift
> slowly....The Lewisohn Commission...developed
> a building program which included new schools
> and shops at Attica, Sing Sing, Elmira and Clinton,
> and new institutions at Wallkill and Woodbourne.
> (MacCormick, 1937, p. 8). ⌒

1932 — "A fine school building was built at Chillicothe" Federal Reformatory,
in Ohio (Wallack, 1939, p. 13). **Austin MacCormick** would later serve
as Chillichothe warden. ⌒

Throughout the country, about 4,000 Federal prisoners were
participating in educational programs. The highest enrollment at
any prison in the U.S. was at the McNeil Island Federal Penitentiary.
(Roberts, 1971, p. 13). ⌒

The several branches of the Mutual Welfare League merged
with the National Society of Penal Information, to form The Osborne
Association, Inc. Throughout most of its history, **Austin MacCormick**
served as executive director of the Association, which is dedicated to
reform of the criminal justice system. **Joseph Callan** later served as
executive director. (Callan, 1981, p. 1). ⌒

The *Prison Library Handbook* was published by a joint American
Library Association/American Prison Association Committee

1932   (MacCormick, in Roberts, 1973, pp. 327-328). It was funded with grants
(cont'd.) from the Bureau of Social Hygiene and the American Association for
        Adult Education (Wallack, 1939, p. 12). ⟐

        The White House Conference on Child Health and Protection
recommended that special education services should be extended to
delinquent juveniles (Wallack, 1939, p. 241). Although many cite this
conference and the legislation of the 1970s as the origin of modern
special education, **Dr. Carolyn Eggleston**'s 1989 dissertation suggests
the real "beginning" was at Elmira Reformatory before the turn of the
20th century. ⟐

        In Denmark, classroom teaching began in 1932. In 1930 the
Danish Civil Criminal Code had been "adopted, resulting in the
establishment of youth penitentiaries in 1933" for offenders between
the ages of 15 and 21. (Nordic Council of Ministers, 2005, p. 26—see
1952 entry). ⟐

        A full-time correctional education program at Wisconsin State
Prison was implemented and managed by the State University system
(Reagen and Stoughton, 1976, p. 60). The next few years would witness a
profound increase of education programs in prisons around the nation,
sparked by new models, increased communication among correctional
educators, and in some cases Federal funding. ⟐

        However, sometimes the systems that are supposed to provide
educational services fail. When that happens, help can come from
unexpected quarters. In 1932 several convicts at Illinois' Stateville
Prison identified problems with the school there:

            ...the inmate grade school teachers were not too
            carefully selected; unless they happened to be a bit
            idealistic...there weren't many rewards or incentives
            for conscientious work. Some of them, for a bribe of
            cigarettes or other store order, would give a student
            whatever marks he wanted, would pass him on to the
            next grade, or would certify that he had reached the
            level required to permit him to leave school. Con ethics
            entered too. What were you going to do if somebody
            in your class just wouldn't make an effort to learn?
            You couldn't go to the officials about it. Unless you
            wanted to take the guy on personally, there was just
            nothing to do but let him go his own way. (Leopold,
            1958, p. 224—see 1933 entry). ⟐

        New York State's program for modernizing and improving
correctional education began (Wallack, 1939, p. iii). **Walter Wallack** was
employed by the Lewisohn Commission as Educational Advisor and

1932   directed to go "to the Elmira Reformatory for the purpose of directing
(cont'd.) as much reorganization of the educational program there as could be
        accomplished in the time allotted and with the limited funds at his
        disposal." (Wallack, 1939, p. 10). The correctional education budget in
        New York State was increased to 150% of the 1931 level—most of the
        increase went to salaries for trained staff (p. 29). The first organized
        correctional education student guidance program was established at
        Elmira (p. 108). By 1937 New York State correctional education had
        progressed: one reporter characterized correctional education during
        1932 as

> a minor element in the institutional program. The
> vitality which had attended the organization of
> the programs thirty years or more ago had largely
> disappeared. The body still lived, but breath was
> slow and the spirit had almost departed. Routine and
> lethargy had a stranglehold on teaching methods and
> materials. The books in use still carried the slogan,
> 'Remember the Maine,' [they were from the 19th
> century] and beyond teaching a few men to read
> and write programs in many institutions were non-
> existent. Vocational training, what there was of it, was
> carried on in sublime disregard of industrial, economic
> and social changes on the outside, and was designed
> largely for output rather than training. (MacCormick,
> 1937, pp. 3, 8).

The increased attention to correctional education prompted
some observers to articulate honest sentiments. At the American Prison
Congress, **Warden Stanley Ashe** made the following observation:

> Every prison administrator will agree that education
> plays a very important part in every man's
> development. He will also agree that education is a
> necessary element in the rehabilitation of criminals.
> Yet, few prison administrators have gone beyond
> a mere gesture, in actual practice, in providing the
> inmates of their respective institutions with adequate
> educational opportunities. We all do lip service to a
> number of modern penological theories, but few of
> us are sufficiently aroused by our temporary bursts of
> enthusiasm to put inspiration into practice. (Gaither,
> 1982, p. 21).

1933 — New York **Governor Lehman** established a Commission for the Study
      of Educational Problems of Penal Institutions for Youth. In 1934 he
      appointed **Professor N.L. Engelhardt**, of Teachers College, Columbia
      University, to chair it. (Wallack, 1939, p. 12). The Commission's name

1933 and mission were later adjusted; its new title was the Commission on
(cont'd.) Education in Correctional Institutions in the State of New York (Kendall, 1981). Wallack, Kendall, and Briggs later reported that "The Engelhardt Commission...[took] up where the Lewisohn Commission left off..." in the process of identifying and correcting problems of correctional education implementation. Some of the Commission's accomplishments included (a) public conferences and exhibits on correctional education, (b) "a training course at Teachers College, Columbia University, for educational workers in correctional institutions," (c) Experimental projects in vocational education and social education, funded "with a $25,000 grant obtained from the Carnegie Corporation, through the American Association for Adult Education," and (d) a new law establishing a Division of Education in the Department of Correction. (1939, p. 12). The statewide correctional education staff consisted of a director and two assistants—one in vocational education and the other in social education (MacCormick, 1937, p. 8). In addition, the schools at Elmira Reformatory (see 1934 entry) and Wallkill and Clinton prisons "stood out as educational systems which provided a model for other systems throughout the country to follow." (Roberts, 1971, p. 13—see 1937 entry). 𝒪

The New York State Vocational Association had its first conference session on correctional education. This practice was continued each year. (Wallack, 1939, p. 31). 𝒪

Concerned inmates founded the Stateville (Illinois) Prison Correspondence School, and were assigned an office—cell #12 on One Gallery, C House (Leopold, 1958, p. 228). **Professor Bailey** "was most gracious in acting as our nominal boss, just as he did in the library." The founders divided up the work of writing curricula, and "after a couple of months we had seventy or eighty students in more than a dozen courses." (p. 229—see 1935 entry). 𝒪

Gorky Colony, in the Ukraine, was consolidated with another juvenile institution (Makarenko, 1973, vol. 1, p. 352—see 1917-1923 entries). The improvements that Anton Makarenko had implemented would have a profound impact on Soviet correctional education, and even on Soviet local school education. 𝒪

Franklin Delano Roosevelt wrote the following words in a biography of **Thomas Mott Osborne** (see 1913 entry):

> Thomas Mott Osborne had courage; even his enemies admit that; he had vision; even those who laughed at him twenty years ago admit that now. Nearly a century ago Charles Dickens [see 1842 entry] and others brought out the physical harms of a prison system which had not changed in a thousand years....Mr. Osborne was the

great pioneer in calling our attention to these physical conditions. His was a voice crying in the wilderness and it has been only in the past half dozen years that society as a whole and leaders of government have heeded the appeal....His deep principle was wholly sound—that human beings who are apprehended and punished by the State for sins against society can, in a very large percentage of cases, be restored to society as law-abiding citizens. He was right in holding that the prisons themselves were the key to the problem...many perfectly well-meaning people were unable to grasp the fundamentals which he advanced....Let us remember that penology as a social science is still in its infancy and that the greatest tribute which we can pay Mr. Osborne's memory will be to carry on the fight relentlessly, and with the high idealism which he so well exemplified. (Roosevelt, in Tannenbaum, 1933, pp. ix-x).

The book that contained the president's message was **Frank Tannenbaum**'s *Osborne of Sing Sing*.

In the career of the criminal, imprisonment served chiefly as an interlude between two periods of crime... Osborne attempted to change that basic experience of the men in prison by turning the penal institution into a community with new interests, stimuli, and activity that would in turn become the source of new ideas and new ideals, new interests and new attitudes.... It is important to remember that Osborne was no mere theorist...[his work] represents a great human adventure. He literally did the impossible. In spite of all the scoffing and ridicule he did what no one had had the courage to do before—to take men in prison as men, to trust them, to work with them as with human beings...[but] the evils Osborne fought against persisted beyond his day and unfortunately still persist in various places. (Tannenbaum, 1933, pp. xii-xiii).

Dr. Felix Adler said

'he [Osborne] stands today as the representative of a great redemptive movement....For Mr. Osborne is not only redeeming the prisoner—that is the obvious view of it—he is trying to redeem us...the spirit of Tom Brown (Osborne's prison name), like that of John Brown, will go marching on until the last vestige of the old system shall be effaced from this fair earth'....Judge Wadhams said: 'Elizabeth Fry [see 1832 entry] visited

1933
(cont'd.)

the prisons, Howard [see entry in the Introduction] suggested reform and Dickens disclosed conditions in jails; but it remained for Osborne to solve the prison problem. He has established a new system of prison management. We must carry it on. (p. 144).

If Osborne's system was so much better, what was the old system? Overcrowding, brutality, rotten food, vermin, etc.

A sentence to Sing Sing for a term of several years is too often equivalent to a slow death sentence. Many become affected with tuberculosis and are sent out into the world too much diseased to earn their livelihood. Often they carry the germs of this malady into their families and become a menace to the health of the community in which they live. (pp. 7-8).

The 'Old Timers' and 'Second Timers' tell [a new prisoner],' says an inmate, 'tales of how they were treated, that he cannot get justice and gradually the leaven of every prisoner enters his heart 'How can he escape.' He becomes shifty, constantly scheming how to outwit his guards and how to make a get away from the Prison'.... Yes, it is true that many are anemic or otherwise ill, all are pallid, listless, inert, silent, moody, furtive and resentful, watching the screws (guards) and shrinking at their approach, thirsting for hot stuff (dope), planning to go back to the old life and with not a shred of hope that starvation can be long warded off by any other manner of life when the grated doors shall open and usher them one by one to freedom....If the system succeeds it destroys all the convict's manly qualities, makes him a spineless nonentity, an imbecile, a suicide. If it fails it makes him a confirmed criminal. (pp. 41-42).

[S]ociety seemed so organized as to make a change in the criminal's career exceedingly difficult if not impossible. Osborne set out to challenge the whole scheme of penal administration not only so as to change the influence of the prison upon the prisoner but so as to change the prisoner before his return to society and in the process change the community's attitude towards the released prisoner. (pp. 55-56). ᗡ

A series of sensational local newspaper articles assaulted **Howard Gill**'s Norfolk Prison rehabilitation experiments. He was also "fending off attacks from...disgruntled politicians...who accused him of

210

1933   'coddling' his inmates." (Serrill, 1982, p. 25). The stories originated with
(cont'd.) unhappy staff members and a state auditor who, Gill is convinced, was
        sent in to dig up evidence of malfeasance that would give the governor
        an excuse to terminate the experiment. In early 1934, Gill was suspended
        "pending an investigation of charges by the auditor and others." A few
        months afterwards, public hearings were held. "Gill says he exonerated
        himself" (p. 31—see 1934 entry). ⌁

        Approximately 60% of all inmates at Federal institutions were
        enrolled in school programs (Roberts, 1971, p. 13—see 1946 entry). The
        following decades would witness great improvements in the school
        programs at Federal institutions. ⌁

1934 — Correctional education programming had become well established in
        two systems—New York State's and the Federal Bureau of Prisons.
        Both adopted compulsory attendance policies. (Reagen and Stoughton,
        1976, p. 60). ⌁

        In its report, the State of New York's Commission for the
        Study of the Educational Problems of Penal Institutions for Youth
        recommended that educational programs should be of a quality and
        scope sufficient to provide reasonable chances for offenders to develop
        necessary skills and attitudes (Roberts, 1971, pp. 13-15). However, the
        record indicates that there were still some problems. A lesson sheet at
        Elmira Reformatory began with this introduction: "If you follow these
        instructions, nothing will happen to you." (Kendall, in Roberts, 1973,
        p. 96). Thirty-four trades were offered at Elmira (Wallack, Kendall, and
        Briggs, 1939, p. 17). The educational reorganization there resulted in
        individualized instruction for each inmate not later than three months
        after he was assigned to the institution (p. 17). Sex offenders were
        no longer tracked into certain vocational classes (p. 18). Fifteen new
        instructional positions were established, and one for a Director of
        Education (p. 19). The major instructional task was defined in this way:
        "to give encouragement without making that his [the teacher's] chief
        business" (p. 20). Compulsory attendance was eliminated at Elmira
        (p. 21—see entries for 1885 and 1934). After the Elmira reorganization
        was completed, efforts were focused on Wallkill and Clinton prisons,
        where social/vocational education experiments were implemented.
        Before opening the new school at Woodbourne Institution for Defective
        Delinquents (see 1915 entry), a group of inmate teachers was selected
        and trained (see 1925 entry). (Wallack, 1939, p. 48). ⌁

        Howard Gill was fired from his job as Massachusetts Prison
        warden, as result of a "political fight that lasted five months" (Murton,
        1976, p. 213—see 1933 entry). Later, Gill "commented that 'society's test
        of prisons is whether men come back again or not, and it is not a fair
        test as long as society fails to clean up its cesspools." (Gill, in Serrill,
        1982, p. 32).

211

Yahkub makes the same point, saying that 'the essential difficulty...in rehabilitative penology is the fact that our very social pattern creates criminals. The criminal on one level is merely carrying out...the spirit of the society in which he exists... (Yahkub, in Serrill, 1982, p. 32—see 1889 entry).

In 1935 a Bureau of Social Hygiene (see 1911 entry) report explained that Massachusetts citizens felt Norfolk was "too extravagant for a criminal population" (Serrill, 1982, p. 30). By 1955 the institution was renamed the State Prison Colony (p. 25). ☁

Father Flanagan reported that even the roughest "boys can detect truth from counterfeit...quickly....They can perceive weakness and hypocrisy in your eyes before you even open your mouth and remove all doubt." (Oursler, and Oursler, 1949, p. 5). There was additional news from Boys Town.

In December 1934 came official recognition by the government of the United States that the place called Boys Town had become an actual municipality, with a postal identity of its own....In September of 1935 an amendment was made to the Articles of Incorporation naming Boys Town as the place of business of the home—an incorporated village with a population of two hundred and seventy-five....When you have a real town you have to have a real government. They would need a mayor, a city clerk, a commissioner of police, and a commissioner of sanitation, and others. The election campaign included parades through the dining hall, with banners, placards, and songs. There were whoop-it-up rallies, and speeches by candidates of just-formed rival parties—the 'Build Boys Town Party' and the 'Help Our Town Party,' known as the BBTs and the HOTs. In the heat of the contest, boy candidates took to making campaign promises, too. Some were assuring the voters that if elected the candidate guaranteed to get the whole school one extra trip a month into town. Others were promising that instead of one movie a week at Boys Town, there would be two. First mayor under the new setup was Tony Villone, who had come into the home in 1931. Today [1949] he has an important job with Metro-Goldwyn-Mayer at Culver City, California. (p. 248).

With the coming of war in 1941, many of the recreational activities of the home had to be curtailed. The powers of the boy government were sharply limited, and a

<table>
</table>

1934
(cont'd.)

military training program for older boys, under the control of an army colonel, continued during the war years. Since then the original powers of the Boys Town government have gradually been restored and strengthened. (pp. 249).

By 1948 'civil authorities' were again in full control. Today's system has changed little from early times; it is a representative form of elective government patterned after the city government of Omaha. Elected for six-month terms are seventeen commissioners and four councilmen. The mayor is chosen by the boys from the four councilmen, who constitute a board of 'elder statesmen.' Voting citizens are the youngest participating in any municipal elections in the nation, probably in the world. Sole requirements of a voter are that he be a citizen of Boys Town and be able to read and write his own name. There have been Negro mayors and white, Catholic and Protestant, and many of these were among the most bedraggled and hopeless when they first came to town. (pp. 249-250).

There is a commissioner for each apartment house in Boys Town, and each commissioner is responsible for order in his territory and for the 'orientation' of new boys... (p. 251—see entries for 1948 and 1949).

McNeil Island Federal Penitentiary was dubbed "the Harvard of our penitentiaries." That year inmate "Reading gained in popularity ...by 133 percent at McNeil" (Tucker, in Keve, 1984, p. 212). The *Island Lantern* inmate newspaper reported that the largest library in the Federal system, at McNeil, had 10,000 volumes. "**Austin MacCormick**... who was responsible for promotion of academic programs in all the federal institutions, gave...successful leadership." "By the 1950s the school program was run by a full-time staff of one principal and four teachers. More than half of the inmates were taking courses..." (Keve, 1984, p. 212; emphasis added). When the Navy gave the institution a 120-foot sub chaser, it was "refitted with a better engine and adapted for passenger service under its new name, the A.H. MacCormick" (p. 230).

1935 — The inmate-founded Stateville (Illinois) Correspondence School was visited by **Prince Louis Ferdinand**, the grandson of former Kaiser Wilhelm II (Leopold, 1958, p. 236). In 1934, the founders had received a letter from **Albert Einstein**, in response to their inquiry regarding appropriate reading material to prepare students for study in higher mathematics (Leopold, 1958, p. 235). In a comparison between Stateville courses and those of the Chicago public schools,

Dr. William Johnson, head of the Chicago Board of Education, and **Dr. Don Rogers**, assistant superintendent, visited the school and took some of our final examinations to administer to five hundred pupils in the Chicago public high schools. The highest grades the Chicago pupils scored were about equal to our lowest. (Leopold, 1958, p. 229; emphases added).

As a result, transfer credit was awarded to Stateville Prison graduates upon request (Leopold, 1958, p. 230). Several public school systems asked to adopt the Stateville English curricula. The program was now funded through the Inmate's Amusement Fund. (Leopold, 1958, p. 231). ⌂

New York State's Correction Law defined correctional education: "the socialization of the inmates through varied impressional and expressional activities, with emphasis on individual inmate needs" (Wallack, 1939, p. 33). The State Commissioner of Education, in cooperation with the Commissioner of Correction and the Director of Education (a Correction employee) were authorized to establish educational criteria for correctional educator licensure. The standards included coursework in "penology, sociology, psychology, philosophy, in the special subjects to be taught, and in any other professional courses as may be deemed necessary by the responsible officers." (p. 35). **Governor Lehman** acted on a recommendation from the Commission on Education in Correctional Institutions, which expressed the need to replace inmate teachers with qualified civilians. As a result, each New York State institution added two civilian instructors to its staff. (p. 192—see 1847 entry). ⌂

At the American Prison Association's 65th Annual Congress of Correction, **Mr. C.J. Francis**, director of education at Southern Michigan State Prison, reported that a wide variety of educational programs were required to meet the objectives of correctional education. These objectives consisted of (a) learning to read and write, (b) developing interests which improve opportunities for advancement, (c) increasing the students' sense of responsibility, (d) acquiring problem solving skills, and (e) developing salable academic and occupational skills. (Roberts, 1971, pp. 15-16). Note: John Gaither later reported that Francis' speech was delivered at the 1938 Congress, which would be the 68th (Gaither, 1982, p. 21). ⌂

The ongoing Depression prompted a rethinking of prison industries. Congress passed the Ashurst-Summers Act, eliminating the sale of prison made goods in the free labor market (Reagen and Stoughton, 1973, pp. 58-59—see 1940 entry). ⌂

1935   With more than 1,500 inmates, the Soviet Union's Bolchevo
(cont'd.) Colony was one of the largest open institutions in the world. See 1924
entry. Its population of "habitual criminals" stabilized—"the average
number of sentences per inmate was at least nine. Special schools were
built for the inmate's children, and teachers were hired to instruct them.
"All working prisoners were paid the same wages as civilian workers...
the institution was self-supporting as of 1930..." Furloughs were often
used for trips to Moscow. "Lectures, concerts, and theatricals succeeded
each other; courses in general studies or special studies in drama; dance
and voice were available...recidivism was believed to be approximately
ten per cent...Bolchevo was closed soon after the outbreak of World
War II, as was the case with a large number of 'Makarenko colonies.'"
(Eriksson, 1976, pp. 149-151). ⌒

There were abiding problems in the local schools to which most
modern correctional educators can relate, associated with the nation's
background of slavery and Jim Crow segregation.

> In Minneapolis [local public schools]...there were
> no black counselors for Negro children, and white
> counselors had little knowledge of the 'job outlook
> for Negroes.' The career choices of Negro schoolboys
> in that city differed sharply from the actual patterns
> of employment of black men: 58.6 percent of the male
> students chose professional jobs, whereas only 4.4
> percent of men were so employed...70.1 percent of
> Negro employees worked in unskilled jobs, whereas
> only 2.5 percent of boys selected unskilled positions.
> Parents shared similarly high aspirations for their
> children's careers. (Tyack, 1974, pp. 222-223). ⌒

1936 — New York State's Lehman Commission (the Commission on Education
in Correctional Institutions) submitted a report that "forms a platform
for correctional education. Copies have been sent gratis to all the adult
institutions in the country." (MacCormick, 1937, p. 8). The Commission
found that

> The basic and ultimate aim of the correctional
> institution may be stated to be 'the social and economic
> rehabilitation of inmates.' This is certainly the major
> objective of education in correctional institutions.
> Delinquents and criminals are socially and vocationally
> maladjusted. They represent a definite and special
> problem for adjustment. The maladjustments result
> from many causes, some of which operated before
> incarceration and some of which are involved in
> confinement away from a normal social environment.
> (Wallack, 1939, first page).

1936 New York State's correctional education system acquired an improved
(cont'd.) supervisory capability when the Department of Correction established
two assistant directors, one in charge of general (academic) education
and another in charge of vocational education (p. 12—see 1937 entry
for information that may explain the contrast between this report and
the one made for 1933, which assigned an assistant director to social
education rather than to general education). The Central Guard School
at Wallkill was organized and directed by the Division of Education in
the Department of Correction (p. 29). The scope of correctional education
in New York State was thus expanded to include officer training.

> During the year 1936-37 (the first year that the Division
> of Education has been fully organized) a large part of
> the time of the Director of Education and the entire
> time of one assistant director has been devoted to
> the Guard School. While this project has somewhat
> delayed development of inmate education it is already
> paying dividends in increased understanding of
> and cooperation with the objectives and work of
> correctional education on the part of all institutional
> personnel. (MacCormick, 1937, p. 8).

In addition to these systemwide improvements, the literature also
includes reports regarding school-based programs. Out of 745 men
committed to Elmira Reformatory, 631 had no previous vocation.
(Wallack, 1939, p. 62). At the Coxsackie Institution an instructor
provided evening classes for the faculty in "Methods of Teaching
Shop Subjects." By 1937 these classes were offered on Saturdays at a
nearby center. (Wallack, Kendall, and Briggs, 1939, p. 69). Furthermore,
two innovative special education programs were implemented. An
experiment was conducted at the institution for defective delinquents
at Napanoch, to determine whether "low grade defectives could and
should be taught to read." (Wallack, 1939, p. 247). At Woodbourne
Institution for Defective Delinquents another experiment focused on
instruction in reading and social concepts (p. 249).

1937 — New York State's Engelhardt Commission reported that the division
of correctional education into "general" (academic) and "vocational"
sections was for administrative purposes only. The Commission's report
focused on the role of education in the socialization and rehabilitation
processes; it emphasized the need to go beyond the "Three Rs" to
meaningful development of values and attitudes. (Roberts, 1971, p.
15). Also in New York, a director of education was appointed at Sing
Sing Prison (Wallack, 1939, p. 284). The Annual Report of the Division
of Education reviewed the changes in legal provisions for correctional
education in the State since 1822 (Kendall, 1939, p. 2). **Mrs. Harvey E.
Stone**, who had served as head teacher at Auburn Women's Prison
from 1910 to 1932, told a reporter that "The real purpose of the school

1937
(cont'd.)
was to correct the attitudes of the prisoners toward society." (Wallack, Kendall, and Briggs, 1939, p. 26). In a similar vein, **Wallack, Kendall,** and **Briggs** wrote in their 1939 book that

> Modern correctional education programs differ from the older programs not so much in stated objectives, although these have been clarified, but in the development of what are believed to be more effective procedures of achieving the objectives—particularly the changing of attitudes. (p. 27).

One school-based improvement this year was at Woodbourne Institution for Defective Delinquents, where Saturday morning classes in related vocational (academic) subjects were established in order to avoid interruption of the work schedule (p. 82). The Engelhardt Commission was still operational in 1941 (New York, 1941, p. 1).

Consistent with the new developments in the field, a new language was emerging to describe its aspirations and problems. **Dr. Ross Pugmire** defined correctional education:

> Correctional Education is the process or the means of achieving the reformation, correction, or rehabilitation of inmates in correctional institutions. It comprehends all of the experiences which such an institution can bring into the lives of those inmates...goes beyond the programs of academic and vocational instruction....It makes prisons and reformatories basically educational institutions. (Wallack, 1939, p. 37).

The first edition of *Correctional Education* (now called the *Journal of Correctional Education*) was published by the American Prison Association Standing Committee on Education. One article included this statement: "In the last ten years there has been a definite trend from correspondence to classroom instruction." (Wallack, 1939, p. 279). That statement may have been premature. The Committee was chaired by **John Cranor**; its membership included *Journal* editor **Austin MacCormick**, as well as New York State's **Walter Wallack** and U.S. education commissioner **J.W. Studebaker**. It was funded by a grant from "the American Association for Adult Education, a child of the Carnegie Corporation and the leading organization in the field of adult education in America." (MacCormick, 1937, p. 4). Commissioner Studebaker was quoted:

> The only possible justification for releasing a prisoner from incarceration is the expectation that he will not again break the law....It is only as the revenge idea of incarceration disappears that we begin to be practical

enough to see that education—adequate education—for prisoners is the obvious answer to our problem... adult education in prisons can salvage and rehabilitate untold numbers of mentally and morally confused persons. When correctional institutions become educational institutions not only will crime drop, but hundreds of thousands of men and women will be lifted to new and useful lives, with corresponding positive benefits to society. (Studebaker, in MacCormick, 1937, p. 5).

Correctional Education served the combined roles of the current CEA *Journal of Correctional Education* and the CEA *News and Notes* newsletter. Every adult institution in the country was surveyed for news for the "Correctional Education Here and There" column.

The educational program of the Federal penal and correctional institutions and that of New York State have been accorded the honor of leading articles because of the fact that these two prison systems appear to have made greater progress in their educational programs during the last decade than any other prison systems in the country. A few individual prisons in other parts of the country have also made outstanding progress but the Federal Government and the State of New York, taking their institutions as a whole, have unquestionably led the way in recent years. (p. 4—see 1934 entry).

The New York article began with a paragraph that included this phrase: "...the education of adult prisoners is progressing in New York State." See 1912 entry—this phrase was used by **Zebulon Brockway** and borrowed by Austin MacCormick as the title of his 1931 book. The article went on to describe New York State's cultural/lecture program at Sing Sing and its handout clearinghouse distribution system of teacher-designed materials (p. 3).

Like Einstein's expanding universe (see 1935 entry), educational programs are never finished....New York's program of Correctional Education has reached a point where it is well-housed in several institutions, and better housed than ever before in all institutions; personnel, supplies and equipment are improved and increased; trained central supervision is directing the work, and keeping it on the move; a new spirit of progress pervades the personnel; new materials and methods are being produced and tried out; administrative cooperation is apparent everywhere. (p. 11).

1937   This paragraph summarized the Federal correctional education report:
(cont'd.)

> For the last three months of the fiscal year 1936-37 more than five thousand prisoners in the Federal penitentiaries, reformatories, jails, and camps, were enrolled in some form of educational work; approximately four thousand were attending regular classes in elementary education or selected special courses; more than twelve hundred men were being supervised as vocational trainees; and a little over sixteen hundred were enrolled in cell-study and correspondence courses. For the same three months' period, an average of 1,560 standardized educational achievement tests were administered. (p. 6). ᐃ

Correctional Education reported that New York City Commissioner of Correction **Austin MacCormick** served as chairman of a new "Friends of Prison Libraries Committee." Many prominent correctional education librarians served on the Committee, including Minnesota's **Perrie Jones**. (MacCormick, 1937, p. 7—see 1928 entry). In New York, "Sing Sing, Wallkill, and Elmira have outstanding libraries in charge of civilians. Wallkill employed the first full-time trained librarian in the state institutions during the past year." (p. 11). The Federal Bureau of Prisons had a supervising librarian and "eight trained full-time librarians distributed among the major Federal institutions." (p. 6). ᐃ

From *Correctional Education* we can also identify some relevant trends: (a) institutional high school instruction was clearly expanding, especially through correspondence courses, (b) chaplains were still in charge of correctional education programming in many facilities, (c) there were a great many inmate teachers (see entries for 1805 and 1932), (d) some wardens resented Federally-supported Works Progress Administration instructors and free instructional materials (see 1938 entry), (e) the Minnesota custom of charging $.25 to visitors and using the proceeds for library books had become established in Iowa (see 1902 entry), (f) at several sites, library books were purchased with fees from inmate "book clubs," (g) the Iowa correctional education library model—state library coordination—had been replicated in most states, (h) many institutional schools offered typing and shorthand courses for male offenders (see 1907 entry), (i) unlikely vocational courses such as "navigation" and "aviation" were sometimes offered, (j) structural linkages between correctional education and state departments of education were being developed, and between correctional education and the state universities, (k) individualized instruction was pursued all around the country in correctional education, and (l) new institutional schools were being established. This edition reported new institutional

1937   schools in Michigan, Montana, New Mexico, North Carolina, and
(cont'd.) West Virginia. (MacCormick, 1937, pp. 12-24). ⌒

          Mettray closed. It had been the innovative French juvenile
institution. Mettray had become "the focus of increasingly bitter public
criticism." (Eriksson, 1976, p. 128—see entries for 1840 and 1900). ⌒

1938 — The American Prison Association established a Standing Committee on
        Libraries (Wallack, 1939, p. 26). It was chaired by **Mildred Methven**,
        who prepared a list of 1,000 Books for Prison Libraries (MacCormick, in
        Roberts, 1973, p. 328—see 1877 entry). The list was "made possible by
        a grant of funds from the Carnegie Corporation through the American
        Association for Adult Education" (MacCormick, 1939, p. 2). It was
        sent gratis to institutions, and was also on sale for $.50 per copy (p.
        5). Methven succeeded Perrie Jones as Minnesota's institution library
        supervisor. In admiration of her work, **Austin MacCormick** wrote that
        "Only those who have served time can fully appreciate what books mean
        in prison, what light they may bring into dark cells, and what powerful
        instruments of mental therapy and education they are." (p. 2). ⌒

          Perrie Jones's article "Institution Libraries—1853-1927," on
Minnesota correctional education libraries, appeared in *Library News
and Notes* (MacCormick, in Roberts, 1973, p. 318). It was followed
by another article in the same issue, by **Mildred Methven**, "Library
Development Since 1927" (Methven, 1938, pp. 177-179). Jones' article
included a history of the library at Minnesota Prison. See 1902 entry.
She reported that at the Red Wing Training School for Boys (established
in 1867, with a library) there was "no privilege connected with the
School more highly prized than that of the library." The library moved
with the school in 1886 and was expanded by a $500 appropriation in
1887. (Jones, 1938, p. 175). One thousand dollars was set aside for a
library at the State Reformatory at St. Cloud, but the institution was not
opened until 1899. Another $1,000 was directed to the same purpose in
1892, but a new superintendent was assigned in 1895—thus began what
Methven described as the "doldrums." (Jones, 1938, p. 176—see 1907
entry for a description of the progress made during Carey's tenure).
Methven's article covered the 1928-1938 period. She reported that the
Minnesota correctional library system was funded at $.52 per reader
in 1937. Miss Jones worked "to further efforts for [the wards'] return
to society, [and] to assist in ameliorating their restricted existence. To
accomplish this our program includes: Trained librarians; adequate
book collections, equipment and housing; furtherance of certain studies
to make the service more effective." Methven wrote of the "spiritual
necessity before us of making every man and woman possible a self-
supporting unit in the community." Jones made the libraries

          more accessible and satisfactory reading rooms were
          secured in eleven institutions....Standard library

1938
(cont'd.)

equipment, in the way of catalog cases, picture files, globes, and shelving, in addition to suitable chairs and tables, were provided by the superintendents....[She established] a very close coordination of the library with the school activities....In the prisons where an active school program is in force, the library is constantly used. Rules have been relaxed and minimized, regular inventories initiated, accurate local shelf lists made, duplicate shelf lists for the headquarters office file provided, regular monthly reports standardized and adequate statistics assembled. (Methven, 1938, p. 177).

Jones reported

an underlying, consistent effort to make each one who comes into the library realize that here is a friendly place, that all libraries will be friendly places, and that when he goes back to his old community, or to a new one, he can feel that already there is one friend waiting for him, the library.

Many of the libraries under Jones' care doubled in circulation. She "was able to secure eight college-and-library trained people for library service in these institutions....This seems the major achievement" of her term as supervisor, since it was the librarian's job "to know her... students and to bring to them all the library has to offer." She also started a professional library at the Board of Control headquarters (the State Library came under the Board), obtained the services of apprentice students and two Works Progress Administration workers, established the informal "Twin City Remedial Reading Discussion Group," and helped to found "a course for hospital librarians...offered by the University of Minnesota, Division of Library Instruction." Jones resigned in 1937 "to become Librarian of the St. Paul Public Library....The cumulative effect of more than 25 years of continuous supervision and direction of the libraries in Minnesota's state institutions by a member of the Board of Control staff is one of unquestionable success." (pp. 178-179).

As in previous years, local school educators were attracted to recent developments in the field of correctional education.

The American Association of School Administrators, at its annual conference in Atlantic City, invited a dozen penologists and educators interested in prison education to address one of its sessions on 'Reduction in Crime Through Improved Public Educational Programs and the Educational Rehabilitation of Prison Inmates.' (Wallack, 1939, p. 31).

1938　　This session marked an important juncture in the local school/
(cont'd.)　correctional education relationship.

> Although seats were available for only approximately
> 700 people in the assigned rooms, fully 2,000 more
> members and guests of the Convention assembled in
> adjoining rooms, corridors, and lobbies, and listened
> in on loud speakers to the program which had been
> prepared. (MacCormick, 1938, p. 8).

The list of speakers reads like a "Who's Who" of 1930s correctional
education. It included Sing Sing warden **Lewis Lawes**, **William
Grady** (see 1939 entry), **Austin MacCormick**, Professor **N.L.
Engelhardt** (see 1933 entry), criminology author **Harry Elmer Barnes**,
Walter Wallack, New York Board of Education vice president **James
Marshall**, and U.S. commissioner of education **John W. Studebaker**
(see 1937 entry). Lawes' speech, "The Products of the Schools as I Find
Them," later appeared in the June, 1938 edition of *Harper's Magazine*,
and Marshall's, "Maladjustment as a Factor in Delinquency," in the
May, 1938 edition of *School Executive*. (p. 8—see entries for 1939 and
1981). 🔺

　　A class in functional psychology was started at Attica Prison in
New York State (Wallack, 1939, p. 177). Deaf inmates at Woodbourne
Institution were taught to read lips (Wallack, 1939, p. 249). 🔺

　　Walter Wallack's book, *The Training of Prison Guards*, was
published by Teachers College, Columbia University (Wallack, 1939,
p. 41—see 1936 entry). It was based on Wallack's dissertation, which
was done in completion of his doctor of education degree at Teachers
College, Columbia University (Wallack, 1937). 🔺

　　The second edition of *Correctional Education* (see 1937 entry)
began with a cover story on the Extension Division at San Quentin (see
1914 entry).

> In our University Extension System mathematics is the
> highest rating interest and English is a close second.
> The system offers approximately 250 different courses.
> Of the enrollments 46 per cent complete their courses,
> although in correspondence courses bought from the
> traditional schools, research indicates that not more
> than 5 percent of those who buy courses complete
> them. (MacCormick, 1938, p. 2).

　　The *Journal* committee expressed the "belief...that correctional
education, in its broadest sense, includes the training of officers as well
as prisoners." Articles on guard training in the New York State and

1938 Federal systems were included. Correctional education use of Works
(cont'd.) Progress Administration resources was a major development.

> Attention is called to the fact that an increasing
> number of institutions report the effective use of
> teachers and other educational personnel supplied by
> the Works Progress Administration. The report from
> North Carolina indicates that its prison is making
> more extensive use of W.P.A. teachers than any other
> reporting. (p. 4).

In the "Correctional Education Here and There" column, several
trends can be identified: (a) social education was emerging around
the country, but mostly without that descriptive title, (b) passage of
the Hawes-Cooper Act (see 1929 entry) led to the establishment of
several new institutional schools to "take up the scheduling slack"
left by curtailed prison industries, (c) new programs were announced
in Delaware, Maine, Oklahoma, and Washington State, (d) programs
were closed in Maine (for use as a dormitory), Montana (because of a
lack of funds), and Vermont (for reorganization), (e) "Americanization"
classes—similar to what we now call English as a second language
programs, were started in some states, (f) the Spanish language was
taught in two Washington State prisons, and a science lab was at one
in Massachusetts, (g) recreation efforts were often coordinated by the
education departments (see 1930 entry), (h) the 1/2 day work, 1/2 day
school inmate schedule was in place at several institutions, and (i) New
York State's correctional education system was moving toward a focus
on "attitudes, skills, and knowledges" (the reverse of the traditional
"knowledge, skills, and attitudes" approach)—see 1897 entry on
Germany. Regarding this last trend, **Mr. Price Chenault** (see 1946 entry)
was in charge of a "study of inmate attitudes" project at State Vocational
Institution at West Coxsackie. (pp. 9-23). ⌒

> **Rosenberger** offered four suggestions for correctional
education improvement. These included (a) programs for adults
should be on an adult level, but (b) provide elementary courses, (c)
high school courses should be provided for those who are ready for
them, and (d) college level correspondence courses should be offered
(Gaither, 1982, p. 21). ⌒

New attention was directed to themes that seem commonplace
today, especially the relation between education and crime. In
England,

> 2.9% of the prison population, or 794 men and 153
> women, were illiterate; 1,672 could read and write only
> imperfectly. In the same year approximately 9.5 per
> cent of some 12,500 inmates of New York state prisons

1938
(cont'd.)
were illiterate; if prisoners in special institutions for mental defectives were omitted, the ratio was still 6 per cent. (Grunhut, 1973/1948, p. 241). ⌒

The average number of library volumes per prisoner in the U.S. was 41.4; roughly 75% of the inmate population were readers, averaging 70 books per year. At Alcatraz, 93% of the inmates read, averaging 102 books per reader. In the Federal institutions, almost 1/3 of the books read were non-fiction; non-fiction borrowing was greater where trained full-time librarians were assigned, some averaging up to 45%. (Grunhut, 1973/1948, p. 243). ⌒

1939 — Columbia University's Teachers College Press published **Dr. Glenn Kendall**'s book on social education, *The Organization and Teaching of Social and Economic Studies in Correctional Institutions* (Kendall, 1939). Kendall wrote of the need for courses in addition to those in reading and writing or vocational skills, "courses...which will improve the inmate's attitudes toward society, broaden his concepts, and deepen his insight.... Unless desirable social attitudes are developed, facts and skills will be useless to the individual and may even be used against society." (p. 6). He recommended that social education should be organized around selected problems or units "preferably...chosen by the class and individual..." (p. 32). Kendall reported that "The ever-present and all-powerful basic problem of every inmate is 'How can I get out of prison soon?'" (p. 33). His analysis of offender attitudes toward education, presentation of illustrative learning units, and discussion of teaching procedures and techniques make this the definitive book on social education. ⌒

At California's San Quentin Prison, "the educational director worked with a staff of one hundred inmate helpers, all of them with practical and theoretical qualifications in education" (Grunhut, 1973/1948, p. 234). This pattern, inherited from the monitorial approach to tutoring in the early 19th century and perfected at Elmira Reformatory during the last decades of that century, would dominate correctional education throughout the U.S. until at least the mid 1960s. ⌒

Some systems were experimenting with outside services. For example, in Wisconsin prisons reading instruction was offered by the public library (Grunhut, 1973/1948, p. 234). ⌒

With regard to replicable models for administering prison education throughout a jurisdiction, New York State and the Federal Bureau of Prisons led the way. "Pennsylvania and New York benefited by the central direction of state bureaux or boards of correction" (Grunhut, 1973/1948, p. 234). ⌒

Walter Wallack, **Glenn Kendall**, and **Howard Brigg**'s book, *Education Within Prison Walls*, was published by Columbia University's

1939   Teachers College Press. The authors focused on correctional education
(cont'd.) progress in New York State since Austin MacCormick's 1931 book.
Regarding vocational education, they wrote that

> The worker released from prison should have acquired
> not only usable skills but that pride in high-grade
> performance which enables one to 'get a kick' out of
> doing a job well. He must be trained to the point where
> he gains more satisfaction from the performance of
> legitimate work than from criminal activities. (Wallack,
> Kendall, and Briggs, 1939, p. 29).

Regarding subject matter they wrote:

> The main effort in improving instructional techniques
> and practices during the present stage of development
> has been concerned with shifting the emphasis from
> traditional subject matter to problems which are really
> vital to inmates. Facts and techniques are of value only
> when they assist an individual to solve his problems.
> (p. 35).

"Grammatical forms as well as certain mathematical puzzles are losing
their sanctity" as a focus of instruction and learning (p. 38). Regarding
recreation, they wrote: "At the present time emphasis seems to be upon
the entertainment of inmates rather than upon the legitimate values
inherent in physical education and recreational activities, a condition
which should be corrected" (p. 43).

The first Handbook of the American Prison Association's
Committee on Education, *Correctional Education Today*, was edited by
Walter Wallack and published by Columbia University's Teachers
College Press. In part, it was reported that "...prisoners are quite
deficient in what might be called 'social intelligence'" (Wallack, 1939,
p. 106). "Too often education in correctional institutions seems to mean
only a few classrooms in which the three R's are taught" (Wallack, 1939,
p. 108). The book was funded by a grant from the Carnegie Corporation,
through the American Association for Adult Education—see 1927
entry. Copies were sent to institutions free of charge, and those with
"extensive programs" received several copies. Otherwise, the normal
cost was $1.00 per copy. (MacCormick, 1939, p. 1). The 1939 journal,
Correctional Education, was less extensive than those of 1937 and 1938
as a result of the additional work and expense of this important book
project (p. 2).

The Division of Education in the New York State Department
of Correction had applied individualized methods exclusively in social
education at Elmira Reformatory. To correct this situation, an adjustment

1939
(cont'd.)
was required. "Elmira no longer depends entirely upon individualized instruction in social education but is utilizing group discussion to very good advantage." (Wallack, Kendall, and Briggs, 1939, p. 37). ⚎

Several New York State correctional education experiments focused on a "neglected field," education for special needs inmates (Wallack, 1939, p. 250). At Elmira Reformatory special education for psychopathic personalities was addressed through self-contained living conditions, professionally trained instructors of demonstrated emotional stability, and individualized attention to facilitate incremental progress (pp. 242-243). Special education for the disadvantaged was offered in self-contained classrooms, and tailored to be attractive to highly distractible students with short attention spans. The emphasis was on the individual, and no stigma was attached to being in these classes. Special material was designed to meet their adult needs. Students were excited about the program—and pleased when remediation was no longer required. (pp. 243-244). The "mentally defective" students at Elmira received instruction in short units, focused on repetition, physical improvement, and individual needs (p. 215). ⚎

In a speech at the 69th Annual Congress of the American Prison Association (APA—**Austin MacCormick** was president), New York City associate superintendent of schools **William Grady** declared that "...the pioneers in...classification and individualization of personality were the prisons rather than the schools. My hat's off to the prisons!" (APA, 1939, p. 61; emphasis in original). ⚎

Austin MacCormick wrote that the best correctional education programs in the U.S. were at Elmira Reformatory and the United States Industrial Reformatory at Chillicothe, Ohio (Wallack, 1939, p. 21). He reported that "Even in the South, where educational work in prisons was virtually non-existent, Virginia was showing what could be done with a trained director of education and some help from a near-by university." (p. 25). The university was William and Mary, where **Dean K.J. Hoke** (see 1913 and 1921 entries) "did more than anyone else to encourage Penitentiary education" (Outten, 1980). Hoke served on the Virginia Prison Board from 1933 to 1942 (Keve, 1982). ⚎

Ernest Outten and **Grover Cleveland Hamilton** became the first civilian instructors at the Virginia State Penitentiary. Auditorium facilities were used for school purposes, and students were excused from work to attend classes for one hour each day. Elementary subjects were taught. Most of the faculty consisted of inmate teachers, as provided in the 1918 Virginia law (see entry). Correctional industries sometimes paid tuition costs, so selected students could take correspondence courses (Outten, 1980). Outten and Hamilton served under Penitentiary education director Paul McElroy (Wallack, 1940, p. 80). ⚎

1939
(cont'd.)   Eight thousand people came to Cleveland for a conference on education similar to the one in 1938 in Atlantic City, attended by public school personnel. The largest attendance was at a workshop on "The Challenge of Crime." (Wallack, 1939, p. 31). ⌒

Lloyd Yepson wrote that "Education is a continuous process.... Education within the prison is not different, basically, from education any place else; education means not only the learning of new activities but the unlearning of old ones as well." (Wallack, 1939, p. 58). ⌒

Correspondence courses were popular at some institutions. For example, 955 men at New York City's Rikers Island Penitentiary were enrolled in correspondence cell-study courses (Wallack, 1939, p. 278). ⌒

A general sense of the protracted failures of prisons and juvenile institutions was gradually working its way to the public consciousness.

> Possibly the most comprehensive look at what penal practices and facilities across the nation constituted [during the 1930s] is contained in the United States attorney general's *Survey of Release Procedures*: 'Punishment for crime through custody in a prison may be the best solution society has yet found to satisfy that feeling for justice which is instinctive with human beings; it may even be of value in shocking some people into a realization of how far from social adaptation they have strayed; it may be the only means of protecting society from the vicious criminal. But...a realistic view of 150 year's experience with imprisonment as a means of rehabilitation, moral, physical, intellectual or industrial, does not incline one to an optimistic conclusion. After all is said and done, imprisonment remains chiefly a custodial and punitive agency.' (Gaither, 1982, p. 21). ⌒

The cost of local public schoolrooms varied from $6,000 in some areas to less than $100 in others.

> The upper 10 percent spent $4,115 to the lowest 10 percent's $500. Worse off than city schools were those in the countryside....Most exploited were the black schools of the states which maintained segregated systems. There the median expense for white classrooms was $1,166, for Negro $477. (Tyack, 1974, p. 273).

1939
(cont'd.)   Capital outlays for education jumped from $53,856,000
              in 1943-44 to $1,477,322,000 in 1951-52....Total
              expenditures for all public schools increased from
              $2,906,886,000 to $10,955,047,000 in the decade after
              1945, far outpacing the growth in the population of
              students. (p. 275).

While expenditures for education were increasing steadily, they were
completely overshadowed by military expansion.

              During one year of World War II the United States
              spent more for military purposes than it had expended
              on public education during the entire history of
              the nation. In 1955, a 'peacetime' year, the federal
              government spent over 40 billion, almost four times the
              total expenditures for public education. (p. 275). ⌬

1940 — The second Yearbook of the American Prison Association's Committee
on Education appeared, *Prison Administration—An Educational Process*.
It began with the words

              Reformation, like education, is an intrinsic thing. It
              must come from within the one who is to be affected. It
              can get its inception, however, from the contacts made
              and the situations arising from a definite program of
              training for work, studies, and the proper use of leisure
              time. (Wallack, 1940, first page—see 1939 entry on the
              first Yearbook).

The following quote from the second Yearbook reflected its main idea:
"The chief factor which will make or break any educational program is
the attitude of the institutional staff toward that program." (Briggs, in
Wallack, 1940, p. 23).

              In many institutions the entire educational organization
              is still on trial; is looked upon as an experiment or
              tolerated as a necessary something to be put up with....
              Once the educational program has been sold to the
              staff, the problem becomes one of keeping it 'sold.' The
              degree to which it succeeds and meets a real need will
              determine how long it remains in existence. (Turner, in
              Wallack, 1940, p. 157).

The book contained practical and useful suggestions about establishing
correctional education programs on a shoestring budget. ⌬

              Approximately 40% of the total prison population in the United
States was engaged in productive labor (Reagen and Stoughton, 1976,

1940   p. 59—see entries for 1885 and 1973). By this time all of the states had
(cont'd.) passed laws prohibiting the sale of prison made products within their
         borders (Reid, 1979, p. 679). ⌒

Harold Williams found that, contrary to many previous reports,
institutionalized delinquents and institutionalized nondelinquents
from the same background demonstrated little difference in intellectual
abilities.

> He summarized the results of the studies: 'The more
> recent studies have yielded, therefore: (1) from 10 to 30
> percent feebleminded, (2) a central tendency of about
> IQ 85, and (3) a very markedly reduced proportion of
> superior intelligence (3 to 12 percent). Though these
> results are much higher than the earlier estimates, they
> range far below the general population, especially at
> the upper levels. There seems to be little difference
> between court and institutional cases.' (Dell'Apa,
> 1973b, p. 17).

These findings were published in Williams' article "Intelligence and
Delinquency," which appeared in *Intelligence: Its Nature and Nurture*,
the 39th Yearbook of the National Society for the Study of Education.
(pp. 17-18—see 1926 entry). ⌒

The movement to house female prisoners in prisons managed
by females had substantially changed North American prisons. By
1940 23 states had established separate women's prisons (Freedman,
1981, p. 144). ⌒

Within the institutions, the legal relationship between education
and the other programs was gaining clarity.

> The hegemony of security over education reached
> its highest point in the case of *Numer v. Miller* in the
> United States [165 F.2d.986 (9th Cir.1940)] in which the
> court upheld a warden's refusal to allow a prisoner
> to undertake a correspondence course because upon
> release he intended to apply his knowledge to writing
> a book about 'brutal' prison officers. (Braithwaite, 1980,
> p. 193—see 1824 entry). ⌒

Even within this context, however, there was a constant
articulation of the need to improve and expand institutional education
programs. At the American Prison Congress,

George Killinger aptly stated an early concern
regarding the need for post secondary education

229

1940
(cont'd.)

programs in prison: 'Every attempt should be made to balance the prison education program so that it will meet the need of each individual incarcerated....To meet the demands of men falling into the upper educational bracket, the cooperation of extension divisions of colleges and universities should be sought.' (Gaither, 1982, p. 22; emphasis added). ⌒

Kenyon Scudder worked as the Los Angeles County chief probation officer. In 1940 the head of the prison directors was impressed with his work, and Scudder was asked "to take a leave of absence from his job to act as a consultant in planning for the new prison." (Brown, 1991, pp. 111-113). Scudder was appalled at the progress that had been made according to the changed, maximum security plans at Chino (p. 114). Nevertheless, he was offered the warden's assignment.

> Scudder did not hesitate. He accepted with alacrity, seeing the job offer as a unique opportunity to be involved in the creation of a new type of penal institution which would develop a different pattern of care and treatment in the handling of youthful offenders. Programs could be developed which would focus on giving young men freedom of choice, acceptance of responsibility while in prison, and preparation for return to the community. (p. 115).

Scudder's condition for taking the assignment was that he would hire the staff. This would preclude the political appointments that frequently frustrated reform wardens. It was also consistent with what has become known as Austin MacCormick's "Red Barn theory." MacCormick maintained he could transform an old red barn into an exemplary institution, provided he could staff it appropriately. Indeed, Scudder

> was determined to hire only the cream of the crop. Judge Pacht [head of the prison directors] assured Scudder that subject to the approval of the Governor, there would be no interference in his plans by the Board of Prison Directors, and any political pressure brought from any source would be vigorously resisted. [Governor Rolph subsequently promised Scudder would have the free hand he needed.] On those conditions, Scudder accepted the job. (p. 115). ⌒

Period Five: 1941-1945

1941 — The first California Institution for Men (CIM) population was transported from San Quentin to the new facility, on July 10, 1941. All the traditional restraints were ignored—they rode in a Greyhound Bus, without handcuffs or chains of any kind, and without armed guards. During the 500 mile trip, **Kenyon Scudder** explained to the mixed group of men that he would not tolerate any racial discrimination at Chino. Everything was peaceful on the bus, so Scudder passed out cigarettes and matches—considered a real luxury—and bought box lunches for everyone at a bus stop on the way. He sat in the front seat part of the time, and visited with each of the men separately the rest of the time, to begin a dialogue that would fix their hope on the future. (Scudder, 1968/1952, pp. 44-52). The governor tried to change the arrangement by which Scudder was hired as warden, but the head of the prison directors was able to maintain the original agreement (Brown, 1991, p. 121). The result was an exemplary prison without walls. At first the constraints of World War II inhibited further construction, since materials were largely unavailable (p. 127). The education program at California Institution for Men began in 1941, and again Scudder diverged from past practice. Consistent with the maxim that "educators should be in charge of educational decisions," he contracted with the Chino School District for teachers. (p. 139). This relationship has been carried into the present. The following passage describes its origins.

> We needed to provide regular courses from the first grade through high school, as nine per cent of men in prison had never learned to read or write and most of the others had dropped out of school early. I did not want to have inmate teachers [the norm at that time], for that plan has never been successful in any prison. Neither did I want to take on a group of teachers full time. We decided to ask the high school district to sponsor the program on an average daily attendance basis as they did the high school and adult education classes in the community, they to furnish the teachers and we to provide the students and equipment. Soon after Chino opened, I called on my good friend, the late Dr. Walter Dexter, State Superintendent of Public Instruction in Sacramento. He immediately grasped the significance of our plan and thought it could be worked out, but when he called one of his department heads, he ran into opposition at once. 'This would be a dangerous precedent to establish,' the man said. 'If we approve it for Chino, San Quentin and Folsom will also want it, and there is no telling where it will end.' Dr. Dexter pressed a buzzer. 'Ask Mr. Lentz

231

to come in,' he said. Mr. Lentz was legal adviser for
the State Department of Education. 'I see no reason
why the plan won't work,' Lentz said. 'It would be
the same as an adult education program in any other
community, with the school district reimbursed
through the average daily attendance fund. There is
no legal barrier to prevent the high school from taking
the institution into its area.' Dr. Dexter concluded the
conference by saying, 'If there is any group of men in
the state that needs this training, it is our prisoners.
Perhaps they would not now be in custody if the
schools had given them better opportunities earlier
in life.' The Chino Board of Education approved the
establishment of day and evening vocational classes
on the premises of...[CIM] under the direction of the
Chino Board of Education. It permitted all instruction
to be by civilian teachers fully certified by the State
Board of Education, which meant that our men could
therefore receive their graduation certificates from
the Chino high school district instead of from a state
prison. This has become a permanent arrangement...
(Scudder, 1968/1952, pp. 149-150).

Although it might seem like a small step today, at the time this action
took great courage and insight. Perhaps that is why, at one point Austin
MacCormick (see above) identified Kenyon Scudder as one of the
best (reform-oriented) wardens in the nation (in Rowles, 1962, p. 341).
Kenyon Scudder's lifework was testimony to the great causes of prison
reform and correctional education. ⌀

     Nathan Leopold wrote "Education in Prison and Success on
Parole," describing one dimension of the inmate-founded Stateville
Prison Correspondence School (Leopold, 1958, p. 235). He reported a
parole violation recidivism rate for 187 students in a sample of 4,517 at
16.04%, as compared to 31.18% for the non-students. When adjustments
for "previous criminal record, intelligence, type of offense, and age"
were worked into the calculations, the figure was reduced to 16.04%
for students and 20.32% for non-students. (Leopold, 1958, p. 234—see
entries for 1933, 1935, and 1958). ⌀

     A survey of 44 state prisons and 17 state reformatories revealed
that approximately 25% of the prison population and approximately
50% of the reformatory population were involved in school programs.
Only about 10% of the prisoners and 20% of the reformatory inmates
were enrolled full-time. (Roberts, 1971, p. 16). ⌀

     Dr. Glenn Kendall was the director of education of New York
State's Department of Correction (New York, 1941, p. iii—see entries

for 1939 and 1953). Elements of the statewide correctional education organization were described.

> In 1940-41, 46 per cent of the inmates in twelve institutions, or 7,137 inmates, were enrolled in organized educational activities. (Organized educational activities are all those in classrooms, shops, maintenance work, industries, recreation, or elsewhere, which have a teacher, a course of study, regular periods of instruction, and a means for checking progress.) There are 158 civilian teachers, instructors, educational supervisors and directors employed in these institutions...the budget for all educational purposes for fiscal year 1940-1941 was $330,911. This represents a total per capita cost for education of $21.36 for each of 15,491 inmates in the total population and $46.36 for each of the 7,137 inmates enrolled... (New York, 1941, p. 2).

There were three positions in the statewide central office (Table I). Male academic and vocational teachers and librarians began at a starting salary of $1,800; females at $1,150 (Table 8). In a report on *Future Plans and Costs,* the Division of Education explained that

> It is natural to make some comparison between public schools and institutional education. However, it is difficult to make such comparisons due to the marked differences between the way public schools operate and the way in which institutional education is carried on... (p. 3)

Six differences were reported, and correctional education was found to be "a combination of general education, vocational education, and physical education. (pp. 3-4). An analysis of New York correctional education law revealed that

> 1) Education cannot be narrowed or limited to teaching the three R's or even actual skills, but must be broad and intensive enough to improve the thinking and social reactions of inmates. Education must affect the inmate mentally, emotionally, vocationally, morally, and socially. 2) Effective education cannot be reduced to a routine prescription for all inmates but must be based on the abilities, deficiencies, and needs of the individual inmate. (p. 6).

Twenty-two percent of the inmates were considered unsuited for correctional education, ranging from 3% at Elmira to more than 30% at some institutions. This group included

1941
(cont'd.)

1) Inmates in reception or observation. 2) ...in the hospital. 3) ...in segregation and punishment. 4) ...who are over age (60 years of age and over.) 5) ...who are physically unfit. 6) ...who are mentally unfit (M.A. [mental age] below 8). 7) ...who are hopeless cases (drug addicts or inmates who have committed over 3 felonies). 8) ...with an adequate education (have completed the 10th grade and earned $1,800 or more in a socially acceptable occupation). (pp. 7-8).

The range of inmates suited for education was from 51% (Attica) to 97% (Elmira). Different types of correctional education schedules had been worked out for the level of security at each institution. The average class size was 20, and the average teaching load was six classes. Formula had been developed to project the number of teachers needed at any site. (p. 9). Two of the recommendations in this report were especially relevant to correctional education nationwide.

#9... The Department and the [Engelhardt] Commission are definitely opposed to any great dependence upon correspondence and cell study and certainly not as the sole method of education...[and] #11... General and academic classes are taught by inmates who should be replaced by civilians so far as possible. (p. 18).

[The] State [should] provide at least five per cent of the total amount appropriated for correctional institutions for the purpose of so changing the attitudes and behavior of inmates so that they will, upon release, serve society rather than be a menace to it. (p. 19).

This well-documented, comprehensive study presented funding alternatives to decision-makers for their review. ⌂

The first vocational correctional education course in England, wrote Burkey, was initiated at Maidstone Prison—in precision engineering fitting.

...[I]n 1942, identical courses were opened with equal success at Wakefield and Wormwood Scrubs Prisons. By 1946 Maidstone, Manchester, Liverpool, Stafford, Wormwood Scrubs and Wakefield Prisons had training courses in five different trades: carpentry, bricklaying, painting and decorating, precision engineering fitting, and boot and shoe repairing. (Burkey, in Forster, 1981, p. 45). ⌂

1942 — During 1942-1943 the California Institution for Men (CIM) emphasis on producing war materiel provided an appropriate theme for the new facility. In particular, CIM's large farm and cannery provided thousands of tons of foodstuffs for the men at the front. (Brown, 1991, p. 128). One of the first prison units to combat forest fires was implemented, a tradition that has been carried on to the present in California institutions (pp. 123-124). Men released from CIM were getting good jobs in the free market (p. 127). By 1943 **Earl Warren** was the governor of California. He appointed a Special Investigation Committee on Penal Affairs. The Committee embarked on a year long study, and the findings supported a previous report by the Osborne Association: "the whole administrative structure needs to be reorganized." (pp. 87-88). Among the recommendations were items that would eliminate the "con boss" system, centralize correctional activities, eliminate inmate idleness, and stimulate interest in education (pp. 99-100). **Kenyon Scudder** began hiring women employees in addition to men (p. 130). He started a reception unit at CIM (p. 131), and launched huge intensive treatment programs that operated at both the individualized and group levels (p. 133). ⌒

     Lloyd Yepson announced to the American Prison Association that Standards for Educational Programs in Corrections could be made more objective. In his paper, Yepson proclaimed that changed attitudes and habits should be used to measure correctional education program success. (Davis, 1978, pp. 10-11—see 1975 entry). ⌒

     In Finland, the Act on Vocational Training Institutions was implemented, making vocational education legally possible in prison. One early improvement that resulted was "the mechanical engineering workshop...opened in 1948 at the juvenile unit of the Riihimaki central prison." (Nordic Council of Ministers, 2005, p. 48).

1945 — The Federal Correctional Institution at Danbury, Connecticut developed a prototypic prerelease program (Roberts, 1971, p. 237). In the next few decades important prerelease programs would be implemented in Texas, the Federal Bureau of Prisons, and other jurisdictions. ⌒

1946 — The Standing Committee on Education (see 1930 entry) became a new affiliate of the American Prison Association. The affiliate was called the Correctional Education Association (CEA). Committee chair **Price Chenault** (see entries for 1937 and 1949) introduced the measure to the APA Congress, reporting the Committee's desire "...to be organized as an allied body of the American Prison Association." (Gehring, 1982, p. 7). Dr. Chenault became the first CEA president. ⌒

The first *Manual of Correctional Standards* was published by the American Prison Association. The Committee was chaired by New York's **Sam Lewisohn**. The chapter on education was written by **Austin MacCormick**, who wrote that education of the handicapped significantly increased the opportunity for successful rehabilitation, and that such programs required a director and faculty with highly specialized training. (Lewisohn, 1946, p. 43). ⌒

Eight thousand and two hundred Federal inmates, or approximately 50% of the Federal Bureau of Prisons population, were enrolled in educational programs (Roberts, 1971, p. 16). Although impressive because of the number of inmates, this figure represented a smaller percentage of the total Federal prison population than had been reported in 1933—see entry. ⌒

The leadership for postwar Virginia correctional education was coming into place. **Ernest Outten** became the principal at Virginia State Penitentiary (Outten, 1980). ⌒

At England's Wormwood Scrubs, psychotherapist **Dr. J.C. Mackwood** experimented "with a selected group of ten patients who were put to live together in a special ward, known as the New Ward, in which they lived, ate, and slept, while working together in the same shop..." (Banks, 1958, p. 106). During the war, "it was found possible only to start classes for young prisoners and illiterates. In all, four prisons maintained a fairly full educational programme, fifteen had something, and twelve had nothing." (p. 36).

> Correspondence Courses...first came into popularity towards the end of the Second World War, when other forms of educational activity had undergone a temporary black-out....Indeed, inmates who persistently pursue correspondence courses at the expense of classes are not usually rated very high in prognosis for subsequent social adjustment. (p. 215).

1946   "The next great landmark in educational history came in 1945 and is
(cont'd.) attributable to the Durham Educational Authority," which established
          a corrections/local education authority (LEA) cooperative program.
          The LEA implemented correctional education, and came to "regard the
          prison as an Evening Institute." By 1953 "the financial responsibility
          was transferred from the Local Education Authorities to the Prison
          Commissioners." (p. 37).

> At the beginning of 1947 a Directorship of Education
> and Welfare was created on the Prison Commission,
> and the appointment fell to **Mr. H.A. Jenkin**...formerly
> one of His Majesty's Inspectors of Schools....Upon his
> retirement at the end of 1950, however 'it was...agreed
> that the Commissioners should in future look for
> specialist advice on...both sides of the work. Accordingly,
> **Mr. C.T. Cape**, an Assistant Commissioner, who had
> experience as a teacher before joining the Service and
> has since governed both prisons and Borstals, was
> transferred to these duties as Assistant Commissioner
> (Education and Welfare).' Mr. Cape is still [1958] the
> 'Teacher's Friend.' (p. 38; emphasis added).

In 1946 the first psychologists and social workers were appointed to
positions at English penal institutions (Forster, 1981, p. 10). **Frances
Banks** later wrote of postwar advances in English correctional
education.

> The spirit of the New Education and its gathering
> impetus could hardly be better illustrated in any field
> of our national life than it is in the records of these ten
> [postwar] years. It marches ahead, the accompanying
> handmaid of all other achievements in prison reform,
> steadily expanding as the ameliorative aspects of
> penology are developed. Often hampered by scarcity
> of funds, it refuses to have its virility quenched. Only a
> prophet could predict what the next ten years will bring
> forth. Probably we shall then marvel retrospectively at
> our present spasmodic, incohesive, and inadequate
> efforts. I am proud to know some of the pioneers who
> have been responsible for the courageous samples of
> advance here chronicled. (Banks, 1958, pp. 43-44—see
> 1958 entry). ⚋

1947 — The conceptual framework of a comprehensive correctional education
       program was emerging in the Canadian Federal system. Canada's
       Gibson Report included a recommendation that prison educational
       opportunities "in their widest scope" should be offered (Weir, in
       Roberts, 1973, p.43). ⚋

1947 "60.8 percent of industrial workers in the nation's twelve
(cont'd.) largest metropolitan areas worked in central cities; by 1970 the figure
had dropped to less than 40 percent." White flight to the suburbs had
begun. There was

> an increase of over 50 percent in [the African American
> populations of] Boston, Newark, Milwaukee, New
> York, and Los Angeles [in the 1960s]. Blacks formed a
> majority of the total population in 1970 in three large
> cities—Atlanta, Newark, and Washington, D.C.—but
> in 1966-67 nonwhite pupils formed a majority in the
> public schools of ten major cities. In part as a result
> of urban migration patterns, central cities in the 1960's
> contained a disproportionate number of the old, the
> poor, and the unemployed. In 1969 one tenth of urban
> whites lived at or below the poverty line, one fourth
> of urban blacks. Among parents of schoolchildren the
> incidence of poverty rose more sharply than in the
> general population. 'In 1950 it was estimated that one
> child out of every ten attending public schools in the
> nation's fourteen largest cities could be considered
> socio-economically disadvantaged,' report Raymond
> Hummel and John Nagle. 'By 1960 this proportion had
> increased to one in three, and it is believed that by the
> early 1970's it had risen to approximately one out of
> every two.' (Tyack, 1974, p. 278). ⌒

1948 — **Austin MacCormick** declared that "Education in penal and correctional
institutions has at last achieved maturity" (Morrison, in Roberts, 1973,
p. 15). Much of the work of making this aspiration consistent with the
reality of the field would unfold during subsequent decades, largely
based on MacCormick's state-of-the-art models. ⌒

> **Dr. Miriam Van Waters'** appeal against a legal assault was
> successful. She was reinstated as superintendent of Massachusetts'
> Framingham Reformatory for Women and retired in 1957. Like
> Osborne in New York State before World War I, she faced trumped
> up legal charges in Massachusetts, instigated by entrenched
> obstructionists in the Department of Correction. Osborne and Van
> Waters were also connected through the enduring friendship and
> support of Dr. George Kirchwey, a criminologist at the New York
> School of Social Work and Dean of Columbia Law School. Kirchwey
> had served as temporary Sing Sing warden while Osborne defended
> himself in court. Osborne had been supported by Franklin Delano
> Roosevelt; Eleanor Roosevelt invited Dr. Van Waters to dine at
> the White House (Rowles, 1962, p. 257). Austin MacCormick once
> summarized Dr. Van Waters' career as a reform warden with the
> phrase "Absolutely tops" (p. 341). In 1962 B.J. Rowles' book on Van

1948   Waters was published, *The Lady at Box 99: The Story of Miriam Van*
(cont'd.) *Water* (Rowles, 1962). 〽

In his book, *Penal Reform: A Comprehensive Study*, **Max Grunhut** wrote that the aim of correctional education "is almost identical with the object of a progressive penal administration" (Grunhut, 1973/1948, p. 231). He considered adult education to be

> a universal spiritual movement in our time. It has created new demands and unforeseen possibilities. **Nikolaj F.S. Grundtvig**, the 'father' of the Danish Folk High School, believed that only barbarians and tyrants could imagine that 'the root and kernel of the people... does not need any more enlightenment than can be obtained behind the plow, in the workshop, on the ship and behind the counter.' (p. 235; emphasis added).

Grunhut wrote that

> There is indeed a genuine desire to strive hard for 'the means for life rather than for sheer livelihood.' New methods of instruction have been developed. Grundtvig propagated the 'living word,' an unorthodox, vivid, and comprehensive presentation of the subject. England developed the tutorial class, Germany the Rundgesprach and Arbeitsgmeinschaft. No longer do pupils exhaust their energies in answering the teachers' questions, but teacher and student unite in a common effort to find out the truth in a gradual progress by mutual contributions. (p. 235).

However, he also wrote that "the prison school—more than other adult education—aims at vocational training" (p. 236). "With the proclamation of such ideals the question suggests itself whether prison education does not lose sight of its primary object of readjusting offenders to a law-abiding life in the community" (p. 238). Grunhut emphasized the role of cultural and art education for prisoners, and discussed that issue in terms of the correctional education literature (pp. 238-239). He wrote that "Since the repudiation of the Lombrosian doctrine of inborn criminal types, the prison population is usually regarded as a negative selection out of the total community....For mental equipment, the evidence is far from being conclusive..." (p. 239—see entries for 1876 and 1895).

> And yet 47.3 percent. of the prisoners had not been able to have a school education of seven to eight years, as against only 28.2 percent. of the army group.... Wm. Moodie [of the London Child Guidance Clinic]

found no difference in general intelligence between delinquents and non-delinquents, but the delinquents were six times more backward in schoolwork than their non-delinquent contemporaries. (p. 240).

He wrote that "An educational approach will often meet with suspicion, a rejection of all that savours of 'preaching,' a resentment against what seems like the whitewashing of those 'on the other side.'" (p. 241). However, he found that "In the long run, a man whose devotion is sincere and pursuit of truth uncompromising will never fail to impress his pupils, within prison walls or in the world" (p. 242). Regarding correctional libraries:

> In a world whose community is artificial because imposed, reading at least is a sanctuary of privacy.... Men read more in prison. It has been estimated that the average prisoner reads five to ten times as many books as the average citizen using public libraries... (pp. 242-243). ⋙

Much of the correctional education advocacy effort is based on the limited education of inmate populations across various types of institutions. In 1948, one third of the prison population in the United States was identified as illiterate (Reagen and Stoughton, 1976, p. 60). ⋙

The Federal Bureau of Prisons used a planned curriculum of various high school subjects, and offered standard high school diplomas. An increased emphasis was assigned to social education, using modalities such as current events, discussion groups, training and documentary films, lectures, and inmate forums. Specific social education classes were structured to provide learning activities in problems of personal adjustment, human relationships, and post release issues. Vocational courses such as airplane mechanics, business machines, commercial art, and typewriter repair were offered. (Roberts, 1971, p. 18). ⋙

Father Flanagan died, the founder of Boys Town. He was succeeded by Monsignor Wegner, chancellor of the Omaha Roman Catholic Archdiocese. (Oursler and Oursler, 1949, pp. 58, 295). Flanagan was born in 1886 (p. 302). Throughout his career Flanagan had consistently maintained "There's no such thing as a bad boy." (p. 7). "There were no bad boys. There were only bad parents, bad environment, bad example. That would be his credo, in full focus....No bad boys. None." (p. 192; emphasis in original). Near the end of his life he explained: "'I can still say that I have never known a really bad boy.... It's wrong even to call it juvenile delinquency. Why not call it what it generally is—the delinquency of a callous and indifferent society?'"

1948 (p. 298). "Without an appeal to the spiritual nature, he declared, you
(cont'd.) would get nowhere with boys." (p. 10). For years Flanagan had been
opposed to the popular media, and "especially incensed because of the
corruption of youth by movies, radio, magazines, and newspapers."
(p. 121). Perhaps General Douglas MacArthur's words were the fittest
summary of his career at Boys Town. At one point MacArthur said
to Flanagan "You have reached millions...where others have reached
only thousands." (p. 288). Earlier, Flanagan had called MacArthur "a
great Christian gentleman." (p. 286). Boys Towns were established
near Shanghai, China (p. 289), in Prestina, a suburb of Rome, and also
in the Italian towns of Santamariella and Palermo (p. 70—see entry for
1949). ⌂

1949 — Oursler and Oursler's book *Father Flanagan of Boys Town* was published
by Doubleday. In it readers learned, among other things, that the
Boys Town chief psychologist had worked with Alfred Adler (p. 20).
Father Flanagan had spoken repeatedly of "The kinship of poverty
and evil." (Oursler and Oursler, 1949, p. 32—see 1929 entry). He wrote
that the "Institutions to which such children were sent, reformatories
and occasionally orphanages as well, were centers of stupidity and
brutality, even bestiality, run by misfits, political hangers-on, and
often enough sadists. Whip them! Birch them! Strike them with a
lash!" (p. 34; emphases in original). However, Flanagan steadfastly
maintained that

> Not then, or ever, could he blame children. The fault lay
> with parents who denied them love, with society which
> exhibited no concern, and with an environment which
> offered temptation and evil example simultaneously. It
> was a heathen setup. The remedy must be democracy,
> the great experiment implementing Christianity in
> political terms; the social structure resting firmly
> upon the foundation of the worth of each individual
> soul. And he was well aware...that many among the
> influential and the powerful disagreed with his simple
> remedy. (p. 42).

Flanagan had died in 1948 (p. 58). Oursler and Oursler focused on
Flanagan's words to a typical delinquent: "'Eddie,' began the leader
of Boys Town, 'you are welcome here. The whole place is run by the
fellows, you know. Boy mayor. Boy city council. Boy chief of police.'"
(p. 64). Flanagan had discussed a theoretical connection with the Junior
Republics, founded by William George (p. 115, 130—see entries for
1895 and 1911). He had reported that leading Boys Town required "...
more even than an open mind. There must also be the open heart. The
scientists shied away from such metaphysics" (p. 116). Oursler and
Oursler wrote that, to Flanagan,

the offenses of juvenile criminals presented a problem not of guilt and punishment but of diagnosis and therapy. He would have to find out why children committed such crimes before he could hope to prevent them. Here of itself was a forbidding study with many factors. Was it an individual problem or a community one?... (p. 125).

In discussing this idea [the community problem of street gangs], former **President Herbert Hoover**, staunch supporter of the Boys Club movement, once pointed out...that the average cost to care for such a boy is forty dollars. That forty dollars would take a boy off the street. Give him his chance to play and some direction in character discipline and you have a fair chance of turning out a good citizen. But if you keep that forty dollars in your pocket, and don't give the boy his chance, within a few years the taxpayers may be called upon to pay ten thousand dollars to burn him in the electric chair. With that thesis Father Flanagan profoundly agreed. (p. 126).

During his lifetime, Flanagan had been expressive about the need to improve conditions in county jails. Oursler and Oursler wrote that

What in Father Flanagan's eyes was the greatest mess of all, a mess clamoring for a cleanup, was the scandal of county jails. In spite of great advances, it still is a scandal. Out of the three thousand county jails in the United States [1949], a few years ago, sixteen hundred had been condemned as unusable—and were still being used. Their sanitary inadequacies were a menace to community health. They were firetraps and their overcrowding was a spectacle to turn the stomach of Lucifer himself. The effect upon young first offenders, thrown into the horrible intimacy of these overcrowded lazarettos, was incalculable in its final effect on society. Yet there they stood! (p. 123; emphasis in original).

Flanagan had maintained a connection with FBI director **J. Edgar Hoover** (p. 118). In their book on Flanagan, Oursler and Oursler quoted Hoover on the topic of probation:

If parole is a scandal, probation is sometimes a horror beyond the conception of decent citizens. What happens when a youth hampered by lack of parental guidance indulges in his first infraction? He receives the benefit of that most necessary and laudatory

1949
(cont'd.)

system known as probation. It is right that he should have probation. It is a crime for any child upon his first offense to be incarcerated without a chance to reform, always excepting the very rare anti-social degenerate. But under our maladministered system we find very often the probation officer is ignorant, that he sometimes is himself a criminal, or that he is merely a political panderer willing to debauch the most sacred of tasks—that of the protection of our youth—merely to keep a job. And so in this modern pilgrim's progress toward the inevitable slough of despond, we find our child criminal sunk deeper and deeper, first through properly administered probation, then into reform schools, which are not reform schools but crucibles where boil the worst instincts of humanity and where innocence vanishes and insolence takes its place. We find him educated step by step, not in law obedience but in law avoidance. We find him traveling from the reform school to the prison, with rarely a thought toward his true reformation but always with the association of the vicious, the foul-minded, and the dangerous older criminals. At last he himself becomes a professor of crime and he, like others, carries on his recruiting in an ever-widening circle which at last has brought us to the degenerating position where each year in America twelve thousand human beings die by murder. (pp. 123-124).

About juvenile delinquency in general, and its relation to Father Flanagan's message, Oursler and Oursler wrote that

...the public was lured by a false sense of security.... Eventually came a bombshell. Professor Sheldon Glueck of Harvard University Law School and his equally eminent wife, Dr. Eleanor T. Glueck, undertook a study of one thousand cases of juvenile delinquents .... (p. 128).

The idea that society, and especially parents themselves, bore primary responsibility for delinquency among children was a bitter pill to swallow. It was more comfortable to believe that no one was responsible but the child himself—that some were just born with the devil in their hearts." (p. 158—see entries for 1919, 1929, 1934, and 1948). ᘓ

The effects of the improvements in the Federal Bureau of Prisons schools was beginning to be felt. In the year 1949, 129 Federal Bureau of

1949   Prisons inmates completed their high school education (Roberts, 1971,
(cont'd.) p. 18—see 1957 entry). ⋒

Approximately 50% of the New York State inmate population
was enrolled in the educational program (Chenault, 1949-1951,
p. 8). **Dr. Price Chenault** (see entries for 1937 and 1946) served as the
Director of Education in the Department of Correction's Division of
Education (Chenault, 1949-1951, p. 1). **Dr. Walter Wallack** (see 1930
entry) and **Dr. Glenn Kendall** (see 1941 entry), had previously served
in that position. ⋒

1950 — The American Group Psychotherapy Association surveyed 109 U.S.
penal and correctional institutions and found that 39 offered group
therapy and ten had plans to start groups soon (McCorkle, in Roberts,
1973, p. 258). Group therapy had emerged as a major correctional
program after World War II. ⋒

The Advisory Corrections Council was established by
Congress. Its mission was to improve "the overall administration of
criminal justice," "promote the prevention of crime and delinquency,"
and "suggest studies to be taken by both public and private agencies"
(Metametrics, 1977, p. III-2—see 1969 entry). ⋒

In Sweden, from the 1950s through the 1970s, prison education
was organized largely around the "folk high school" model.

> [F]olk high schools were the main arrangers of prison
> education. These institutes of adult education, as
> representatives of society external to the correctional
> services, were considered the natural organisation to
> take on the task of providing prisoners with further
> adult education. In practice, a folk high school in
> geographical proximity to the prison would set up
> a branch in the prison, using the school's teaching
> staff to run courses corresponding to those offered at
> the folk high school in Swedish, mathematics, civics,
> English, and Swedish for immigrants. To some extent,
> each folk high school left its own characteristic mark
> on the content and organisation of education in the
> prison where it had a branch. During the same period,
> there were also teachers employed by The Prison and
> Probation Service who ran practical, vocational courses,
> mainly at youth penitentiaries. (Nordic Council of
> Ministers, 2005, pp. 98-99—see 1974 entry). ⋒

A Swedish visitor to California's Chino Prison (California
Institution for Men) reported that

244

1950	Special problem films are extensively used in the group
(cont'd.)	therapy sessions ('You and Your Family,' 'Act Your

1950
(cont'd.)
Special problem films are extensively used in the group therapy sessions ('You and Your Family,' 'Act Your Age,' 'The Feeling of Rejection,' 'Shy Guy,' 'The Feeling of Hostility,' 'The Feeling of Depression,' 'Problem Drinker,' for example.) After the men have seen the film they discuss its contents. The group leader must be much more active in this form of group therapy than is usually the case. (Eriksson, 1976, p. 188).

A treatment team approach had been implemented for "all prisoners with sentences of more than one year," with each "team consisting of a psychiatrist, a psychologist, a sociologist, a social case worker, and a teacher." (p. 188). ⌂

In England, 1950-1958, His Majesty's Inspector of Schools became directly involved in correctional education. "**Ritchie** visited every [penal] establishment at least twice, many more often, and took part between 1952 and 1958 in sixty-two full-scale inspections..." (Forster, 1981, pp. 37-38—emphasis added). ⌂

1951 — The first English edition of **Anton S. Makarenko**'s book *The Road to Life* was published, about the 1920s Soviet Gorky Youth Colony (Makarenko, 1973, vol. 1—see entries for 1917, 1920-1923, and 1933). All three of the volumes were republished, in English, in the early 21st century. ⌂

In Norway the first prison workshop schools were implemented, though the law that enabled them—for education including vocational and other types of correctional education at institutions for young offenders—was passed in 1928. The legislation was revised in 1963 but abandoned in 1975. (Nordic Council of Ministers, 2005, p. 68—see 1958 entry). ⌂

1952 — Danish prison education regulations were adopted.

...as a rule education is to be offered on a group basis and, whenever possible, outside working hours. All prisoners under the age of 30 are required to participate in the basic education courses in written and oral proficiency in Danish, and in mathematics, writing and civics, arranged by the prison where they are serving their sentences. The prison Governor [warden] may determine, after consultation with the head teacher, to include other areas in the obligatory courses. (Nordic Council of Ministers, 2005, p. 27).

By 1973 a report by a commission appointed by the Ministry of Justice formulated the following objective for prison education:

The prison authorities should strive to provide prisoners with a range of Educational options corresponding to that available to the citizens in society at large. Whenever possible, this teaching should take place as participation in courses, etc. held outside the prison. However when necessary, for reasons of security or other special, prison-related considerations, educational opportunities should be offered on the prison premises. (pp. 27-28).

In 1986 a nationwide plan to improve all education, "in and outside prisons," was implemented. Called the Skadhauge plan, its focus in correctional education was to "integrate prison education into the state educational system." Two pilot prison projects were implemented to make use of learning opportunities in the communities. (p. 28). In 1986 a new wave of reform was directed to the development of work, education, and leisure time. "Production schools" were a central element of this initiative, to further consolidate prison education within the state education system (p. 29). But by 2002 another report recommended these production schools should be phased out. This report also recommended the following lines of development: (a) a focus on secondary education, both at the lower and upper levels, (b) "flexible, adaptive teaching," and (c) distance learning as both an independent subject and as a supplement to the other courses. (pp. 30-31).

1953 — The University of Maryland established an extension at the Maryland Penitentiary. Requirements for admission included a good record and a high school or GED diploma. (Roberts, 1971, p. 21). College-level courses for credit were also offered at the U.S. Penitentiary at Leavenworth, Kansas (Gaither, 1982, p. 22).

Speaking at the 83rd Annual Congress of the American Prison Association, **Glenn Kendall** identified the development of social education as the most significant correctional education trend of the 1950s because it promoted insight about personal attitudes and enhanced social adjustment. He recommended that correctional education programs should emphasize the development of inmate motivation to learn and improve. (Davis, 1978, p. 11). Metametrics later reported that

In the early 1940's and particularly after World War II, corrections education was increasingly seen as a rehabilitative tool. 'Reformation' of the offender became 'rehabilitation' and the concept of the criminal nature changed dramatically. It was during this era that the social sciences, in particular psychology, had a profound impact on correctional thinking. The criminal

1953
(cont'd.)
was no longer viewed as a free willed, although deficient being, but as a determined one—'propelled by a neuroses, psychoses, psychopathologies, sub-cultural commitment, or other problems which occurred in his childhood or teenage years.' (Salimony, in Metametrics, 1977, p. II-9).

1954 — A new *Manual of Correctional Standards* was published by the American Prison Association. Chapter 20, on "Education," established criteria by which institutional schools would be assessed when correctional facilities applied for Association accreditation. Standards were provided for comprehensive programs of vocational, academic, physical, cultural, and social education housed in "adequate" facilities and staffed by "competent" personnel. (Roberts, 1971, p. 20).

New York correctional education director **Price Chenault** (see 1946 entry) published a *Successful Living* curriculum. Focusing on "morals and ethics," it helped inmate students "to withstand the evil influences which they will inevitably confront"—see 1840 entry. Sections were devoted to "worship, clean speech, what is right, honesty, sincerity, development of character, constructive thinking and purposeful living, by example, home...sense of duty," etc. (Chenault, 1954).

In its *Brown v. Board* decision, which struck down the "separate but equal" segregated local public school rule, the U.S. Supreme Court

affirmed belief in the central 'importance of education to our democratic society' as 'the very foundation of good citizenship.' 'Today,' said the Court, schooling 'is a principal instrument in awakening the child to cultural values, in preparing him for later professional training, and in helping him to adjust normally to his environment. In these days, it is doubtful that any child may reasonably be expected to succeed in life if he is denied the opportunity of an education. (Tyack, 1974, p. 279).

Tyack later remarked that

Segregation, of course, denied the professed ideology of the common school, which in theory sought to mix all kinds of children under the unifying roof of the public school. Hence the Supreme Court was not so much stating a new principle as correcting an old abuse. (p. 279).

1955 — Cook County (Chicago) Jail chaplain Wesley Kosin visited Emmaus Bible School, where **John Erwin**, a former delinquent and ward, was studying. Kosin challenged the students to support prison work, and Erwin began Sunday volunteer efforts at the Jail. (Erwin, 1978, p. 93—see 1957 entry). ⌒

1956 — The Medical Center for Federal Prisoners began a cultural program, bringing in guest lecturers, discussion leaders, and men of prominence in the community. The Federal Youth Center in Englewood, Colorado established a social education program for vocational students, including sociodrama techniques. Federal reformatories started courses in social relations. (Roberts, 1971, p. 21). ⌒

A University of Southern Illinois Extension was established at Menard Prison (Morrison, in Roberts, 1973, p. 19). Even bigger innovations would soon be established at Southern Illinois—see 1957 entry below. ⌒

1957 — The "first college program of live education in a prison" was developed by Southern Illinois University president **Delyte W. Morris** for rehabilitative purposes (Metametrics, 1977, p. II-11). This was an important model that attracted widespread attention and helped to shape many postsecondary prison education programs in later decades. ⌒

More than 40% of the inmate population in Federal prisons was enrolled in correspondence courses (Davis, 1978, p. 11). Readers will notice the shift between the figures presented in entries for 1933, 1948 and this one for 1957. ⌒

Two hundred and forty-five Federal Bureau of Prisons inmates completed their high school education while incarcerated (Roberts, 1971, p. 18—see 1949 entry). See GED completion numbers for the same system in the 1949 entry. ⌒

John Erwin became chaplain at Chicago's Cook County Jail (Erwin, 1978, p. 99). In 1958 the warden gave him the chapel broom closet to use as an office (p. 113—see entries for 1955 and 1967). Erwin would play an important role in the dissemination of prototypic correctional education models during the next few decades. ⌒

North Americans compared their public schools to those of the Soviet Union. "Sputnik dramatized concerns that began to emerge in the late 1940's." The "cold war intensified debate and action in a... sort of crisis: was American schooling too soft, too inefficient, too unselective to sustain the nation in its conflict with Russia" (Tyack, 1974, p. 270). ⌒

1958 — The Maryland Penitentiary school was directed by **Zigmund Maciekowich**. This year the school hosted Johns Hopkins University courses and established classes in Great Books and the Dale Carnegie material (Roberts, 1971, p. 21—see 1928 entry). ◿

In his book *Alexander Maconochie of Norfolk Island*, **John Barry** wrote the corrections mission in Maconochie's own words: "The first object of prison discipline should be to reform prisoners and thus prepare them to separate [from prison] with advantage both to themselves and to society after their discharge" (Murton, 1976, p. 195). "There is hardly a reform, in the correctional field in our epoch that cannot be traced, at least partially, to the fertile imagination of Maconochie" (Barry, 1958, p. xi—see entries for 1840 and 1870). Note: In the 1830s a ship named the "John Barry" was used to transport convicts to Australia (Hughes, 1987, p. 405). ◿

Nathan Leopold's book *Life Plus 99 Years* was published, describing, in part, the establishment and growth of the Stateville Correspondence School (Leopold, 1958—see entries for 1932, 1935, and 1941). Inmate Leopold made lasting contributions to the field of correctional education. ◿

Throughout the postwar period social education programming dominated much of the correctional education scene. In 1958 **U. Samuel Vukcevich** implemented a model social education program at New Jersey's Bordentown Reformatory, with content in the areas of self-study, personality development, and attitudes (Roberts, 1971, p. 22). ◿

A new Prison Act was passed in Norway. Its main function in regard to correctional education was to emphasize work programs. "[E]ducational activities were to take place outside working hours," and "cooperation between the prison and educational authorities was to be strengthened." Consolidation of the programs progressed during the 1950s and '60s. (Nordic Council of Ministers, 2005, pp. 68-69—see 1969 entry). ◿

In her book *Teach Them to Live*, **Frances Banks** wrote of "... the civilizing force of education within the walls. For the history of prison education is an unbroken record of trust answering trust, of human response to human approach." (Banks, 1958, p. 6). "No activity in prisons is more dependent upon the personal enthusiasm of the governors [wardens] and staff concerned, who, in turn, are somewhat dependent upon local goodwill and accessibility." (p. 43). Banks wrote that "during the war years the figures for [incarcerated] women practically doubled themselves, and then returned to 'normal'" (p. 237—see 1860 entry). Banks' outlook on correctional education personnel issues was direct: "never by mere paper qualification will

1958   the post be appropriately filled" (p. 274). Banks was education officer
(cont'd.) at Maidstone Prison—see 1941 entry. In 1981, Forster wrote that to read
her book "is to realise something of the excitement, enthusiasm, and
dedication which inspired all the parties concerned, especially at the
institutional level" during the post-World War II period (Foster, 1981,
p. 38). 🔾

1959 — The Missouri legislature created the Division of Inmate Education, with
"general supervision over the planning, establishment and conduct
of academic and vocational educational programs in the several
institutions within the department of corrections." Its director was
appointed by the corrections head, and charged with responsibility to
plan and implement "a long-range program and courses of instruction
for the education of the inmates" including (a) academic curricula
for grades 1-12, (b) vocational education for marketable skills,
and (c) library services. The legislation provided a rationale for the
Division's activities, established a formal liaison with the commissioner
of education, and gave the inmate education director authority in
correctional education personnel decisions. (Missouri, 1959). Important
advances were made in student achievement testing, teacher tenure,
strengthening the retirement system, and expanding interest in the
Correctional Education Association. **Tom Hageman**, who served as
inmate education director for many years, was elected Correctional
Education Association president for two years. The Division was
dismantled in 1968 (Hageman, 1982). These developments represent
the most sophisticated level of correctional education bureau activity—
see 1930 entry. 🔾

1960 — Based largely on Austin MacCormick's 1931 model, social education
programs were becoming increasingly popular. In 1960 a model social
education program was established at the U.S. Penitentiary, Terre
Haute, Indiana (Roberts, 1971, p. 24). 🔾

The American Correctional Association updated its Declaration
of Principles, which had been originally drawn up in 1870 (Murton, 1976,
p. 10—see entries for 1930 and 1970). Originally intended to be a guide
for transforming prisons into reformatories, the Declaration gradually
became a statement of ideals for maintaining safe prisons. 🔾

1961 — **Dr. John McKee** founded the programmed instruction model at Draper
Correctional Institution, in Elmore, Alabama. Dr. McKee's work
documented the success of the individually prescribed instruction
strategy with prisoner students. It was sponsored by the Rehabilitation
Research Foundation, a private, non-profit organization. (Yahraes, in
Roberts, 1973, p. 182—see entries for 1964, 1969 and 1972). 🔾

The U.S. Department of Health, Education, and Welfare received
authority to provide categorical grants to institutions for innovative

1961   correctional training programs through the Juvenile Delinquency and
(cont'd.) Youth Offenses Control Act. Approximately 47 million dollars were
           spent by 1967 through this Act, which was extended in 1964 and 1965.
           It was transferred to the Office of Economic Opportunity in the mid
           and late 1960s. (Metametrics, 1977, pp. III-11-12). ⌒

1962 — The first *Guide to Better Living Program,* sponsored by the Stone-Brandel
       Foundation, was established at the Chicago House of Corrections
       (Roberts, 1971, p. 24—see 1979 entry). Throughout this period the
       Guide was considered a model curriculum material for social education
       in corrections. ⌒

1963 — The Texas Department of Corrections, directed by **George Beto**,
       initiated a statewide prerelease program (Cohen, in Roberts, 1973, p.
       143). Although this was not the first prerelease program, it did help set
       the pace for subsequent improvements. ⌒

           The university influence in Illinois prompted additional
       advances. In 1963 a follow-up study of social education students at
       the Illinois State Penitentiary indicated a substantial improvement in
       recidivism rates among program graduates (Roberts, 1971, p. 141). ⌒

           "Congress passed Public Law 89-333, the Amendments to the
       Vocational Rehabilitation Act." These amendments helped correctional
       education service agencies improve specific programs through Federal
       resources for institutional schools. (Carlson, 1980a). ⌒

1964 — In 1964, when George Wallace was governor, **John McKee** prepared a $400,000 grant application for the Federal Manpower Development Training Agency (MDTA), to initiate vocational education at Draper Correctional Center in Elmore, Alabama. He eventually heard from the MDTA management team in Washington, DC that the project would be funded, but that it could only be implemented if Black inmates participated in the program along with White inmates. Unsure how the concept of integration would be received in his State, McKee first dialogued Draper Warden John Watkins. When he first heard the term "integration," the warden asked what it meant, and McKee explained. The warden's response was "You'll need to take this matter to the Commissioner." McKee then discussed the matter with the Commissioner of Corrections, Frank Lee. After hearing the situation, Lee said "I'd lose my job tomorrow if I have anything to do with integrating the prison. I can't do it." So McKee took the matter to Alabama's Department of Labor. The director of this department said, "I'd be glad to take this bid to Governor George Wallace, but I can't give you any encouragement." When the governor heard about the prospect of the program improvement and the issue of integration, he approved the project and commented that "the black prisoners need training, too, but you tell Dr. McKee not to get me into trouble." So hearing of the approval, the warden took the issue to the Draper Inmate Council—"We're going to get big resources for training, but we've got to integrate the institution to qualify for the funds. What do you think about this matter?" Their response: "We support you in this warden." In summary, the initial episode of turning back Jim Crow segregation at a major prison in an Old South state was initiated because of a strategic effort to improve and consolidate correctional education by a major contributor to our field, Dr. John McKee. This episode was especially dramatic and auspicious, but Dr. McKee has been a steady contributor to the field of correctional education over the decades; his instructional designs and clinical strategies have provided great encouragement for generations of institutional teachers and administrators. (McKee, J., and McKee, S., 2005—see entries for 1969 and 1972). ⌒

In England, 1964 Home Office Prison Rule #1 helped shape subsequent correctional education developments. It declared that "The purpose of the training and treatment of convicted prisoners shall be to encourage and assist them to lead a good and useful life" (Forster, 1981, p. 75). ⌒

In the local public schools, a new emphasis on compensatory education for the disadvantaged was taking shape, although various members of the educational community approached the problem from various perspectives. "Psychologists and educators argued that

252

1964   the reason poor children often failed in school was that they lacked
(cont'd.)   certain experiences in the home and community that enabled others to
succeed—in short, that they had a 'cultural deficit.'" A Boston assistant
superintendent of schools explained his perspective.

> Many of these children have low aspirational levels....
> By virtue of their limited background [they] fail to
> meet the expected outcomes as defined in Curriculum
> Guides....It is our hope to raise the achievement of
> these pupils closer to their potentials which have for
> too long been submerged by parental lack of values.
> (Tyack, 1974, p. 281).

The chairman of the Boston school board had another perspective. "We
do not have inferior schools; we have been getting an inferior type of
student." (pp. 281-282). ⟠

1965 — Prison colleges were started in Texas (Roberts, 1971, p. 25). "There were
an estimated 40,000 offenders ready [nationwide] for college work in
1965" (Gaither, 1982, p. 22). ⟠

     Bowen's book on *Soviet Education* appeared, with some good
summary information on the contributions of **Anton Makarenko** (see
entries for 1919-1923; 1933). During the tsarist years, Makarenko studied
to be a teacher (Bowen, 1965, p. 9). Later, World War I, the revolution, and
the civil war left terrible devastation. Many orphaned children became
juvenile delinquents (pp. 47-49). In the Ukraine, Makarenko addressed
this problem by establishing special youth institutions, and a social
education model that became the pattern for future institutions (p. 64).
Maxim Gorky influenced Makarenko's writing skill by critiquing his
book drafts about social education (p. 11). Out of gratitude, Makarenko
named several of his first correctional schools "Gorky Colonies." His
most popular book, *The Road to Life*, was published in the mid 1930s.
Written like a novel, it presents social education strategies for the
development of "the new Soviet man." Soviets studied this book not
only for its educational message, but also as fine literature (pp. 3-4)—just
as students in the U.S. read *Moby Dick*. In addition, Makarenko's books
established the foundations for modern Soviet pre-school to secondary
education (p. 44). When confronted by a problem, Makarenko immersed
himself in the issue and its literature until he found a solution. One
such problem was the Bolshevik concept of the family. Marx and Engels
had seen the nuclear family as an expression of male domination that
would wither when women were free to pursue their own careers.
The Bolsheviks did not initiate anti-family actions, but "the family had
been singled out as the prime bourgeois institution... antithetical to...
true society" (p. 36). Distressed by this problem, Makarenko studied it
intensely. His solution was a new view that presented families as "social
education collectives." As a result of his work the family emerged from

1965   the period of insecurity, and Soviet policy became very supportive of the
(cont'd.) family structure (p. 172). ⌒⌒

The post World War II social climate facilitated unionization of various occupational groups, including teachers. In the local public schools

> From 1946 to 1965 NEA-affiliated groups [the National Education Association] conducted twenty-two 'work-stoppages' enlisting 16,450 teachers; almost double that number of teachers in NEA groups stopped work in 1966 alone. In September 1967, about 100,000 teachers went out in union strikes in a number of cities, including Detroit and New York. Although the AFT [American Federation of Teachers, an AFL-CIO affiliate] was much smaller in membership than the NEA—about 135,000 to 1,000,000 in 1969—the union won power in many big cities by winning elections to represent the teachers in salary negotiations. The distinction between union and professional association became less and less sharp as the decade of the 1960's progressed. In an NEA poll of teachers...nine tenths favored group action in bargaining with employers; by 1968 two thirds of teachers in another NEA poll believed that strikes were acceptable. At mid-decade an NEA official observed that public school teachers worked in 'a state of ferment bordering on rebellion.' (Tyack, 1974, p. 287).

In 1947 a Buffalo, New York teacher expressed his sentiment:

> I've always been opposed to strikes....I don't think it's right to keep the children out of school. But it looks as though the city wants it this way. Aren't teachers supposed to be human beings? How long do you think we can be stepped on? (p. 274).

"In 1969 Alan Rosenthal reported that 185 teacher leaders in five large cities believed that teachers had minimal influence over personnel policy, curriculum, and school organization." (p. 288). ⌒⌒

The first halfway house was established (Geary, 1975, p. 304). During the 1970s this model would be implemented in many states. ⌒⌒

1966 — "Title I of the Elementary and Secondary Education Act of 1965 was amended...by Public Law No. 89-750, to include education or educationally related services to children living in state and locally administered institutions for neglected or delinquent children"

1966 (Metametrics, 1977, p. IV-3—see 1977 entry). Federal legislation to
(cont'd.) help support institutional libraries was proposed (MacCormick, in Roberts, 1973, p. 332—see 1969 entry). Congress also passed the Adult Education Act this year; in corrections, Title VI has assisted by providing relevant programs for many illiterate offenders (Metametrics, 1977, p. 7). ⌒

The social climate in North America during this period fostered an emerging focus on all forms of education, including correctional education. **Daniel Glaser** found that

> If one compares only inmates of similar age and criminality, and only those confined for long terms, those in prison school for an appreciable portion of their term have higher postrelease success rates than those in prison school only briefly or not at all (Glaser, in Roberts, 1973, p. 351). ⌒

This receptivity generalized though all the developed Western nations. In England the Prison Department,

> under the stimulation of the Mountbatten Report on prison escapes, was shocked into new life and financially helped to repair its then worst deficiencies. Education underwent the biggest expansion in all its long history. Reimbursements to local education authorities, for example, rose from less than 1/2 million £ in 1964/65 to over 8 million £ today [1981], and there were increases in related expenditure. Some of the growth, of course, represents inflation, but much of it stands for real development, representing a full-time organisational element in institutions, regional offices and headquarters; growing integration within management in all three tiers; improving accommodation, equipment and material resources generally; and increasing education staff induction and in-service training. There is a more professional approach to prisoners' and trainees' educational needs and interests, particularly in remedial education (where a good twenty-two per cent of the whole custodial population has a reading age of less than ten years), in vocational training, and amongst young offenders of compulsory school age. All these are areas where what is done has attracted favourable acclaim. To maintain the momentum here and the element of innovation, the closest possible involvement of prison education staff in mainstream education is essential. (Forster, 1981, p. 41). ⌒

1966   In her book, *The Testing of Negro Intelligence*, **Audrey Shuey**
(cont'd.)   reported errors in intelligence testing resulting from racial bias. She

reviewed 28 comparative studies that had been
conducted between 1919 and 1965. The following
excerpts from the studies illustrate the point very well:
'Findings indicate that delinquent Negro boys, as a
group, are both intellectually and emotionally retarded'
(1941). 'Weighting of scores at lower end of scale may
be accounted for by drunkenness, lack of interest,
anxiety, but mostly in terms of the general inferiority
of the group' (1923). 'White offenders are significantly
more intelligent than Negro offenders' (1936). The
results support the idea that inadequate motivation
is an extremely important factor in Negro inmates'
intellectual test performance' (1965). (Dell'Apa, 1973b,
p. 18). 🔺

1967 — The first Project Newgate college program was established in Oregon
(Metametrics, 1977, p. II-10—see 1969 entry).

The President's Commission of Law Enforcement and
Administration of Justice examined the role of post
secondary education in prisons. In 1967 the Commission
argued that Universities have an indispensable role to
play in filling the knowledge gap that exists throughout
corrections. (Gaither, 1982, p. 22). 🔺

Reverend John Erwin received support from Cook County
Jail warden **John Ogilvie** and **Senator Charles Percy** in his effort to
establish PACE Institute (Programmed Activities for Correctional
Education). Erwin began soliciting private and Federal resources for
the construction of a school at the Jail, a project which was not funded
through the institutional or State budgets. (Erwin, 1978, p. 125—see
entries for 1955 and 1957). 🔺

Winthrop Rockefeller took office as Arkansas governor. He had
been elected on a platform of prison reform, in response to a State police
report that documented cruelty in Arkansas prisons. Rockefeller hired
Tom Murton, who had worked in the Alaska corrections system, to
evaluate the charges, and subsequently appointed him as Tucker Prison
superintendent. (Murton, 1976, pp. 213-214). Murton established a self-
governing Inmate Council, improved the food and medical services,
hired some female teachers and work supervisors, started academic
and vocational education programs, integrated the death row prisoners
into institutional activities, and sponsored male/female inmate dances.
(pp. 213-220). 🔺

1968 — **Tom Murton** was transferred and promoted from Tucker Prison warden to Cummins Prison Farm superintendent. Cummins was a larger institution (Murton, 1976, p. 220). He excavated the remains of several inmate bodies from the yard there—they had allegedly been tortured and murdered by officers and inmate guards. See 1920 entry. Murton was subsequently informed by the Prison Board that he would probably not be appointed as Arkansas Corrections Commissioner (pp. 149-150). Five days after he was assigned to Cummins Farm, Murton was fired, with one day's notice (p. 220). He was placed under house arrest until his departure from the prison (pp. 149-150). ⌂

   The Federal Law Enforcement Assistance Administration (LEAA) was established when the Omnibus Crime Control Act and the amended Safe Streets Act were consolidated (Metametrics, 1977, p. 7). LEAA discretionary funding helped to develop many correctional education programs. However, 85% of LEAA funding went to the states in block grants, which tended to preclude school programming because correctional education was often not a state priority. The Department of Health, Education, and Welfare and other Federal agencies "were requested to leave the active development of corrections related programs to the new agency." (p. 1). ⌂

   Abbott's book *The Child and the State* was published. In part, Abbot wrote that it was not until the twentieth century that the juvenile court movement got under way, starting with the first juvenile court law, passed in Illinois in 1899. The passage of this law was largely the work of **Julia Lathrop**, **Lucy Flower**, and **Jane Addams**, all noted for philanthropic work. They exemplified the middle class reformer women of the time. (Abbott, 1968, vol. #2, pp. 323-328). ⌂

   Robert Roberts' book *Imprisoned Tongues* was published, about literacy education in English prisons. It touches on many of the universal aspects of correctional education. "An almost indispensable aid in my own classes is a stock of duplicated worksheets on English and arithmetic." (Roberts, R., 1968, p. 98). "'It's nice,' said one student, as he entered the classroom...'to come in 'ere out of the nick [prison]!'" (p. 113; emphasis in original). "A tutor in prison soon gets used to gibes about teaching men to read and write, then seeing them return for forgery" (p. 67). "Their experience of education has contributed to a fear and hatred of learning" (p. 4). "Student idiosyncrasies show themselves oftener than in classes outside" (p. 41). "The first few days after coming to prison many are at their bitterest; wretched, brooding over 'injustice' done, worrying about a possible appeal, they feel in no mood for chit-chat on education" (p. 13). "Frequently [the prisoner's] sense of time, space, direction, and relationship is distorted, leaving him by turns confused, loudly aggressive, or mute with muddle and doubt" (p. 9). "The commonest failing with illiterates is an inability to concentrate for longer than a few minutes together" (p. 45).

Inadequacy is often reflected in the illiterate's lack of ordinary skills. A surprising number admitted that they had never learned to swim, dance, use simple household tools, or even ride a bicycle. Very few have taken part of their own accord in any team games, or know childish pastimes like ludo or snakes and ladders. (p. 6).

"One finds the [audio] tape most useful of all in demonstrating and helping to correct blurred, slovenly, and inarticulate speech" (p. 112). "In literacy, teaching success depends mainly not on the book nor on the method but on the teacher's ability to stimulate the student's interest and will to learn" (p. 22).

In the early stages of learning adult illiterates require individual attention, but as soon as possible one should begin to take the group as a whole, for part of the time, at least. The tutor, of course, is not merely teaching men to read and write, he is offering them a basic education. (p. 108).

The purpose of correctional education can be "to encourage them to think (the opposite to the present institutionalisation that takes place in prison) to accept responsibility, and to undertake a leadership role—if only the role of leading themselves" (Hauser, in Roberts, R., 1968, p. 162). "The gaoler [jailer] has never been popular.... Of all civil servants the prison officer is perhaps the one held in lowest esteem." (Roberts, R., 1968, p. 151). "Officers live in a confined society....In his more pessimistic moods the officer at a large local gaol sees himself as little better than the turnkey of a century ago." (pp. 153-154).

It is always worth while keeping an illiterate's earliest work. To let him see it again when he is striving, perhaps, towards a junior standard of reading and writing gives both a shock and a very real sense of achievement. (p. 27).

"*The Guiness Book of Records*, easily the most sought after volume in a prison library, is looked upon as the repository of modern knowledge and the winner of a television quiz game is considered a 'real genius'" (p. 53).

War stories and junior adventure attract the greatest number of readers; romantic novels may be avoided. Conversation about sex is less frequent among the unlettered than with literates in the same age groups. When it arises one sometimes notices a prudishness

1968
(cont'd.)   and an embarrassment seldom indeed found among
                         the more educated students. (p. 73).

"Prison is one of the few places in Britain where verse-writing is a respected occupation" (p. 75). "Tattoos" are "the hallmarks of virility" (p. 60). ⚹

A survey by **S. Adams** entitled *College-Level Instruction in U.S. Prisons* revealed that 75% of the institutions polled offered some type of college program, including correspondence courses, study release, extension divisions, and instructional television (Metametrics, 1977, p. II-25—see 1973 entry). "Seven state prison systems offered Associate degrees to offenders in conjunction with local junior colleges" (Gaither, 1982, p. 22—see 1971 entry). ⚹

Between 1940 and 1968 only six doctoral dissertations were published on correctional education (Reid, 1979, p. 674). Although correctional educators have benefited from the research and scholarship of many over the decades, there is still a great deal of work to be done. At present (2006) there are no terminal degree programs (for Ed.D.s or Ph.D.s) in the field of correctional education. ⚹

At Marburg, Germany, Phipps University's Research Center for Comparative Education established an **Anton Makarenko** Department—"its sole aim the study of Anton Makarenko's life, work, and international reception" (Edwards, 1991, p. 1). Makarenko (1888-1939), "the father of Soviet correctional education," had been compared to Rousseau, Pestalozzi, and Tolstoy (p. 2; see entries for 1917, 1920-23, 1933, 1935, 1951, and 1965), and Dr. Benjamin Spock (p. 9). In 1933 John Dewey "suggested that the West could learn from Makarenko's work with juvenile delinquents" (p. 10). Throughout Scandinavia "an expanding number of 'intentional communities' for alienated youth (such as alcohol and drug addicted youngsters, or adolescents with severe adjustment problems), [are] modeled on Makarenko's collectives" (p. 11). ⚹

In his book on *Soviet Education*, Grant wrote that in the Soviet Union, "Intelligence tests are condemned as 'bourgeois pseudo-science,' while the whole concept of 'intelligence' as innate ability is viewed with deep mistrust. The Marxist believes that human nature is not basically pre-ordained, but rests in the hands of man himself..." (Grant, 1968, p. 46). ⚹

1969 — Windham School District, Texas' correctional school district, was established as a component of the Texas Department of Corrections. **Dr. Lane Murray** was appointed superintendent of schools. (Murray, 1975). ⚹

Connecticut established a correctional school district for adults, with **Edmund Gubbins** as superintendent of schools (Miller, 1978, p. 267). Eventually, two additional school districts were started in Connecticut, one for confined juveniles (p. 281), and another for mentally retarded students (pp. 283-284). Later, the State's prison industries and correctional education programs were administratively merged for a few years (p. 270). ⌒

The need for nationwide planning in corrections was emerging. In 1969 the Inter-Agency Council on Corrections was formed in the executive branch of the Federal government, to develop recommendations and strategies to improve corrections (Metametrics, 1977, p. III-2). ⌒

Delaware **Governor Peterson** ordered that henceforth the whipping post at the Delaware Correctional Institution would be stored in the basement. It had not been used since 1952. (Murton, 1976, p. 132). ⌒

The U.S. Department of Labor funded **Reverend John Erwin's** PACE Institute for one year at $200,000 (Erwin, 1978, p. 140). The PACE program concept was based, in part, on the results of **Dr. John McKee's** educational experiments at Draper Correctional Institution in Elmore, Alabama (Reagen and Stoughton, 1976, p. 77—see 1961 entry). ⌒

The U.S. Office of Education funded a project sponsored by the Educational Research and Development Center of the University of Hawaii. **Dr. T.A. Ryan** facilitated the project meeting in Arlington Heights, Illinois, where correctional education practitioners discussed program goals. The result was the Adult Basic Education, Corrections (ABEC) program, in which many people were later trained. (Ryan, 1970, p. v). Dr. Ryan's contributions in the areas of correctional career education, correctional education curriculum development, the systems approach to correctional education, and ABEC have been substantial. ⌒

Dr. Thomas Gaddis, author of *Birdman of Alcatraz*, reported on the Project Newgate effort which he designed in cooperation with the Division of Continuing Education, Oregon State System of Higher Education. First implemented at Oregon State Penitentiary (see 1967 entry), Newgate was an experimental program for inmates who had potential for college education. "It combines pre-college and college level instruction with counseling and pre-release training." Newgate quickly spread to Minnesota, Pennsylvania, New Mexico, and the Federal System. It was designed to demonstrate the value of postsecondary education as a rehabilitative program. (OEO, 1970, pp. 3-4—see 1973 entry). Newgate was the name of old prisons in London (see 1817 entry), and New York City (see 1797 entry). ⌒

1969   The Library Services Act of 1956 was expanded to include
(cont'd.) support for institutional libraries (Lewis, L. 1977). In the years that
followed this became an important source of funding for correctional
library services. ⌒

In Norway, "the educational authorities took over responsibility
for prison education." The Ministry of Educational, Cultural and Church
Affairs "already felt quite overwhelmed by all its responsibilities and
was not being proactive about taking on new ones." The purpose of the
change was "to provide education for young offenders of school age
and for young offenders with inadequate educational backgrounds."
(Nordic Council of Ministers, 2005, p. 69). Much of this attention was a
result of criminologist **Nils Christie**'s "import model."

> Christie considered the import model as a way of
> opening up the system, but placed responsibility for
> all functions not related to prison care outside the
> prisons. According to Christie, the most dangerous
> aspect of the self-supply model is the likelihood that
> various groups of professionals will lose contact with
> the general expertise of their disciplines, as well as
> losing their own identities by becoming too adapted
> to the security measures applying in prisons. This
> philosophy paved the way for putting medical,
> library and many other services offered in prisons in
> the hands of external providers in the community...
> (p. 70). ⌒

The *Guide to Better Living Program* was operational at the
correctional schools in Illinois, Connecticut, and Washington State, at
the Kentucky Reformatory, and McNeil Island Federal Penitentiary.
It was also being used at several jails and prisons across the country
(Roberts, 1971, p. 24—see 1962 entry). ⌒

The boom in postsecondary programs for inmates was about
to take off. Thirty-two inmates at the District of Columbia Youth Center
were attending Federal City College (Roberts, 1971, p. 25). ⌒

1970 — Construction on the new PACE school at Chicago's Cook County
Jail was completed, and 60 students were immediately enrolled
(Erwin, 1978, p. 143). The school continued to grow, and **Reverend
John Erwin**'s work was a source of encouragement to correctional
educators around the country. In addition, he served as director of
the National Advisory Council on Vocational Education (NACVE)
during the period when **Dr. Richard Carlson** reported his findings
for the NACVE study on vocational education in corrections (Carlson,
1980b—see 1980 entry). ⌒

1970   Stephen Duguid later explained a series of perceived "causes"
(cont'd.) for crime that extended from 1840-1970.

>   The biological approach [to delinquency and crime]
>   is 'resurgent' because it...has a long tradition, much of
>   which its current advocates...prefer to see forgotten.
>   Nassi and Abramovitz [in their 1976 article "From
>   Phrenology to Psychosurgery and Back Again," *American
>   Journal of Orthopsychiatry*, (4), p. 605] list an impressive
>   array...'scientific curiosa'...starting in the mid-nineteenth
>   century: Phrenology (1840-70), Criminal atavism—
>   Lombroso—atavistic reversal to the primitive revealed
>   physiologically [around the turn of the 20th cen.], Heredity
>   and crime—Jukes and Kallikaks—1910—bad gene theory,
>   Crime and mental deficiency—IQ—1920s, Constitutional
>   psychiatry—behavior a function of body structure—
>   1930s, Hormonal imbalance—1930s, Twin studies—
>   1940s, Physique and delinquency—1950s—mesomorphs
>   and delinquency, Neurological disorders—EEGs—1950s,
>   XYZ genes—1960s—extra Y and aggression, Epilepsy
>   and violence—1960s, Brain dysfunction—episodic
>   dyscontrol syndrome—1960s, [to these Duguid added]
>   Testosterone—1970s. (Duguid, 2000, p. 29; note—the list
>   is rearranged chronologically). ⌒

The American Correctional Association updated the Declaration
of Principles, its 1870 position paper on prison reform (Murton, 1976,
p. 10). Many of the corrections leaders from around the nation gathered
at the marker that designated the 1870 Cincinnati Congress, including
Austin MacCormick. ⌒

A 1949-1968 cumulative index to the *Journal of Correctional
Education* was prepared by teams of correctional educators in New York
State and Illinois. University Microfilms began making back issues
available on 35mm microfilm. (Ryan and Hagen, 1970). ⌒

1971 — Lehigh University established the Social Restoration Education teacher
training program. **Dr. Raymond Bell** managed the program (Gehring
and Clark, 1979, p. 45). The Lehigh Program became an important center
of correctional education activity. Together with Dr. Bell, **Elizabeth
Conrad** and **Thomas Laffey**, helped shape correctional education
evaluation. (Bell and Laffey, 1978). Dr. Bell was active in international
correctional education, special education in corrections, counseling,
and the Correctional Education Association. ⌒

Albert Roberts' first correctional education textbook was
published, *Sourcebook on Prison Education* (Roberts, 1971). Roberts'
books became a benchmark for several subsequent writers. ⌒

262

1971   An unusual departure from normal management practice
(cont'd.) in one state prompted concern regarding community sentiment on
           juvenile justice.

> All juvenile institutions in Massachusetts were closed
> in the course of a single year in 1971-1972. Youth were
> diverted to halfway houses in the community. The
> abrupt transition provoked a harsh public reaction and
> generated opposition from the police and the courts as
> well. (Dell'Apa, 1973b, p. 70). ⌂

Within a consortium of Federal agencies another innovation
resulted in a reconfigured alliance for improvement of the criminal
justice system.

> [An] extraordinary cooperative venture into corrections
> education was undertaken by LEAA, HEW, and the
> Department of Labor. The Comprehensive Offenders
> Program Effort (COPE) was to be jointly funded and
> administered by the three agencies. In 1972 HEW
> withdrew from the effort. LEAA and DOL remained
> committed to the program and jointly sponsored 12
> three-year grants to the states. (Metametrics, 1977,
> p. 8). ⌂

Fully 121 institutions were "...collaborating with prisons to
provide college level instruction to inmates."

> **Adams** and **Connolly**...summarized [community
> college correctional education involvement] in their
> article 'The Role of Junior Colleges in the Prison
> Community.' The following excerpt is of special interest:
> 'Many characteristics of community and junior colleges
> make them especially suited to conduct educational
> programs for prisoners, and parolees. Most public
> institutions are 'open door' so admissions problems
> are few. Their offerings range broadly, from the purely
> vocational to the primarily intellectual and esthetic.
> The occupational curriculums are varied and can
> accommodate a wide array of student needs, interests,
> and abilities. The colleges are relatively experienced
> in meeting the special requirements of disadvantaged
> persons. They are ubiquitous, and, therefore, readily
> accessible to more of the nation's correctional facilities.
> Finally, community functions of the community college,
> and a cooperative prison educational program falls
> into either of these categories.' (Adams and Connolly,
> in Gaither, 1982, p. 22; emphasis added). ⌂

1971   New York governor Nelson Rockefeller appointed **Austin**
(cont'd.) **MacCormick** co-chairman of the special committee to study the Attica
Prison uprising (Reagen and Stoughton, 1973, p. 2). This was the last
major project with which MacCormick was associated in the public
mind. ⌂

In *Juvenile Reform in the Progressive Era* (1971), **Jack Holl** prefaced
his three stage sequence by considering the Pennsylvania system
which predated Auburn; he further adjusted it by labeling the Junior
Republic "anti-institutional." Thus Holl discussed four patterns of
prison discipline: (a) Pennsylvania, (b) Auburn, (c) reformatory prison
discipline, and (d) anti-institutional institutions. He implied that other
systems were either derived from these or historically inconsequential.
Holl's four part review is a refreshing change from traditional prison
histories. See 1910 entry. ⌂

1972 — The U.S. General Accounting Office found that there were 11
agencies involving more than 70 funding programs to assist offender
rehabilitation, and no overall coordination of the $192 million expended
annually (Metametrics, 1977, p. III-13). "Nearly 20% of the programs
were not able to identify the amount of funds expended for activities
directly benefiting offenders" (p. III-14). ⌂

Dr. John McKee submitted the Environmental Deprivation
Scale (EDS) to the Department of Labor. Sponsored by the Rehabilitation
Research Foundation, the EDS is a reliable predictor of recidivism
(Jenkins, 1972, title page). ⌂

Virginia's compulsory school attendance law was made
applicable to children at State institutions (Virginia Code Commission,
1981). Support for compulsory, or mandatory, attendance became
popular in Maryland and the Federal Bureau of prisons. ⌂

The modern model of correctional education administration
that was established in Texas and Connecticut was attracting attention.
In 1962 Illinois and New Jersey established correctional school districts
(ABA Bulletin #22, 1973, p. 3). ⌂

The **(Tom) Murton** Foundation for Criminal Justice, Inc. began
publication of *The Freeworld Times*, a national prison reform newspaper.
Publication ended in 1974. (Murton, 1976, p. XIV). ⌂

1973 — **Frank Dell'Apa** surveyed 150 adult institutions with a total population
of 110,000 inmates, to ascertain the extent of correctional education
programming. The survey was sponsored by the Western Interstate
Commission for Higher Education, and funded in part by a grant from
the Office of Education. "Based on the survey...findings that over 75% of

1973 the total inmate population were not high school graduates, Dell'Apa
(cont'd.) concluded that the primary thrust of academic programming should
be centered on very basic education." (Metametrics, 1977, pp. II-15-16).
"Dell'Apa found that...slightly more than one-third participated in at
least some educational programs. More than twice as many inmates
were involved with prison industry type programs." (Metametrics, 1977,
p. II-18). Dell'Apa reported that there was a "groundswell of concern
about education for the offender" but a "shocking lack of knowledge
about the state of education in correctional settings" (Dell'Apa, 1973a,
p. ii). His survey was conducted in collaboration with the Correctional
Education Association and focused on academic instruction (p. 1).
More than 75% of the total population had not completed high school;
over 50% had not reached grade ten; almost half had not reached grade
seven; the median educational attainment was around grade eight (p. 8).
The amount spent on correctional education varied substantially from
institution to institution (p. 10). In most states, the Federal government
funded approximately 20% of this cost, and the state 80% (p. 11). There
were more part-time students than full-time, with part-time students
comprising more than 50% of the total (pp. 15-16). Correctional
education programs in Federal institutions reached more students than
those in state institutions (p. 13). Approximately 70% of all teachers
were certified, and inmate teachers amounted to nearly 11% of the total
(p. 21). The average student/teacher ratio was 11/1 (p. 22). In addition
to being trained in special education, guidance/counseling, abnormal
psychology, the emotionally disturbed, and sociology, Dell'Apa found
that the teacher respondents listed necessary personal characteristics
of successful correctional educators. These included maturity, stability,
self-control, respect for individuals and cultural differences, patience,
creativity, a desire to experiment, flexibility, empathy, firmness and
fairness, a variety of real-world experiences, a desire to help people,
and an accepting and open mind (p. 26). Individualized teaching and
diagnostic techniques were found to predominate (p. 28). Most of the
schools reported that they needed more money and more facilities
(p. 30). ⌒

In a parallel survey on correctional education in institutions for
juveniles, Dell'Apa's sample included 36 facilities, with 2,905 students
and 381 teachers. "The smallest school had an enrollment of 31; the
largest had 1,080....Only two institutions report less than 100 percent of
['school age'] students in school....About one-third of the institutions
conduct programs for handicapped or special students." (Dell'Apa,
1973b, pp. 24-25). The average student/teacher ratio was 8.93/1 (p. 26).
Dell'Apa explained that juvenile institutions were established originally
to "get children out of the adult penitentiaries," and to care for "the ever
increasing mass of children who were not transgressors but who were
simply homeless, vagrant, or destitute" (pp. 10-11). This combination
of offenders and nonoffenders required individualized treatment
(p. 12). Approximately 80% of the institutional schools surveyed used

1973 individually prescribed instruction methods (p. 28). A "short span of
(cont'd.) attention...is entirely suited to the step-by-step learning of programmed
materials" (p. 53). Approximately 75% of the students were boys. Their
mean age was 16.68 years—normally they would be halfway through
high school, but their academic average was around 7th grade (p.
35). Dell'Apa found that four % of the students had disabilities that
were physical; 43% emotional; 46% had reading difficulties; 47% were
remedial problems; 48% were culturally disadvantaged; 71% had
behavioral or social problems; 35% were not motivated to learn; and
six % appeared mentally retarded (p. 37). Fully 88% had one or more
special learning problem (p. 39). He reported that the average teacher
salary was $11,363, with a range from $6,000 to $16,000 (p. 33). Twelve
percent of the teachers had completed their bachelor's degree; 50% had
done some graduate work; 25% had masters degrees or "above" (p. 34).
Yet one education director said "We have plenty of teachers, but not
necessarily the right kind" (p. 31). Student needs did not correspond
with traditional teacher preparation competencies: "My experience
with this group has led me to believe that their educational problems
are the least of those that confront them" (p. 31). "By and large, teachers
have adequate educational background on the basis of their academic
degrees, although their training has not generally been appropriate to
teaching in correctional education" (p. 34). 〰

In *An Evaluation of Newgate and Other Prisoner Education
Programs,* **John Irwin, et. al.** reported that "prison college programs
pay for themselves." The survey was funded by the Office of Economic
Opportunity, and based on a 20-year income tax projection after the
release of student participants (Irwin, in Metametrics, 1977, p. II-44).
The Newgate Resource Center of the National Council on Crime and
Delinquency conducted the *National Survey of Post Secondary Educational
Programs for Incarcerated Offenders.* Three hundred and five institutions
were polled; 218 (71%) reported that they offered higher education
programs, in which approximately 5% of the inmates were enrolled
(Metametrics, 1977, p. II-25—see 1977 entry). 〰

Attention was once again shifting to needed improvements.
The National Advisory Commission on Criminal Justice Standards and
Goals reported that

> The role, quality, and relevance of educational programs
> in major institutions have not kept pace with the
> social, economic, political and technological changes
> and expectations of society....Offenders typically lack
> marketable skills for employment as well as the basic
> education necessary to develop these skills. They have
> been 'losers' in school and are caught up in the cycle
> of cultural and economic deprivations. (Metametrics,
> 1977, p. 1). 〰

1973   Western Illinois University established the Corrections and
(cont'd.) Alternative Education Teacher Training Program, which was directed
by **Dr. Joseph Kersting** (Gehring and Clark, 1979, p. 46). With emphases
in elementary education learning content and the foundations of
education, Dr. Kersting was an important contributor to the literature
of the Correctional Education Association and the field of correctional
education. ⌒

The American Bar Association's Clearinghouse for Offender
Literacy Programs disseminated bulletins advocating the consolidation
of correctional schools into statewide nongeographical school districts
(ABA Bulletins #4 and 22, 1973). These Bulletins became essential to the
states that subsequently implemented the innovation. ⌒

Arkansas and Ohio established correctional school districts
(ABA Bulletin #22, 1973, p. 3). Some observers identified a correctional
school district advocacy movement. However, although implemented
by some states after Arkansas and Ohio, this improvement was never
pursued with vigor, largely a result of caution on the part of the
corrections systems. ⌒

Albert Roberts' second textbook on correctional education was
published, an anthology entitled *Readings in Prison Education* (Roberts,
1973). Most readers find the chapters, written by the various experts in
the field, to be especially useful. ⌒

Congress passed the Comprehensive Employment and
Training Act (Coward, 1980). This Department of Labor program
assisted many correctional education agencies in the delivery of
needed services. ⌒

Syracuse University Research Corporation published the
descriptive overview *School Behind Bars*. In part, the report included
this statement:

> The goals and purpose of correctional education are, at
> present, vague, inadequate, and somewhat defensive.
> Correctional education speaks not with a single voice.
> In fact, the most vocal elements are persons not working
> in education in penal systems but in other agencies.
> The Correctional Education Association has yet to
> state a goal, a purpose, a philosophy for correctional
> education....The goals, purposes, and philosophy of
> correctional education have been stated almost entirely
> by correctional administrators, with little or no input
> from educators. (Marsh, in Reagen and Stoughton,
> 1976, pp. 27-28—see 1983 entry). ⌒

1973   A "Gallup pole on [local public school] education reported
(cont'd.) once again, as in four of the previous five years, that citizens are most
worried about 'lack of discipline'" (Tyack, 1974, p. 290). **David Tyack**
found that "urban teachers and students often went to work amid
bureaucratic breakdown" (p. 272). His book, *The One Best System: A
History of American Urban Education* was published in 1974, and included
this summary of public schooling in the U.S. up to 1940:

> The search for the one best system has ill-served the
> pluralistic character of American society. Increasing
> bureaucratization of urban schools has often resulted
> in a displacement of goals and has often perpetuated
> positions and outworn practices rather than serving
> the clients, the children to be taught. Despite frequent
> good intentions and abundant rhetoric about 'equal
> educational opportunity,' schools have rarely taught
> the children of the poor effectively—and this failure
> has been systematic, not idiosyncratic. Talk about
> 'keeping the schools out of politics' has often served
> to obscure actual alignments of power and patterns
> of privilege. Americans have often perpetuated social
> injustice by blaming the victim, particularly in the case
> of institutionalized racism. (p. 11). ⚋

1974 — Virginia's General Assembly enacted Senate Bill #500, establishing the
Rehabilitative School Authority (Virginia Code Commission, 1981). In
1985 the agency's name was changed to the Department of Correctional
Education (DCE). An independent State agency that functions like a
correctional school district, DCE is organizationally separate from the
youth and adult agencies that operate correctional institutions, and
from the State Department of Education (Gehring, 1979, p. 172). ⚋

Two Florida Technological University sociologists reported
their research findings regarding the suicide rate among confined
adult offenders, which was 159% of the average rate among "free
world" North Americans (Murton, 1976, p. 24). **Tom Murton** helped
disseminate this data. ⚋

In Sweden, the criminal justice system was overhauled
and reorganized, "based on the principles of normalisation and
proximity."

> Pursuant to these principles, the correctional service
> was to use the regular community services whenever
> possible rather than constructing parallel systems of
> their own, with an emphasis on the proximity of the
> outside world for prisoners. Therefore, the Prison and
> Probation Service began to cooperate with the National

1974
(cont'd.)

Agency for Education and the National Labour Market Board. Theoretical education in prison was to be organized under the auspices of the municipal adult education authorities and the national adult education establishments, and vocational education in prison was to be provided on Equal terms as in the community, i.e. in the form of labour market training courses. The National Labour Market Board allocated funding for the vocational training, and the National Agency for Education earmarked funding for municipalities with prisons. Towards the end of this phase, the county boards of education took over responsibility for education at the Swedish national prisons and remand centres [which function somewhat like local jails in the U.S.]. (Nordic Council of Ministers, 2005, p. 99—see 1985 entry). ⌒

Marie Buckley's handbook for prison volunteers was published *Breaking Into Prison*. Based on the principle that volunteers prompt prison reform by opening institutions to public scrutiny, the book offered many useful tips for correctional educators who are considering service expansion through volunteers. (Buckley, 1974). The chapter entitled "For Bleeding Hearts" is especially helpful; other chapters explain key dimensions of prisons and their target populations. ⌒

1975 — Congress passed the Education of All Handicapped Children Act, P.L. 94-142, to ensure free, appropriate, public education (FAPE) for all children with disabilities, aged five to 21. It included provision for identifying students, wherever they were being served, including corrections. Later it was reauthorized under the title Individuals with Disabilities Act, IDEA. ⌒

An estimated $94 million of federal funds were expended for corrections education and closely related programs. Approximately $12 million of this amount was used for federal prisoners. Of the remaining $82 million, 9 million or 11% was derived from the Law Enforcement Assistance Administration Program. HEW accounted for $72 million or 88% of the total and the Department of Labor provided $1 million or 1%. (Metametrics, 1977, p. 7).

The U.S. General Accounting Office reported that "Administrative problems resulted because of overlapping roles for HEW and the Law Enforcement Assistance Administration." The findings were included in *How Federal Efforts to Coordinate Programs to Mitigate Juvenile Delinquency Proved Ineffective* (pp. 8-9). The National Endowment for the Arts spent approximately $210,000 on prison art and art related projects under the Expansion Arts Program (p. IV-40). The states collectively

1975   spent $428 million for correctional education programming, which was
(cont'd.) approximately 80% of the total correctional education budget (p. IV-
44—see 1973 entry). 🐘

Approximately 8,000 Federal inmates, or about one third of
the Federal inmate population, were enrolled in educational programs
(Metametrics, 1977, p. II-19). In addition, "Over 8,000 Federal inmates
completed a variety of occupational education type of programs
that covered a diverse area including medical technology, welding,
dental technology, retailing, business administration and many other
occupational fields" (p. II-21). A report by **G.W. Levy, R.L. Abram,**
and **D. La Dow** for the Department of Labor focused on vocational
education in Federal institutions. Entitled *Vocational Preparation in
U.S. Correctional Institutions*, its findings revealed that only four %of
inmates participated in work release programs—and only one %in
vocational education release, and over 40% of the vocational education
programs had not been reviewed or accredited by outside agencies.
(p. II-22). 🐘

"The Martinson Study," *The Effectiveness of Correctional
Treatment*, was published by Praeger. Written by D. Lipton, and
Judith and R. Martinson, the team analyzed 231 evaluation studies
on prison rehabilitation programs, and found that "with isolated
exceptions, the rehabilitative efforts that have been reported so far,
have no appreciable effect on recidivism." (Metametrics, 1977, p. II-
31). In a study that was released in 1974, **K. Baker, et. al.** concluded
that "recidivism is, in fact, a poor measure of program effectiveness
in reducing criminality because it is 1) conceptually a poor index of
criminal behaviors, 2) an insensitive measure, and 3) contaminated by
other factors and measures things other than criminal behaviors." The
report was entitled *Summary Report: Project Newgate and Other Prison
College Education Programs*, and was funded in part by the Office of
Economic Opportunity. (pp. II-38-39). 🐘

The effort to establish women's prisons, managed by women—
which had begun before the turn of the 20th century—had acquired
a record of success. By 1975, only six states lacked separate women's
prisons (Freedman, 1981, p. 144). 🐘

Texas' Windham School District superintendent **Dr. Lane
Murray** wrote "The School District Concept." The article appeared in
Adult Leadership (Murray, 1975). 🐘

1976 — In his article, "Education: Weapon Against Crime," **E. Herschler** wrote

Poor education does not necessarily cause crime. We
can say, however, that the greater the problems of the
people, including educational problems, the more

1976
(cont'd.)

likely it is that they would resort to crime, either out of frustration or because of economic needs. This is particularly true if people do not have skills to secure jobs. (Herschler, in Metametrics, 1977, p. V-1).

The Criminal Personality, Volume I: A Profile for Change appeared in print, by **Samuel Yochelson** and **Stanton Samenow**. Studying inmates at Saint Elizabeths in Washington, D.C. and other hospitals for the criminally insane, Samenow and Yochelson found that "a criminal was not a victim of impulses or compulsions—he made choices." (Samenow and Yochelson, 1976, p. 20).

In our interviews, we saw contradictions within a given criminal's thinking and action. He appeared both fearless and fearful, grandiose and meek, independent and parasitic, sentimental and brutal, suggestible and rigid. In addition, his attitudes towards his own criminal activities were puzzling. Occasionally, these men viewed what they had done with disgust, but this disgust did not last long enough to deter them from a repetition. More commonly, a criminal took the position that he was justified in what he did. These men, who had been in crime all their lives, regarded themselves as good people. Astoundingly, to a man they told us that they had never viewed themselves as criminals. A crime was an offense that someone else committed. Although what they did was against the law, they believed that it was right for them at the time. Such a psychology was totally baffling to us....We paid considerable attention to the mental mechanism whereby a criminal was able to rid himself of concerns of conscience and fears of apprehension. It was through this 'shutoff mechanism,' as we called it, that a man could change from sentimental to brutal. During our discussions of 'idea through execution' thinking, we learned that some criminals heard a voice just before committing a crime. As they described this phenomenon, it was clear that it was not a manifestation of psychosis. Rather, it was an internal conscience deterrent, which a criminal could choose to heed or disregard. He did not think he was being directed by outside forces. (p. 19).

"Some criminals use drugs to 'shut off' fear, so that they have the 'heart' or courage to commit a crime" (p. 20).

The greatest fear of these criminals was that others would see some weakness in them....Another trait in all was the inclination to view oneself as worthless...'nothings.'

These 'zero feelings,' as we termed them, were present very early in life. Though intelligent, good-looking, and talented, these men often viewed themselves as stupid, ugly, and total failures....To these men, lying was nearly as essential—indeed, automatic—as breathing...concrete thinkers...every criminal regarded himself as totally unique...very suspicious of others...unlike those of true paranoids, the suspicions of these men were grounded in fact.... (pp. 22-23).

This information caused Samenow and Yochelson to adjust their orientation toward criminals.

Instead of being viewed as the exploited, they were the exploiters. Instead of suffering from past traumas, they were the ones who had traumatized others. Instead of focusing on what others had done to them, we examined what they had done to others.... (pp. 28-29).

...[W]e formulated what we called 'tools for responsible thinking and action,' a set of concepts that were to form the foundation of a new set of thinking processes. We were teaching criminals concepts that were second nature to a responsible schoolchild, but totally new to them. (p. 37).

We came to recognize that a criminal needed two types of education: self understanding and knowledge about the outside world. We insisted on conversion as an indication that a criminal meant business, and was not just giving lip service to change. However, we could not produce a conversion as a result of our direct effort to convert by education.... (p. 44).

Samenow and Yochelson developed terminology descriptive of their findings: "automatic errors of thinking," "the 'I can't defense,'" "external deterrents," "internal deterrents," "cutoff" ("elimination from the mind of deterrent considerations"), "superoptimism," "big score," "celebration," "getting caught is itself [seen as] an injustice," etc. "Some criminals hold respected positions in society, which they exploit in their own self-serving ways. They pursue power for its own sake, but do it in ways that are acceptable to society or, at least, avoid breaking any laws." (pp. 52-53). Their book contains a good review of the standard criminality literature. ⌂

New Jersey's Garden State (correctional) School District (see 1972 entry) was transferred from the Department of Institutions and Agencies to the Department of Education (MacNeil, 1979,

1976   p. 215). "The original placement of the school district in the
(cont'd.) Department of Institutions and Agencies was unique to New Jersey.
          In Connecticut, Texas and Illinois the correctional school district
          was housed in the Department of Corrections, and Pennsylvania's
          within the Department of Education." (pp. 217-219). By 1978 a bill
          was introduced to the New Jersey legislature to abolish the Garden
          State School District because of "conflicts between the bureaucracies
          of the two agencies"—the school district and the Department of
          Corrections (p. 216). ⌒

          The National Correctional Education Evaluation Project, a
          part of the Education Commission of the States, published *Correctional
          Education: A Forgotten Human Service* (Correctional Education Advisory
          Committee, 1976). This publication helped get useful information,
          wrapped in a pro-education sentiment, to interested readers. ⌒

          McGraw-Hill normed the revised Tests of Adult Basic Education
          (TABE) on a population that included many inmates (Shearin, 1981).
          Over the years the TABE and its accoutrements have been an important
          diagnostic instrument at many correctional education programs. ⌒

          Tom Murton's book, *The Dilemma of Prison Reform*, was published.
          In part, Murton wrote: "Reform of the prison must precede any plan
          to reform the inmate." (Murton, 1976, p. 173; emphasis in original). In
          his chapter on "The Medical Model: The 'Treatment' Game," Murton
          reported that "...the treatment is not directed toward attitudinal change,
          but the facade of behavioral change" (Murton, 1976, p. 73). ⌒

          Albert Roberts (see entries for 1971 and 1973) and **Osa Coffey**
          (see entry for 1980) completed their *State of the Art Survey for a Correctional
          Education Network*. Their project was funded through a Law Enforcement
          Assistance Act grant to the American Correctional Association. The
          team sent out questionnaires to correctional education programs all
          across the country, and interviewed many correctional educators. Their
          purpose was to describe the technological support systems in use, and
          project a comprehensive model for system improvement consistent
          with identified student needs. The results focused on media hardware
          and software, especially television, communications satellites, and
          computer-assisted instruction. (Roberts and Coffey, 1976). ⌒

          Bo Lozoff's book, *Inside Out*, was published. Subtitled
          A Spiritual Manual for Prison Life, it includes chapters on Hatha
          Yoga, meditation, "saints in cells," etc. Much of Lozoff's work has
          been through the Prison-Ashram Project. "Ashram" is a word for
          a monastery; *Inside Out* helps prisoners maximize the benefits of
          incarceration through the pursuit of spiritual development, much as
          monks might do in a monastery. (Lozoff, 1976). In 1995, Lozoff wrote

If we forget that in every criminal there is a potential saint, we are dishonoring all of the great spiritual traditions. Saul of Tarsus persecuted and killed Christians before becoming Saint Paul, author of much of the New Testament. Valmiki, the revealer of the Ramayana, was a highwayman, a robber, and a murderer. Milarepa, one of the greatest Tibetan Buddhist gurus, killed thirty-seven people before he became a saint. Moses, who led the Jews out of bondage in Egypt, began his spiritual career by killing an Egyptian. If we forget that Charles Manson is capable of transformation, that doesn't reveal our lack of confidence in Manson, it shows our lack of confidence in our own scriptures. We must remember that even the worst of us can change. (in Swift, 2002, pp. 84-87, 154-159).

Marjorie Seashore and **Steven Haberfeld**'s book was published, *Prisoner Education: Project Newgate and Other College Programs*. The study "reveals some clear and positive relationships between prison college programs and success among participants after release from prison" and "very definite conclusions about what type of prison college programs...have the greatest impact on participants' postprison success" (Seashore and Haberfeld, 1976, p. 184). Important variables such as student success, institutional programming, and social background were discussed; *Prisoner Education* is the definitive book on higher education in corrections. However, the authors' examination of critical institutional variables was equally important, and relevant to all levels of correctional education service delivery.

Many prison personnel initially object because they see it [college-level correctional education] as 'giving the inmate too much.' They are accustomed to believing that no experience during incarceration should be made enjoyable. They also fear that the inmate might get more of an education than they themselves have and that, as a consequence, the staff will lose some of its authority. (p. 149).

"No staff member should work more than three years in any prison college program. Such work is so thoroughly taxing that no person can possibly remain vital and innovative after a three-year period" (p. 157). "Initially, there was great resistance [from the prison staff] to the newcomers [teachers], who threatened status quo relationships." Seashore and Haberfeld labeled correctional education programs that relied on relationships external to the institution "expansionist," and those with a "narrow [institution-only] influence base" as "isolationist." (p. 41). "In Oregon, the struggle was resolved by the Newgate director resigning. In Pennsylvania, the prison took full control over the college program." (p. 43).

1976
(cont'd.)

In certain ways the goals of program quality and program survival work at cross purposes. Many of the features suggested in the report as enhancing program quality (for example, college atmosphere, semiautonomy, involvement of outsiders, programmatic links with the university) serve to exacerbate tensions between the new program and the prison and ultimately threaten the integrity, if not the actual survival, of the original program.... (p. 44).

"...[H]eavy reliance on the individual who is warden leaves it [the program] unprotected when the warden is succeeded by a new man..." (pp. 181-182). Therefore, the authors found that one measure of program quality was "The degree of integration of the program into the prison: This refers to the absence of conflict between program staff and participants on one side and the prison staff and administration on the other." (p. 126). At several programs

...the prison administration's concern with security and routine tended to dominate, and to an extent stifle, concerns for educating the inmates. Moreover, participants' interest in education was aroused when the program had more of the atmosphere of a real college and less the atmosphere of a prison. The prison atmosphere tended to prevail in those programs that were more integrated into the rest of the correctional institution....A program that works closely with the prison administration can be a good one if it manages to influence the rest of the prison to move in its direction, rather than the other way around. (p. 130). 🔺

Alexander R. Luria's book on *Cognitive Development: Its Cultural and Social Foundations* appeared in an English version. From original research in the 1920s, Luria found that simple acquisition of literacy skills improved six major cognitive processes: perception, generalization and abstraction, deduction and inference, reasoning and problem solving, imagination, and self-analysis/self-awareness. (Luria, 1976). When offered activities to develop social attitudes, literacy programs may therefore help correctional students rethink some of the problems that resulted in incarceration. 🔺

1977 — Metametrics, Inc. submitted its report to the U.S. Department of Health, Education and Welfare. Entitled *A Review of Corrections Education Policy*, it outlined the Federal sources of assistance for correctional education and recommended greater coordination of existing programs (Metametrics, 1977). Metametrics reported that

Corrections programming has traditionally been a step-child among state agencies which has often resulted in low budgets, inadequate staff and facilities. In many cases, corrections agencies are extending their resources just to maintain security and have no resources, either manpower or financial, to initiate and develop innovative rehabilitative programs. (p. V-10).

Metametrics recommended

the establishment of a Representative of Corrections Education within the Office of the Secretary [of Health, Education, and Welfare] with the function of representing the interests of the corrections clientele similar to the representation provided other minority and disadvantaged groups. This special office should be provided with the responsibilities, resources, and powers required to collect, store and distribute information on corrections education programs and to accomplish the coordinated development of program rationale, planning implementation and evaluation. (p. 11—see 1980 entry).

Metametrics found that "There are eight...[correctional] school districts in existence" (Metametrics, 1977, p. V-7). ⌒

"...43.3 million was spent for corrections education programs under Title I of the Elementary and Secondary Education Act" (Metametrics, 1977, p. V-9). Approximately $9.2 million of the $801.9 million total Basic Education Opportunities Grant budget (BEOG, now known as Pell Grants) went to offenders (p. IV-2). The BEOG program operated under the Higher Education Act of 1965. Metametrics reported that six % of the prisoners in the U.S. were involved in college programs. (p. II-24—see 1982 entry). ⌒

Largely a result of **Dr. Charles Whitson**'s work, the Ohio State University Center for Vocational Education published the results of a national survey, *Vocational Education in Corrections* (Whitson, et al., 1977). Over the years the Center for Vocational Education has been an important crucible for research and the dissemination of useful findings. ⌒

Joseph Skok reported to the Pennsylvania Department of Education on *The Selection of a System for Providing Correction Education for Adjudicated Persons in Pennsylvania*. Skok studied four alternative organizational formats for correctional education: (a) an operating unit of the Department of Education, (b) a contractual monitoring unit of the Department of Education, (c) a Department of Education

1977
(cont'd.) "pass through" organization, with local education agencies delivering correctional education services, and (d) a separate correctional school district. (Skok, 1977, p. 2). Variables studied included cost of administration, accountability, coordination capacity, visibility, operational flexibility, authority, ease of enactment, social cost, simplicity, and the public interest (p. ii). The school district option was described as

> nearly autonomous. Existing local school district operating procedures would apply to the operation of the Separate School District, and those procedures are well established, and school administrators are well trained in following the system. A great deal of latitude is provided in the system because of the high degree of autonomy provided the local boards of school directors by *The Pennsylvania School Code*. (p. 88).

According to the criteria Skok applied, the school district organizational pattern rated a total "score" of 231.5; contract monitoring unit, 172.5; pass through organization, 165; and Department of Education operating unit, 160 (p. 95).

> Tabulations of the weighted values of the criteria assessments shown on the summary matrix indicate that alternative four—the Separate School District—is clearly the superior means for delivering correctional education in Pennsylvania. Numerous indications from the literature of corrections corroborates the conclusion established by the analysis procedure. Discussions with persons involved with correctional education in Texas, Illinois, New Jersey [see 1976 entry], Virginia, and Connecticut, where separate school districts now operate, and with persons from Maryland, where there is no separate school district [see 1978 entry], add the weight of informed professional opinion to the choice of the Separate School District alternative. It is therefore recommended that concerted efforts of the Department of Education be directed toward the establishment of a Separate School District for the purpose of providing educational services to both adults and juveniles who are under the supervision of the courts of the Commonwealth of Pennsylvania. (p. 97). ◿

The Correctional Education Association announced that approximately 20,000 people in the U.S. were involved in various correctional education jobs (Barrum, et al., 1980, p. 15). Despite phases of expansion and contraction, the currently accepted number (2005) has risen to approximately 30,000. ◿

1978 — Congress passed the Educational Amendments of 1978, including a Correctional Education Demonstration Act. President Carter did not budget funds for it, however, and the demonstration projects were never implemented. (Carlson, 1980c). ⌂

      Laura Means Pope Miller wrote an outstanding article which appeared in the *Harvard Journal on Legislation,* on the legal implications of the correctional school district concept (Miller, 1978). Miller's analysis of the concept was direct and useful; as a result some additional research on the subject was implemented. ⌂

      W. Reason Campbell's book, *Dead Man Walking* (Campbell, 1978), presented the experiences of a correctional education practitioner in an interesting, episodic, and documentary style—almost like a novel. It was on the best-seller list. ⌂

      Senators Bayh and **Metzenbaum** introduced a bill entitled "The Federal Correctional Education Assistance Act." **Robert Terhune**, Correctional Education Association president, worked steadfastly to bring it to public attention. **Senator Pell** strongly advocated the measure, and **David Evans**, from Senator Pell's Office, devoted a great deal of energy and organizational support to that cause. (Gehring, September, 1980, p. 4). ⌂

      Sam Houston University's Correctional Education Teacher Training Program began graduate-level studies (Gehring and Clark, 1979, p. 48). Most of the correctional education degree programs during this period were based on locally identified needs for institutional teacher education. ⌂

      System Development Corporation issued its National Evaluation of Title I Elementary and Secondary Education Programs, *Programs for Neglected or Delinquent Youth in State Institutions.* The report recommended that better evaluation designs would substantially improve correctional education program effectiveness. (System Development Corporation, 1978—see 1979 entry). ⌂

      In *Perspective on Education in Prisons,* **Douglas Ayers** wrote that a Federal Canadian correctional school district should be established.

> A country-wide unit, centralized in Ottawa, that would be responsible for educational programs in all prisons, similar to several state-wide school districts providing educational services to all of the prisons within a state's jurisdiction. Such a structure would allow some coordination in the development of programs and the implementation of ones found effective. It could lead to more effective selection and

278

1978
(cont'd.)

training of teachers. But its primary thrust would be to make programs more independent of local prison administration except for day-to-day operations. In this way, it would help in establishing an identity for the school separate from that of the prison such that the prisoners would perceive the teachers as being from 'outside,' somewhat in the way they view the instructors in the [college] Program. This requirement is a prerequisite for the establishment of conditions that facilitate learning in a prison setting.... (Ayers, 1978, p. 4). 🐾

Maryland implemented a correctional education office in the State Department of Education, which functions like a correctional school district (Linton, 1980). This improvement resulted in years of subsequent initiatives, despite limited funding. 🐾

By this time the postsecondary programming for inmates movement had grown tremendously. At McNeil Island Penitentiary, graduation ceremonies "were held...for thirty-one inmates, who received a variety of certificates and degrees from Tacoma Community College, and eight bachelor of arts degrees and one master's degree from Pacific Lutheran University" (Keve, 1984, p. 264). 🐾

Reverend John Erwin's book, *The Man Who Keeps Going to Jail,* was published. It focused on both his early life as a juvenile delinquent and his later work, the founding of PACE Institute at Cook County Jail (Erwin, 1978—see 1967 entry). 🐾

In Iceland "Since 1978 all the prison education at Litla-Hraun [Prison] has been organized under the auspices of the vocational school near Selfoss."

In 1979, according to an agreement on co-financing between the Ministry of Justice and the Ministry of Education, the latter took responsibility for teachers' salaries and the former covered all other expenses related to educational activities. In 1981 the school in Selfoss became a combined comprehensive and upper secondary, and since that year this school has also organized all the prison education at Litla-Hraun, with the prison teachers commuting daily between the village school and the prison.(Nordic Council of Ministers, 2005, pp.121-122).

In 1990 a school was constructed at the institution, "and since then most education for prisoners has taken place there. In special cases, prisoners are allowed to attend school outside the prison to study subjects not available at the prison school." Similar arrangements have been operational at the Kopavogur Prison since 1997. (p. 122). ⌒

1979 — An important national survey report was published, *Correctional Education Programs for Inmates*, by **Dr. Raymond Bell**, et. al. (Bell, 1979). It offered revealing information regarding the relationship between institutional administrations and correctional education, and emphasized the importance of improved program evaluations. See 1971 entry. ⌒

    Austin MacCormick attended his last American Correctional Association conference. He died in New York in October (Pecht and Gehring, 1980, p. 1). ⌒

    Virginia's Rehabilitative School Authority *1980-86 Master Plan* proposed a comprehensive and systematic approach to institutional education (Gehring, 1979). The plan was not implemented, but it inspired several similar initiatives in different states. ⌒

    A major effort to systematize and standardize prison education service delivery was under way. **Dr. Robert Pierce** reported that

> Competency-Based Adult Education (CBAE) is beginning to make a significant impact in the field of correctional education for adults. The current trend of implementing CBAE in prisons is gaining momentum. Not only are state institutional administrators examining competency-based education for possible adaptation, but some city and county jail officials are also beginning to express an interest in CBAE. (Pierce, 1979, p. 229).

CBAE was a system for learning GED-required skills through life experience curricula. Pierce served as learning coordinator for Texas' Windham (correctional) School District (see 1969 entry). His article, "Competency-Based Adult Education in Correctional Institutions: State of the Scene" appeared in the Fall edition of *Adult Literacy and Basic Education*. Windham "was one of the original pilot sites in Texas to use the Adult Performance Level (APL) program developed by the APL Project at the University of Texas." A contingent of Windham staff were assigned to "adapt the APL program to a prison environment." (pp. 229-230). Similar correctional education adaptations were subsequently implemented in Missouri, Illinois, Kentucky, Michigan, Georgia, Kansas, Massachusetts (at Norfolk— see 1928 entry), Oklahoma, and Pennsylvania, and other states (pp. 230-233). Texas and Missouri program administrators listed the positive aspects of APL:

1979   [a] Think and discuss rather than memorize,
(cont'd.)   [b] Relate basic skills to everyday life skills,
              [c] Breaks monotony for ABE and GED programs,
              [d] Increases awareness of the world,
              [e] Clarifies preconceived notions,
              [f] Opportunity to expose students to values,
              [g] Emphasis on learning rather than grades,
              [h] Curriculum materials supplement other areas,
              [i] Gives students opportunity to be heard, and
              [j] Flexibility. (p. 231). ⌒

Ron Clark and **Thom Gehring** wrote the Virginia correctional education Teacher Training Program Proposal and worked with Virginia Commonwealth University (VCU) to establish a format for implementation (Gehring and Clark, 1979). The plan was not implemented, but in 2005 VCU began hiring to establish a similar program. ⌒

The U.S. General Accounting Office reported to Congress how *Correctional Institutions Can Do More to Improve the Employability of Offenders*. Much of the report focused on correctional education needs, especially in social education and on-the-job training. (General Accounting Office, 1979). ⌒

Canada's **Doug Griffin** (see 1983 entry) brought together **Stanton Samenow** (see 1976 entry), **Reuven Feuerstein** (see 1980 entry), **Carl Haywood**, and **Doug Ayers** (see 1978 entry), to produce a videotape on *Crime and Reason*. The tape offered theory and practical suggestions about how correctional educators can assist offenders to overcome cognitive deficits. (Griffin, 1979). It provided an excellent link between the ideas of Feuerstein (see 1980 entry) and the Samenow/Yochelson team (see 1976 entry). ⌒

Felony convictions in Chicago's Cook County Jail increased 470% between 1972 and 1979. "Between January and July [1982], Mississippi's prison population grew at an annual pace of 44%." Anderson remarked that incarceration "is too precious a resource, too expensive and damaging, to waste on the run of criminals." (Anderson, 1982, p. 40—see 1982 entry). ⌒

1980 — Congress established the U.S. Department of Education, with a Secretary on the President's cabinet. The Correctional Education Association launched an advocacy effort for the implementation of a Correctional Education Office in the new Department. (Gehring, September, 1980). This approach paralleled the findings of the National Institute of Education (Carlson, 1980b) and the National Advisory Council for Vocational Education (Carlson, 1980a), and supported by findings presented by Metametrics in 1977 (see entry). The Corrections

281

1980   Program was established "within the Office of Special Projects
(cont'd.) under the Assistant Secretary of Vocational and Adult Education"
(Hufstedler, 1981). **Dr. Richard Carlson**, a correctional education
supporter of nationwide acclaim in the field of vocational education,
was appointed to head up the Special Projects Office (Gehring,
September, 1980, p. 1). Carlson obtained a grant from the National
Institute of Corrections (NIC) through NIC director **Allen Breed**,
to establish a position for **Dr. Osa Coffey** (see 1976 entry), who
coordinated the new Corrections Program in the U.S. Education
Department (Carlson, January, 1981). **Thom Gehring**'s article on the
subject reported how opinions and resources aligned to establish the
new office (Gehring, 1980). 〇

More than 300 correctional institutions provided postsecondary
education programs (Gaither, 1982, p. 22). Most of these were funded
with Basic Educational Opportunity Grants (BEOGs—the funding
source was later renamed the Pell Grant Program, after **Senator
Claiborne Pell**, who was a consistent friend of correctional education).
BEOGs and Pell Grants were for all indigent postsecondary students;
inmates qualified not because of their incarceration but because of their
poverty. 〇

A 1982 article in *Time* magazine proclaimed that by 1980 many
policy makers had agreed that

> Determinate sentencing ends the ambiguity [of varying
> sentences for similar crimes]. The plan considered
> wisest is the one adopted by Minnesota in 1980.
> Basically, that state's 'grid' formula quantifies a convict's
> criminal past and his current offense, and assigns the
> appropriate sentence. A judge who occasionally wants
> to impose any lesser or greater penalty must justify
> his divergence in writing. Most appealing is the cool
> simplicity embodied in the guidelines, which help to
> restore an aura of fairness and strictness to criminal
> justice. Deterring crime is a murky business, but it can
> work well only if the sanctions threatened are credible,
> consistently applied and within society's means.
> 'The certainty of punishment,' says Norman Carlson,
> director of the Federal Bureau of Prisons, 'is more
> important than the length of punishment.' (Anderson,
> 1982, p. 40).

In 1982 Anderson quoted Franklin Zimering, a sociologist at the
University of Chicago: "There are two strains in penology now....The
liberals, stressing equality, draw the sentencing grids. Conservatives
say 'Fine, but let's erase this four years and put in eight.'" (p. 41—see
1982 entry). 〇

John Braithwaite's book about Australian correctional education was published, *Prisons, Education, and Work*. Most of it is about the organization of correctional education in the various states and territories, especially New South Wales, which had several exemplary programs. Braithwaite outlined the principle of lesser eligibility: "prisoners should not be entitled to any benefits which exceed the benefits enjoyed by the lowest classes among the free community." He also outlined the principle of greater eligibility: since prisoners are generally disadvantaged and incarceration is a further disadvantage, justice and equity require that the state do everything possible to help releasees obtain suitable employment. (Braithwaite, 1980, pp. 15-18).

> Most prisoners have missed out on the excitement of learning, the sense of achievement at mastering a branch of human knowledge, the wonderment of discovering new ideas and challenging old ones, the feeling of being able to contribute to a democracy as an informed citizen (p. 191).

"Let us not attempt to make prisoners the scapegoats for the nation's economic problems. They have a right to work and make a productive contribution to the nation equal to that of any citizen." (p. 18).

> At Geelong prison, whenever the guard is called away from the tower overlooking the prison schoolroom (something which happens frequently) classes must cease immediately....Because of the unimportance of education in the normal priorities of prison administrations, it is possible for prison teachers to have an easy ride. No one in the administration cares much if they do their job badly. Prisoners to whom I spoke often had harsh words to say about teachers not attending classes and appointments as agreed, failing to organize timetables or textbooks, and generally being more interested in prison teaching as a 'novelty' or a 'glamour' job than in the prisoners themselves. An example of this is teachers visiting high schools giving talks on prisons rather than being at work. (p. 193).

Consistent with Maconochie's guiding principles, Braithwaite suggested that prisoners should spend the last month of their sentences out looking for jobs, without escort (p. 221).

> Rossie et al. asked 2002 Americans the following question: 'At the present time [1980], most men when released from prison throughout the country receive between $20 and $50 to start life over. Would you be in favour of or opposed to providing released prisoners

with some form of financial support, for example, like
unemployment insurance, until they found a job?'
Only 24 percent of the sample said that they would
be opposed. Even more surprisingly, when those who
were not in favour were asked 'If it were shown that
such support reduced crime among men coming out
of prison, would you be in favour of it or no?', only 22
percent said they would still not be in favour. (p. 232).

"The most staggering finding of Roux's research was that the most
common source for an employer being told about their past criminal
record was the police" (p. 212). Ultimately, he recommended that "the
most effective solutions to crime lie...in transforming the society which
produces the grist for the criminal justice mill" (p. 231). ◢◣

A major book by **Reuven Feuerstein** was published, *Instrumental
Enrichment: An Intervention Program for Cognitive Modifiability*. It was
about "learning to learn" and focused on what students "can learn
rather than have learned" (Begab, in Feuerstein, 1980, p. xv). Feuerstein
explained some problems in education: (a) psycho-analysis—"Theorists
of this school often maintained that behavior is a function largely of non-
intellectual factors that may bypass or even neutralize cognitive process"
(Feuerstein, 1980, p. 4); (b) behaviorism—"behaviorism emerged as a
reaction against any form of introspection and 'outlawed' the concept
of the mind. Only those behaviors directly observable were regarded
as worthy of scientific endeavor" (p. 5); (c) psychometry—"The focus
was the issue of prediction...based on those very characteristics that are
most likely to remain stable and constant over time...to this very day we
still do not have any real understanding of what the IQ test measures."
(p. 6).

> ...[C]ognitive modifiability...is directed...at changes of
> a structural nature that alter the course and direction
> of cognitive development...brought about by a
> deliberate program of intervention that will facilitate
> the generation of continuous growth by rendering
> the organism receptive and sensitive to internal and
> external sources of stimulation. (p. 9).

Regarding cultural deprivation—"It is not the culture that is depriving,
but...the fact that the individual, or his group, is deprived of his own
culture that is the disabling factor...a failure on the part of a group to
transmit or mediate its culture to the new generation" (p. 13).

> By mediated learning experience (MLE) we refer to
> the way in which stimuli emitted by the environment
> are transformed by a 'mediating' agent, usually a
> parent, sibling, or other caregiver. This mediating

1980
(cont'd.)

agent, guided by his intentions, culture, and emotional investment, selects and organizes the world of stimuli [for the student]...the more and the earlier an organism [learner] is subjected to MLE, the greater will be his capacity to efficiently use and be affected by direct exposure to sources of stimuli....MLE, therefore, can be considered as the ingredient that determines differential cognitive development...in otherwise similarly endowed individuals, even when they live under similar conditions of stimulation. (pp. 15-16).

It is an interesting book, well worth reading. See 1983 entry.

1981 — South Carolina established a correctional school district (Murphree, 1981). It was named Palmetto School District, and was managed for years by **Layne Coleman** (Rankin, 1982, 3rd page).

In a February speech before the American Bar Association, Supreme Court **Chief Justice Warren Burger** said recidivism rates of corrections are similar to product recalls in factories.

> The dismal failure of our system to stem the flood of crime repeaters is reflected in part in the massive number of those who go in and out of prisons. In a nation that has been thought to be the world leader in so many areas of human activity our system of justice— not simply the prisons—produces the world's highest rate of 'recall' for those who are processed through it. How long can we tolerate this rate of recall and the devastation it produces? (Burger, 1981a, p. 7).

"We must accept the reality that to confine offenders behind walls without trying to change them is an expensive folly with short term benefits—a 'winning of battles while losing the war....'" He recommended that correctional institutions

> provide a decent setting for educational and vocational programs...make all vocational and educational programs mandatory with credit against the sentence for educational progress—literally a program to 'learn the way out of prison,' so that no prisoner leaves without at least being able to read, write, and do basic arithmetic [see 1888 entry]....In the interest of billions of dollars lost to crime and blighted if not destroyed lives—we must try to deter and try to cure. (p. 8).

Later that year, Burger further developed these ideas in public addresses presented in Washington, D.C. and Lincoln, Nebraska. In May he said

> I have long believed—and said—that when society places a person behind walls and bars it has a moral obligation to take reasonable steps to try to work with that person and render him or her better equipped to return to a useful life as a member of society....To try to make these people good citizens is also for our own proper self interest....Without...basic skills, what chance does any person have of securing a gainful occupation when that person is released and begins the

search for employment—with the built-in handicap of a criminal conviction? (Burger, 1981b, pp. 2-6).

However, he was cautious about a problem that related directly to the correctional education teacher preparation issue: "Without special training, prison personnel can become part of the problem rather than part of the solution" (Burger, 1981b, p/ 4). ⌂

During the previous years an extensive repertoire of correctional education organizational capabilities had emerged. This level of social and institutional support had not been experienced by correctional educators since the late 1930s.

> The new Secretary of Education, **Dr. T.H. Bell**, speaking for the [Reagan] Administration, announced to a packed auditorium on Correctional EducationActivities Day, March 26, 1981, 'I am here to make a commitment on behalf of this Department to lend our efforts in doing something about this problem....Education must not stop at the prison gate. For some, that may even be where it can begin.' (Bell, in Gehring, 1981, p. 7; emphasis added). ⌂

Estelle Freedman's book was published, *Their Sister's Keepers: Women's Prison Reform in America, 1830-1930* (Freedman, 1981). It made historical information regarding correctional education in women's institutions more accessible, and helped to revise many narrow views on the dynamics of prison reform and correctional education. ⌂

A major book by **Lawrence Kohlberg** was published, *The Philosophy of Moral Development: Moral Stages and the Idea of Justice*. In it, Kohlberg explained the definition of moral stages (Kohlberg, 1981, pp. 17-19), the motives in each stage (p.19), and definitions for the value of human life in each stage (pp. 19-20). Reporting that criminals tend to be retarded in cognitive-moral development, Kohlberg suggested activities to develop relevant skills. ⌂

Stephen Duguid's article, "Moral Development, Justice and Democracy in the Prison" appeared in the *Canadian Journal of Criminology*. It was probably the most concise, early statement of the way Duguid applied Kohlberg's theories in western Canadian prisons. "Kohlberg insists that justice (moral reasoning) can only be taught in just schools. The implications of this are indeed profound for the prison and a direct challenge to a prison education program based on moral development." (Duguid, 1981, p. 5).

> The prison as an institution and a community creates a clear Stage 1 or 2 [low level] environment. It is

authoritarian by nature and encourages the formation of social relations among individuals for the purpose of self-protection (Stage 2) or outright deferral to unquestioned authority or force (Stage 1). Prison staff, like police officers and military personnel, can be seen to function at a Stage 2 level while on the job, responding in part to the rules of the institution and in part to the situation. In terms of moral development, within the prison, staff and prisoners are two sides of the same coin. (p. 7). ⌀

In **William Forster'**s book *Prison Education in England and Wales*, correctional education was discussed as "a window on the world" for inmate students (Forster, 1981, p. 82). Regarding correctional education professionalization, the author indicated that "it would be unwise...for the education officer's [principal's, or education director's] thinking to be influenced purely by institutional considerations..." (p. 128). The book was written as the May Committee was preparing its recommendations for the entire English local/Federal system to

move...away from the notion of humane containment as being too narrow a definition of the objectives of imprisonment and posit...the alternative objective of 'positive custody'....The scope of education, it was argued, should be enlarged substantially; it should be regarded as a full-time alternative to work; rates of pay should be the same whether a prisoner was at work or at education; and educational facilities should be made available to prison staff and their families, as well as to prisoners. (pp. 20-21).

The book's summary of the five major schools of criminological thought—classical, positivist, sociological, socialist, and radical—is especially concise and useful.

As so often happens, the central tenets of the positivist school reversed, in almost all respects, those of its rival. Where the classicists concentrated upon the crime, the positivists concentrated upon the criminal. Where the classicists saw the offender as rational and responsible, free to choose whether or not to break the law, the positivists saw his behaviour as strongly influenced, if not completely determined, by his innate constitution and immediate environment. Where the classicists insisted that the punishment must be strictly related to the crime, the positivists took the line that it must be related to the offender. Where the classicists saw the sentence primarily as proportionate to the crime

1981
(cont'd.)

already committed, the positivists saw it as measure for the prevention of future crimes. Where the classicists rejected adaptation of the penalty to the individual personality of the criminal the positivists insisted upon it. Where the classicists ruled out attempts to reform the law-breaker, the positivists advocated them. Where the classicists prohibited consideration of whether he threatened future danger, the positivists insisted that his future dangerousness should be the central criterion for deciding whether or not a criminal must be detained for the protection of others. The contrast between the two schools has been well summed up in the aphorism 'The classical school exhorts men to study justice, the positivist school exhorts justice to study men.' (Radzinowicz and King, in Forster, 1981, p. 12). ⚎

Lucien Morin's anthology was published, *On Prison Education*. Most of the great Canadian correctional educators contributed chapters: **Duguid, Ayers, Griffin, Parlett**, etc., as well as **Forster** from the United Kingdom. The themes of value-oriented education, the humanities, democracy, education (as opposed to socialization), and cognitive-moral development are emphasized, in line with correctional education thinking throughout Canada. In sum, "...educational development in prison is obviously a 'good thing.'" (Forster, in Morin, 1981, p. 66). ⚎

The U.S. Department of Justice released an important monograph by **John Conrad**, *Adult Offender Education Programs*. Conrad's honest approach was critical, in part, of institutional administrations that did not emphasize educational priorities. (Conrad, 1981). ⚎

1982 — U.S. Education Department Corrections Program coordinator **Dr. Osa Coffey** reported that 8% of the total non-Federal U.S. prison population were enrolled in postsecondary education programs (Coffey and O'Hayre, 1982—see 1977 entry). U.S. Congressman William Whitehurst (R, VA) proposed legislation to exclude inmates from the Pell Grant Program for postsecondary education and establish an alternate system with a fund ceiling of $6 million (Whitehurst, 1982). ⚎

A new "tough on crime" sentiment was developing. In a *Time* Magazine article, "What Are Prisons For?" Kurt Anderson reported that

The public wants to 'get tough' with criminals, and legislators, prosecutors and judges are obeying that diffuse mandate by sending more people away for longer stretches. Prisons have nearly doubled their

<table>
<tr><td>1982
(cont'd.)</td><td>population since 1970. Last year's 12.1% increase was the fastest in this century. Now the Inmate Nation is growing by more than 170 a day, and during the next few weeks will probably edge over 400,000, not quite half black, about 4% women. At the current rate of growth the number of inmates would double again by 1988. Today more than one out of every 600 Americans is in prison—not jail or reform school, but prison. Only the Soviet Union and South Africa have a higher percentage locked up. (Anderson, 1982, p. 38).</td></tr>
</table>

"In 30 states, prisons are under court orders to end unconstitutionally cruel conditions and practices, whether inadequately treating sick inmates, improperly ventilating cellblocks or simply jamming in too many prisoners (p. 39). "In Texas, where until a year ago 2,000 inmates had to sleep on the floor, officials for one week in May simply stopped admitting new prisoners rather than flout Judge Justice's order" (p. 40). "During the first eight months of 1982, California's inmate population grew nearly 12%. Illinois prison officials plan to build space for 1,500 additional inmates by 1985; unfortunately, they expect by then to have 3,500 additional inmates to house." (p. 39). The shift to mandatory sentencing intensified the problem—see entries for 1869, 1876, 1900 and 1980.

> Since 1977, 37 states have passed mandatory sentencing laws for certain crimes, which inflexibly deny judges the right to shorten or suspend sentences....Some states have already been pressed by high volume toward a strategy of reserving prisons for the most violent. More than 70% of the inmates in Illinois and New York are doing time for homicide, kidnapping, rape, arson, robbery, assault or weapons possession. Nationally, however, just over half of all prisoners are locked up for such crimes, and in Georgia, for instance, the overwhelming majority of prisoners are serving time for non-violent crimes. The rest are not angels with dirty faces but crooks, to be sure—thieves mostly—stupid or bad or both. Yet they are not generally the outlaws who make it scary even to think about going downtown for dinner and a movie. (pp. 40-41). ⚋

1983 — A special double edition of the *Journal of Offender Counseling Services and Rehabilitation* was devoted to "Current Trends in Correctional Education: Theory and Practice." Edited by **Sol Chaneles**, it had chapters on various types of program implementation. The editorial board included **John Braithwaite** (see 1980 entry), **John Conrad** (see 1981 entry), **Daniel Glasser** (see 1966 entry), **Lane Murray** (see 1969 entry), and **Anthony Travisono** (see 1984 entry). (Chaneles, 1983). ⚋

1983   Canada's **Doug Griffin** (see 1979 entry) interviewed **Reuven**
(cont'd.) **Feuerstein** (see 1980 entry) and **Ron Miller** in an extensive videotape
presentation entitled *Learning to Think*. In part, Feuerstein explained
that he was

> interested in cognitive modifiability. By cognitive
> we refer to all the perceptual and thought processes,
> thinking, which gives the individual the way by which
> he behaves...the form of behaviour and...the ways the
> individual chooses and makes certain decisions as to
> how to behave and in order to adapt... (Feuerstein, in
> Griffin, 1983). 🝑

Stephen Duguid's (see 1981 entry) *Humanities Core Curriculum:
Human Nature and the Human Condition* was published. It had units
on "The Individual and Society," "Science, Technology and Human
Progress," "20th Century Utopias," and "Language and Literature."
(Duguid, 1983, pp. ii-iv). Each unit was divided into parts, which
included introductory tips for the instructor, summaries of discussion
topics, and reading lists. The curriculum was indicative of correctional
education thought in contemporary Canada—especially its emphasis on
ideas from **Ayres, Feuerstein, Griffin, Kohlberg,** etc. This curriculum
is worth reading. "The teacher should aim to be an equal participant
in the discussion[s]...to be successful, there can be no preaching by
authority figures." (pp. 25-26). Designed to help change "a series of
misconceptions about the nature of the relationship of the individual
to society," (p. 13) the course established a link between the prisoner
student and the great themes of Western culture.

> Following the English tradition of curriculum design
> rather than the American model, it places content and
> student needs and attitudes ahead of specific learning
> objectives....Exponents of General Education have
> difficulty with objectives because they are less able
> to quantify the ends of education than are their more
> narrow peers. (pp. 4-5).

"A humanities program in Great Britain used the following as a working
definition: 'The Humanities are understood as any subject, or aspect of a
subject which contributes to the rational or imaginative understanding
of the human situation.'" (Shipman, in Duguid, 1983, p. 8). "...[B]eing
human is not a natural condition, but rather is an historic one....To be
human is to make choices; not just choices of a career but fundamental
choices which collectively make up our personalities and govern our
lives." (Duguid, 1983, p. 9).

> In the right context...critical insight should enable the
> individual to literally 'escape' from their own history.

1983
(cont'd.)

This is a lofty goal but throughout these curriculum materials the instructor is urged to have students question assumptions, re-think arguments, discuss evidence, and participate in reaching new conclusions. (p. 10).

The Humanities can help us understand an important dimension of our lives: "that we are responsible within the bounds of our responsibility (or the failure to do so) is the fundamental problem of the human condition" (p. 19). The

> function of education is to ameliorate savage man. To pass on the culture of our forefathers, to inculcate morals, faith and so on. In a word to civilize. Unfortunately much of the education which takes place in our correctional institutions is posited on the preparation of workers for the industrial world, yet there is no evidence that the industrial world ameliorates man. (Parlett, in Duguid, 1983, p. 15).

> The criminal, making consistently ill-informed choices in a variety of situations, living in a superficial world of polar opposites, preoccupied with private emotional conflicts, lacking an informed or adequate frame of reference within which to evaluate society as a whole, and crippled by poor educational achievement, literally cannot 'figure out' a way out of the cycle of decision making which keeps leading him back to prison. (Duguid, 1983, p. 17).

> If criminal activity is the rational outcome of individual decision making, then the character of the individual criminal assumes a more prominent position in society's attempts to address the problem. My own work has tended to focus on the issue of 'developmental lags' in the cognitive and moral reasoning domains, in weaknesses in reasoning skills, awareness of cause and effect relationships, and generally poor levels of self-esteem. Other similar analyses focus on problems with perception, knowledge of right and wrong and problem solving skills. (p. 16). ⌒

A correctional education manifesto and goals/objectives statement was completed, the *CEA Resolutions*. Correctional Education Association president **Rod Ahitow** appointed **Thom Gehring** Resolutions Committee chair at the Baltimore International CEA Conference in 1982; the Committee consisted of **Osa Coffey**—Washington, D.C., **Doug Griffin**—Ottawa, **David Jenkins**—Maryland, **Tom Moy**—

1983   California, Bob **Pierce**—Texas, and **Tom Thorpe**—New York. Ten
(cont'd.) central issues were addressed: 1) definition of correctional education, 2)
        characteristics of exemplary correctional education delivery systems, 3)
        relevant accreditation systems, 4) recommended funding structure, 5)
        coordination of Federal support, 6) teacher skills and characteristics, 7)
        teacher training needs, 8) interface with the related professions, 9) status
        of education within the institution, and 10) Correctional Education
        Association objectives. The Committee surveyed the literature, reading
        1,310 pages from over 100 books and articles; facilitated regional hearings
        and gathered facts and opinions from interested members; solicited
        statements from 68 identified correctional education leaders; and kept
        the profession abreast of its activities through the *Journal of Correctional
        Education* and the Association's *Newsletter*. Hundreds of pages of
        testimony and findings, collected and processed throughout FY 1982-
        83, were synthesized into a seven and a half page report submitted to
        the CEA Executive Board in May, 1983 (Gehring, 1983—see 1976 entry).
        The Correctional Service of Canada had the *Resolutions* translated into
        French in 1984, and the English version appeared in a December *Journal*
        article that same year. ⌁

        In her article, "Texas' Commitment to Education," **Dr. Lane
        Murray** (see entries for 1969 and 1975) wrote:

> The Texas Department of Corrections has long been
> known for its work ethic. With the proliferation of
> the Windham School System, an education ethic has
> emerged as well. The board's and director's policy is
> for a 10 percent increase in education participation
> each year. Wardens view education as a management
> tool. Work bosses see vocational and apprenticeship
> training as an aid to getting the job done. And inmates,
> well, inmates have different views toward educational
> opportunities. One inmate...mused, '...and education is
> the big hope...' (Murray, 1983, pp. 54-60). ⌁

1984 — **Dr. Joan Fulton**'s book, *Learning Power*, was published. It was based
        on a cognitive instruction model called "Developmental Teaching."
        Designed to accompany inservice training, the book outlined brain-
        compatible strategies that help the left and right hemispheres work
        together. Developmental Teaching helped disadvantaged students
        develop schemas (patterns of association), thereby facilitating the
        coping and learning processes—assimilation of directions, long-term
        memory, characterization of life experiences, goal-setting, problem-
        solving, etc. "If students do not know the pattern for the concept, the
        concept is not teachable." (Fulton, 1984, p. 63). Test scores collected
        over several years demonstrated substantial student learning gains
        and improvement in self-concept. Fulton presented at the International
        Correctional Education Association Conference in Philadelphia.

<table>
<tr><td>1984
(cont'd.)</td><td>Intelligence can be taught!....What is intelligence?... the ability to adapt to the situation or task. From the student's score on an intelligence test, we predict his ability to adapt to classroom tasks. Intelligence is measured by several abilities. However, this is not the way we understand it. We think of intelligence as one general ability, instead of several components, or separate abilities. This is why intelligence is not being taught in the classroom. (pp. 64-65; emphasis in original). ⌒</td></tr>
</table>

Philip Priestly edited an English correctional education book, *Social Skills in Prison and the Community: Problem-Solving for Offenders.* It was a description of an experiment to include prison guards as teachers of pre-release training classes for inmates. Parts of the book offered thought-provoking characterizations of phenomena that many correctional educators take for granted.

> 'Gate fever' is the name of a non-medical syndrome said to infect men in prison as the day of their discharge draws near. Its symptoms are euphoria and anxiety mixed with irrational thinking; and the unfailing cure of the condition is the cold douche of reality which awaits the victim outside the prison gate. (Priestly, 1984, p. 2).

> From the inside, prison life is most often seen, and felt, in terms of frustration; of being at the mercy of a blind bureaucracy, and of personal helplessness. Personal adaptations to this situation can assume radically alternative forms. A few prisoners rebel, either in individual campaigns of insubordination, or collectively in riots. Most adopt a posture of passive conformity towards a system which is clearly beyond their control. In extreme cases this passivity can become what has been recognised as 'institutional neurosis.' And even in cases which fall short of this diagnosis there may be perceptual attrition of the personality and character. (p. 4). ⌒

Thom Gehring initiated a study to identify the relevant competencies (skills and characteristics) of successful, veteran, correctional education classroom teachers (Gehring, 1984). The product of this study has been refined over the years. It currently (2005) includes both the updated and refined version of the skills and characteristics and **Dr. Patricia Arlin**'s findings on the attributes of wise teachers. ⌒

1985 — The **Robert Ross** and **Elizabeth Fabiano** team, out of the University of Toronto, published *Time to Think: A Cognitive Model of Delinquency Prevention and Offender Rehabilitation*. Along with MacCormick's 1931 book, this is one of the definitive volumes on our field. Ross and Fabiano's theme was about "what works?" in rehabilitation, in response to Martinson's premature announcement that "nothing works" (see 1975 entry). In the process they outlined attributes of the most effective correctional education programs in North America, and compared and contrasted among them. After some important articulation of underlying principles, the heart of Ross and Fabiano's material is rooted in elements of criminal thinking, and how programs can work to improve interpersonal cognition. The whole presentation accrued from Ross' famous meta-analysis reports, which were exhaustive in their scope. ◢◣

The Swedish Code was amended—municipalities "were no longer obliged to provide prison education." The previous trend had decentralized prison education services (see 1974 entry) by putting much of the programming under the National Labour Market Board, which in turn delegated them to local employment services. In 1985 however, "The Adult Education Act was...amended to clarify that municipalities were no longer obliged to provide prison education." The problem that sparked this change was that the funding flow from the national to the local level "had failed to follow the directives stipulated in the Public Procurement Act"—services "had been procured from the municipal education providers without being open to competition from other providers of education." (Nordic Council of Ministers, 2005, p. 100). Until the early 1990s the law had required that "prisoners had the same rights to basic education as all other citizens. After funding was transferred from the Ministry of Education to the Ministry of Justice [in association with the problem regarding procurement], this legal right no longer applied." "Chapter 11 of the Adult Education Act," which ensured general access to education, was amended: "The stipulations in this article do not apply to prisoners." (p. 101).

1987 — On March 21 the *La Porte Herald-Argus* reported a recidivism idea described by Indiana Corrections chief John Shettle: "If [offenders] aren't educated or rehabilitated, they will only cause problems again." Shettle's summary transcends the relationship between education, rehabilitation, and recidivism and depends on the words "educated or rehabilitated." (La Porte Herald-Argus). Another comment, by British Columbia correctional educator **Steve Duguid**, transcended the "nature/nurture," environment vs. free will issue about crime, which often bogs down correctional education advocacy. For education to work, Duguid wrote, "it has to get at the root of the problem, in this case the causes of people's decisions to commit crimes (not the causes of crime, which is another question altogether)." (Duguid, 1987, p. 7; emphases in original). ◢◣

1989 — The idea of establishing a European Prison Education Association (EPEA) was first discussed at the international conference on Prison Education at Wadham College, Oxford University that was planned and implemented largely as a result of an initiative by **Gerald Norme** and **Stephen Duguid.** Many of the participants were in regular correspondence with Dr. Duguid and were eager to help foster the international theme of the conference.

> Working on a model already established in America (the Correctional Education Association [CEA]), they were keen to do something similar, and suggested the idea of setting up an organization that would also help to turn the aspirations of the new Council of Europe report 'Education in Prison,' into a working reality. Among other important recommendations, that report had identified a need for contact by prison educators across national boundaries. Under an ancient copper beech tree, this idea was explored by a group of five—**Pam Bedford** from England, **Gayle Gassner** (then President of the CEA), **Henning Jorgensen** of Denmark, **Asbjorn Langas** of Norway and **Kevin Warner** of Ireland. A larger, hurried meeting in a garden gave enthusiastic backing to the project. (Rocks, 2003, first page—emphases added).

The Recommendations of the Council of Europe (R[89]), which have been at the center of EPEA activities, follow:

1. All prisoners shall have access to education, which is envisaged as consisting of classroom subjects, vocational education, creative and cultural activities, physical education and sports, social education and library facilities;

2. Education for prisoners should be like the education provided for similar age groups in the outside world, and the range of learning opportunities for prisoners should be as wide as possible;

3. Education in prison shall aim to develop the whole person bearing in mind his or her social, economic and cultural context;

4. All those involved in the administration of the prison system and the management of prisons should facilitate and support education as much as possible;

5. Education should have no less a status than work within the prison regime and prisoners should not lose out financially or otherwise by taking part in education;

1989   6. Every effort should be made to encourage the prisoner to participate
(cont'd.)   actively in all aspects of education;

7. Development programmes should be provided to ensure that prison educators adopt appropriate adult education methods;

8. Special education should be given to those prisoners with particular difficulties and especially those with reading or writing problems;

9. Vocational education should aim at the wider development of the individual, as well as being sensitive to trends in the labor market;

10. Prisoners should have direct access to a well-stocked library at least once per week;

11. Physical education and sports for prisoners should be emphasised and encouraged;

12. Creative and cultural activities should be given a significant role because these activities have particular potential to enable prisoners to develop and express themselves;

13. Social education should include practical elements that enable the prisoner to manage daily life within the prison, with a view to facilitating the return to society;

14. Wherever possible, prisoners should be allowed to participate in education outside prison;

15. Where education has to take place within the prison, the outside community should be involved as fully as possible;

16. Measures should be taken to enable prisoners to continue their education after release;

17. The funds, equipment and teaching staff needed to enable prisoners to receive appropriate education should be made available. (Nordic Council of Ministers, 2005, pp. 132-134).

The EPEA has emerged as one of the most important correctional education professionalization organizations. Its international conferences are held every other year. 🔼

Dr. Carolyn Eggleston completed a study on the first special education programs for inmates in an adult prison in the U.S., Elmira Reformatory. (See References for citation, and various entries on Elmira during the 1876-1900 period.) 🔼

2000 — **Stephen Duguid**'s book appeared, *Can Prisons Work?: The Prisoner as Object and Subject in Modern Corrections*. It offered a useful interpretation of the events that resulted in the remarkable rise, and subsequent adaptation of Canadian correctional education. Duguid insisted "correctional education" is a euphemism and "prison education" might be more direct. Of course he is accurate in this, though the historical tendency in the U.S. has favored the former term. Gehring wrote a review of the volume for the *Journal of Correctional Education*.

> Although Duguid is a major contributor to international thinking in our field, he worked most closely with the British Columbia postsecondary program. Since that program was phased out in 1993 an alarming trend is unfolding: newer Canadian prison educators are largely unfamiliar with the exemplary traditions that Duguid and the people around him ushered in. The Canadian contributors were magnificent, but in a single decade many correctional educators forgot that tradition of work. I am alluding to **Cosman**, **Parlett**, **Griffin**, **Morin**, **Ayers**, **Ross**, **Knights**, **Fabiano** and others, as well as **Duguid** himself. If you want to learn about these contributors, read this book. (Gehring, 2002, p. 5; emphases added).

Can Prisons Work? summarized and synthesized 20 years of longitudinal data on student learning in the British Columbia postsecondary program for inmates. It is especially pertinent because the data are presented incrementally, an approach that allows readers to extract from his findings aspects that might be relevant in their own programs. In part, Duguid wrote that to reduce recidivism for high risk students

> ...prison education programs should aim to encourage a culture of academic achievement, focus...on those students who show signs of improvement, provide opportunities for participation in program administration and governance, offer extracurricular activities such as theatre, and...encourage and facilitate a continuing engagement with education after release. (Duguid 2000, p. 223).

In another part of the book, Duguid presented what might be called a literature review that addresses the breadth of correctional education but focuses on four programs: (a) the University of California, Santa Cruz Women's Prison Program, (b) Project Newgate, (c) Scotland's Barlinnie Special Unit, and (d) his own University program in British Columbia. The context for all this was what Duguid called the "era of opportunities" (1972-1992). Throughout, it is a good read, and has helped encourage many to improve correctional education programs. ⌂

References

(ABA) American Bar Association. (October, 1973). *Law reform coordination bulletin #4: Correctional school district legislation and programs*. Washington, D.C.: Resource Center on Correctional Law and Legal Services.

(ABA) American Bar Association. (December, 1973). *Coordination bulletin #22: Potential of correctional school district organizations*. Washington, D.C.: Clearinghouse for Offender Literacy Programs.

Abbott, G. (1968). *The child and the state*. New York: Greenwood. (two volumes).

Allen, F.C. (1927). *A Hand book of the New York State Reformatory at Elmira*. Elmira: Summary Press.

Anderson, K. (September 13, 1982). What are prisons for? *Time*, 38-41.

Angle, T. (September, 1982). The development of educational programs in American adult prisons and juvenile reformatories during the nineteenth century. *Journal of Correctional Education, 33*(3), 4-7.

(APA) American Prison Association. (1930). *Proceedings of the sixtieth annual congress of the American Prison Association*. Louisville, Kentucky: APA.

(APA) American Prison Association. (1939). *Proceedings of the sixty-ninth annual congress of the American Prison Association*. New York: APA.

Ayers, J.D. (1978). *Perspective on education in prisons*. Victoria, British Columbia: University of Victoria.

Baker, J.E. (1985). *Prisoner participation in prison power*. Metuchen, New Jersey: The Scarecrow Press.

Banks, F. (1958). *Teach them to live: A study of education in English prisons*. New York: International University Press.

Barnes, H.E., and Teeters, N.K. (1959). *New horizons in criminology*. Englewood Cliffs: Prentice-Hall.

Barrum, J., Harris, C., and Lawless, H. (March, 1980). Correctional education: A new program. *Journal of Correctional Education, 31*(1), 15-17.

Barry, J. (1958). *Alexander Maconochie of Norfolk Island: A study of a pioneer in penal reform*. Melbourne: Oxford University Press.

Beaumont, G., and de Tocqueville, A. (1964/1833). *On the penitentiary system in the United States and its application in France.* Carbondale: Southern Illinois University Press.

Bell, R., Conrad, E., and Laffey, T. (1978). Correctional education: A summary of the national evaluation project. *Quarterly Journal of Corrections, 2,* 14-20.

Bell, R., et al. (June, 1979). *National evaluation program phase I report: Correctional education programs for inmates.* Washington, D.C.: U.S. Department of Justice.

Bellows, H.W. (1948). *John Howard: His life, character, and service.* Illinois State Penitentiary.

Bowen, J. (1965). *Soviet Education: Anton Makarenko and the years of experiment.* Madison: University of Wisconsin.

(BPDS) Boston Prison Discipline Society. (1972). *Reports of the Prison Discipline Society of Boston, 1826-1854.* Montclair, New Jersey: Patterson Smith.

Braithwaite, J. (1980). *Prisons, education, and work: Towards a national employment strategy for prisoners.* Queensland, Australia: University of Queensland Press.

Brisbane, A.S. (July 15, 1984). Prison editors struggle for free press behind bars. *Washington Post,* A-1.

Brockway, Z. (1969/1912). *Fifty years of prison service: An autobiography.* Montclair, New Jersey: Patterson Smith.

Brown, M.D. (1991). *The history of Chino Prison: The first fifty years of the California Institution for Men 1941 to 1991.* Chino, California: California Institution for Men.

Bryson, B. (2000). *In a sunburned country.* New York: Broadway Books.

Buckley, M. (1974). *Breaking into prison: A citizen guide to volunteer action.* Boston: Beacon Press.

Burger, W. (1981a). *Annual report to the American Bar Association by the chief justice of the United States.* Washington, D.C.: Public Information Office of the Supreme Court of the United States.

Burger, W.E. (1981b). Remarks... Washington, D.C.: George Washington University School of Law, commencement exercises.

Caldwell, C. (1829). *New views of penitentiary discipline and moral education and reform.* Philadelphia: William Brown.

Callan, J. (April, 1981). Lecture on Thomas Mott Osborne and Austin MacCormick. Richmond: Virginia Commonwealth University.

Callan, J. (Fall, 1980). The Osborne Association, Inc.: Past and present. *The Osborne Association, Inc. Newsletter.*

Campbell, W.R. (1978). *Dead man walking: Teaching in a maximum security prison.* New York: McGraw-Hill.

Carlson, R.E. (December, 1980c). Telephone interview by Thom Gehring.

Carlson, R.E. (January, 1981). The birth of corrections education in the U.S. Education Department. *CEA Newsletter.*

Carlson, R.E. (1980a). *Vocational education in correctional institutions.* Washington, D.C.: National Advisory Council on Vocational Education.

Carlson, R.E. (1980b). *Vocational education in the prison setting.* Washington, D.C.: National Institute of Education.

Carney, L.P. (1973). *Introduction to correctional science.* New York: McGraw-Hill.

Carpenter, J.E. (1974/1881). *The life and work of Mary Carpenter.* Montclair, New Jersey: Patterson Smith.

Carpenter, M.(1969/1864). *Our Convicts.* Montclair, New Jersey: Patterson Smith.

Carpenter, M. (1872). *Reformatory prison discipline, as developed by the rt. hon. Sir Walter Crofton, in the Irish convict prisons.* London: Longmans, Green, Reader, and Dyer.

Carpenter, M. (1970/1851). *Reformatory schools for the children of the perishing and dangerous classes and for juvenile offenders.* Montclair, New Jersey: Patterson Smith.

Chamberlain, R.W. (1935). *There is no truce: A life of Thomas Mott Osborne.* New York: Macmillan.

Chaneles, S. (ed.) (Spring/Summer, 1983). Current trends in correctional education: Theory and practice. *Journal of Offender Counseling Service and Rehabilitation.*

Chenault, P. (director). (1949-1951 reprints). Inmate education in the Department of Correction of New York State, 1847-1949. *Correction Magazine.*

Chenault, P. (director). (1954). *Successful living.* Albany: New York Department of Correction.

Clay, J. (2001). *Maconochie's experiment*. London: John Murray.

(Clinton) (1846). *Annual report of the agent of the Clinton State Prison to the Legislature of the State of New York*. Albany: New York Senate.

Coffey, O. and O'Hayre, B. (1982). *The current utilization of Pell Grants by men and women incarcerated in state correctional facilities*. Washington, D.C.: U.S. Education Department.

Commonwealth of Pennsylvania. (1928). *Correctional education and the delinquent girl*. Harrisburg: Department of Welfare.

Compayre, G. (1907). *The history of pedagogy*. London, England: Swan Sonnenschein & Co.

(Connecticut). (1830). *Report of the directors and warden of the Connecticut State Prison*. New Haven: Hezekiah House.

Conrad, J.P. (1981). *Adult offender education programs*. Washington, D.C.: U.S. Department of Justice.

Corder, S. (1855). *Life of Elizabeth Fry: Compiled from her journal*. Philadelphia, Pennsylvania: Henry Longsteth.

Correctional Education Advisory Committee. (1976). *Correctional education: A forgotten human service*. Denver: Education Commission of the States.

Coward, F., Comprehensive Employment and Training Administration Planner. (June, 1980). Richmond: telephone interview by Thom Gehring.

Davis, E.K. (1978). Offender education in the American correctional system: An historical perspective. *Quarterly Journal of Corrections*, 2, pp. 7-13.

Dell'Apa, F. (1973b). *Education for the youthful offender in correctional institutions: Issues*. Boulder: Western Interstate Commission for Higher Education.

Dell'Apa, F. (1973a). *Educational programs in adult correctional institutions: A survey*. Boulder: Western Interstate Commission for Higher Education.

Dewey, J. (1929). *Impressions of Soviet Russia and the revolutionary world*. New York: New Republic, Inc.

Dickens, C. (1957/1842). *American notes*. London: Oxford University Press, 97-111.

Dodge, C. (July-August, 2005). Knowledge for sale: Are America's public libraries on the verge of losing their way? *Utne*, pp. 72-7.

Duguid, S. (2000). *Can prisons work?: The prisoner as object and subject in modern corrections*. Toronto: University of Toronto Press.

Duguid, S. (1983). *Curriculum guide: Humanities core curriculum—Human nature and the human condition*. Burnaby, British Columbia: University of Victoria.

Duguid, S. (April, 1981). Moral development, justice, and democracy in the prison. *Canadian Journal of Criminology*.

Duguid, S. (1987). *University prison education in British Columbia*. Burnaby, British Columbia: Prison Education Program, Simon Fraser University.

Dyer, D. (1867). *History of the Albany Penitentiary*. Albany: Joel Munsell.

Dykhuizen, G. (1973). *The life and mind of John Dewey*. Carbondale: Southern Illinois University Press.

Edwards, R. (1991). *A.S. Makarenko's general educational ideas and their applicability to a nontotalitarian society*. Chicago: Loyola University of Chicago. (unpublished doctoral dissertation).

Eggleston, C. (1989). *Zebulon Brockway and Elmira Reformatory: A study in correctional/special education*. Richmond: Virginia Commonwealth University (unpublished dissertation).

Encyclopedia Americana. (1979). MacCormick, Austin Harbutt. Danbury, Connecticut, 18, 28.

Eriksson, T. (1976). *The reformers: An historical survey of pioneer experiments in the treatment of criminals*. New York: Elsevier.

Erwin, J. and D.C. (1978). *The man who keeps going to jail*. Elgin, Illinois: David C. Cook.

Feuerstein, R. (1980). *Instrumental enrichment: An intervention program for cognitive modifiability*. Baltimore: University Park Press.

Fisher, N.A. (1970). History of correctional education. In Ryan, T.A. (ed.) *Collection of papers prepared for the 1970 national seminars: Adult basic education in corrections*. Honolulu: University of Hawaii, 183-196.

Forster, W. (ed). (1981). *Prison education in England and Wales*. Leicester: National Institute of Adult Education.

Freedman, E. (1981). *Their sister's keepers: Women's prison reform in America, 1830-1930*. Ann Arbor: University of Michigan Press.

Fulton, J.L. (1984). *Learning Power: Program I training manual.* Richmond: Joan Fulton.

Gaither, C.C. (June, 1982). Education behind bars: An overview. *Journal of Correctional Education,* 19-23.

Geary, D. (1975). *Community relations and the administration of justice.* New York: John Wiley and Sons.

Gehring, T. (January, 1982). An identified need: The development of a CEA rationale statement. *Journal of Correctional Education,* 32(4), 4-8.

Gehring, T. (March, 2002). Book review: Duguid, Stephen. (2000). *Can prisons work?: The prisoner as object and subject in modern corrections. Journal of Correctional Education,* 53(1).

Gehring, T. (1983). *CEA resolutions.* Richmond: Correctional Education Association (unpublished).

Gehring, T. (September, 1980). Correctional education and the United States Department of Education. *Journal of Correctional Education,* 31(3), 4-6.

Gehring, T. (1981). *Correctional education teacher training program: A proposal for the William T. Morris Foundation, Inc.* Virginia Commonwealth University (unpublished).

Gehring, T. (1979). *Rehabilitative School Authority (RSA) master plan: 1980-86.* Chesapeake, Virginia: RSA.

Gehring, T. (1984). *Relevant competencies survey.* Richmond: Rehabilitative School Authority (unpublished).

Gehring, T., and Bowers, F. (September, 2003). Mary Carpenter: 19th century English correctional education hero. *Journal of Correctional Education,* 54(3), 116-122.

Gehring, T. and Clark, R. (1979). *A proposal from the Rehabilitative School Authority for correctional education teacher certification and teacher training program(s).* Richmond: Rehabilitative School Authority (unpublished).

General Accounting Office (GAO). (1979). *Correctional institutions can do more to improve the employability of offenders.* Washington, D.C.: GAO.

George, W. (1937). *The adult minor.* New York: D. Appleton.

George, W. (1911). *The Junior Republic: Its history and ideals.* New York: D. Appleton.

George, W., and Stowe, L.B. (1912). *Citizens made and remade: An interpretation of the significance and influence of George Junior Republics*. Boston: Houghton Mifflin.

Grant, N. (1968). *Soviet education*. Baltimore: Penguin.

Griffin, D. (moderator). (1979). *Crime and reason*. Ottawa: Canadian Penitentiary Service (videotape).

Griffin, D. (moderator). (1983). *Teaching to learn: Feuerstein's theory of instrumental enrichment*. Ottawa: Canadian Penitentiary Service (videotapes).

Grunhut, M. (1973/1948). *Penal reform: A comparative study*. Montclair, New Jersey: Patterson Smith.

Hageman, T., former Missouri Correctional Education Chief. (November 24, 1982). Interview by Carolyn Eggleston and Thom Gehring.

Heilbron, W.C. (1909). *Convict life at the Minnesota State Prison—Stillwater, Minnesota*. St. Paul: W.C. Heilbron.

Hicks, C.B. (1925). *The history of penal institutions in Ohio*. Columbus: F.J. Heer.

History of the Ohio Penitentiary Annex and prisoners. (1891). Columbus: Ohio Penitentiary.

Holford, G. (1821). *Thoughts on the criminal prisons of this country*. London: Rivington.

Holmes, C. (1912). *The Elmira Prison Camp*. New York: G.P. Putnam's Sons.

Holl, J.M. (1971). *Juvenile reform in the Progressive era: William George and the Junior Republic movement*. Ithaca, New York: Cornell University Press.

Holt, M.I. (1992). *The orphan trains: Placing out in America*. Lincoln: University of Nebraska Press.

Hufstedler, S.M., U.S. Secretary of Education. (November 3, 1981). Letter to Senator Pell.

Hughes, R. (1987). *The fatal shore*. New York: Alfred A. Knopf.

(Illinois). (1834). *Report of the Select Committee on the Penitentiary, submitted to the [Illinois] House of Representatives*. Vandalia: William Walters.

Jenkins, W.O. et al. (1972). *A manual for the use of the environmental deprivation scale (EDS) in corrections: The prediction of criminal behavior*. Springfield, Virginia: National Technical Information Service.

Jones, P. (June, 1938). Institution libraries—1853-1927. *Library News and Notes*, 174-176.

Kendall, G. (August 4, 1981). Letter to Thom Gehring.

Kendall, G. (1939). *The organization and teaching of social and economic studies in correctional institutions*. New York: Bureau of Publications, Teachers College, Columbia University.

Keve, P. (July 16, 1982). Telephone interview with Thom Gehring.

Keve, P. (1984). *The McNeil century: The life and times of an island prison*. Chicago: Nelson Hall.

Kingsmill, J. (1854). *Chapters on prisons and prisoners and the prevention of crime*. London: Longman, Brown, Green, and Longmans.

Kohlberg, L. (1981). *The philosophy of moral development: Moral stages and the idea of justice*. San Francisco: Harper and Row.

La Porte Herald-Argus. (March 21, 1987).

Leopold, N.F., Jr. (1958). *Life plus 99 years*. Garden City, New York: Doubleday.

Lewis, O.F. (1967). *The development of American prisons and prison customs, 1776-1845*. Montclair, New Jersey: Patterson Smith.

Lewis, D. (1965). *From Newgate to Dannemora*. Ithaca, NY: Cornell University Press.

Lewis, L. Richmond City Jail Librarian. (1977). Interview by Thom Gehring. Richmond, Virginia: Rehabilitative School Authority.

Lewisohn, S. (ed.) (1946). *Manual of suggested standards for a state correctional system*. New York: American Prison Association.

Linton, J., Maryland Chief of Correctional Education. (August, 1980). Telephone interview by Thom Gehring.

Lozoff, B. (director) (1976). *Inside out: A spiritual manual for prison life*. Nederland, Colorado: Prison-Ashram Project. Note: Prison-Ashram is now located in Durham, North Carolina.

Luria, A.R. (1976). *Cognitive development: Its cultural and social foundations*. Cambridge: Harvard University Press.

MacCormick, A. (ed.) (1937). *Correctional Education*. New York: Committee on Education of the American Prison Association.

MacCormick, A. (ed.) (1938). *Correctional Education*. New York: Committee on Education of the American Prison Association.

MacCormick, A. (ed.) (1939). *Correctional Education*. New York: Committee on Education of the American Prison Association.

MacCormick, A. (1931). *The education of adult prisoners*. New York: The National Society of Penal Information.

MacNeil, P. (1979). Organizational barriers to the administration of correctional education: An analysis of a correctional school district. *Adult Education*, 30 (4), 208-221.

Maggill, S. (1810). *Remarks on prisons*. Glasgow, Scotland: Hedderwick.

Makarenko, A.S. (1973). *The road to life: An epic in education*. New York: Oriole. (Three volumes).

Martin, J. (2002). *The education of John Dewey: A biography*. New York: Columbia University Press.

McKee, J, and McKee, S., Institute for Social and Educational Research/Pace Learning Systems. (July 12, 2005). Interview by Thom Gehring. Des Moines, Iowa: International Correctional Education Association.

McKelvey, B. (1977). *American prisons: A history of good intentions*. Montclair, New Jersey: Patterson Smith.

Metametrics, Inc. (1977). *A review of corrections education policy for the Department of Health, Education, and Welfare: Final report*. Washington, D.C.: Metametrics.

Methven, M.L. (June, 1938). Library development since 1927. *Library News and Notes*, 177-179.

Miller, E.P. (M.D.) (1867). *A treatise on the cause of exhausted vitality, or, abuses of the sexual function*. Boston: E.P. Woodward.

Miller, L.M.P. (1978). Toward equality of educational opportunity through school districts in state bureaus: An innovation in correction education. *Harvard Journal on Legislation*, 15(2), pp. 221-296.

(Missouri) Missouri State Statutes. (1959). Division of inmate education. 216.555 through 216.565.

Monroe, P.M. (1912). *A brief course on the history of education*. New York: MacMillan.

Morin, L. (ed.) (1981). *On prison education.* Ottawa: Canadian Government Publishing Centre.

Mountjoy Prison. (1866). *Head school master's journal.* Dublin, Ireland (unpublished journal).

Murphree, D., Florence, South Carolina Adult Education Director. (November 7, 1981). Letter to Thom Gehring.

Murray, L. (June, 1983). Texas' commitment to education. *Corrections Today,* 52-60.

Murray, L. (June, 1975). The school district concept. *Adult Leadership.*

Murton, T.O. (1976). *The dilemma of prison reform.* New York: Holt, Rinehart and Winston.

Nelson, C.M., Rutherford, R.B., and Wolford, B.I. (1987). *Special education in the criminal justice system.* Columbus, Ohio: Merrill.

(New York). (1941). New York State Department of Correction and the Commission on Education in Correctional Institutions in the State of New York. *Future plans and costs for education in institutions in the New York State Department of Correction.* Sing Sing.

Norcott, A. (1979). *A documentation and analysis of the historical development of educational programs in the state prisons of New Jersey.* New Brunswick, NJ: Rutgers University (unpublished dissertation).

Nordic Council of Ministers (2005). *Nordic prison education: A lifelong learning perspective.* Copenhagen, Denmark: Norden.

Office of Economic Opportunity (OEO). (October, 1970). *NewGate: A way out of the wasted years.* Washington, D.C.: OEO (appears in ERIC as ED 064 554).

O'Hare, K.R. (1923). *In prison.* New York: Knopf.

Osborne, T.M. (1924b). *Prisons and common sense.* Philadelphia: J.B. Lippincott.

Osborne, T.M. (1975/1916). *Society and prisons: Some suggestions for a new penology.* Montclair, New Jersey: Patterson Smith.

Osborne, T.M. (1924a). *Within prison walls.* New York: D. Appleton.

Oursler, F. and Oursler, W. (1949). *Father Flanagan of Boys Town.* Garden City, NJ: Doubleday.

Outten, E., Rehabilitative School Authority Board Member. (May 13, 1980). Interview by Thom Gehring and Richard Massey.

(PANY) *Second report of the Prison Association of New York*. (1846). New York: W. Newell.

(PANY). *Third report of the Prison Association of New York*. (1847). New York: Burns and Banes.

(PANY). *Twenty-eighth annual report of the Executive Committee of the Prison Association of New York, and accompanying documents for the year 1872.* (1873). Albany: Argus.

Pecht, H.E., and Gehring, T. (April-May, 1980). A tribute to Austin MacCormick: The number one hero of correctional education. *CEA Newsletter*.

Pierce, R.P. (Fall, 1979). Competency-based adult education in correctional institutions: State of the scene. *Adult Literacy and Basic Education*, 229-233.

Priestly, P., et al. (1984). *Social skills in prison and the community: Problem solving for offenders*. London: Routledge and Kegan Paul.

Quick, R.H. (1916). *Essays on educational reformers*. New York: D. Appleton.

Quinby, H. (1873). *The prison chaplaincy, and its experiences*. Concord, New Hampshire: D.C. Guernsey.

Rankin, K. (June, 1982). Region VIII. *CEA Newsletter, 3.*

Reagen, M.V. and Stoughton, D.M. (eds.). (1976). *School behind bars: A descriptive overview of correctional education in the American prison system*. Metuchen, New Jersey: The Scarecrow Press. See also the ERIC version, 1973.

Reid, S.T. (1979). *Crime and criminology, second edition*. New York: Holt, Rinehart, and Winston.

Roberts, A. (ed.). (1973). *Readings in prison education*. Springfield, Illinois: Charles C. Thomas.

Roberts, A. (1971). *Sourcebook on prison education: Past, present, and future*. Springfield, Illinois: Charles C. Thomas.

Roberts, A. and Coffey, O. (1976). *A state of the art survey for a correctional education network*. College Park, Maryland: American Correctional Association.

Roberts, R. (1968). *Imprisoned tongues*. Manchester, England: University of Manchester Press.

Rocks, P. (May, 2003). History (of the European Prison Education Association). Obtained online at http://www.epea.org/history.htm on August 11, 2005.

Roscoe, W. (1819). *Observations on penal jurisprudence and the reformation of criminals*. London: J. Cadell.

Ross, R., and Fabiano, E. (1985). *Time to think: A cognitive model of delinquency prevention and offender rehabilitation*. Johnson City, Tennessee: Institute of Social Sciences and Arts.

Rowles, B.J. (1962). *The lady at box 99: The story of Miriam Van Waters*. Greenwich, Connecticut: Seabury Press.

Ruggles-Brise, E. (1901). *Report to the secretary of state for the Home Department on the proceedings of the fifth and sixth international penitentiary congresses*. London: Darling and Sons.

Rule, L.V. (probably 1920). *The city of dead souls and how it was made alive again*. Louisville: Kentucky Printshop.

Ryan, T.A., and Gehring, T. (eds.). (June, 1995). *Journal of Correctional Education* (special edition on the history of the field of correctional education), 46(2).

Ryan, J.A., and Hagen, P.E. (probably 1970). *Journal of Correctional Education: Cumulative index, 1949-1968*. Menard: Illinois State Penitentiary.

Ryan, T.A., and Sivern, L.C. (eds.). (1970). *Goals of adult basic education in corrections*. Honolulu: University of Hawaii.

Samenow, S., and Yochelson, S. (1976). *The criminal personality: A program for change*. New York: Aronson.

Schama, S. (1989). *Citizens: A chronicle of the French Revolution*. New York: Alfred A. Knopf.

Scott, W. (August 19, 1984). Walter Scott's personality parade. *Parade Magazine*.

Scudder, K.J. (1968/1952). *Prisoners are people*. New York: Greenwood Press.

Seashore, M., and Haberfeld, S. (1976). *Prisoner education: Project NewGate and other college programs*. New York: Praeger.

Secretary of State. (1899). *Rules for the government of local prisons*. London: Darling and Son.

Serrill, M.S. (August, 1982). Norfolk: A retrospective. *Corrections Magazine*, 25-32.

Shearin, F., Rehabilitative School Authority director of vocational education. (June, 1981). Richmond: interview by Thom Gehring.

Skok, J. (1977). *The selection of a system for providing correction education for adjudicated persons in Pennsylvania.* Wilkes-Barre: Wilkes College (unpublished dissertation).

Smith, P. (May, 1982). Collecting true crime literature. *AB Bookman's Weekly.*

Smith, R.M., Aker, G.F., and Kidd, J.R. (Ed.s). (1970). *Handbook of adult education.* New York: Macmillan.

Snedden, D.S. (1907). *Administration and educational work of American juvenile reform schools.* New York: Teachers College, Columbia University.

Solzhenitsyn, A.I. (1974). *The gulag archipelago.* New York: Harper and Row.

Statutory Provisions. (possibly 1887). British—no author or publisher listed.

Suerken, R., Gehring, T., and Stewart, J. (June, 1987). Special bulletin: how to establish a correctional school district. *Journal of Correctional Education,* 38(2), 84-90.

Sullivan, R.D. (1975). *An historical perspective of education in Massachusetts correctional institutions.* Boston: Boston University (unpublished dissertation).

Swift, W.B. (Sept/Oct, 2002). The kindness cure. *New Age Journal,* pp. 84-87.

Sydney Herald [Australia]. (Wednesday, July 1, 1840). Supplement: Fete at Norfolk Island, p. 1.

System Development Corporation (SDC). (February, 1978). *Examples of components of Title I programs for neglected or delinquent youth in state institutions.* Santa Monica, California: SDC.

Tannenbaum, F. (1933). *Osborne of Sing Sing.* Chapel Hill: University of North Carolina Press.

Teeters, N.K. (1955). *The cradle of the penitentiary: The Walnut Street Jail at Philadelphia, 1773-1835.* Philadelphia: Pennsylvania Prison Society.

Teeters, N.K. and Shearer, J.D. (1957). *The prison at Philadelphia: Cherry Hill.* New York: Columbia University Press.

Topping, C.W. (1929). *Canadian penal institutions.* Toronto: Ryerson Press.

Tyack, D.B. (1974). *The one best system: A history of American urban education.* Cambridge, Massachusetts: Harvard University Press.

Van Waters, M. (April-May, 1938).Incentive and penalty in education. *Educational Trends,* 4(5), 27-31.

Virginia. (1914). *Annual report of Board of Directors of the Penitentiary.* Richmond: Board of Directors.

Virginia. (1922). *Annual report of Board of Directors of the Penitentiary.* Richmond: Board of Directors.

Virginia Code Commission. (1981). *Code of Virginia.* Charlottesville, Virginia: The Michie Company.

Wallace, I., Wallechinsky, D., and Wallace, A. (September 5, 1982). Edison and the electric chair. *Parade Magazine.*

Wallack, W. (ed.). (1939). *Correctional education today.* New York: American Prison Association.

Wallack, W. (ed.). (1940). *Prison administration—An educational process.* New York: American Prison Association.

Wallack, W. (ed.). (1937). *The training of prison guards.* New York: Teachers College, Columbia University (unpublished dissertation).

Wallack, W., Kendall, G., and Briggs, H. (1939). *Education within prison walls.* New York: Bureau of Publications, Teachers College, Columbia University.

Whitehurst, W. (1982). *HR 5993.* Washington, D.C.: U.S. Congress.

Whitson, C.M., et al. (1977). *Standards for vocational education programs in correctional institutions: National study of vocational education in corrections.* Columbus: The Center for Vocational Education, Ohio State University.

Wines, E.C. (ed.). (1871). *Transactions of the National Congress on Penitentiary and Reformatory Discipline.* Albany: Argus.

Wines, F.H. (1889). *Crime, the convict, and the prison.* Springfield, Illinois: Springfield Printing Company.

Wines, F.H. (1888). *The restoration of the criminal: A sermon.* Springfield, Illinois: H.W. Rokker.

Wright, R.J. (January-February, 1980). Austin H. MacCormick, April 20, 1893- October 24, 1979: A memorial statement. *Corrections Today,* 60-61. ⌂

Acknowledgements

Excerpts from *Nineteen Eighty-Four* by George Orwell, copyright 1949 by Harcourt, Inc. and renewed 1977 by Sonia Brownell Orwell, reprinted by permission of the publisher. ⌘ Excerpts from *Social Skills in Prison and the Community. Problem Solving for Offenders* by Priestly, P., et al., copyright © 1984 Routledge and Kegan Paul. Reproduced by permission of Taylor & Francis Books UK. ⌘ Reprinted by permission of the publisher from *The One Best System: A History of American Urban Education* by David Tyack, Cambridge, Mass.: Harvard University Press, Copyright © 1974 by the President and Fellows of Harvard College. ⌘ Reprinted by permission of the publisher from *Prisoner Education: Project Newgate and other College Programs* by M. Seashore and S. Haberfield, New York: Praeger, copyright © 1976 by Greenwood Publishing Group, Inc. Westport, CT. ⌘ Reprinted by permission of the publisher from *Their Sister's Keepers: Women's Prison Reform in America, 1830-1930* by E. Freedman, copyright © 1981 by University of Michigan Press Ann Arbor, MI. ⌘ From A. Roberts, *Readings in Prison Education*, copyright © 1973. Courtesy of Charles C Thomas Publisher, Ltd., Springfield, Illinois. ⌘ From A. Roberts, *Sourcebook on Prison Education*, copyright © 1971. Courtesy of Charles C Thomas Publisher, Ltd., Springfield, Illinois. ⌘ From *Life Plus 99 Years* by Nathan F. Leopold, copyright 1958 by Nathan F. Leopold, Jr. Introduction by Erle Stanley Gardner. Used with permission from Doubleday, a division of Random House, Inc. ⌘ From *In a Sunburned Country* by Bill Bryson, copyright 2000 by Bill Bryson. Used by permission of Broadway Books, a division of Random House, Inc. ⌘ From *Father Flanagan of Boys Town* by Fulton Oursler and Will Oursler, copyright 1949 by Fulton Oursler and Will Oursler. Used by permission of Doubleday, a division of Random House, Inc. ⌘ Excerpts from *A Preface to History* by G. Gustavson, copyright © 1955 by McGraw-Hill. Reproduced with permission of the McGraw-Hill Companies. ⌘ From *Personality Parade: Capt. James Cook* by Walter Scott, Parade Magazine August 19, 1984. Copyright 1984 Parade Publications. All rights reserved. ⌘ From *Intelligence Report: Edison and the Electric Chair* by I. Wallace, D. Wallechinsky and A. Wallace, Parade Magazine September 5, 1982. Copyright 1982 David Wallechinsky. All rights reserved. ⌘ Reprinted with permission of the publisher from *Prisons, Education, and Work: Towards a National Employment Strategy for Prisoners* by J. Braithwaite, Queensland, Australia. Copyright © 1980 by the University of Queensland Press. ⌘ Cover photo of Walnut Street Jail instructional scene courtesy of Pennsylvania Prison Society. ⌘ Reprinted by permission of the publisher from *Soviet Education: Anton Makarenko and the Years of Experiment* by J. Bowen, Madison, Wisconsin: University of Wisconsin, Copyright © 1965. ⌘ Reprinted by permission of the publisher from *The Child and the State vol. 2* by Grace Abbott. Copyright 1938 by the University of Chicago. ⌘ Reprinted from *The Orphan Trains: Placing out in America* by Marilyn Irvin Holt by permission of the University of Nebraska Press. Copyright © 1992 by the University of Nebraska Press. ⌘ Excerpts from *Impressions of Soviet Russia* by John Dewey first published in 1929 by the New Republic. ⌘ Excerpts from *Austin H. MacCormick, April 20, 1893-October 24, 1979: A Memorial Statement* by Randall J. Wright, Corrections Today, January-